ISLAMISING INDONESIA

THE RISE OF JEMAAH TARBIYAH AND THE PROSPEROUS JUSTICE PARTY (PKS)

ISLAMISING INDONESIA

THE RISE OF JEMAAH TARBIYAH AND THE PROSPEROUS JUSTICE PARTY (PKS)

Yon Machmudi

A thesis submitted for the degree of Doctor of Philosophy
of The Australian National University, Southeast Asia Center
Faculty of Asian Studies, July 2006

Published by ANU E Press
The Australian National University
Canberra ACT 0200, Australia
Email: anuepress@anu.edu.au
This title available online at: http://epress.anu.edu.au/islam_indo_citation.html

National Library of Australia
Cataloguing-in-Publication entry

Author:	Machmudi, Yon, 1973-
Title:	Islamising Indonesia : the rise of Jemaah Tarbiyah and the Prosperous Justice Party (PKS) / Yon Machmudi.
ISBN:	9781921536243 (pbk.) 9781921536250 (pdf)
Series:	Islam in Southeast Asia series.
Notes:	Bibliography.
Subjects:	Partai Keadilan Sejahtera.
	Political parties--Indonesia.
	Islam and politics--Indonesia.
	Islam and state--Indonesia.
	Indonesia--Politics and government.
Dewey Number:	324.2598082

All rights reserved. No part of this publication may be reproduced, stored in a retrieval system or transmitted in any form or by any means, electronic, mechanical, photocopying or otherwise, without the prior permission of the publisher.

Cover design by ANU E Press

This edition © 2008 ANU E Press

Islam in Southeast Asia Series

Theses at The Australian National University are assessed by external examiners and students are expected to take into account the advice of their examiners before they submit to the University Library the final versions of their theses. For this series, this final version of the thesis has been used as the basis for publication, taking into account other changes that the author may have decided to undertake. In some cases, a few minor editorial revisions have made to the work. The acknowledgements in each of these publications provide information on the supervisors of the thesis and those who contributed to its development. For many of the authors in this series, English is a second language and their texts reflect an appropriate fluency.

Table of Contents

Foreword	xi
Acknowledgments	xv
Abstract	xvii
Glossary and Abbreviations	xix
Notes on Transliteration, Spelling and Referencing	xxix
Introduction	1
1. The Emergence of the New Santri in Indonesia	21
2. Jemaah Tarbiyah and Islamisation in Indonesia	51
3. Flourishing in A hostile Political Environment	81
4. Patterns of controlling Institutions: from campus to state	107
5. Indonesian and Egyptian Brothers	133
6. The sufi influences: in Pursuit of an Islamised Indonesia	165
7. A Vision of Shariah–Led Prosperity: PKS Attitudes to the Implementation of Islamic Law	191
Conclusion	217
APPENDICES	
1. Piagam Deklarasi Partai Keadilan	223
2. Deklarasi Partai Keadilan Sejahtera	227
3. Anggaran Dasar Partai Keadilan Sejahtera	231
4. Anggaran Rumah Tangga Partai Keadilan Sejahtera	241
5. Susunan Pengurus Pusat PKS 205-2010	255
6. Susunan Penempatan Anggota F-Pks Di Alat-Alat Kelengkapan Dpr/Mpr Ri Dan Kabinet Periode Tahun 2004/2005	259
Bibliography	263

List of Tables

Table 1: Attitudes of New Santri in Indonesia — 31
Table 2: Models of Islamic Reform in Indonesian Religious Movements — 55
Table 3: Traditionalist and Modernist Affiliation of PKS Committees — 65
Table 4: Educational Background of Members of DRR RI(2004-2009) — 126

List of Illustrations

Syahrir accompanied by other Indonesian delegations met with the General Guide of the Muslim Brothers, Hasan al-Banna, in Cairo — 143

H. Agus Salim and H.M. Rasyidi discussed with Hasan al-Banna in Cairo — 144

Foreword

The Prosperous Justice Party (PKS) is the most interesting phenomenon in contemporary Indonesian politics. Not only is it growing rapidly in membership and electoral support, it is also bringing a new and markedly different approach to Islamic politics, one which has no precedent in Indonesian history.

There are several interrelated elements to this new approach which deserve mention. First, more than any other Islamic party, PKS's primary source of ideological and organisational inspiration is external and draws heavily upon the thinking of Egypt's Muslim Brotherhood. Other parties, in particular Masyumi during the 1950s, had a high awareness of developments in the Middle East and South Asia, but their internal discourses and doctrines were largely domestic. In the case of PKS, one need only look at the number of Brotherhood texts translated and published by party members, the frequency of references to Hasan al-Banna or Sayyid Qutb in party documents or websites, and the popularity of images from the Middle East, such as Hamas badges or T-shirts depicting Palestinian youths throwing stones at Israeli soldiers during the Intifada, to find evidence of the depth of Middle Eastern consciousness. Other parties such as Nahdlatul Ulama, Masyumi, Parmusi, the United Development Party (PPP), the National Awakening Party (PKB) and the Crescent Moon Party (PBB) have been much less influenced by such external forces.

Second, PKS is the only genuine cadre party in present-day Indonesian politics. It has a strict process of induction, training and promotion of members which produces a disciplined and committed corps of cadre. Whereas most other parties have low routine involvement of grassroots members outside of campaign periods, PKS has regular branch meetings, discussion groups, community activities and religious outreach. Moreover, most PKS office holders and legislators have usually gained their positions on the basis of merit and through a internal democratic process. This stands in contrast to the vote-buying, intimidation, patronage considerations and favouritism that so often besets other parties. Indeed, with the possible exception of the former Soeharto-regime party Golkar, PKS is the only party to develop the kind of internal culture and organisational discipline which political scientists deem desirable for the proper functioning of a consolidated democracy.

Third, it is the only party with an extensive and ongoing community service program. This can take various forms from emergency relief for the victims of natural disasters such as tsunamis, earthquakes, floods and fire to the provision of regular and often free medical and dental services to poorer communities. While some parties offer occasional services, particularly in the run-up to elections, PKS has made its welfare programs an integral part of its outreach.

Thus, PKS has been able to promote itself as a 'caring' party and one which has good track record of community assistance.

Fourth, PKS has made morality in public life central to its political program. All the major parties of the post-Soeharto era declare their commitment to 'clean' and 'transparent' politics but in most cases this is for rhetorical effect rather than a statement of intent. Indeed, corruption and collusion pervade most Indonesian political parties and the prospect of quick enrichment remains an important motivation for many politicians. By contrast, PKS is relatively (but not entirely) free of 'money politics' and it enforces strict anti-corruption regulations for its leaders and legislators. In recent years, the party has imposed tough sanctions on members found to be taking money illicitly and branches have also been quick at withdrawing support for leaders who are seen to have benefited excessively from their positions. Moreover, PKS legislators have strived to expose and prevent corruption and abuse of office in the national and local parliaments, often incurring the ire of other parties. On occasions, this has even led to the kidnapping of PKS politicians.

Finally, PKS is more serious about ideology and policy than any other large political party. At a time when most parties are unashamed about their lack of internal discussion about the values and policy objectives to which they should aspire, PKS is notable for the richness of its intra-party discourse on key conceptual and doctrinal issues. The sheer number of books, magazines and web-based materials produced by PKS members far exceeds the output of any other party.

For all these reasons, PKS can be seen as broadening the choices available to Indonesian voters and as offering a fresh alternative to more 'traditional' parties such as PPP, PKB and Megawati's Indonesian Democratic Party of Struggle (PDI-P). Though PKS is often criticised in both the Indonesian and foreign media, there are grounds for welcoming its presence in Indonesian politics and its ability to provide a new paradigm of Islamic political behaviour.

Despite its successes in dramatically increasing its electoral support and membership, PKS is entering into a more challenging phase of its development that will test its ability to maintain its ideological focus and moral integrity. The party's victories in recent direct elections of provincial and district head (pilkada) have brought its leaders into positions of direct authority in regional administrations, with all the temptations and dilemmas which such positions involve. In the past, most parties have been heavily compromised and corrupted by the holding of executive power. It will be interesting to see if PKS can avoid a similar fate. Also, PKS leaders have made clear their plans for the party to double or triple in size over the next few elections. Such a rapid expansion risks diluting the purity of the Brotherhood-inspired ideology, which the party has until now held dear. While PKS leaders may hope to 'convert' the influx of new members to their way of thinking and behaving, it could be that the new 'recruits' change PKS, making it more like other parties and less distinctive in Indonesian politics.

Understanding PKS and analysing its political behaviour presents challenges to scholars and observers. This is partly due to the fact that the party represents a new trend within Indonesian Islam which has few parallels with preceding movements. It is also a reflection of PKS's own success in tightly managing the party's image, particularly to emphasise its 'moderate' and 'pluralist' aspects and play down the more Islamist elements. Thus, any analysis of PKS needs to (1) consider carefully how to characterise the party, particularly whether existing typologies of Indonesian Islam are adequate to describe it, and (2) probe behind the party's self-image to examine the origins and contours of its thinking.

In this regard, Yon Machmudi has rendered us a valuable service. In this book, he provides a thoughtful and authoritative context for viewing PKS. He critiques the existing categorisations for Indonesian Islam and points to their inadequacy when describing the PKS and the campus-based Tarbiyah movement from which it sprang. He reworks the santri typology, dividing it into convergent, radical and global sub-streams. This offers new possibilities for explaining the PKS phenomenon and assists in differentiating between various types of Islamic revivalism in contemporary Indonesia. It also allows a more understanding of the accommodatory stance which PKS has towards the state and other political forces.

Yon Machmudi's account, which is based on his doctoral thesis, is also notable for his analysis of the religious and organisational background of PKS leaders. Contrary to the assertions of some scholars, who claim that the party is modernist dominated, he argues that PKS actually draws cadre from a broad cross-section of the Muslim community, including the traditionalist community.

Yon's text provides a good overview of the development of PKS from its Tarbiyah movement origins to its impressive success at the 2004 general elections. It considers the party's attitude towards the issues of sharia implementation and community welfare and closes by examining the future challenges facing PKS. It is a well written and authoritative account from a scholar who has done wide-ranging research on the party. It is a valuable contribution to the literature on PKS and I am happy to recommend it to readers.

Greg Fealy
Canberra
5 November 2008

Acknowledgments

My first thanks go to my supervisor, Dr. Greg Fealy of the Research School of Pacific and Asian Studies, The Australian National University. I have benefited greatly from the experience of being his student for four and half years. His wide ranging knowledge of Indonesian politics and Islam has helped me in structuring and making better analysis in this thesis. His critical and careful reading of various drafts has been most valuable in making the thesis more accessible to broader intellectual communities. Professor Virginia Hooker read several chapters and provided detailed and valuable comments. Professor Harold Crouch of The Australian National University has given his precious time to discuss preliminary drafts of my research proposal and offered important comments.

Particular thanks also go to my editor, Dr. Wendy Mukheerje of the Southeast Asia Centre, Faculty of Asian Studies, ANU, who has been very kind in reading, editing and polishing my drafts. Without her assistance I would not have been able to finish my study on time.

I am very much indebted to the Indonesian community and student associations in Canberra that have provided wonderful moments of social gathering which relieved me for a moment from a long and tiring process of writing up the thesis. My gratitude, especially, goes to all my best friends in ANU, Agus Abdullah, Arif Zamhari, Daryono, Della Temenggung, Deny Hamdani, Din Salehuddin, Firman Noer, Hamdan Juhannis, Jonery, Kacung Marijan, Lukmanul Hakim, Mokhamad Mahdum, Muhammad Yasir Yusuf, Rusan Nasruddin, Muhammad Yasin, Nashihin, Taufiq Prabowo, Yogi Vidyattama and those whose names are not mentioned here but contributed so much support to me and my family during our stay in Canberra. Especially to Dr. Amin Samad and Jajang Setiadi, thank you for your kind hospitality.

I also thank the Yayasan Bina Bangsa in Jakarta which facilitated my study in Australia. Thanks, too, to Ausaid and its committees who helped me by providing a scholarship and generous assistance during my study at The Australian National University. Thanks to all respondents in Indonesia, particularly from the Prosperous Justice Party, Partai Keadilan Sejahtera (PKS) who gave of their time to enable me to conduct my research. Thanks also to Dr. Muhammad Luthfi, Head of the Arabic Department, Faculty of Humanities, The University of Indonesia in Jakarta who has always encouraged me to deepen my knowledge.

My lasting and deepest thanks go to my beloved wife, Soraya and children, M. Hakan Enayata and Hilwa Taqiyya for their patience and forbearance in accompanying me and supporting my study. I am very thankful to have been granted such a wonderful wife and children.

Abstract

This thesis presents a study of the emergence of a new Islamic force in Indonesia, Jemaah Tarbiyah and its political vehicle the Prosperous Justice Party, Partai Keadilan Sejahtera (PKS). Jemaah Tarbiyah emerged in the mid 1980s, mainly on campuses, and in 1998, it transformed itself into political party known initially as the Justice Party, Partai Keadilan (PK) and then since 2003 it changed its name into PKS. This study focuses on their origins, ideology and efforts to Islamise Indonesia. It also attempts to analyse the relations of the movement with the existing Islamic groups in Indonesia and its stance towards the implementation of *shariah*, Islamic law.

In general, I argue that its emergence has contributed to shaping a new variant of *santri*, or observant Muslims in Indonesia which has gone beyond the modernist and traditionalist classifications. Its emergence has contributed in shaping new forms of Islamisation in Indonesia, both in society and the state. In this thesis, I propose other classifications of *santri* in contemporary Islam: convergent, radical and global. Jemaah Tarbiyah is categorized as a movement of a global *santri*. In contrast to fundamentalist features of other Islamist forces in the Islamic world that have been influenced by the Muslim Brothers of Egypt, Jemaah Tarbiyah has shown an accommodative and flexible approach in responding to religious and political questions. It has been an agent of Islamisation that has followed a course between accommodationist and purificationist reformism. Jemaah Tarbiyah demonstrated its non-violent approach in responding to the political repression of Soeharto's New Order. Jemaah Tarbiyah sought to avoid direct confrontation with the regime and focused its activities on predication.

Since becoming a political party, the movement has had to adjust its Islamic aspirations to political realities. A pragmatic approach has become its choice in order to attract popular support. In fact, this too has been largely influenced by the ideas of Hasan al-Banna of the Muslim Brothers, who laid the foundations of reform within the system. al-Banna Sufi influence of Islam shaped his method of gradually bringing change to society and the state. This has been the approach adopted by activists of Jemaah Tarbiyah and is manifest also in PKS's political praxis.

The heterogeneity of Jemaah Tarbiyah activists has been understudied but it has activists from a traditionalist background - in addition to modernists and revivalists. All have contributed to domestication of a trans-national movement into the Indonesian context. In this regard, the role of campus Islam activists in promoting the ideas of al-Banna and using them as a guideline for political activities is very significant. On the issue of the implementation of *shariah* in Indonesia, Jemaah Tarbiyah, through its political party, PKS has not tried to impose *shariah* but rather it has attempted to revise its image by focusing on the issues of prosperity and justice. An analysis of the experiences of Jemaah Tarbiyah and PKS in Indonesia is crucial to an understanding of how an Islamist group can influence the state within the democratic system.

Glossary and Abbreviations

Abangan: Nominal Muslim

Adat (Ar. *al-'Adah*): Custom.

Ahl al-Zimmi: "People of Book" who get protection under the Islamic state.

Akhafuddurarain (Ar. *al-Akhaf al-Durrarayn*). Reducing harm; choosing the lesser of two evils.

Akhlaq (Ar. *al-Akhlaq*): Moral, etiquette.

Al-Adah Mu'adalah (Ar. *al-'Adah Mu'addalah*): a jurisprudential precept meaning a custom is the law.

Aliran Kepercayaan: Religious sect.

Al-Qaedah (Ar. Al-Qa'idah): A network engaged in terrorism, associated with Saudi exile Osama bin Laden.

Al-Qur'an: Muslim Holy book.

Amar Ma'ruf Nahi Munkar: (Ar. *Amr bi al-Ma'ruf wa Nahy 'an al-Munkar*) enjoining good and preventing evil.

Aqidah (Ar. *al-'Aqidah*): Faith.

Arkanul Bai'ah (Ar. *Arkan al-Bay'ah*): Requirements of allegiance.

Baiat: (Ar. *al-Bay'ah*): Allegiance.

BEM: Badan Eksektutif Mahasiswa or Student Executive Board.

Bid'ah (Ar. *al-Bid'ah*): religious innovation.

BKAM: Badan Koordinasi Amal Muslimin or Forum for Muslims' Action and Coordination. It was founded by former activists of Masyumi in preparing the establishment of an Islamic party in 1967.

BMKI: Bina Masjid Kampus Indonesia or Indonesia Campus Mosques Supervision.

CGMI: Central Gerakan Mahasiswa Indonesia or Concentrated Movement of Indonesian Students. Student organisation affiliate of the Communist Party of Indonesia.

Dakwah (Ar. *ad-Da'wah*): Islamic Predication or propagation.

Daulah (Ar. *ad-Dawlah*): State

Daurah (Ar. *ad-Dawrah*): Training.

DDII: Dewan Dakwah Islamiyah Indonesia or Indonesian Council for Islamic Predication. An Islamic missionary organisation founded in 1967 by M. Natsir, a former leader of Masyumi.

Dema: Dewan Mahasiswa or Student Council.

DI: Darul Islam or the House of Islam. An Islamic movement founded by Kartosuwiryo in 1949 aiming to establish an Islamic state.

Din wa daulah (Ar. *al-Din wa al-Dawlah*): Religion and State.

DPR: Dewan Perwakilan Rakyat or People Representative Council.

Dzikir: (Ar: *al-Dhikr*): Remembrance of God, liturgies.

Fardhiyah (Ar. *al-Farziyyah*): Personal, individual.

Fatwah (Ar. *al-Fatwah*): Formal legal opinion.

Fi Zilalil Qur'an (Ar. *Fi Zilal al-Qur'an*): In the shade of the Qur'an. An Qur'anic exegesis written by Sayyid Qutb.

Fikrah (Ar. *al-Fikrah*): Idea, thought.

FIS: Forum for Islamic Study.

Formasi: Forum Amal dan Studi Islam or Forum for Application and Study of Islam.

FPI: Fron Pembela Islam or Islamic Defender Front.

FSLDK: Forum Silaturahmi Lembaga Dakwah Kampus or Forum of Coordination of Campus Predication.

Golkar: Golongan Karya. A secular political party founded by the regime of Soeharto.

Golput: *Golongan Putih* or non voter. An Indonesian citizen who declares not to vote during the general election.

GPI: Gerakan Pemuda Indonesia or Indonesian Youth Movement. A youth organisation has affiliation with Masyumi.

GMNI: Gerakan Mahasiswa Nasional Indonesia or Indonesian National Students Movement.

Gemsos: Gerakan Mahasiswa Sosialis or Socialist Students Movement

Hadith (Ar. *al-Hadith*): the Saying of the Prophet Muhammad.

Haji (Ar. *al-Haj*): Pilgrim; a title of man who has performed *hajj* while for woman it is used title *hajjah*.

Hajj (Ar. *al-Haj*): Pilgrimage to Mecca.

Halal (Ar. *al-Halal*): allowable.

Halaqah (Ar. *al-Halaqah*): Circle

Haram (Ar. *al-Haram*): Prohibited.

Hizb (Ar. *al-Hizb*): Party, group.

Hizbut Tahrir: (Ar. *al-Hizb al-Tahrir*): A trans-national movement founded by Taqiyyuddin al-Nabhani in Jordan which has promoted the establishment of an international caliph.

HMI MPO: Himpunan Mahasiswa Indonesia – Majelis Penyelamat Organisasi or Indonesia Students Association – Safeguarding Committee of the Organisation.

HMI: Himpunan Mahasiswa Islam or Indonesian Students Muslim Association. Predominantly modernist students' association founded in 1947.

HTI: Hizbut Tahrir Indonesia or Indonesian *Hizbut Tahrir*.

Hudud (Ar. *al-Hudud*): Islamic punishment.

IAIN: Institut Agama Islam Negeri or State Institute of Islamic Religion.

ICMI: Ikatan Cendekiawan Muslim Indonesia or Indonesian Intelectual Muslim Association.

IIFSO: International Islamic Federation of Student Organisation.

IIRO: International Islamic Relief Organisation. An Islamic humanitarian organisation founded in 1978 based in Saudi Arabia.

Ijtihad (Ar. *al-Ijtihad*): Legal reasoning.

Ikhwah (Ar. *al-Ikhwah*): Brother. It has two derivations, *ikhwan* (Brothers) and *akhawat* (Sisters).

Ikhwanul Muslimin (Ar. *al-Ikhwan al-Muslimun*):.The Muslim Brothers founded by Hasan al-Banna in Egypt in 1928.

IKIP: Institute Kejuruan Ilmu Pendidikan or Higher Education for Education Sciences.

Imam: (Ar. *al-Imam*): Leader.

Insan Kamil (Ar. *al-Insan al-Kamil*): Perfect human being, a Sufi concept.

Iqtisadi (Ar. *al-Iqtisad*): Economy

Islam Kultural: Cultural Islam, referring to Muslim groups who promote Islam at the level of the state through substantialist approaches. They prefer to influence the state based on Islamic general values (substance).

Islam Politik: Political Islam, referring to Muslim groups who promote Islam at the level of the state though legal formalist approaches. Islam must be considered as the only source of legislation.

ITB: Institut Teknologi Bandung or Bandung Institute of Technology.

ITS: Institut Teknologi Sepuluh Nopember or Technology Institute of Tenth November in Surabaya.

Jemaah (Ar. *al-Jama'ah*): Movement; group.

Jamaah Takfir wal Hijrah (Ar. *al-Jama'ah at-Takfir wa al-Hijrah*): A radical splinter group of the Muslim Brothers in Egypt.

Jamaat Islami (Ar. *al-Jama'ah al-Islamiyyah*): Islamic Party founded by Abu A'la Maududi in Pakistan.

JI: Jemaah Islamiyah (Ar. *al-Jama'ah al-Islamiyyah*): Islamic Group. A radical Islamic group founded by Abdullah Syungkar and Abu Bakar Ba'asyir.

Jihad: (Ar. *al-Jihad*): Strife, Struggle.

JIL: Jaringan Islam Liberal or Islamic Liberal Network. A liberal-minded organization founded by activists of the younger generation of NU.

JIMM: Jaringan Intelektual Muda Muhammadiyah or Muhammadiyah Young Intellectual Network. An association for the younger Muhammadiyah intellectuals and activists who promote the idea of liberal Islam.

Kafah (Ar. *al-Kaffah*): Total and comprehensive.

Kahfi (Ar. *al-Kahfi*): A name of cave referring to the story of *ashab al-Kahfi* (cave dwellers) who were forced to hide in a cave for hundreds years due to the repression of a tyrant king.

KAMI: Kesatuan Aksi Mahasiswa Indonesia or Indonesian Student Action Union). An association of student organisations founded in 1966 to prevent the influence of the communist student movement.

KAMMI: Kesatuan Aksi Mahasiswa Muslim Indonesia or Indonesian Muslim Student Action Union. An extra campus organization founded by activist of Jemaah Tarbiyah in secular campuses in 1998.

Kantor Catatan Sipil: Marriage Registrar.

Katibah (Ar. *al-Katibah*): gathering of many members of *usrah*.

Kaum Muda: Young group (progressive).

Kaum Tua: Old group (conservative).

Kelompok Sempalan: Splinter group.

Khilafah: (Ar. *al-Khilafah*): Caliphate. United grouping of Islamic countries.

Khilafiyah (Ar. *al-Khilafiyyah*): Disputes concerning religious matters.

Khurafat (Ar. *al-Khurafah*): Mysticism which is not pemitted.

KISDI: Komite Indonesia Solidaritas Dunia Islam or Indonesian Committee for Solidarity with Islamic World.

KKN: *Korupsi, Kolusi dan Nepotisme* or Corruption, Nepotism and Collusion.

KMI: Korp Muballigh Islam or Islamic Preacher Corps.

KNPI: Komite Nasional Pemuda Indonesia or National Committee of Indonesian Youth.

Kolot: old or traditional. It usually refers to a traditionalist Muslim group.

Komji: Komando Jihad or Command of Jihad. It refers to radical groups in 1980s that were associated with DI factions.

KPPSI: Komite Persiapan dan Penegakan Syariat Islam or Committee for Preparing and Upholding Islamic Shariah.

Kyai: Muslim leader, cleric.

LDKU: Lembaga Dakwah Khairu Ummah or Predication Institute of Khairu Ummah. A Jemaah Tarbiyah affiliated-Islamic preachers' association.

LDMI: Lembaga Dakwah Mahasiswa Islam or Board of Muslim Student Proselytising. An Islamic missionary organisation founded by HMI.

LIPIA: Lembaga Ilmu Pengetahuan Islam dan Arab or Institute for Islamic Knowledge and Arabic.

LMD: Lembaga Mujahid Dakwah or Institute of Predication Struggler.

LSM: Lembaga Swadaya Masyarakat or Non Governmental Organisation (NGO).

Ma'had (Ar. *al-Ma'had*): Islamic higher education.

Maishah (Ar. *al-Ma'ishah*): Income

Majelis Syurah (Ar. *al-Majlis al-Shurah*): Consultative Council.

Martabat Tujuh: Seven stages of human based on Sufi teachings.

Maslahat Dakwah (Ar. *Maslahah al-Da'wah*): Benefit of the common good for the sake of Islamic predication.

Maslahat (Ar. *al-Maslahah*): Necessity, benefit.

Masyumi: Majlis Syura Muslimin (Ar. *al-Majlis al-Shurah al-Muslimun*), Muslims' Consultative Council.

Mazhab (Ar. *al-Madhhab*): School of Islamic jurisprudential thought

Mihwar (Ar. *al-Mihwar*): Stage

Minhajul Hayah (Ar. *Minhaj al-Hayah*):: Way of life.

MMI: Majelis Mujahidin Indonesia or Indonesia Fighters Council.

Moderen: Modern. It refers to a modernist Muslim group.

MPR: Majelis Permusyawaratan Rakyat or People's Consultative Assembly.

MSA: Muslim Student Association. A student association founded in 1975 based in the United States.

Mu'assasi (Ar. *al-Mu'assasy*): Politicisation.

Mualim (Ar. *al-Mu'allim*): Teacher.

Muhammadiyah: A modernist group association influenced by the ideas of Muhammad Abduh in Egypt founded in 1912.

Mukhayam (Ar. *al-mukhayyam*): Camp.

Muktamar (Ar. *al-Mu'tamar*): Conference

Murabbi (Ar. *al-Murabb*): Teacher, mentor.

Murid (Ar. *al-Murid*): Pupil, student.

Mursyid (Ar. *al-Murshid*): Religious guide of Sufi order.

Mushalla (Ar. *al-Mus}alla*): A place for prayer.

Musyarakah (Ar. *al-Musharakah*): Cooperation, coalition.

Mutarabbi (Ar. *al-Mutarabb*): Pupil, student.

Nadwah (Ar. *al-Nadwah*): Seminar.

NII: Negara Islam Indonesia or Indonesia Islamic State.

Nizham Islami (Ar. *al-Nizam al-Islamiy*): The Islamic system.

NKK/BKK: Normalisasi Kehidupan Campur/Badan Koordinasi Kampus or Normalisation of Campus Life/Committee for Campus Coordination.

NU: Nahdlatul Ulama or Renaissance of Islamic Scholars. A mass organisation associated to traditionalist group founded in 1926.

Opsus: *Operasi Khusus* or Special Operation.

PAN: Partai Amanat Nasional or Party of National Mandate. A party linked to Muhammadiyah.

Pangkopkamtib: Panglima Komando Pemulihan Keamanan dan Ketertiban or Supreme Military Operation Commander for Security and Order.

PBB: Partai Bulan Bintang or Party of Moon and Crescent. A party linked to Masyumi.

PDIP: Partai Demokrasi Indonesia Perjuangan or the Indonesian Democratic Party – Struggle.

PDS: Partai Damai Sejahtera or Party of Prosperity and Peace. A party linked to Christian groups.

Perpu: *Peraturan Pemerintah* or Government Policy.

Persis: Persatuan Islam or Islamic Union. A revivalist movement group founded by A. Hasan in 1923 in Bandung.

Perti: Persatuan Tarbiyah Islamiyah or Islamic Education Association. Traditionalist organisation based in West Sumatra.

Pesantren: Islamic boarding school.

Petisi 50: Fifty Petition. An oppositional group criticising the regime policy in Indonesia declared in 1981.

PHI: Persatuan Haji Indonesia or Indonesian Pilgrim Association.

Piagam Jakarta: the Jakarta Charter

Piagam Madinah: Medina Charter, an agreement between Muslims and non-Muslims in Medina under the rule of the Prophet Muhammad.

PII: Pelajar Islam Indonesia or Indonesian Muslim Pupils. A modernist association for Muslim students in High schools.

PK: Partai Keadilan or Justice Party. A party established by members of Jemaah Tarbiyah in 1998 and changed its name into PKS, Partai Keadilan Sejahtera or Prosperous Justice Party in 2002.

PKB: Partai Kebangkitan Bangsa or Party of National Renaissance. A party linked to NU.

PMI: Partai Muslimin Indonesia (Parmusi) or Indonesia Muslims' Party. The party aimed to continue the struggle of Masyumi after it failed to be revived.

PMII: Pergerakan Mahasiswa Islam Indonesia or Indonesia Islamic Students Movement. A tertiary student organisation affiliate with NU.

PMKI: Perhimpunan Mahasiswa Kristen Indonesia or Indonesian Christian Students' Association.

PNDI: Penanaman Nilai Dasar Islam or Cultivating of Basic Islamic Values.

PPP: Partai Persatuan Pembangunan or Unity and Development Party.

Pribumisasi: Indigenisation.

Priyayi: Javanese aristocrat.

PRRI: Pemerintah Revolusioner Republik Indonesia or Revolutionary Government of the Republic Indonesia.

PSI: Partai Sosialis Indonesia or Indonesia Socialist Party.

PSII: Partai Syarikat Islam Indonesia or Indonesia Islamic Union Party. A Muslim trader based association.

PTDI: Pendidikan Tinggi Dakwah Islam or Higher Education for Islamic Predication.

Qaul (Ar. *al-Qawl*): Saying, opinion. In Islamic jurisprudence has two categories, *al-Qawl al-Qadim* (old opinion) and *al-Qawl al-Jadid* (new opinion).

Rabat (Ar. *ar-Rabat*): Profit.

Rabitah (Ar. *ar-Rabitah*): Binding, association.

Rihlah (Ar. *ar-Rihlah*): Recreation.

Riwaq (Ar. *ar-Riwaq*): Dormitory.

Rohis: *Rohani Islam* or Islamic Spirituality.

RPKAD: Resimen Para Komando Angkatan Darat or the Army Para Commondos.

Salafi (Ar. *al-Salaf*): Old, ancient. A movement that claims to follow the teachings of Islam through ancient trusted scholars.

Salafus Salih (Ar. *al-Salaf al-Salih*): ancient trusted scholars. It refers to three generations of Muslim scholars after the death of the Prophet Muhammad.

Sanlat: Pesantren Kilat or Short Islamic Training.

Santri: Devout Muslim

Sekoci: A small boat. The term used to name splinter groups of DI.

Sema: Senat Mahasiswa or Student Senate.

Shalat (Ar. *al-Salah*): prayer.

Syariah (Ar. *al-Shari'ah*): Islamic Law.

SIDIK: Studi dan Informasi Dunia Islam Kontemporer or Study and Information for Contemporary Islamic World.

SII: Studi Islam Intensif or Intensive Islamic Study.

Sisdiknas: Sistem Pendidikan Nasional or National Education System.

Sya'bi (Ar. *al-Sha'biy*): Society, community or socialisation.

Syamil (Ar. *al-Shamil*): Comprehensive; general, universal, perfect, complete.

Ta'aruf (Ar. *al-Ta'aruf*): Introduction.

Tabligh (Ar. *al-Tabligh*): Preaching.

Tafa'ul (Ar. *al-Tafa'ul*): Assistance, insurance.

Tafahum (Ar. *al-Tafahum*): Mutual understanding.

Tahlilan (Ar. *al-Tahlil*): Recitation of the creed, *La ilaha Illa Allah* (There is no god but God), at ceremonies to commemorate the dead.

Takhayul: Superstition

Tanzim (Ar. *al-Tanzim*): Organisation

Tarbiyah (Ar. *al-Tarbiyyah*): Education or training model of Jemaah Tarbiyah in disseminating its ideas.

Tariqah (Ar. *al-Tariqah*): Path, Sufi order.

Tasawwuf (Ar. *al-Tasawwuf*): Islamic mysticism.

Tawasul (Ar. *al-Tawassul*): Intercession, intermediary. A prayer mediated by holy persons.

Tawhid (Ar. *al-Tawhid*): Theology of the oneness of God.

UGM: Universitas Gadjah Madah or Gadjah Madah University in Yogyakarta.

UI: Universitas Indonesia or University of Indonesia.

Ukhuwah (Ar. *al-Ukhuwwah*): Brotherhood.

Ulama (Ar. *al-'Ulama'*): Religious scholars, jurists.

Ummah (Ar. *al-Ummah*): Society, community and nation.

Unair: Universitas Airlangga or University of Airlangga in Surabaya.

Unpad: Universitas Padjajaran or Padjajaran University.

Ushul Fiqh (Ar. *al-'Usul al-Fiqh*): Jurisprudential basis.

Usrah (Ar. *al-Usrah*): Family

UUD: Undang Undang Dasar or Indonesia Constitution.

Wirid (Ar. *al-Aurad*): Set of prayer formula recited regularly. It is also called *wadzifah*.

Wahabi: A movement influenced by Muhammad Abd al-Wahab in Saudi Arabia.

Yarsi: Yayasan Rumah Sakit Islam Indonesia or Indonesian Islamic Hospital Foundation.

Zawiyah (Ar. *al-Zawiyyah*): Meditation room

SEMMI: Serikat Mahasiswa Muslimin Indonesia or Indonesian Muslim Students Association. A student movement associates with PSII.

Somal: Sekretariat Bersama Organisasi-Organisasi Lokal or Collective Offices of Local Organisations.

Pelmasi: Pelopor Mahasiswa Sosialis Indonesia or Pioneer of Indonesian Socialist Students.

Mapantjas: Mahasiswa Pancasila or Students of Pancasila.

Notes on Transliteration, Spelling and Referencing

For Arabic words and names, this thesis uses the system of transliteration, which is applied in the discipline of Islamic studies, as employed The Institute of Islamic Studies, McGill University, under following principles:

Consonants:

b = ب	z = ز	f = ف
t = ت	s = س	q = ق
th = ث	sh = ش	k = ك
j = ج	s = ص	l = ل
h = ح	d = ض	m = م
kh = خ	t = ط	n = ن
d = د	z = ظ	h = ه
dh = ذ	' = ع	w = و
r = ر	gh = غ	y = ي

Vowels:

Short: a = ́ ; i = ˏ ; u = ˚

Long: a< = ; i> = ي ; = و

Diphthong: ay = ي ; aw = او

Arabic terms translated to English follow their original meanings, such as *al-Ikhwa>n al-Muslimu>n* is translated as the Muslim Brothers, rather than the Muslim Brotherhood. Indonesian phrases referring to proper names, names of persons, places and institutions are not italicized. Partai Keadilan, Jemaah Tarbiyah, Muhammdiyah, Partai Persatuan Pembangunan and the like are not italicized.

All references use the footnote system applied by Kate L. Turabian.[1] Starting with the name of the author and then followed in order by the title of the work, the place of the publication, the name of the publisher, the date of publishing, and page number. The three elements before the last are given in brackets, as shown here:

Michael Gilsenan, *Saint and Sufi in Modern Egypt: an Essay on the Sociology of Religion* (Oxford: The Clarendon Press, 1973), 25.

Reference to a work that has already been cited in full form, but with intervening references, uses the author's last name, a shortened title of book and page that is: Gilsenan, *Saint and Sufi in Modern Egypt*, 25.

ENDNOTES

[1] Kate L. Turabian, A Manual for Writers of Term Papers, Thesis, and Dissertations (Chicago and London: The University of Chicago Press, 1996).

Introduction

> "Again, the Prosperous Justice Party [Partai Keadilan Sejahtera, PKS] held a demonstration. And again, it involved thousands of participants, and it was amazing because the demonstration was peaceful and orderly. That's what happened yesterday - thousands of PKS cadres poured on to the streets. They launched a demonstration calling for the United Nations to acknowledge the independence of Palestine. They condemned the United States and denounced Israel."[1]

The post-Soeharto era of government in Indonesia, beginning in 1998, has witnessed the emergence of various Islamic groups and movements. The emergence of these new groups has not only displayed diversity in terms of their political and religious orientation, but they have also brought new actors and agendas to the fore. Greater space for political expression and political participation has been opened up. Interestingly, the Justice Party (PK) that did not have popular front figures, either from traditionalist or modernist camps, performed well but did not meet the electoral threshold during the 1999 general elections. However, it produced a remarkable achievement after changing its name into the Prosperous Justice Party, Partai Keadilan Sejahtera (PKS) in the 2004 general elections.[2]

PKS is an interesting phenomenon in Indonesia. Its educated cadres, drawn mainly from university campuses, lead a dedicated membership. Its low profile performance and non-violent strategies have raised it to become the sixth largest political party in Indonesia. Its peaceful orientation, yet its criticism of Western domination of the global political order have been apparent during its many demonstrations, as the excerpt from an editorial in *Media Indonesia* above illustrates. PKS members have not hesitated to bring their families, including their small children, to their public demonstrations. "Bringing along children to a demonstration is an obvious guarantee that it will be peaceful and safe. That is something that has been shown by the Prosperous Justice Party."[3] The emergence of such a new force of political Islam represented by PKS is on the surface a recent phenomenon; in fact it has had a long history in Indonesia, which will be elaborated.

During the sustained political repression by Soeharto's New Order regime towards organised Islam, Muslim activists who joined a new informal religious movement called Jemaah Tarbiyah were able to revive Islamic activities on many university campuses. They focussed on cultivating religious understanding and practice among students. They set up informal religious circles, or *halaqah*, using small prayer rooms and other student facilities to conduct their activities. In order to consolidate their programs they founded intra-campus organisations under the umbrella of a body called the Forum for Islamic Study (FIS).

Jemaah Tarbiyah gained momentum and attracted many students during the 1990s. In this decade, many of its activists won control of student executive bodies and placed their best cadres in the position of head of student senates. In 1993, a Jemaah Tarbiyah cadre, Mustafa Kamal, won the student elections in the Faculty of Humanities of the University of Indonesia and became the first member of Jemaah Tarbiyah to gain highest position of the student government at the faculty level. The following year, Jemaah Tarbiyah activist Zulkieflimansyah secured the position of general chairman of the student senate at university level in the same institution. Since then, student governments at the university and faculty levels in other prestigious universities have come under the control of Jemaah Tarbiyah activists, pushing aside candidates from the existing Muslim student associations, such as Muslim Student Association, Himpunan Mahasiswa Islam (HMI) or Indonesia Islamic Students Movement, Pergerakan Mahasiswa Islam Indonesia (PMII).

Jemaah Tarbiyah has also expanded its influence in an extra-campus predication network, called the Forum for Coordinating Campus Predication, Forum Silaturahmi Lembaga Dakwah Kampus (FSLDK) throughout secular universities in Indonesia. Through this campus predication net, members of Jemaah Tarbiyah seized the advantage to establish the Indonesian Muslim Student Action Union, Kesatuan Aksi Mahasiswa Muslim Indonesia (KAMMI) in Malang, East Java in 1998. In April 1998 KAMMI, under the leadership of Fahri Hamzah, organised a huge demonstration calling for the resignation of President Soeharto.

After the collapse of the Soeharto regime, Jemaah Tarbiyah, as an informal social movement, decided to transform itself into a formal organisation. This decision was taken when the movement had to choose whether to establish a mass organisation, or a fully political party. The majority of members agreed to form a political party, named the Justice Party, Partai Keadilan (PK) accommodating all of Jemaah Tarbiyah's activities. PK was established on 28 July 1998 and publicly announced on 9 August 1998. Nurmahmudi Ismail, a PhD graduate from the American Texas A & M University, was elected as the party's first president.

In 1999 PK participated in the general legislative elections and gained 1.4% (1.436.565) of the total vote. Nurmahmudi Ismail was appointed Minister of Agriculture and Forestry. On 20 May 2000, Hidayat Nurwahid, who held a doctorate in Islamic Studies from Madinah University, Saudi Arabia, replaced Ismail as president of PK. Since PK did not meet the electoral threshold of 2%, activists of Jemaah Tarbiyah then prepared a new political party, the Prosperous Justice Party, Partai KeadilanSejahtera (PKS). On 20 April 2003, PKS, led by Al-Muzammil Yusuf, a former activist in campus predication, was formally declared a political party to take part in the 2004 general elections.

On July 2003, PK formally merged with PKS and Hidayat Nurwahid was elected president. During the general elections of 2004 PKS succeeded in gaining 7.34% (8.325.020) of the total vote and this has placed its cadres in seats in the national and local parliaments. Nurwahid was chosen as Chairperson of the People's Consultative Assembly (MPR) and left his position as president of PKS. On May 2005, Tifatul Sembiring, another former activist in campus predication was selected as the new president of PKS.

The emergence of this new Islamic party has surprised many observers and scholars of Indonesian politics and Islam. The dramatic success of PKS participation in the 2004 general elections also continues to puzzle many. For instance, the Indonesia Survey Institute, Lembaga Survei Indonesia (LSI) issued the results of its national survey conducted in September 2003, stating that if the general elections had been held at the time of the survey, PKS would have been predicted to gain about 2.3%.[4] Surprisingly, in the 2004 elections it succeeded in gaining 7.34%; that is, significantly above the LSI's predictions. Even though PKS appears to have had little support, it still succeeded in achieving a significant share of votes in 2004.

PKS has raised new issues about the ability of a political party that apparently maintains Islam as its political and ideological basis to attract votes. PKS phenomenon has puzzled not only foreign observers but Indonesian scholars as well. This is largely because PKS has no precedent in the past and it has shown itself to be unique in the Indonesian democratic system. Its campaigns for clean government and against corruption and the abuse of power, in addition to its commitment to religious aspirations have surprised observers and merit further examination.

PKS represents a younger generation of Indonesian Muslims from various backgrounds who no longer follow their parents in political participation. They have begun to create their own political party to represent the Muslim *ummah* (Muslim community). Thus PKS presents an alternative political vehicle for Muslim activists who have not been accommodated by their parents' political parties, such as PKB, PAN, PPP and PBB. They are, in the main, educated outside the traditional educational system and have taken different paths to learn about Islam. They now claim to struggle for the interests of an Islam undivided by the traditionalist and modernist dichotomy. The concept of a universal and total Islam has become their religious framework and orientation. Within their image of themselves as Muslims they lean towards a global and universal Islam that brings together all different Muslim identities for the triumph of Islam.

As the backbone of PKS, Jemaah Tarbiyah has also actively implemented a proselytising mission focussed on improving Indonesian Muslims' understanding of their faith. Inspired by a religious movement in the Middle East, the Egyptian Muslim Brothers, Jemaah Tarbiyah has played a role as the agent of religious reform and at the same time has embarked on political activities to present itself as a united force of *ummah* regardless of individual religious orientations within its ranks. In carrying out its reform, Jemaah Tarbiyah has shown an accommodative strategy in order to avoid religious disputes and resistance among Indonesian Muslims in general.

Jemaah Tarbiyah's inclusive attitude to accommodate Muslims from various backgrounds and to invite them to follow its ideas has been heavily influenced by Hasan al-Banna, the founder of the Muslim Brothers.[5] Al-Banna's inclination towards accommodation in religious matters has influenced Jemaah Tarbiyah's stance in dealing with politics. Rather than demonstrating any fundamentalist views, the ideas of Jemaah Tarbiyah have been channelled through PKS in "accommodative ways" that tend to downplay its ideology. Its coalition with the Prosperity and Peace Party, Partai Damai Sejahtera (PDS), a Christian Party, to run for the election of governor of the Province of Papua in 2006, indicates PKS efforts to be accepted by the broader population of Indonesia.[6] The views of PKS on *shariah*, or Islamic law and its implementation in Indonesia is also a good example of its pragmatic approach and will be analysed in Chapter VII.

Jemaah Tarbiyah's practical attitude to religious and political issues has their historical origins during the years of Soeharto's New Order. Instead of identifying themselves as a resistance group, the activists of Jemaah Tarbiyah deliberately avoided open confrontation with the regime and kept their distance from domestic and political issues. The commitment of Jemaah Tarbiyah to non-violence within its mass events on the university campuses began to bear fruit when the regime introduced a policy of political openness, picking up momentum when the regime's situation became critical and finally collapsed in 1998. Jemaah Tarbiyah was able to transform itself into a political party and to set up branches throughout the country.

In order to gain an adequate insight into PKS phenomenon, a study of its informal religious movement, Jemaah Tarbiyah that has become the voting mainstay of the party, is crucial. We need to focus on the historical record of the Jemaah Tarbiyah, as well as on its ideological and political orientations. This will be done in this thesis by analysing the intellectual and religious origins of the movement and by placing it in the context of the dynamics of Islam in Indonesia. Whilst the transmission of intellectual influences from the international arena of Islam into Indonesia is significant, the contribution of local dynamics to the process of shaping the final ideology must be understood. The social and religious affiliations of the Jemaah Tarbiyah membership are also important factors in Jemaah Tarbiyah's response to Indonesian realities. These will be taken into consideration in our analysis of the possible moves of the party in its efforts to Islamise the state.

A. Recent Studies on Jemaah Tarbiyah and the Prosperous Justice Party

The emergence of Jemaah Tarbiyah and its political vehicle, PKS has excited the curiosity of scholars of Indonesian Islam. In general, there have been three approaches in the many studies depicting the phenomenon of Jemaah Tarbiyah and PKS. Unfortunately, however, each approach has been significantly misleading in its view of the reality of Jemaah Tarbiyah and its political party.

First, some writers, such as Ali Said Damanik, Abdul Aziz and Azyumardi Azra try to depict Jemaah Tarbiyah as an entirely new movement and do not attempt to relate it to the broader process of continuing Islamisation in Indonesia. It has been also described as a splinter group apart from mainstream Islam. A second group of authors, such as Aay Muhammad Furkon and Andi Rahmat claim that the movement is merely a continuation of the modernist history of Indonesian Islam. Some exaggerate this belief and go so far as to state that PKS is the direct inheritor of Masyumi, and that the history of PKS is no less than part of Masyumi's development. A further issue regarding the phenomenon of PKS is its attitude towards democracy. Most observers, such as Martin van Bruinessen, Sadanand Dhume and Zachary Abuza still question its commitment and integrity towards an agenda of democratisation in Indonesia. They assert that that PKS, born from a religious movement as it is, has so far taken no obvious stance on democracy.

The following section will elaborate how the three approaches give an inaccurate picture of Jemaah Tarbiyah and PKS. I try to bridge any gaps by suggesting new approaches and perspectives in analysing this phenomenon.

1. The "Splinter Group" Approach

The main concern of this approach has been with the roots and historical origins of PKS and its alleged links with a trans-national Islamic movement in the Middle East. The mere fact that PKS rests on the support of Jemaah Tarbiyah offers little further insight. Because of a general lack of information, Jemaah Tarbiyah has been viewed as an entirely new movement, without historical connections to existing Islamic groups in Indonesia, perhaps a group set apart from Indonesian mainstream Islam. And to some extent, it has indeed aroused suspicion in the two largest established Muslim organizations, Nahdatul Ulama (NU) and Muhammadiyah about its connection with splinter groups, since its appearance in Indonesia coincided with the emergence of Islamic radicalism.

So Jemaah Tarbiyah has not only been considered to lie outside mainstream Islam but it is also regarded by some as one of the illegal Islamic sects (*aliran-aliran terlarang*) or splinter groups (*kelompok-kelompok sempalan*) - such new movements being labelled "fundamentalist" without any serious research having been given them.[7] For instance, a preliminary study of Jemaah Tarbiyah by Azyumardi Azra, though not exclusively addressing it, puts Jemaah Tarbiyah in the same category as several deviant groups which stray from the general understanding of Islam in Indonesia.[8]

The significant international influences upon Jemaah Tarbiyah are the main reasons for its categorisation as an exclusive and alienated movement. The members of the group behave in ways (such as in their mode of dress and their restricted socialising) which set them apart from many other observant Indonesian Muslim groups. They display their spiritual symbols by self-consciously following the Prophet's examples, such as keeping beards, wearing Arab style clothing, and the like. They have been labelled by mainstream Muslims as *kelompok sempalan* (splinter groups).[9]

However, the term "*sempalan*" in Indonesian discourse about Islam is not unproblematic. As suggested by Martin van Bruinessen, it is translated into English as "splinter group", and has been adopted by Indonesian scholars to identify various new Islamic groups or religious sects that have been considered "alien" or deviating from the mainstream.[10] In the context of Indonesia, "mainstream" and "orthodox" refers to recognised organisations such as MUI, Muhammadiyah, NU and others. New Islamic movements that are not associated with these have been labelled *kelompok sempalan*. The term is also applied to groups which deliberately dissociate themselves from the mainstream, develop exclusive attitudes and are critical of established Muslim scholars.[11] It is perhaps understandable that early studies of Jemaah Tarbiyah have tended to view it in the frame of splinter groups in Indonesia that adopt an *usrah*, or "family" approach in disseminating their ideas. Among these are, as mentioned by Azra, Jamaah Takfir wal Hijrah, Hizbut Tahrir, and Jemaah Tarbiyah.[12]

Depicting the phenomenon of Jemaah Tarbiyah as lying outside mainstream Islam may lead to the assumption that the movement, politically and culturally, has raised serious problems for and challenged the government and mainstream Islam. Admittedly, the adoption of the *usrah* model, borrowed from the Muslim Brothers, its links with international networks and its idea of Islam as *al-nizam al-islamiy* (the Islamic System) might lead such a movement into exclusive and radical directions.[13] However, the transformation of Jemaah Tarbiyah into a political party and its integration with broader Indonesian society has not only reduced its fundamentalist image but has also made possible a new model of an Islamic movement that is not necessarily a splinter or dissident group.

A book on Jemaah Tarbiyah by Ali Said Damanik, entitled *Fenomena Partai Keadilan Transformasi 20 Tahun Gerakan Tarbiyah di Indonesia* (The Phenomenon of the Justice Party: the Transformation of Twenty Years of the Tarbiyah Movement in Indonesia) explains something of the context behind the establishment of Partai Keadilan.[14] Damanik does not try to link the new movement with mainstream Islam. He sees Jemaah Tarbiyah as a unique group that has no historical association with existing Islamic groups and parties. It is an entirely new movement, born of the ideas of the Society of Muslim Brothers in Egypt. In his introduction, Damanik expresses his confusion in identifying the movement. "The author does not know how he should name this movement that has been initiated by young Muslims, and which is very active in setting up Islamic circles (*halaqah*) for training and preaching on the university campuses. They are like a wind, it is easy to feel their presence but their shape is still not clear."[15]

2. The "Modernist Heritage" Approach

Recent studies of PKS often attempt to relate it to the heritage of Islamic modernism, in particular by directing it to the Star and Crescent Family *(Keluarga Bulan Bintang)* or Masyumi. In these studies, PKS is regarded as a continuation of the old Masyumi of the 1950s. However, rather than acknowledging PKS as an heir of Masyumi, *Keluarga Bulan Bintang,* through the Board of Indonesian Islamic Predication, Dewan Dakwah Islamiyah Indonesia (DDII) prefers to formally ratify the Star and Crescent Party (PBB) as Masyumi's successor.[16]

Aay Muhammad Furkon, in his book *Partai Keadilan Sejahtera: Ideologi dan Praksis Politik Kaum Muda Muslim Indonesia Kontemporer* (The Prosperous Justice Party: Ideology and Political Praxis of Contemporary Young Indonesian Muslims) concludes that PKS has obviously historical modernist roots.[17] Culturally, it is an organic part of DDII in carrying on the struggle of Islam bequeathed by Masyumi.[18] According to Furkon, in its earlier stage, most of the Justice Party activists were well connected to modernist figures from DDII, even being known as young cadres of DDII.[19]

However, the accuracy of this claim is questionable, since the establishment of PKS was the result of the contributions of Muslims of various backgrounds and affiliations. As stated by Anis Matta, an influential figure in Jemaah Tarbiyah who holds the position of Secretary General of PKS 2005-2010: "The Justice Party is like a growing tree, and modernist Muslims have contributed to its watering; but many other Muslims have played the same role. They have been watering PK with the spirit and the 'water' of struggle."[20]

Furkon is exaggerating when he makes the claim that the modernist family is the only group which deserves to acknowledge PKS as its legitimate son. He overlooks the fact that Masyumi was not only represented by modernist figures – even though after NU broke from Masyumi in 1952 it was still supported by traditionalist figures who firmly believed in the significance of politics and power in the struggle for an Islamic agenda. Some *pesantren,* or traditionalist Islamic boarding schools in Java, and others in the Outer Islands as well, continued to be strongholds of Masyumi supporters. Two influential traditionalist figures who owned large *pesantren* in Java, Abdullah Syaifii of the Pesantren

Assyafiiyah in Jakarta and Yusuf Hasyim of the Pesantren Tebuireng in East Java are still accorded a high reputation among the "family" of *Bulan Bintang*. On the other hand, many of the younger generation of NU which are not formally associated with NU organisations joined Jemaah Tarbiyah and have supported the Justice Party.

The weakness of Furkon's account is that he fails to focus on the remarkable generational change in Muslims which took place towards the end of the Soeharto regime. The decades of the 1970s and 1980s witnessed a process of convergence among the successors of Indonesian traditionalism and modernism. They worked together, either in developing new directions in Islamic thought or in promoting Islamic predication movements. In this era, the embryo of PKS, Jemaah Tarbiyah developed and attracted both traditionalists and modernists. Examining these trends during the New Order regime will help us to understand the possibility of linkage between traditionalist and modernist groups and PKS.

Another book, *Perlawanan dari Masjid Kampus* (Resistance from the Campus Mosque) by Andi Rahmat, an activist of the Association of Indonesian Muslim Students, Kesatuan Aksi Mahasiswa Muslim Indonesia (KAMMI) offers a broader explanation of the involvement of the students and their opposition to the Soeharto regime.[21] KAMMI is known for its close affiliation with PKS. Rahmat tries to connect the spirit of political opposition with the heritage of modernist groups, which dominated the student movements. This became the central point in the emergence of Jemaah Tarbiyah and the establishment of KAMMI. The use of the mosque as a centre of opposition was obviously an effort to connect the new movements with DDII history in which the mosques had become the venue for veterans of Masyumi to criticise the regime.

Following on in this vein, it is generally recognised that mosques were used as sites to express Muslim opposition to the state during the 1980s. In contrast to DDII, however, which made frequent use of the mosques in urban areas to criticise government policies, the case of Jemaah Tarbiyah is somewhat different. Once the New Order had wrested control of all mosques and maintained censorship of the contents of sermons, the mosques were no longer safe sites for dissident groups.[22] In order to keep apart from the regime's oppression, Jemaah Tarbiyah preferred to initiate their activities through Islamic study groups and training sessions, using campus facilities, such as classrooms, halls and small prayer rooms. They avoided confronting government policies and concentrated on developing Islamic morality and ethics and on upholding the performance of the daily prayers. During this era, Jemaah Tarbiyah also tried to keep its distance from DDII in order to develop a non-political predication totally different from that of their predecessors of the modernist groups. They confined their activities of Islamisation to the campuses. They only moved into campus mosques after the regime opened up political space for Muslims in the 1990s, extending the Islamic activities and training that before had always come under official surveillance.

In general, the modernist image that seems to characterise PKS is due to the fact that most of the earliest outspoken activists of Jemaah Tarbiyah came from modernist families, whilst figures from a traditionalist background had a low profile. Moreover, the latter had not been active members of the traditionalist organizations. It is understandable that in the early development of Jemaah Tarbiyah connection with modernist mentors was strongly established, particularly with DDII. However, contrary to this "superficial" impression about PKS, my research into the background of its activists shows a great number of figures connected to traditionalist traditions. Traditionalist figures now dominate the membership and appear as a force within PKS that will bring change in the strategy and appearance of the party in the future. PKS represents an alternative vehicle for young Indonesian Muslims of differing religious origins united by a vision to make Islam more applicable to every aspect of daily life, including politics.

3. The "Compatibility with Democracy" Approach

As was mentioned above, the shadow and influence of the Muslim Brothers movement in Egypt over Jemaah Tarbiyah has given rise to suspicions among scholars about the commitment of PKS to democratic ideals. Was this possible for a political party almost solely supported by a religious movement, which in the beginning preferred to promote Islam as an alternative to democracy? Can the two different agendas go hand in hand in Indonesia? Will it be the role of Jemaah Tarbiyah to drive the party to promote a more Islamist programme and to downplay the value of the democratic system?

Martin van Bruinessen, in his article entitled "Post-Suharto Muslim Engagements with Civil Society and Democratisation" describes the phenomenon of the *usrah* group (Jemaah Tarbiyah), the embryo of PKS, as an interesting case representing different aspects of certain civil society groups.[23] Of these, he classifies the Muslim groups into three categories: first, the civil society based on the mainstream Islamic organizations, such as Nahdlatul Ulama (NU) and Muhammadiyah; second, the civil society represented by non-governmental organizations, Lembaga Swadaya Masyarakat (LSM), which are mainly offshoots from NU or Muhammadiyah activism; and third, a relatively a new kind of civil society represented by the *usrah* group. Since the latter tends to appear in underground forms with a tightly monitored membership, it is more likely to be viewed as a threat to the government of the day, even though it ultimately serves to strengthen "civil society."[24]

Proceeding from this analytical framework as he does, it is understandable that van Bruinessen has no clear explanation regarding the emergence of PKS in the national political process towards democratisation in Indonesia. As a political party grown from a once exclusively religious movement, PKS still has not positioned itself into an open commitment to democracy. Yet this uncertain position of PKS is likely to be something of a paradox, since for van Bruinessen it represents at the same time "imperfect democrats but perhaps Indonesia's strongest force for democratisation."[25]

Sadanand Dhume, in his article entitled "Radical March on Indonesia's Future" has presented a more sceptical and hostile attitude toward PKS.[26] Since the Justice Party, according to Dhume, has been inspired by the ideology of the Muslim Brothers in Egypt, it is likely to pose a serious threat to Indonesia's democracy.[27] Further, Dhume states that PKS shares a radical ideology with the Jemaah Islamiyah, an underground Islamic organisation alleged to have links with the terrorist group, al-Qaedah. The difference between them stems from their approaches to achieving their goals. Jemaah Islamiyah has used revolutionary and violent ways; PKS has preferred to use evolutionary and peaceful approaches.[28]

However, Dume also shows a lack of insight into the dynamics of radicalisation and Islamism in Indonesia. He does not distinguish between "moderate" and "radical" in Indonesia. Since most Islamic groups have shared ideas about the need to struggle for Islam at the levels of society and the state, Dhume has conflated the groups and simplified reality. His overestimation of the fundamentalist nature of political Islam has led him to neglect the possible contribution of political Islam in the democratisation process in Indonesia. Islamic democracy, as expounded by PKS, finds no room in Dhume's analysis.

Further misleading information about Jemaah Tarbiyah and PKS is presented by Zachary Abuza in his article "Muslims, Politics and Violence in Indonesia: an Emerging Jihadist-Islamist Nexus?"[29] This study describes the emergence of the Tarbiyah movement as the vehicle of the oldest and most established Wahabi Islam in Indonesia, one that has always reflected the interest of the Arab minority. According to Abuza, the main goal of Jemaah Tarbiyah is the establishment of an Islamic state.[30] Therefore, he classifies Jemaah Tarbiyah and its political party as extension of Indonesian radical Islam, even though neither entity has ever clearly stated what the *shariah* or an Islamic state would look like in practice.[31]

B. New Perspectives on Jemaah Tarbiyah

In this thesis I attempt to present the phenomenon of Jemaah Tarbiyah in a broader context by framing and analysing its existence within the post-independence history of Indonesia. I will introduce new perspectives that have been lacking in earlier researches. In contrast to much other recent work as mentioned above, this thesis will also present new findings on the phenomenon of Jemaah Tarbiyah and PKS. Firstly, Jemaah Tarbiyah and PKS are born from a process of convergence between traditionalist and modernist generations of Indonesian Islam. Secondly, the emergence of Jemaah Tarbiyah in the discourse of Indonesian Islam provides a new direction for study, particularly in their ability both to adopt a foreign influence (that of the Egyptian Muslim Brothers) and to accommodate local elements (earlier traditionalist and modernist movements). Thirdly, even though PKS is a transformation of a religious movement it is necessary to see it within political perspectives. In other words, the commitment of Jemaah Tarbiyah to its participation in the political process compels it to abide by political rules and to be willing to compromise its religious agenda with political realities. This is to be seen especially in its response to the issue of implementing Islamic law.

1. The Historical Context of Jemaah Tarbiyah

Studying the phenomenon of PKS calls for historically informed research, since only focussing on its superficial appearance reveals the fact that this political party has no historical precedent in Indonesia. It is true that its political elites and key figures are not well known among the Indonesian people. However, they are mainly of the latest generation of Indonesian Muslims from families of either a traditionalist or modernist background who have been raised in the historical situation where differences between the two religious orientations no longer exist. They have benefited from the New Order's economic achievements, which have enabled them to pursue their studies in universities, either in Indonesia or in foreign countries (Western and Middle Eastern). In these new academic environments, they have encountered Islamic activism and milieus dominated by the slogan of universal Islam[32], whilst home-grown traditionalist and modernist tensions have been reduced. They remain part of the process whereby Indonesian Muslims promote Islam into broader contexts.

The decade of the 1980s was a crucial one for Jemaah Tarbiyah, particularly because it saw the emergence of new variants in Indonesian Islam, which had their roots in the 1970s. It was during this period that the demarcation between "old" and "new" *santri* became apparent, the latter being less interested in political activity and distancing themselves from the heritage of their predecessors. This change has prevailed not only for Muslims who shifted their agenda into cultural and intellectual movements but also for the proponents of political Islam, who channelled their activities into predication movements. The difference is that while the cultural and intellectual groups have blamed the political activities of their predecessors as the source of Muslim problems, the predication groups still hold the ideal that one day political Islam will reappear and gain momentum.

The ability of Jemaah Tarbiyah to manage predication activities and avoid practical political issues enabled it to develop during the mid 1980s without any significant repression from the New Order. Even though the activists came under surveillance from the regime, they were able to run their Islamic circles and training sessions on the campuses. Such campus predication enabled the students to distance themselves safely from radical activities and political confrontation. According to Jemaah Tarbiyah, the only way to influence those in power was to eschew conflict; their goals could be reached by *dakwah,* or missionary activity that would have a long term impact.[33]

The rising generation of the 1980s has contributed to initiating various kinds of Islamic activities on the Indonesian campuses, ranging from discussion programmes to outward bound ventures. Students from both modernist and traditionalist backgrounds joined these programs. The challenging dynamics of Islam faced by this "new generation of Muslims" since the 1980s has in turn borne fruit in new orientations in the intellectual and political movements of the 1990s.

The 1980s generation has not only avoided disputes in religious issues but it has also not experienced the harsh battles between the nationalist and Islamist factions of the past. In general, their ideas on Islam were not to be trapped in the "old issues" of their predecessors, such as establishing an Islamic state or even restoring the caliphate; rather, they formulate new ideas compatible with the current socio-political conditions of Indonesia. They also differ from other Muslim groups in Indonesia in so far as they are able to accommodate the two inherited orientations, as well as legal formalist and substantialist approaches to Islamic questions and politics.

This trend of convergence among the Jemaah Tarbiyah activists can indeed be observed in politics and religion. For instance, during the discussions and debates on the issue of the 1945 Constitution in the 2000 parliament meetings, PKS did not support the amendment of chapter 29 of the Constitution, which aimed to revive the Jakarta Charter. PKS proposed an alternative, called "the Medina Charter," which, according to the party, was more suited to the Indonesian context. In order to comply with the demands of some Muslims for the implementation of *shariah,* PKS has attempted to encourage individuals to practise Islamic teachings at the personal level.

Activists of PKS believe it is insufficient merely to observe Islamic doctrines and teachings in ritual and religious ceremonies - they must be manifested and internalised within individuals and lead to a commitment to morality and a sense of social concern. The programme of *shariah* is not merely understood as an effort to impose Islamic laws; rather it must become part of the internal character and power of the cadres who campaign against corruption and promote a clean government. It also aims to bring justice and social welfare to the Indonesian people.

In this historical context, Jemaah Tarbiyah is best described by following three approaches. First, by putting Jemaah Tarbiyah within the framework of the dynamics of the *santri* of Indonesia. The activists of Jemaah Tarbiyah are of a different character from the "old" *santri*. Second, Jemaah Tarbiyah is part of a continuing process of Islamisation in Indonesia that combines the two dimensions of accommodation and purification. This will determine a political praxis that is pragmatic in nature. Third, Jemaah Tarbiyah is part of a social movement that opposed the hegemonic regime of the New Order by establishing more space for Islamic cultivation and education *(tarbiyah)*. It is through this strategy that Jemaah Tarbiyah has been able to develop itself as an alternative to Islamic radicalisation that increasingly took hold during the decade of the 1980s.

2. Internationalisation and Internalisation

As a result of its decision to withdraw from national political issues and to avoid any confrontation with the New Order regime, Jemaah Tarbiyah shifted its sights towards international issues. Ideas coming in from the Middle East became more interesting, particularly international issues involving the role of the US and Israel in the Middle East.

The phenomenon of PKS itself shows clearly the influence of Middle Eastern ideas in Indonesia. PKS activists adopted the ideas of Hasan al-Banna, while accommodating the local dynamics of Indonesian Islam. At this superficial level, the role of the Middle East as the sender of ideas and Indonesia as the receiver is immediately apparent. However, since the process also necessarily involves the role of the receiver, in which the ideas from the Muslim Brothers are domesticated, a different, modified movement has resulted. The political and cultural situation of Indonesian society has tempered the process of adaptation. The main intellectual ingredients were imported from the Middle East, but were enhanced to suit an Indonesian taste. Indonesian Islam, activists of PKS believe, will set an example about the contribution of an Islamic movement to participate in the democratic system to other Muslim countries, including those of the Middle East.[34]

This process of interaction between the international source and Indonesian local dynamics which produced the Jemaah Tarbiyah has had the effect of diluting the perceived fundamentalist character of the Muslim Brothers. The involvement of Jemaah Tarbiyah activists in the realm of politics has forced them to deal with the heterogenous nature of Indonesia. As a result, the political agenda of PKS in promoting Islamic aspirations (the major discourse of Jemaah Tarbiyah) has been played down; it has passed through a process of domestication in which local contexts become determinant factors in the promotion of its aspirations.

This is not to say that the international face of Jemaah Tarbiyah is not still apparent, in particular when it places the issue of "experiences of injustice" in the Islamic world, particularly the Middle East, as a high priority in its international policy. PKS is very critical of the role of the US and its ally, Israel on the plight of the Palestinian people. This strong criticism is often misunderstood as merely an anti-Western and anti-Semitic stance; it has not yet been recognised to be the feeling of disenchantment of the *ummah* towards the perceived injustices in the global acts of the superpower nation and its allies.

3. Reformulation of *Shariah*

The commitment of Jemaah Tarbiyah to participate in politics has altered its religious orientation. A new paradigm in viewing relations between Islam and the Indonesian state has evolved.[35] Conformity between the movement's belief and popular issues is something that cannot be avoided by its party if it is to win mass support. Inclusive and pluralistic attitudes are also promoted in order to change the exclusive and fundamentalist image of Jemaah Tarbiyah. These new directions, however, are grounded in a deep religious reasoning, and the significant achievement of PKS in the 2004 general elections is an important example of how the party has been able to apply its new paradigm.

The case of the 2004 general elections proved the ability of PKS to broaden its domain of support. This accomplishment has differentiated PKS from other Islamic parties in the past, whose supporters were concentrated in particular regions where the *santri* community was dominant. The support base of PKS has formed not only within the old strongholds of Islamic parties, but has extended into areas where Islamists were not popular before. However, the strongholds of PKS are still specifically in urban areas where the lower middle class and the urban poor are numerous. People from the lower middle class in Jakarta, for instance, have given their support to the party. In the Province of DKI Jakarta PKS won power and defeated other major parties such as Golongan Karya (Golkar) and The Party of Indonesia Democracy Struggle, Partai Demokrasi Indonesia Perjuangan (PDIP).

The main reason for PKS' achievement is that as long as the party makes promises for a better life, regardless of ideology, the people will give it their support. Although PKS is an Islamic party, it is able to respond to people's interests and it also succeeds in areas where Islamic slogans and aspirations are not dominant. The people are concerned with the party's programs and performance. Here, PKS shows its readiness to accommodate popular problems, particularly in responding to the interests of the little people of the cities.

A reformulation of Islamic *shariah,* by emphasising PKS' role in improving welfare, a commitment to care and a clean government have become central issues within the discourse of PKS activism. A new understanding of the *shariah,* highlighting other than its purely punitive aspects, is part of the new paradigm to implant the *shariah* into popular consciousness. The party is well aware that imposing the issue of *shariah* in the form in which it has been understood in the past and as it is promoted by other Islamic parties will not find much public favour in Indonesia.

On the other hand, incorporating the spirit of Islam into issues that are apparently secular, such as clean government and anti-corruption, and using them in political campaigns is also part of PKS' effort to carry out a reformulation of *shariah*. Secular issues are being framed within the new paradigm to reveal their Islamic nature. Every attempt is made to relate Islamic teachings to worldly issues in order to bring the party closer to popular aspirations.

C. Objectives and Methodology

My thesis aims to contribute to the analysis of the current phenomena of Islamic movements and Islamic parties in Indonesia, particularly by understanding the emergence of Jemaah Tarbiyah movement and its transformation into the political party of PKS. The achievement of PKS during the 2004 general elections indicates that the party has attracted voters who see it as a real alternative to existing parties. However, PKS and Jemaah Tarbiyah are not merely interesting phenomena in themselves; they offer an ideology and religious experience which is making a unique contribution to Indonesian politics by testing the nature of the relationship between Islamically based politics and the secular state.

The contribution of PKS as an Islam based party will always be determined by its ability to uphold its Islamic vision and to conform with the realities of Indonesia. The new direction in Indonesian Islamism represented by PKS progresses towards justice, social care and good governance for all Indonesians. The use of Islamic symbols and slogans must also meet the expectations of the masses, so that if the party is unable to work for the people's interests, PKS will lose its significance in Indonesian politics.

In order to understand and provide a comprehensive picture of Jemaah Tarbiyah and PKS, I have used a variety of approaches and methodologies from several disciplines. The chapters of the thesis draw on theories from anthropology, political science, social movement analysis, history and Islamic Studies. Relying on political science and neglecting religious and socio-cultural features is patently insufficient for an understanding of Islamic parties such as PKS. More elaboration is needed, since up to now there have been no authoritative sources to satisfy the need of readers regarding this phenomenon. Individual key figures and leaders of PKS may present different descriptions of their organizations; each has their own experience and story. My task has been to structure the oral narratives into an academic analysis.

I present the thesis in the following form: there are seven chapters, which are divided into three parts. Each part employs a particular approach to shape the analysis. Part One presents the historical context and consists of two chapters, the first of which deals with the dynamics of the *santri*, or observant Muslims in Indonesia, focussing on the emergence of new variants of *santri* (convergence, radical, and global) and aims to describe Jemaah Tarbiyah in its global context. Chapter One applies an anthropological approach as developed by Geertz and Koentjaraningrat to describe Indonesian Muslims in the 1950s, to which I add the further development of the different variants of *santri*. Chapter Two deals with the patterns and types of Islamisation of Indonesia, focussing on how the emergence of Jemaah Tarbiyah offers a new perspective on the process of Islamisation. In this chapter, I use mainly a sociological approach in analysing the strategy of a religious movement that aims to influence society and the state to meet its Islamic goals.

Part Two deals with development of Jemaah Tarbiyah during the repression of the New Order and comprises two chapters. Chapter Three focusses on the historical events that coincided with the emergence of Jemaah Tarbiyah and describes how Jemaah Tarbiyah managed to survive and even expand within a hostile political environment. In this chapter, social movement theory is used to examine the relationship between the regime's repression and Jemaah Tarbiyah's response. Chapter Four analyses the significance of "campus Islam", in particular how Jemaah Tarbiyah established itself on secular campuses in Indonesia and made them bases for its political caderisation. This chapter takes a political approach that attempts to depict the elite recruitment of PKS and its role within student governments during the New Order period up to its collapse in 1998. In this chapter it becomes clear that the party's origins "will affect its organisational structure, internal dynamics, functions and ideological principles."[36]

Part Three of the thesis also contains three chapters, both focussing on aspects of the religious and political ideology of Jemaah Tarbiyah and PKS. Chapter Five studies the influence of the Muslim Brothers of Egypt in Indonesia, how the process of transmission of ideas occurred and what type of relationship the central movement and its associates have built. The approach here is political, highlighting the influence of a foreign ideology on a local social movement and political party. Chapter Six deals with the Sufi influences of the Muslim Brothers upon Jemaah Tarbiyah activists and then how to use them in responding to Indonesian issues. Why do Jemaah Tarbiyah activists believe it is important to return to the ideas of the Egyptian activist and social philosopher, Hasan al-Banna? Social movement theory is used to analyse the role of ideology in driving political practice, it is the internal factor that leads PKS to play a pragmatic role in Indonesian politics. Chapter Seven is then dedicated to a critical analysis of the sensitive issue of *shariah* - how PKS addresses this issue and what strategies are brought into play to gain broad support from society, at the same time maintaining the solidity of PKS cadres. The discipline of Islamic Studies helps to clarify the significance of *shariah* and its importance to Muslims. When the results of Islamic Studies analysis are combined with those of the political science analysis, it becomes clear that the demand to implement *shariah* in Indonesia still needs to gain popular support; it is essential for PKS to successfully bridge the gap between Islamic ideals and political realities.

The data to support my arguments in this thesis are mainly derived from field research, which I conducted from 23 January 2003 to 15 January 2004 and from 15 November 2005 to 20 January 2006 in Surabaya (East Java), Depok (West Java), Jakarta (DKI Jakarta), Padang (West Sumatra) and Makassar (South Sulewesi). The research was based on in-depth interviews and my direct observations. During the periods mentioned, I met with most PKS leaders and figures holding high positions in the party. I interviewed them regarding their religious background and education as well as their activities in the party. I asked them to tell of their experiences during the early development of the informal movement of Jemaah Tarbiyah under the Soeharto regime and how they responded to the regime's policy of oppression. During the interviews I also tried to gather information about the views of PKS activists on the implementation of *shariah* in Indonesia. I was fortunate to have the chance to observe PKS political activities and some sessions of its religious training, *halaqah*. In addition, I collected primary source materials, such as books, articles and official documents written by activists of Jemaah Tarbiyah and PKS.

My familiarity with primary sources written by PKS activists on religion and politics has been important in helping me to understand the movement and its political praxis. Before the establishment of PKS, during my studies towards my bachelor's degree at The University of Indonesia (UI), Jakarta in 1992-1997 I was able to interact directly with members of Jemaah Tarbiyah and other Islamic groups on campus. These valuable experiences helped me to understand the characteristics of the movement under study. My close acquaintance with a number of PKS figures helped me gain further insight into the movement and its political activities. However, I have endeavoured not to allow this closeness to interfere with the critical analysis of my subject matter. I have tried to be objective but also to develop "empathy" with the movement. In this sense, my "empathy" towards my subject lies in fully engaging with the phenomenon of PKS so as to understand all its facets, ideals and strategies. In doing so, I do not necessarily mean that "empathy" evolved into "sympathy."

ENDNOTES

[1] See "Demonstrasi itu Tertib dan Damai," *Media Indonesia*, 15 September 2003.

[2] In 2004 general election PKS gained 45 seats at the national parliament, 165 seats at provinces and 849 seats at districts, compared to 1999 general election when PK only attained 7 seats at national

parliament, 26 seats at provinces and 158 seats at districts. During direct elections of mayors (*Bupati* or *Walikota*) in provincial and district level PKS also won in 61 regions. See "PKS Perkirakan Raih 48 Kursi DPR," *Gatra*, 21 April 2004 and "61 dari 112 Pilkada telah Direbut PKS," *Gatra,* 10 June 2006.

[3] *Media Indonesia*, 15 September 2003.

[4] See "Pemilih Islam dan Partai Keadilan Sejahtera (PKS): Hasil Survey LSI tentang Partai Politik dan Calon Presiden 2004," LSI, September 2004, 8.

[5] Al-Banna was born in Egypt in 1906. He founded his movement, *al-Ikhwa>n al-Muslimi>n* (the Muslim Brothers) in 1928, to become a force within Egyptian social movements. On 12 February 1949 he was assassinated by the Egyptian secret police. See John L. Esposito, ed. *The Exford Encyclopedia of the Modern Islamic World Vol. 1* (New York: Oxford University Press, 1995), 195-198. Further details about al-Banna and the society of Muslim Brothers will be presented in Chapters V and VI.

[6] See "Klaim di Luar Survei LSI," *Jawa Pos*, 26 March 2006.

[7] See Tholkhah and Abdul Aziz, "Gerakan Islam Kontemporer di Indonesia: Sebuah Kajian Awal," in *Gerakan Islam Kontemporer di Indonesia* (Jakarta: Pustaka Firdaus, 1996), 11 and see also Azyumardi Azra, *Islam Reformis Dinamika Intelektual dan Gerakan*, (Jakarta: PT RajaGrafindo Persada, 19990, 46.

[8] See Azyumardi Azra, "Kelompok Sempalan di Kalangan Mahasiswa PTU: Anatomi Sosio Historis" in *Dinamika Islam di Perguruan Tinggi Wacana Tentang Pendidikan Agama Islam* (Jakarta: Logos, 1999), 227.

[9] Ibid.

[10] See Martin van Bruinessen, "Gerakan Sempalan di Kalangan Umat Islam Indonesia: Latar Belakang Gerakan Sosial Budaya," in *Artikulasi Islam Kultural: dari Tahapan Moral ke Periode Sejarah* (Jakarta: RajaGrafindo Persada: 2004), 206.

[11] Ibid., 206.

[12] Azra, "Kelompok Sempalan di Kalangan Mahasiswa PTU," 227.

[13] Ibid.

[14] See Ali Said Damanik, *Fenomena Partai Keadilan: Transformasi 20 Tahun Gerakan Tarbiyah di Indonesia* (Bandung: Mizan, 2002).

[15] Ibid., x.

[16] See Firdaus Syam, *Ahmad Sumargono:Dai dan Aktifis Pergerakan Islam Yang Mengakar di Hati Umat* (Jakarta: Millenium Publiser, 2004), 74.

[17] See Aay Muhammad Furkon, *Partai Keadilan Sejahtera: Ideologi dan Praksis Politik Kaum Muda Muslim Indonesia Kontemporer* (Bandung:Teraju, 2004).

[18] Ibid., 281-282.

[19] Ibid.

[20] Ibid., vii.

[21] Andi Rahmat and Mukhammad Najib, *Gerakan Perlawanan dari Masjid Kampus* (Surakarta: Purimedia, 2001).

[22] The government censored the contents of sermons in response to increasingly harsh criticism of the regime by Muslim preachers. See Faishal Ismail, "Pancasila as the Sole Basis for all Political Parties and for all Mass Organizations; an Account of Muslim's Responses," *Studia Islamika* 3 no. 4 (1996), 55.

[23] See Martin van Bruinessen, "Post-Suharto Muslim Engagements with Civil Society and Democratisation," in *Indonesia in Transition: Rethinking 'Civil Society', 'Religion', and 'Crisis,'* (Yogyakarta: Pustaka Pelajar, 2004), 52.

[24] Ibid.

[25] Ibid.

[26] Sadanand Dhume, "Radical March on Indonesia's Future," *Far Eastern Economic Review* 168 No. 5 (May 2005), 11-19.

[27] Ibid., 18.

[28] Ibid and see also Sadanand Dhume, "PKS and the Future of RI's Democracy," *Jakarta Post,* 5 December 2005.

[29] Zachary Abuza, "Politics and Violence in Indonesia: an Emerging Jihadist-Islamist Nexus?" *NBR Analysis* 15 no. 3 (September 2004), 1-54.

[30] Ibid., 38-39.

[31] Ibid., 48.

[32] In this sense, Islam is understood as a country and citizenship that eliminates all differences. Islam recognises neither geographical frontiers nor racial divisions. See Esposito, ed., *The Oxford Encyclopedia of the Modern Islamic World Vol 1*, 198.

[33] Interview with Rahmat Abdullah, Jakarta, 11 May 2003.

[34] Interview with Nursanita Nasution, Canberra, 25 October 2005.

[35] Ibid.

[36] See Joseph Lapalombara and Jeffrey Anderson, "Political Parties," in *Encyclopedia of Government and Politics Vol. 1* (London and New York: Roudledge, 1992), 399.

Chapter 1: The Emergence of the New *Santri* in Indonesia

To an extent never seen before, following the collapse of the Soeharto regime in 1998 Islamist groups in Indonesia began to express themselves vocally and explicitly. Islamic discourse has developed apace, ranging from demands that the state lift the ban on the role of Islamic ideology in political parties and mass organizations to accommodate Muslim interests up to calls for the implementation of Islamic *shariah* to replace the laws of the state. As well, the issue of a global Islamic state, the *khilafah*, once not of great interest, has now been promoted by a section of Indonesian Muslims. There is also growing impetus within political Islam to review the significance of cultural Islam in Indonesia. The agenda of Islamisation no longer rests only on the intellectual and cultural aspects of Islam. Islam needs to play a greater role in Indonesian politics.

These recent phenomena indicate the emergence of a new type of devout Muslim, the *santri*, differing from their parents in terms of political orientation, religious ideology and in their attitude towards inherited traditions. The new *santri* are not only influenced by the local and changing dynamics of Indonesian politics, society and culture but they are also subject to international influences in Islam. Within Indonesia, some of them retain their links with traditionalist or modernist groups, some keep their distance from them and yet others show radical orientations. They have become very influential within certain sections of Indonesian society and have gained attention from many observers and researchers.

This chapter analyses the early development of the new *santri* during the time of the consolidation of Soeharto's New Order up until its collapse in 1998. We introduce three types of new *santri*: convergent, radical and global. While these are not rigid classifications, the three variants can be explained by affiliation with different groupings within Indonesian Islam. *Santri* described as "convergent" are both traditionalist and modernist activists who tend to merge with each other. The "radical" *santri* are usually pessimistic about the traditionalist and modernist struggles in Islam and demand radical change in Indonesia. The "global" *santri* are more influenced by trans-national movements in the Middle East, yet still form part of both traditionalist and modernist groupings at home. Our approach is based on an analysis of the doctrinal origins and the religious agendas of these contemporary *santri* in order to better understand the emergence of the Jemaah Tarbiyah. The activists of PKS are mainly drawn from members of Jemaah Tarbiyah, who fall into the category of global *santri*.

A. Old and New Santri

Generally speaking, in the past, the term *santri* was used by scholars of Indonesian Islam, such as Geertz[1] and Koentjaraningrat[2] to refer to observant Muslims; they might have come from either a traditionalist or a modernist background. Indonesian Muslims were first divided theoretically between nominal Muslims and the devout. The latter, the *santri,* were likely to be affiliated with Islamic parties, while nominal Muslims were known by their connection with the secular factions of politics. In this regard, being *santri* was to support political Islam in which the Islamic political parties were perceived to be the only valid means of struggle for Muslim interests. However, the divisions of Muslims in terms of political and religious orientation were sharply distinctive - not only between the nominal and the devout but also among kinds of Muslims themselves.

By contrast, since the beginning of the New Order in 1966, and in part after the failure of the Islamic political parties to win benefits for Muslims (which resulted in critical relations between the regime and Muslim political activists in general) the influence of religious and political streams on the new generation of Muslims declined. In this era, many younger Muslims tended to disengage from political activities and were little concerned with traditionalist or modernist connections. They showed a capacity to integrate the two once opposite poles while remaining devout; they simply sought different ways to promote Islam in the society and the state.

An identification of the *santri* in Indonesia was made through the useful work of the anthropologist, Clifford Geertz. In his study of the religious life in the town of "Mojokuto", East Java, during the 1950s, Geertz classified the Javanese into three variants, *priyayi, santri* and *abangan*. Although his work has drawn criticism from many scholars, the *santri-abangan* dichotomy is still important for an understanding of the religious and political orientations of Muslims in Indonesia. *Santri*, or observant Muslims are further divided into two groups, *kolot* (traditionalist) and *moderen* (modernist).[3] The former, following Geertz, accommodated local practices and rituals in their Islam and affiliated politically with Nahdlatul Ulama (NU) whilst the latter were determined to purify Islamic teachings from local syncretic practices and preferred to join Masyumi.[4]

About twenty years later, another distinction between traditionalist and modernist was made by Allan A. Samson. He described them as politically accommodationist or reformist in nature. Samson then added a further type of *santri,* which he named "radical fundamentalist". This new category is indeed helpful for our understanding of the reality of *santri* in Indonesia, in addition to the two already acknowledged variants.[5] The fundamentalist element of *santri* was attributed to the Darul Islam movement of the 1950s, which launched a rebellion against the new Indonesian state, aiming to establish an Indonesia

Islamic State.[6] The continuation of fundamentalist groups from the past, as classified by Samson, bears a correlation to radical groups of the present which has contributed to violent actions. In this thesis we call this category of *santri*, "radical" *santri*.

However, merely relying on the received insights of Geertz, Samson and other scholars will not provide us with a satisfactory picture of the recent face of Islam in Indonesia. Various events have taken place since the New Order period, which have changed the face of the old *santri*; a new concept, which I present in this thesis, is needed to explain these recent developments.

The new *santri* do not represent one single phenomenon. The generation of Muslims of the 1970s tended to combine traditionalist and modernist features, while the subsequent generation of the 1980s and the 1990s took different directions. This generation expressed their disillusionment towards both traditionalist and modernist heritages and began to search for an alternative religious expression. They took their religious references, either from existing radical groups in Indonesia, such as the Darul Islam just mentioned, or from global movements, such as Ikhwanul Muslimin, Salafi and Hizbut Tahrir.

In order to explain this emerging phenomenon, the three variants of the new *santri* will be employed. With no intention of neglecting other prominent factors, such as the emergence of liberal movements, my categorization is intended to explore the features of political Islam in Indonesia. The views of the three new types of *santri* on the relation of Islam to the state and their practical strategies in implementing their ideas will be analysed. In general, the emergence of new *santri* since the beginning of regime consolidation in 1966 is the result of both local and international dynamics.

B. Factors behind the Emergence of New *Santri*

The emergence of the new *santri* dates from the 1970s, when the younger generation of Indonesian Muslims began to demonstrate a growing distance from their elders. This phenomenon resulted either in the process of convergence between traditionalism and modernism or in a process of alienation. The former contributed to a new strategy in promoting Islam through democratic structures, while the latter tended towards a radical orientation. The New Order regime's repression of political Islam, the extension of religious education in public schools and the prominence of international events in the Middle East were important factors contributing to the gulf between the younger generation and their predecessors.

1. Repression and the Failure of Political Islam

The two-pronged policy of the New Order towards Islam in Indonesia was responsible for the decline of the forces of political Islam. The regime repressed "organised Islam" and maintained cooperation with and co-option of Islamic representation that was non-political in nature. It was eager to exclude politicised Muslims because of the threat to the stability of the regime, should they increase their influence in society and in government affairs.[7] Since Muslim politicians enjoyed "genuine popular support", they indeed posed potent threats. On the other hand, nominal Muslims accused them of having an agenda to establish an Islamic state and to impose the *shariah* on those who did not wish to comply with the tenets of Islam.[8] The heavy-handed policies of the New Order towards political Islam led some Muslims to adopt a more pragmatic approach, avoiding formal political struggle and turning instead to cultural and social activities. Some of them even preferred to join government-sponsored associations and to become outright supporters of the regime.

To cast our eyes further back in time, the fall of Soekarno and the establishment of the New Order in 1966 were welcomed optimistically by former members of Masyumi, which had been banned by Soekarno. In their view, the New Order promised to accommodate the forces of Islam, since they had contributed to the campaign to destroy the Communist Party of Indonesia. Islamic groups, particularly the modernists, hoped that the new regime would open up political opportunities to them. In August 1966, thousands of Muslims attended a public gathering held in Jakarta's al-Azhar mosque, welcoming the release of political prisoners such as Hamka, Isa Anshary and Burhanuddin Harahap.[9] Other important figures, such as Syafruddin Prawiranegara, Prawoto Mangkusasmito, Mohamad Roem, Kasman Singodimejo and M. Natsir appeared and gave orations appealing to the government to immediately rehabilitate Masyumi.

The demands of the modernist activists did not gain much attention from the government, however. The military-backed regime affirmed its stance that its ally, the army, would not allow any political groups which had carried out "illegal actions and rebellion" against Pancasila and the Constitution of 1945. The Communists, Darul Islam, Masyumi and the Indonesian Socialist Party (Partai Sosialis Indonesia – PSI) were counted among such dissenting groups.[10]

In preparing a new Islamic party, some former activists of Masyumi established a Co-ordinating Forum for Muslim Action (Badan Koordinasi Amal Muslimin, BKAM) and, with the support of sixteen other Islamic organizations, proposed a new political party, Partai Muslimin Indonesia (Parmusi). In February 1967 the ruling elite permitted the establishment of Parmusi but rejected the involvement of former Masyumi figures. The establishment of Parmusi was "recompensed" by the appointment of a Parmusi chairman who was chosen by the regime itself. The 1971 general elections then showed an ineffective performance by the party, when it gained only about 5 % of total votes, far below the achievement of the traditionalist party of Nahdlatul Ulama (19%).

The success of the new regime in controlling modernist Muslim activists was followed by repression towards traditionalist groups as well. The NU, which had maintained a good rapprochement with the Old Order regime, had immediately joined forces with the army against the PKI during the tragic bloodshed of 1965. Even though NU was able to cooperate with other parties, including the PKI, under the Guided Democracy of Soekarno, in fact at the grassroots, members of NU were in deep conflict with the Communists. When armed clashes took place, NU was among those who harshly attacked Communist sympathisers. However, events around the 1971 general elections showed political competition between NU and the regime's party, Golkar, which involved a terrorising of NU, when many NU campaigners were kidnapped and tortured by the supporters of the regime.[11] NU then shifted its attitude from collaboration to confrontation, a turnabout that caused the government to respond by hardening its stance towards NU and the Muslim community in toto.[12]

Nonetheless, the political struggle of the old *santri* had by no means ended. Both old traditionalist and modernist *santri* still channelled their aspirations through political means, as was indicated by the survival of some Islamic parties, such as NU, Parmusi, PSII and Perti which merged into the United Development party, Partai Persatuan Pembangunan (PPP) in 1973. Subsequently, in 1984, PPP was compelled to adopt Pancasila as the only basis of political ideology, diminishing its Islamic stance. This was the moment when the regime succeeded in breaking the links between the Muslim parties and their genuine constituents, whilst proponents of formal Islam suffered an inevitable failure under the regime's suppression.[13] The success of the New Order regime was proved by its economic and development performance, by which it appeared able to increase national economic growth, regardless of chronic corruption and the abuse of power, and to serve as a strong symbol of political stability and the protection of the people.[14]

Under these conditions, the shift of the Islamic struggle from political into cultural orientations, focussing on intellectual life or on predication, enabled the two opposed traditionalist and modernist groups to encounter each other and to develop social networks. While the intellectually-oriented group tended to denounce Islamic parties, the predication-oriented group, with its non-partisan strategy, further chose not to vote during the general elections as *golput* (*golongan putih*, non voters). Thus it was that the two generations of traditionalists and modernists found themselves inclined to merge. They were able to dissolve the schism between traditionalist and modernist *santri* through intra-organisational interaction, developing a growing acceptance of the idea that the truth might lie in synthesis rather than in antithesis.[15]

2. The Impact of Religious Education

Despite its policies adverse to politically organised Islam, the New Order regime served to expand the social role of Islam in other ways. The Soeharto government offered considerable support to missionary activities and religious education. Robert W. Hefner has presented a remarkable counter example of the process of Islamisation in his research on the region of Tengger in East Java.[16] Bambang Pranowo has also illustrated a similar trend in a rising Islamisation in Central Java during the era of political restriction on the *santri* in general.[17]

The double-edged policy of the New Order government towards Islam has created many speculations of its motives. Yet it was not a new policy. During the first half of the 20th century the Dutch colonial government of the East Indies practised precisely the same policy when it made the distinction between Islam as a religion and Islam as politics. The difference is that the Dutch government did not support the growth of Islam among the Indonesian people, while the Soeharto government did indeed cultivate a process of Islamisation.[18]

The establishment of the Ministry of Religious Affairs, Departemen Agama (Depag) was part of the role of the government to promote Islam.[19] The function of this ministry was to ensure and preserve practice and belief within the five formal religions recognised in Indonesia. The first pillar of Pancasila, "the Oneness of God", reflects the implicit responsibility of the state in maintaining the existence of these religions. Even though the Ministry of Religious Affairs was charged to serve the interest of all religions, since Islam is embraced by the majority, it is obvious that the ministry became an affective agency in carrying out the agenda of Islamisation. During the 1950s and the 1960s much attention was given to the organization, education and internal reinforcement of the Muslim community, as well as to the spread of Islam to the non-literate parts of the country. The Christians initially did not like the Ministry and opposed the intervention of the government in their affairs. Hinduism and Buddhism obtained a directorate within the Ministry not long after the late 1950s.[20]

Few can deny that this ministry has served the interests of the *santri* at the levels of both government and grassroots.[21] Nevertheless, B.J. Boland has disagreed about any dominant role of Islam within the Ministry of Religious Affairs and has argued that the department has served as an important medium in resolving problems between Islamic and secular oriented groups in the heated debate over the foundations of the Indonesian state.[22] The involvement of the government in the area of religious practice among its citizens has contributed to eliminating barriers among the adherents of five legal religions in Indonesia.[23]

One of the main implementations of state support is to ensure that students in public schools and universities receive religious education from teachers of their own religion. However, the commitment of the government to promote religion in educational institutions was a longstanding one, dating from the 1950s. It was Soekarno who issued the governmental decision *Peraturan Pemerintah* (Perpu) No. 4/1950, regulating universal instruction in religion through the collaboration of both the Department of National Education and the Department of Religious Affairs.[24]

President Soeharto confirmed this regulation at a meeting of People's Consultative Assembly, Majelis Permusyawaratan Rakyat (MPR) in 1966. It is stated that religious education is a core subject for all students from primary school to university.[25] Recently, on 11 June 2003 through debate and rejection from non-Muslim schools, this regulation has been validated by the government as the System of National Education Law (*Undang-Undang Sistem Pendidikan National, UU Sisdiknas*).[26] This policy has brought about change in religious trends within schools and universities, so that many students have been able to learn and practise their religion. Along with the facilitation of religious instruction in public schools, religious activities involving both students and teachers have become more apparent. For instance, students may celebrate the high religious days (*Hari-Hari Besar Keagamaan*) and observe their religious obligations during the course of their studies.

The vital role of the Ministry of Religious Affairs in providing and supervising religious courses has made this ministry an arena of conflict between traditionalist and modernist Muslim groups. Motivated by the need to preserve their specific religious practices, which are based on the jurisprudential schools (*al-madhhab*), both traditionalists and modernists are in competition to secure the position of Minister of Religious Affairs for one of their own. Holding the position of Minister means securing more influence over thousands of teachers who are responsible for delivering the religious message to students. When, in 1971, NU lost the top leadership of the Ministry of Religion, its influence over religious training in the primary schools gradually diminished. Religious courses of instruction and textbooks published by the Ministry of Religion were perceived by the traditionalist group as substantially promoting non-traditionalist views.[27]

However, teachers of religion in primary schools have the right to teach Islam in a way that is suited to their students. The teaching of religion in the universities is more open and might well accommodate both traditionalist and modernist views of Islam. Lecturers are not able to impose their own understanding of religious matters, rather it is expected that they maintain a balance and discuss fairly the various understandings of Islam.

Through their religion classes, university students are no longer concerned with sectarian differences and tend to share traditionalist and modernist practices equally. Thus government policy has been responsible for the dilution of traditionalist-modernist antipathies. Students tend to practise Islam in simple ways that are suited to their needs. Since the campuses also provide many extra-curricular Islamic training courses and activities, students are at an increased risk of being diverted from mainstream Islam. They feel no need to visit mosques outside their campus to interact with traditionalist or modernist organizations.[28] However, since they are not sufficiently trained in traditional and classical Islam, in deriving the laws of Islamic jurisprudence, they tend to be more literal in their understanding of Islam.[29]

In the 1980s, Islamic student organizations were barred from the campuses. The Islamic Students Association, Himpunan Mahasiswa Islam (HMI) which had been very prominent during the 1960s and 1970s, was no longer able to recruit the best students from the prestigious secular campuses.[30] Leading student association figures became more interested in organisational issues and campus politics in order to control student executives, abandoning their duties of religious training and predication.[31]

However, it was not only Muslim groups that saw the Minister of Religious Affairs as a crucial post, the regime also found that the ministry was a significant tool of intervention in the daily affairs of Indonesian Muslims. Since the Soeharto regime was able to control the department, its minister could be kept in line with the government's national policies. Soeharto discarded the influence of Islamic forces, traditionalist or modernist, by appointing the minister from elsewhere - the professional class, or even from the ranks of the armed forces.[32]

3. International influences

The encounter of Indonesians with global issues and ideas occurred not only in the 1980s, particularly after the 1979 Iranian Revolution, but it had developed centuries ago. Historically, since the late 15th century it was the *haramayn*, the two holy Arabian cities of Mecca and Medina that were considered to be the hub of the global network of Islam.[33] Scholars in both cities developed their authority throughout the Muslim world. They not only judged to issues within their region but also gave responses to many questions sent by Muslims from around the world. Contact between Muslims of the Indonesian archipelago and the Middle East had become significant since the late 16th century and developed intensively in the late 19th century.[34] Certain Meccan scholars, for instance, were involved in religious issues arising in Indonesia, including the sending of a decree to topple a woman, Sultanah Kamalat Syah of Aceh of the late of 17th century, from rule in accordance with the prohibition against a woman leading a kingdom.[35] The capacity of Indonesian Muslims to accommodate foreign and local elements together resulted in the internalising of the global element into local beliefs. Indonesian Islam was thus distinct in nature in from its Middle Eastern counterpart.[36]

Since the 1980s, the global influences of Islam on Indonesian Muslims have become more apparent. This "globalised" phenomenon of Indonesian Islam is the result more of a direct imitation of international orientations than a reliance on local traditions. Socio-political events in the Middle East, including religious conflicts and scholarly schisms, have had a large impact upon Indonesian Muslims.

Since the adoption of international ideas is not monopolised by any single figure or source of religious authority, their manifestations in Indonesia have been varied. Middle-East-replicated movements have mushroomed in Indonesia, each developing its own channels of contact and networks with Egypt, Yemen, Jordan, India and Pakistan. The emergence of movements such as the Muslim Brothers (Egypt), the Salafi groups (Saudi Arabia), Hizbut Tahrir (Jordan) and Jemaah Tabligh (Indo- Pakistan) are significant evidence that trans-national movements have seeded their influences in Indonesia.

Thus one of the most salient characteristics of Indonesian Muslims since the 1980s has been their tendency to connect themselves with global issues and movements. This has undermined the authority of local scholars in dealing with religious issues. They were considered to have been co-opted by the governing regime and so not to speak for the interest of the *ummah*. The younger generation of Indonesian Muslims has been attracted to foreign movements because of their "original" and "authentic" cachet and their image of not having been manipulated by the state.[37] Jemaah Tarbiyah has adopted new models in carrying out its *dakwah* activities derived from the Muslim Brothers of Egypt, while other segments of Indonesian Muslims have blatantly imported the modus operandi of Middle Eastern movements into Indonesia, and the Salafi, Hizbut Tahrir and Jemaah Tabligh are examples of trans-national movements at work in Indonesia.

Historically, the more apparent influence of the Middle East-based movements in Indonesia was due to the outreach of Dewan Dakwah Islamiyah Indonesia (DDII) under the leadership of M. Natsir, who personally established good relations with Middle Eastern leaders. Concerned about the expansion of the renewal movement and its secular orientation, DDII sent many students to study in Middle Eastern universities, in order to balance the Ministry of Religious Affairs' program led by Munawir Syadzali (1983-1993) who preferred to send young scholars to educational institutions in the United States and to Western Europe.[38] Barred from domestic political participation, Natsir earned a high reputation in Middle-East Muslim countries. He has won credentials recognised by most international Muslim leaders and DDII has benefited from connections with donors in Saudi Arabia, Kuwait and Pakistan to finance its domestic programs. To some extent, the sponsorship of DDII has meant that hundreds of Indonesian students have obtained international degrees, in turn helping to maintain cadres who are committed to global awareness and to anti-liberal Islam.[39] Since the 1970s and 1980s, the oil boom has permitted more funds for religious scholarship programs and the number of Indonesian students in Middle-Eastern countries has multiplied.

The era since the 1970s has also witnessed the translation of hundreds of books from Arabic into Indonesian. In Nasir Tamara's observations of the 1980s Islamic revival, he was amazed at the numbers of Islamic publications and the extent of publishing activity. Most books were not just about ritual obligations but carried a concern for social and political problems as well. For instance, translations of the writings of Sayyid Qutb were very popular.[40] Subsequently, during the mid-1980s, the influence of the Muslim Brotherhood's ideas was not confined to the medium of translated of books, but direct personal contact between Indonesian students and Middle Eastern mentors was also very likely to occur.[41]

The homecoming of Middle Eastern graduates and their interactions with the younger Muslim generation in the secular campuses of Indonesia introduced more comprehensive and systematic models of Islamic movements and thought. The Middle Eastern graduates became actively involved in predication, preferring neither to become government employees nor to return to their old Islamic institutions (*pesantren*) to teach. They remained independent and set up their own Islamic institutions, called *ma'had*, in urban centres where they became involved in providing informal religious instruction to students in their surrounds. Rahmat Abdullah, a Jemaah Tarbiyah activist, acknowledged the role of one Middle Eastern graduate:

> In 1980, my teacher returned from his study in Egypt. He had joined IM [Ikhwanul Muslimin, The Muslim Brothers] training, and had brought back many IM books. One of his books was written by Sayyid Hawa [and translated to Indonesian as] *Risalah Perjuangan* (Message of Struggle). My teacher and I then established an Islamic boarding school, Rumah Pendidikan Islam Darut Tarbiyah (the House of Islamic Education)...[42]

C. Variants, Characteristics and Groupings

Viewing the 1970s and 1980s political and intellectual phenomena among Indonesian Muslims, Syafii Anwar indicated the significant growth of a younger generation that differed from their predecessors. He called this new type of *santri* "neo-*santri*". While the "old *santri*" kept their links with established Islamic parties and groupings, the "neo-*santri*" are identified by their disengagement from political activity.[43] In general, what Anwar means by "old *santri*" is the grouping of political Islam, whilst "neo-*santri*" stands for cultural Islam. In addition, the neo-*santri*, according to Anwar, has not directly experienced the political repression of the New Order regime; they learned politics chiefly from their involvement with Islamic student organizations.[44] They have not held hard and fast attitudes on ideology, but have inclined towards more pragmatic, rational and receptive approaches. Their attitude towards Islam is based on its substance and functions, not on Islamic symbols or a literal understanding of texts. The new *santri*, Anwar claims, are the new Muslim middle class and the embryo of what he calls *"cendekiawan muslim"* (Muslim intellectuals) who were later to form the organization, Indonesian Muslim Intellectual Association, Ikatan Cendekiawan Muslim Indonesia (ICMI).[45]

However, Anwar appears not to have been aware of the different character of the new *santri* that developed within the university campuses after the mid 1980s. The neo-*santri* variant as described by Anwar puts more emphasis on only one side of the convergence phenomenon, that is, the intellectual convergence between the traditionalist NU and the modernist Muhammadiyah, which has lessened the differences between them. He pays little attention to the development of the predication movement, which is quite separate from the renewal movement in its orientation. This is the specific character of younger Muslims who have not only loosened their ties with both NU and Muhammadiyah but also show a tendency to be attracted to international ideas. All of these different variants, characters and groups of new *santri* deserve more elaboration in explaining the phenomena of contemporary Islam in Indonesia.

The table 1 below shows the types of new *santri* in Indonesia, their character and attitudes toward traditionalist and modernist traditions. It also shows how they are diverse in responding contemporary issues, including democracy.

Table 1: Attitudes of New *Santri* in Indonesia

Types of New Santri	Mainstream Scholars	Traditionalist and Modernist Practice	Salafus Salih (trustworthy ancient scholars)	Muslim world issues	Democracy
Convergent (1970s)	Critical	Agree	critical	critical	Strongly agree
Radical (1980s)	Strongly disagree	disagree	Strongly Agree	agree	Strongly disagree
Global (1990s)	Critical	critical	Agree	Strongly agree	Critical

Level of acceptance: 1. Strongly Agree 2. Agree 3. Critical 4. Disagree 5. Strongly disagree.

1. Convergent *Santri* (1970s)

To some extent, the convergence between traditionalist and modernist groups signified the trend of new generation of Indonesian Muslims in the 1970s. They initiated modifications in religious practices and sought to enrich their understanding of Islam by reading alternative Islamic books from overseas (Middle East and the West).[46] In addition, having witnessed the poor relations between the regime and Muslim activists, which were due to the unwillingness of the New Order regime to accommodate their political interests, the new generation of Indonesian Muslims in the 1970s, particularly the modernists, focussed their energy into two types of activities: renewal and a missionary movement. Many Islamic activities were embarked upon, such as discussion groups, seminars and dialogue that brought figures from both traditionalist and modernist camps to discuss Islamic and national issues. More and more, the younger generation were involved in formal and informal meetings to discuss Indonesian and Islamic issues in a broad context.[47]

a) Renewal Movement

Initiated by Nurcholish Madjid, the chairman of the Muslim Student Association, Himpunan Mahasiswa Islam (HMI) the advent of the renewal movement in the 1970s gained momentum and drew much attention from Muslim activists who had become disinclined to continue the struggle of Islam through political party channels.[48] They changed their structural approach into a more cultural one, from a symbolic and formalistic approach to a substantive one. By promoting political accommodation, the prevailing tension between Muslims and the regime was gradually reduced. It was this cultural method of cooperation that enabled Muslims to influence the existing political system from within.[49] Bachtiar Effendy pointed out that this change led to what he called the emergence of a "new Islamic intellectualism" in Indonesia. According to Effendy, the movement contributed to better relations between Muslims and the regime by focussing on three activities - religious renewal, political reformism and social transformation.[50]

Religious renewal was carried out in an effort to solve theological and philosophical problems of political Muslims in their relations with the state. The understanding of the old generation of Muslims towards the lack of separation between Islam and the state was the main concern for the renewal group. Effendy explains that the older theological stance, which tended to be more formalistic, legalistic and literal for the younger generation needed to be adjusted to respond to the social and political realities in Indonesia. They did not intend to change the doctrines of Islam, but rather to mount an effort to refresh Muslims' understanding of their religion. They did not believe that Islam constitutes an ideology, since the Qur'an and Hadith do not command Muslims to establish a state based on Islamic ideology. Therefore, Muslims had to be committed to the universal values of Islam, not to institutions and organisations, including political parties.[51]

In addition, in order to revise critical relations between the state and Islam, the renewal movement's solution was through involvement within the system. This political reformism meant that Islam should not represent an oppositional force against the state; the most important effort for Muslims was to push the state to guarantee their freedom in observing Islamic teachings. These required its activists to play a role in the policy making process by joining the state's bureaucrats and political parties.[52]

This approach brought a significant change that led most former activists of Islamic organisations to accept the ideology of Pancasila and some even became part of the regime.[53] The chairman and secretary-general of the Partai Muslimin Indonesia (Parmusi), Mintaredja and Sulastomo, served as the Minister of Social Affairs and was a bureaucrat in the Soeharto regime during the 1970s. After that other former Muslim activists have joined the regime. Among them were Sularso, Bintoro Tjokroaminoto, Barli Halim, Bustanul Arifin, Madjid Ibrahim, Norman Razak, Zainul Yasni, Omar Tusin, Sya'adilah Mursid, Mar'ie Muhammad, Hariry Hadi and many others.[54] In fact, their involvement within the system has not only brought about reconciliation between the state and Islam but also contributed to the bringing together other elements of Muslim forces from various backgrounds to exert influence on the state.

Another aspect of the renewal movement was the social transformation movement. The transformation movement aimed to strengthen the capacity of society in terms of social, cultural, political and economic improvement. Since the New Order regime was so effective in controlling the socio-political dimensions of the people at the grassroots, the transformation movement had to build communication and cooperation with the regime's apparatus in order to run their programs.[55] In addition, this approach also created good relations between traditionalist and modernist groups. Dawam Rahardjo, Sudjoko Prasodjo, and Adi Sasono were among the pioneers of the social transformation movement. For instance, the Institute of Social and Economic Research, Education and Information, Lembaga Penelitian, Pendidikan dan Penerangan Ekonomi dan Sosial (LP3S) was established in 1971 to strengthen the role of society and has become an important avenue for traditionalist and modernist activists to cooperate each other.

Many figures from modernist-affiliated movements have supported the idea of renewal Islam, such as Usep Fathuddin dan Utomo Dananjaya from the Indonesian Muslim Students, Pelajar Islam Indonesia (PII), Dawam Rahardjo, Djohan Effendi and Ahmad Wahib from the "limited group" discussions in Yogyakarta. Although the traditionalist camp had been absent in the earliest days of the discourse, many from a traditionalist background subsequently contributed to shaping and expanding the new intellectual orientation after the arrival home of Abdurahman Wahid in 1971 from his study in Baghdad. Through discussions and intellectual exercises among the new generation of *santri* in the 1970s, those involved succeeded in bringing Muslim resources together and contributing to the Indonesian developmental program. This was the arena of the phenomenon of convergence, in which traditionalist and modernist views and groups reached mutual understanding and cooperation. These younger Muslim intellectuals held regular series of discussion in Jakarta.[56] As former chairman of HMI, Nurcholish Madjid enjoyed good relations with influential figures from the modernist Masyumi, whilst Abdurahman Wahid had impeccable "blue blood" (*darah biru*) in the eyes of traditionalist NU stakeholders.[57]

Criticism has been directed towards the renewal movement and other associated movements, because they have not engaged with wider public issues but tend to be elite and urban oriented. They have not been able to respond the needs of the grassroots, most of the Indonesian people. In order to be understood by ordinary Muslims, their discourse has needed to be "translated" by a second layer of spokesmen.[58] For this reason, Islamic predication movements emerged to respond the needs of grassroots in understanding Islam.

b) Predication Movement

The predication movement represents yet another type of convergent *santri*. Disillusioned by the failure of their efforts to resurrect the Islamic party of Masyumi, certain modernist Muslims, led by M. Natsir, embarked on programs of propagation and predication. In May 1967 Natsir established an Islamic missionary institution, called the Indonesian Islamic Missionary Board, Dewan Dakwah Islam Indonesia (DDII). By promoting Islamic preaching, activists of DDII hoped to persuade more Muslims to be aware of their religious and political obligations as citizens. Since they were unable to participate in formal political activity or to take part in influencing the state, *dakwah* activity became an alternative strategy to prepare cadres who would struggle for Islam in the future. It was believed that this kind of predication project would have a longer-term impact on the formation of the national leadership in Indonesia. As stated in the organisational goals of DDII, the institution itself originally aimed to serve as "laboratory and consultation for the effective propagation of Islam in modern society."[59] The inclination of the organization to become engaged in political issues has contributed to the weakening of its progress in general.[60] Nevertheless, DDII became fertile ground to seed oppositional attitudes against the New Order regime.

To realise its long-term goals, DDII needed to improve the social and educational levels of Muslim communities. DDII then worked closely with the Medical College of the Islamic Hospital Foundation, Yayasan Rumah Sakit Islam (Yarsi), a modernist oriented institution in Jakarta, in providing medical services for the urban poor and in helping to support the development of libraries in mosques, universities and in *dakwah* institutions. In addition to these programs, DDII assisted in developing modernist-oriented *pesantren* associations in Java and other areas, combining both Islamic and secular subjects.[61] A private agriculture Pesantren of Darul Falah in Bogor, Dana al-Falah in Bandung, Wisma Tani in Payakumbuh and Yayasan al-Falah in Surabaya are examples of DDII-supported projects that are still well known up to the present time.

Another of the important developments in DDII's predication program was its success in expanding its role in the secular university campuses. DDII held many cadre-training programs in order to support this campus predication. One of these was held in Jakarta, organised by Z.E. Muttaqin and Imaduddin Abdurahim, both important figures in Masyumi. Since the training took place on the premises of the Indonesian Pilgrim Committee, Panitia Haji Indonesia (PHI) in Jl. Kwitang, it was called the PHI training. More than 40 delegates, mostly from prestigious universities in Bandung, such as the Institute of Technology of Bandung (ITB), the University of Pajajaran (Unpad) and the Institute of Education (IKIP) attended the training. The recruitment process was conducted through a network of modernist organizations, such as HMI, PII and Muhammadiyah. This PHI training first aimed to provide campuses with religious lecturers to be posted in the state universities and subsequently to become informal liaison officers of DDII on the campuses.[62]

In response to a growing numbers of PHI alumni, a campus network named the Indonesia Campus Mosque Supervision, Bina Masjid Kampus Indonesia (BMKI) was established throughout the universities of Java. Regional coordinators were appointed in order to manage predication programs and communications among the members. There were, for instance, Amien Rais, Kuntowijoyo and M. Mahyuddin as the coordinators for Yogyakarta; Ahmad Sadali, Rudy Syarif Sumadilaga and Yusuf Amir Feisal for Bandung; M. Daud Ali and Nurhay Abdurahman for Jakarta, Halidzi and Abdurrahman Basalama for Ujung Pandang, Kafiz Anwar for Semarang, and AM Saefuddin and Abdul Kadir Jaelani for Bogor.[63] These leading figures subsequently have been widely acknowledged by university students, from both traditionalist and modernist families alike, as their patrons and main reference.

Within other DDII liaisons, it was Imaduddin Abdurahim who succeeded in expanding campus predication in the 1970s. Besides his involvement in campus networks managed by DDII, Imaduddin initiated mental training sessions at the Institute of Technology in Bandung (ITB). These were called Latihan Mujahid Dakwah (LMD) and succeeding in drawing many students into the programs. Their alumni were widespread throughout universities in Java and the outer islands. Until the 1990s, Imaduddin was recognised as the "grand mentor" of Muslim student activists in the secular campuses. In terms of political stance, LMD was similar to DDII, in so far as both became opposition forces against the New Order regime. Imaduddin developed close contact with M. Natsir. He was not only from a modernist family background but he was active in modernist organizations, such as the Indonesian Islamic Students, Pelajar Islam Indonesia (PII) and the Islamic Student Association, Himpunan Mahasiswa Indonesia (HMI) in Bandung. He occupied a central position on the Board of Muslim Student Proselytising, Lembaga Dakwah Mahasiswa Islam (LDMI) of HMI.

LMD was known for its opposition to the development of Islamic renewal and was to some extent considered to be a counterbalance to the rising renewal movement led by Nurcholish Madjid. Imaduddin opposed the liberal ideas promoted by Madjid,[64] so that a serious polemic between the two men ensued. The polemic was actually sharpened by Endang Syaiffuddin Anshari, Imaduddin's assistant at LDMI. It was Anshari who attacked Nurcholish Madjid, not Imaduddin.[65] This is why, when Imaduddin put forward Madjid's name as candidate chairman of ICMI in the 1990s, many of his followers who had opposed Madjid since the beginning were surprised and disappointed.[66]

The mental training at ITB contributed to improving the image of Islam among the students and lecturers. Islam was no longer regarded as a backward-looking religion but was able to attract increasing numbers of educated people and professionals, of both traditionalist and modernist leanings, with its challenge to solve the social problems of modern times.[67] However, LMD not only raised the religious consciousness of Muslim students in observing the obligatory practices but it also gave rise to a major threat to the political regime. Fired with modernist political aspirations, Imaduddin's predication program was aimed at preparing leaders who would "take over" non-Islamic national leadership in Indonesia. He believed that the regime could not be changed unless there were dedicated and qualified Muslims, "the new generation to replace all of this."[68] According to Sugiat Ahmadsumadi, surprisingly both an activist of Muhammadiyah and a member of the Central Consultative Board of the traditionalist party, PKB, LMD in fact produced militant cadres who were critical of the regime.

> In Bandung, Bang Imad was very active in carrying out the mission of *amar ma'ruf nahi munkar* (promoting the good and discouraging the bad) by establishing LMD to train hardline Muslim students to become fiercely opposed to the government. Many of the LMD cadres who occupied vital positions in HMI would often trigger tensions with other committees supporting Pancasila. For this reason then, it is understandable that Imaduddin was imprisoned by the regime.[69]

In fact, both the renewal and predication movements contributed to shaping the face of Indonesian Islam, in which young Muslims became more interested in making Islam "more relevant to life in the modern world."[70] They were no longer attracted to either the traditional, ritualistic dogma of the conservative *ulama* or the "messianic fervour of some modernists who want Indonesia to become a theocracy."[71]

2. Radical *Santri* (1980s)

"Radical" here means "favouring or effecting fundamental or revolutionary changes in current practices, conditions or institutions".[72] The establishment of an Islamic state, therefore, would be the main agenda - to replace the existing state. I apply the term "radical" in this thesis to Islamic groups in Indonesia who believe in the significance of force and violence to challenge society and the state. In contrast, Islamic groups with a belief in the democratic systems, who channel their agendas through political parties and constitutional means, are considered to be "moderate".

The Soeharto regime's favouring of "secular views", which largely neglected the role of religion in the process of national development[73] and its preference for secular and non-Muslim political allies, led to frustration and an intensification of radical feeling in Indonesian society. Some Muslims perceived that society was overwhelmed by an un-Islamic environment and felt that the impact of the government's development programs was to blame. The era of the 1980s witnessed the growing of radical activism and violent actions from a certain section of Indonesian Muslims.

In some cases, "countries with non-secular political regimes are less likely to face the rise of an Islamist movement or a breakout of Islamist violence than their secular counterparts, since they already profess to follow the precepts of Islam."[74] Therefore, the Indonesian regime of the New Order indeed provided grounds for certain Muslims to justify their radical actions. They considered the regime sinful and saw themselves to be the genuine bearers of Islam. The intensification of religiosity among Muslim youths, which was fuelled by their political and social grievances, provoked a clash between the regime apparatus and the radical Muslims. Inevitably, there was spontaneous action by Muslims as a response to conditions and to the regime itself. Many grievances were expressed through the destruction of sinful places (*tempat maksiat*).[75] Radical groups, allegedly in close association with the militant Darul Islam (DI) also gained momentum in channelling social grievances and disillusionment.

Apart from the tendency to merge traditionalist and modernist thought and praxis in Indonesia, there has appeared a generation of Muslims who are disappointed with both of these mainstream views. They have developed their own ideas regarding religious, social and political issues. This type of *santri* has been much influenced by DI. What is more, this group is best identified by its close relations with ex-leaders of DI. Many reports about them in Indonesian newspapers and magazines have named this phenomenon, emerging since the mid 1970s, in the form of neo-NII (Negara Islam Indonesia, the Indonesia Islamic State) due to their close doctrinal and ideological affiliations with radical figures of DI.[76]

Most radical Muslims are totally different from mainstream groups.[77] Their understanding of the teachings of Islam and their radical views are the result of instant training and short courses. Some of them are even eager to simplify reality by making a basic contrast between what they term "Islamic" and "un-Islamic."

However, they are not well equipped with the foundations of the scholarship of Islamic jurisprudence or the Traditions of mainstream Islam, such as NU and Muhammadiyah possess; instead they rely on their own direct interpretations of the Qur'an and Hadith.

According to Kuntowijoyo, the tendency to keep a distance from mainstream Islam in terms of ideological and physical interaction has led these younger Muslims to be further detached from the *ummah*, the Islamic community as a whole. This trend is part of an urban phenomenon in which alienation from wider society and exclusiveness in embracing religion become common. Peer groups and school affiliations become more important than association with conventional Islamic organizations. The *kyai* and *ulama* can no longer attract them to study and understand Islam in depth; rather they gain their information and religious knowledge from anonymous sources, such as cassettes, the internet, radio, television and books.[78] Even though a number of them have gained some mastery of Islamic knowledge, it has not been gained through intensive academic training. Objections to the authority of conventional Islamic organizations and scholars are not uncommon.

Identified by their militancy and strict adherence, as well as their detachment from their elders, this younger generation make themselves more "pious" in their actions than the norm, without necessarily following the views and doctrines of established *ulama*. Kuntowijoyo refers to this type of *santri* as *Muslim Tanpa Masjid* (Muslims without Mosques)[79] or, as the weekly magazine *Tempo* put it, as "Muslims without Custodians."[80]

On the other hand, during the 1980s, the increasing number of young Muslims attending the Friday prayers or joining Islamic organizations surprised many observers.[81] The mosques were filled with younger Muslims, while Islamic study groups mushroomed on the campuses; many young women students wore the headscarf. Concurrent with this religious phenomenon, outside the campus, radical and violent actions escalated. It is understandable that, as William Liddle observed, some campus mosques of leading universities began to be known as centres of "fundamentalism."[82] In view of Liddle's description of religious trends within the campuses, it was obvious that what he referred to as the emergence of a "fundamentalist" orientation was the growing phenomenon of radical *santri* of middle-class urban family backgrounds, who have received little religious education and were studying the exact sciences.[83]

However, Liddle's interpretation of the reality of campus life in the 1980s solely as a fundamentalist phenomenon is misleading. Rather than taking place within the range of student activities, most cases of Islamic radicalisation involved ordinary people and occurred outside the campuses. The only instance that involved a Muslim student was in 1974 at the University of Indonesia, Jakarta, when Fahmi Basya, an engineering student, was found in possession of some explosive materials. There were many more varied aspects of religious awareness on the campuses; the radical trend was only a very small part of the broader dynamics. In this era, Sufism moved out of the mosque and *pesantren*, even beyond common Islamic institutions, to establish strong influences in the secular universities. For example, Sufism became a popular topic among student Islamic study groups at the Bandung Institute of Technology and Gadjah Madah University.[84] In fact, adherents to radical groups kept their distance from the campus mosques, which came under the strict control of the rectorate administration. The fundamentalists tended to run doctrinal dissemination, recruitment and all of their associated activities in clandestine ways.

In contrast, the campus mosques of secular universities have played a role in integrating Muslim students with the Islamic community in general. This is because to hold a sermon during the Friday prayers, the campus mosques need to invite speakers from outside, gaining the endorsement of the mosque committees. These committees have been careful to filter out political issues and to avert the entry of radical views. However, it has not only been radical views and hard-line orientations, such as are held by the activists of DI and Masyumi that were targeted; every attempt was made to eliminate the influence of so-called "deviant" Islamic groups (*aliran-aliran sesat*).[85] The mosque committees, usually appointed by the rector of the university, screened all speakers, carefully investigating their curricula vitae. Only those who embraced moderate views or had affiliations with the government were permitted to deliver the sermons.

All religious activities and programs mounted by the students had to be reported, and endorsement for them gained first through the rector or the deans of faculties. Students were required to include in their proposals all details of their religious activities, including name of program, speaker, syllabus and venue.[86]

The process of alienation among campus Muslims, according to Kuntowijoyo, took place when students failed to integrate with the broader Islamic community and organizations in general. Campus mosques could however play a role in bridging the gap between students and broader society. Further, Kuntowijoyo states

> The mosque, with its congregation, will generate a need for Islamic study clubs, art associations and the like. Through these programs students need to communicate with the society outside campus. For instance, the *Shalahuddin* congregation of UGM has to invite many speakers in their need for religious teachers to conduct the Intensive Islamic Course, whilst its theatre group learns from artists outside the campus. Indeed, the invitation to guest speakers will obviate the rigid exclusiveness of the campus.[87]

Even so, it is understandable that some secular campuses, with their exclusive character, have provided space for some radical groups to disseminate their influence. They carry out their activities and recruit new members through underground secret activities away from the campus mosques. Students become attracted to radical groups after having interacted closely with clandestine groups outside. Strictly speaking, these radical groups are still tiny in number compared to mainstream Islam; however, at times their radical views have prevailed over other more moderate groups. They are not popular among students or Muslim society in general; therefore, when acts of Islamic extremism occur, involving certain elements of radical groups and their actors are caught, the violence usually stops and broad support or popular sympathy for them is lost.[88]

Strictly speaking, the groups allegedly associated with radical activities in Indonesia since the 1980s are mainly referred to under the general name, NII, which later shifted into the more violent global movement of Jemaah Islamiyah (JI). Besides the movements working for an Islamic state, there are also a number of radical organizations that have targeted their actions towards places of vice. They have launched campaigns against prostitution, gambling, alcohol and drugs, sometimes resorting to physical attacks on places where such unlawful services are provided, such as massage parlours, bars, nightclubs and other sites of entertainment.[89] Among these, the Front for the Defence of Islam, Front Pembela Islam (FPI), Laskar Jihad and Laskar Jundulllah are radical groups that are not ideologically driven by the goal of an Islamic state but their presence in Indonesia has caused disturbances and has been cause for concern among many non-Muslims.

a) The Islamic State of Indonesia, Negara Islam Indonesia, NII

The Darul Islam movement, founded and led by Kartosuwiryo, who established an Indonesian Islamic State, Negara Islam Indonesia (NII) on 7 August 1949, was finally crushed by the Indonesian army in the early 1960s. However, its informal network has never been totally destroyed. DI-associated underground movements have persisted until the present day.[90] Instead of uniting themselves under a single leadership, they became separated and fragmented under different leaders. Each group has tried to annul other groups while claiming still to represent the "real" DI.[91]

When the *imam* of Darul Islam was captured and many of his top deputies pledged allegiance to the government in exchange for amnesty, DI became leaderless.[92] There was no single person who was considered qualified to take over the leadership. According to DI regulations on the issue of the central leadership, it was stated that any successor to the *imam* must be chosen from among the regional commanders and the members of the high command.[93] Since all of these had taken an oath of loyalty to the national government in 1963, the only person who remained committed to the struggle was Abdul Fatah Wirananggapi, but he had been in prison since 1953.[94] This uncertainty surrounding the central leadership has resulted in confusion among DI veterans in determining to whom loyalty must be given. Some local leaders of DI, who did not abandon the struggle for an Islamic state, started to exercise independent leadership. For instance, Ahmad Sobari who was DI district head of Priangan Timur, West Java, founded the Islamic State of Tejamaya.[95]

Many splinter groups of Darul Islam are not linked directly to DI leaders, but they carry on the struggle for an Islamic state under the leadership of independent, low-ranking comrades. The policy of repression of the New Order towards the movement has led it into considerable disorientation. The important concern for the remaining activists is how to maintain the survival of the struggle for an Islamic state.[96] They use this analogy: "since the loss of the big ship of DI, which carried out the struggle of the Islamic State, small lifeboats – called *sekoci* (an Indonesian term) must be immediately responsible for saving the struggle of the movement."[97] Some Islamic activists of the 1980s have called those DI-associated movements that have recruited members from the campuses the *Kelompok Sekoci* (*Sekoci* Group), and therefore successors to NII. Among those *Sekoci* groups known for their involvement in violent action during the 1970s and 1980s was the Komando Jihad.[98] Other groups have developed up to the present time under various leaders, such as Abdullah Sungkar, who died in Bogor, West Java in 2000 and was subsequently replaced by Abu Bakar Ba'asyir. *Sekoci* groups nowadays are known by their clandestine activities. They continue to recruit new members and to obtain financial support to carry out their struggle. Newly inducted members are obliged to make monetary contributions. "Paradise is cheap, my brother. It only costs 20% of our income."[99] Those who cannot comply with this obligation will receive some form of penalty. Some members even go as far as stealing or robbing banks.[100]

b) Jemaah Islamiyah

The two best-known and allegedly central figures of Jemaah Islamiyah (JI) are Abdullah Sungkar and Abu Bakar Ba'asyir, both of Hadhrami Arab descent. Even though many Indonesian Muslims still question the existence of JI, it has become clear that both Sungkar and Ba'asyir developed a Muslim group, called Jemaah Islam in the 1980s (not Jemaah Islamiyah).[101] Both terms, *"Jemaah Islam"* and *"Jemaah Islamiyah"* have the same meaning; the difference is that the first is Indonesian whereas the second follows Arabic grammar (*al-jama'ah al-islamiyyah* in full). JI is an expanded version of the Darul Islam organization, formed in part when Ajengan Masduki was appointed to hold the caretaker leadership of DI when most of its leaders were arrested during the case of the Komando Jihad.[102]

The main focus of the Masduki cabinet was to develop international linkages and to support and strengthen DI military capacity. Abdullah Sungkar was appointed to assist Masduki in raising funds from Saudi Arabia and the *Rabitah*, while another member of the top staff, Mia Ibrahim was asked to send DI recruits to Afghanistan. In 1988, Masduki, accompanied by Abdullah Sungkar, Abu Bakar Ba'asyir and two others, left Indonesia with a DI delegation for Pakistan and Afghanistan. This travel linked DI with Abdul Rasul Sayaf of the Philippines and Abdullah Azam, a senior Mujahidin commander in Afghanistan.[103] It exposed DI leaders to the challenge of extending their goals towards a broader, international caliphate. The trip gave rise to friction between Masduki and Sungkar, when Masduki, who could not speak Arabic, asked Sungkar to act as spokesman on behalf of the group. Sungkar did all the talking and deliberately excluded Masduki. This competition was intended to demonstrate the dominance of Sungkar over all Afghan veterans.[104] What is more, Masduki, who was of traditionalist NU inclination, became the target of criticism from the more "pure" Salafi-oriented contingent; Abdullah Sunkar and his networks often accused Masduki of practising what they called "un-islamic mysticism."[105]

In the event, the Afghan veterans joined in strengthening JI on their return to Indonesia and contributed to defining the targets of violence as not limited to the local enemy (the Soeharto regime) but to include attacks on what they perceived as the global enemies of Islam, such as the United States, the West and the Zionist conspiracy. Since then, radical Islamic groups in Indonesia have shown their international concerns in terms of their networks and alliances.

3. Global *Santri* (1990s)

In contrast to their fellow Muslims who have embarked on radical action, there are some of the younger Muslim generation who find themselves unable to identify with either traditionalist or modernist life; they are more interested in trans-national movements. This new type of *santri* is known by its tendency to take on global issues within the Islamic world and to pay little attention to issues of national interest.[106] It is a strategy to avoid repression by the regime in power.[107]

Observing the varying orientations of the growing number of Islamic movements in Indonesia, Azyumardi Azra identifies the religious trends of the 1990s as the emergence of a "neo-Islamic revivalism" whose members differ from their predecessors of earlier revivalist movements.[108] The term "neo" is used to distinguish contemporary revivalist movements (i.e. post modern) from revivalist movements of the past. However, these contemporary movements, according to Azra, still have continuing links with the older movements. Despite their detachment from mainstream Muslim institutions, neo-Islamic revivalists are identified by their critical attitudes towards Western institutions, by a concern with international issues and a lack of a social and cultural basis.[109] In general, this trend has gained momentum since the 1990s, attracting mostly the students of secular universities. The neo-revivalist groups in Indonesia with this international orientation are termed "global *santri*".

Having realised the fact that DDII's model of political *dakwah* and the radical bent of Darul Islam failed to challenge the New Order, global-oriented movements chose to focus their activities in cultivating the religious knowledge of individuals. Instead of being able to promote the interests of Muslim communities, the radical and hardline Islamic groups, such as DI and DDII hardliners, have been blamed by the younger generation for their role in sharpening tensions between Indonesian Muslims and the government, causing the latter to suppress the former.[110] Conversely, the regime succeeded in suppressing them and curtailed their organizations. These Global-oriented Islamic movements originated from the encounter of certain *dakwah* activists with international Islamic movements and figures, mainly from Saudi Arabia.[111]

In line with the above strategic reasoning, since the 1990s, many younger Muslim activists have withdrawn from an interest in domestic politics. They have shifted their attention to international issues, devoted their time to absorrbing the fundamental Islamic teachings and to reading the Qur'an. They have begun to single themselves out from radical groups and have established their own ways of understanding intricate realities. Even though most of them have been frustrated and dissatisfied with the regime and its policies, they have sought to choose a different kind of resistance, setting themselves apart from political and social conditions through covert Islamic cultivation and predication, or *tarbiyah*.[112]

They have attracted many Muslim youths to their new perspectives in understanding social and political realities, by focussing on an Islamic dissemination that is more visionary and organised.[113] Instead of spending their energies in attacking the government, they have preferred to devout themselves to practising the basic teachings of their religion. They have tried to re-Islamise fellow Indonesian Muslims, particularly the youth and students, by improving the "quality" of individuals in terms of morality and behaviour. Having witnessed the process of forced de-politicisation and Muslim ineffectuality, they have eschewed political struggle in the short term, in order to build gradual and small clusters of cells leading eventually to a massive network.[114]

In his research into this new phenomenon, Abdul Aziz also had difficulty in identifying the orientation of the various groups of campus Islam, in so far as they differed from the established Islamic organizations in Indonesia.[115] Even while strictly observing the basic teachings of Islam, they have not been able to attach themselves to existing organizations. And since they have been unable to accommodate their new religious awareness in return, these global *santri* have developed their own ways of observing their situation, based on their own interpretation of the conditions of Muslims abroad, either by reading books translated from Arabic into Indonesian or by listening to lectures delivered by preachers graduated from Middle-Eastern institutions.[116]

a) Jemaah Tarbiyah

One of the most interesting phenomena of Indonesian Islam in the 1990s has been the rise of the religious movement called Jemaah Tarbiyah in the campuses of secular universities. This name is not a formal name of a movement but rather Muslim activists in campuses reportedly acknowledged this group as Jemaah Tarbiyah or *ikhwan*.[117] One activist of Jemaah Tarbiyah stated:

> We do not name our group and even the name "Jemaah Tarbiyah" did not come from us, it is other groups who have named us.[118]

It emerged in the mid 1980s, when certain cadres made first contact with and experienced religious training under the moderate wing of the Muslim Brothers of Egypt. Jemaah Tarbiyah proved itself able to channel enthusiastic Muslim students in the state universities by providing religious training and outreach programs. Since the 1990s, activists of Jemaah Tarbiyah have succeeded in gaining control of intra campus student organisations. They have organised Islamic programs and activities for students based in small prayer rooms in campuses and have founded a Forum for Islamic Studies in many faculties. In order to organise Islamic activities among the universities in Java and the Outer Islands, they also began to control the Forum for Coordinating Campus Predication, Forum Silaturahmi Lembaga Dakwah Kampus (FSLDK). Subsequently, through student general elections, they have been able to take over the central leadership of student senate organisations at the faculty and university level. In 1998, after the fall of the Soeharto regime, Jemaah Tarbiyah activists who were active in FSLD founded an extra-campus organisation, the Indonesian Muslim Student Action Union, Kesatuan Aksi Mahasiswa Muslim Indonesia (KAMMI).

The pioneers of Jemaah Tarbiyah are neither from *abangan* families nor secular backgrounds. They have inherited *santri* traditions but have gone through different religious and intellectual experiences from their forbears. They are the children and grandchildren of both traditionalist and modernist *santri* of the 1950s and 1960s. In describing his family's religious background, one Jemaah Tarbiyah activist who was a student of the Institute of Technology, ITS, Surabaya in 1982, stated

> My family is a transitional one. My grandfather was a religious leader associated with Masyumi and a pious person. In contrast, my father and mother probably had changed [their orientation]. They are like ordinary

people in general. [They were] actively involved in non-religious organizations and middle class groups.[119]

On relations between Islam and the state, this group tends to believe that Islam contains both dimensions of religion and state (*al-din wa al-dawlah*). While holding the view of the inseparable links between Islam and politics, Jemaah Tarbiyah believes that Islam does not provide a detailed explanation of political and governmental matters. The function of the state is to assure and maintain the survival of religion, while the Islamic parties are a necessary means to bring gradual changes in the state to take a more open stance towards Islam. It was for that reason that after Soeharto's resignation and the end of his regime in 1998, Jemaah Tarbiyah transformed itself into a political party, assuming the name of the Justice Party, Partai Keadilan (PK). This was later changed in 2003 into the Prosperous Justice Party, Partai Keadilan Sejahtera (PKS).

b) Salafi Groups

The Salafi groups in Indonesia have much in common with Jemaah Tarbiyah in terms of its ideological and religious views – they are somewhat apart from mainstream Islam. They show a tendency to adhere strictly to the religious doctrines and views of "the virtuous forefathers" of the early Muslim scholars of two generations after the Prophet's life (*al-Salaf al-Salih*) and other scholars from Saudi Arabia and Yemen.[120] The members of Salafi groups make little or no acknowledgement of the authority of either traditionalist or modernist religious scholars in Indonesia.

However, in terms of achieving its aims, the Salafi groups differ from the Muslim Brothers-influenced Indonesian movement. In order to Islamise the state, adherents to this group reject involvement within any existing political regime that is democratically inclined. The system of political parties and other democratic practices have no legitimacy in Islam; so the integration of the group is unlikely. The reasoning behind this, they claim, is that the democratic system is one of human invention and has no precedence in the lives of the Prophet Muhammad and his Companions. Rather than directly involving themselves in any political system not based on the example of the great Traditions, the proponents of Salafism tend to withdraw from politics, yet they have developed a definite policy of compliance with the existing political rule. They believe in the significance of upholding the *shariah* in private and individual practice but do not urge for the establishment of an Islamic state. "As long as we can survive to follow our *shariah*, even though the government does not practise it, we do not care."[121] No matter how oppressive or unjust the ruler, he is deemed deserving of respect and obedience. Consequently, this group is more in favour of upholding the status quo than rebellion.[122] It should not be thought that the Salafi's convictions are by any means exploited by the regime. The group may be keen to give its support to the regime, as long as it envisions the introduction of *shariah*.[123]

c) Hizbut Tahrir

As a global orientated movement, Hizbut Tahrir is more political in so far as it holds to the ideal of the establishment of a global Islamic rule, the caliphate, throughout the Muslim world. In working towards this end, it prefers to effect radical changes in Muslims' views and to propagate its ideas through very provocative *dakwah*. The caliphate is the only solution for the Muslim *ummah*. The establishment of an Islamic state, the implementation of Islamic law and the caliphate in all Muslim regions is obligatory. Since the members of HT have no faith in democracy, they will not carry out their ideas through political participation or urge to change the Indonesian democratic system with an Islamic one.[124]

Be that as it may, the followers of this group denounce the use of violence and radical action. They believe in the process of transforming society through their predication activities. Inevitably, though, their rejection of existing political systems raises the question of just how they will implement their beliefs and ideologies. In fact, the key means to achieve their ideas has been through recruitment and the exertion of extra-parliamentary political pressure.[125] In some cases, they have been involved in running strikes against rises in the price of fuel and oil and other non-religious issues. So even though they may deny their participation in current political developments, they still actively engage in some form of political praxis.[126]

The emergence of various categories of *santri* dating from the early establishment of the Soeharto regime to the current situation in Indonesia has shown the dynamics of the *santri* in Indonesia. This phenomenon is not monolithic but rather has involved many forms of cultural interaction and adaptation. The case of Jemaah Tarbiyah also has shown this tendency, its global inclination, meeting at the interface with local Indonesian traditions. The processes of Islamisation in Indonesia are an interesting subject to study, as will be elaborated in our next chapter.

ENDNOTES

[1] See Clifford Geertz, *The Religion of Java* (New York: the Free Press, 1960).

[2] See Koentjaraningrat, *Javanese Culture* (Singapore: Oxford University, 1985).

[3] Geertz, *The Religion of Java*, 129.

[4] Ibid.,148-176

[5] Allan S. Samson, "Army and Islam in Indonesia," *Pacific Affairs* 44 no. 4 (Winter 1971-1972), 549.

[6] Ibid.

[7] Harold Crouch, "Islam and Politics in Indonesia," in *Politics, Diplomacy and Islam: Four Case Studies* (Canberrra: Department of International Relations The Australian National University, 1986) 15.

[8] Guy J. Pauker, "Indonesia in 1980: Regime Fatigue?" *Asian Survey* 21 no. 2 (February 1981), 240.

[9] B.J. Boland, *The Struggle of Islam in Modern Indonesia* (The Hague: Martinus Nijhoff, 1971), 148.
[10] Ibid.
[11] Ken Ward, *The 1971 Election in Indonesia: An East Java Case Study* (Clayton: Centre of Southeast Asian Studies Monash University, 1974), 112.
[12] Robert W. Hefner, *Civil Islam: Muslim and Democratisation in Indonesia* (Princeton and Oxford: Princeton University Press, 2000), 92.
[13] Crouch, "Islam and Politics in Indonesia," 21.
[14] R. William Liddle, "Soeharto's Indonesia: Personal Rule and Political Institutions," *Pacific Affairs* 58 no. 1 (Spring, 1985), 74-84.
[15] R. William Liddle, "The Islamic Turn in Indonesia: a Political Explanation," *The Journal of Asian Studies* 55, no. 3 (August 1996), 623.
[16] Robert W Hefner, Robert Hefner, "Islamising Java? Religion and Politics in Rural East Java," *The Journal of Asian Studies* 46 no. 3 (1987), 533-554.
[17] Bambang Pranowo, "Islam and Party Politics in Rural Java," *Studia Islamika* I no. 2 (1994), 1-19.
[18] For further details about the Dutch policies in Indonesia, see Harry J. Benda, "Christian Snouck Hurgronje and the Foundations of Dutch Islamic Policy in Indonesia," *The Journal of Modern History* 30 no. 4 (December 1958), 338-347.
[19] The establishment of Depag has been also considered as a political compensation for Muslims after the defeat of the Jakarta Charter (Piagam Jakarta).
[20] Jacques Waardenburg, "Muslim and Other Believers: The Indonesian Case" in *Islam in Asia II* (Boulder: Westview Press, 1984), 32-33.
[21] Geertz, *The Religion of Java*, 200.
[22] Boland, *The Struggle of Islam*, 105.
[23] Ibid.
[24] Ibid., 110
[25] Ibid.
[26] See "Tidak Mudah Bagi Pemerintah Penuhi Amanat UU Sisdiknas," *Kompas*, 17 June 2003.
[27] Andree Feillard, "Traditionalist Islam and the State in Indonesia" in *Islam in an Era of Nation States: Politics and Religious Renewal in Muslim Southeast Asia* (Honolulu: University of Hawaii Press, 1997), 143.
[28] Kuntowijoyo, *Muslim Tanpa Masjid* (Bandung: Mizan, 2001), 133.
[29] Azyumardi Azra, "Islam in Southeast Asia: Tolerance and Radicalism" (Paper presented at The University of Melbourne, 6 April 2005), 5.
[30] Liddle, *Islamic Turn*, 625.
[31] Interview with Nur Mahmudi, Depok, 8 May 2003.
[32] Sidney Jones, "It Can't Happen Here: A Post-Khomeini Look at Indonesian Islam," *Asian Survey* 20 no. 3 (March 1980), 319.
[33] Azyumardi Azra, *Jaringan Global dan Lokal Islam Nusantara* (Bandung: Mizan, 2002), 64.
[34] Azra, "Islam in Southeast Asia," 7.
[35] Azra, *Jaringan Global dan Lokal Islam Nusantara*, 67.
[36] Ibid., 18.
[37] Interview with Akswendi, Surabaya, 13 March 2003.
[38] Robert W. Hefner, *Civil Islam: Muslims and Democratization in Indonesia* (Princeton and Oxford: Princeton University Press, 2000), 110.
[39] Ibid.
[40] Nasir Tamara, *Indonesia in the Wake of Islam: 1965-1985* (Kuala Lumpur: Institute of Strategic and International Studies, 1986), 6.
[41] Interview with Sholeh Drehem, Surabaya, 13 March 2003.
[42] Interview with Rahmat Abdullah, Jakarta, 11 May 2003.
[43] Syafii Anwar, *Pemikiran dan Aksi Islam Indonesia: Sebuah Kajian Politik Tentang Cendekiawan Muslim Order Baru*, (Jakarta: Paramadina, 1995), 128-133.
[44] Ibid.

45 Ibid.

46 Kuntowijoyo, "Konvergensi Sosial dan Alternatif Gerakan Kultural," *Pesantren* 3 no. 3 (1986), 6-7.

47 Anwar, *Pemikiran dan Aksi Islam di Indonesia*, 125.

48 Nurcholish Madjid was considered as the pioneer of the Islamic renewal movement. See Bahtiar Effendy, *Islam dan Negara: Transformasi Pemikiran dan Praktik Politik Islam di Indonesia*, (Jakarta:Paramadina, 1998), 136.

49 Anwar, *Pemikiran dan Aksi Islam di Indonesia*, 8.

50 Effendy, *Islam dan Negara*, 125.

51 Ibid., 136.

52 Ibid., 155.

53 The spirit of reconciliation between the state and Islam evinced by Muslims' acceptance of the ideology of Pancasila not only prevailed within modernist circles but was also followed by traditionalist organisations.

54 Effendy, *Islam dan Negara*, 163.

55 Ibid., 165.

56 Greg Barton, "Islam and Politics in the New Indonesia," in *Islam in Asia Changing Political Realities* (New Brunswick and London: Transaction Publishers, 2002), 19.

57 Recent developments of this *santri* stream have generated two further and complicated trends of neo-traditionalism and neo-modernism. The Liberal Islam Network, Jaringan Islam Liberal (JIL) and the Muhammadiyah Young Intellectual Network, Jaringan Intelektual Muda Muhammadiyah (JIMM) are recent phenomena resulting from the long intellectual journey of the renewal movement.

58 See *Tempo*, 3 April 1993.

59 Muhammad Kamal Hasan, *Muslim Intellectual Responses to New Order Modernisation in Indonesia* (Kuala Lumpur: Dewan Bahasa and Pustaka, 1980), 70.

60 Ridwan Saidi, "Dinamika kepemimpinan Islam," in *Islam in Indonesia: Suatu Ikhtiar Mengaca Diri"* (Jakarta: CV Rajawali, 1986), 134.

61 See Hasan, *Muslim Intellectual Responses*, 70.

62 AM Lufhfi, "Gerakan Dakwah di Indonesia," in *Bang Imad Pemikiran dan Gerakan Dakwah* (Jakarta: Gema Insani Press, 2002), 161.

63 Ibid.

64 Nurhayati Djamas, "Gerakan Kaum Muda Islam Masjid Salman," in *Gerakan Islam Kontemporer di Indonesia* (Jakarta:Pustaka Firdaus, 1996), 207.

65 Jimly Assidiqie, eds., *Bang 'Imad Pemikiran dan Gerakan Dakwahnya* (Jakarta: Gema Insani Press, 2002), 34.

66 Ibid.

67 Adam Schwarz, *A Nation in Waiting: Indonesia's Search for Stability* (St. Leonards: Allen and Unwin, 1999), 174.

68 See V.S. Naipul, *Among the Believers: an Islamic Journey* (London: A Deutsch, 1981), 351.

69 See Dr. H. Sugiat Ahmadsumadi, SKM, "HMI, LMD, AMT, ICMI, DI dan Akhirnya Sufi," in *Bang 'Imad Pemikiran dan Gerakan Dakwahnya*, 248.

70 Schwarz, *A Nation in Waiting*, 173.

71 Ibid.

72 *The American Heritage® Dictionary of the English Language*, 4th ed. (Boston: Houghton Mifflin, 2000).

73 In the early era of regime consolidation in 1966, Indonesian development policy was focussed on material advancement and neglected the spiritual dimension so vital in the character of the Indonesia people.

74 Gul M. Kurtogle, "Toleration of the Intolerant? Accommodation of Political Islam in the Muslim World" (Ph.D. diss., University of Chicago, 2003), 30.

75 See *Tempo*, May 30, 1987.

76 Splinter groups of DI are Komando Jihad, Isa Bugis, Islam Jamaah, Islam Murni and Jemaah Islamiyah while figures, such as Abu Bakar Ba'asyir and Irfan S. Awwas are allegedly known to be associated with DI/NII. Interview with Ismail Yusanto, Canberra, 1 August 2004.

77 Tamara, *Indonesia in the Wake of Islam*, 6.

[78] Kuntowijoyo, *Muslim Tanpa Masjid*, 130.

[79] Kuntowijoyo used the term, "*Muslim Tanpa Masjid*," to identify the phenomenon of young Muslims in 1998. However, the 1970s and 1980s also witnessed the same trend, when many Muslims kept their distance from mainstream Islam. See Kuntowijoyo, *Muslim Tanpa Masjid*, 130.

[80] *Tempo*, 11 April 1981.

[81] Geertz himself was surprised with the younger generation of *abangan* who were becoming *santri* as quoted by van der Mehden, *Christian Science Monitor*, 2 Jan 1986. Nonetheless, Geertz' observation on *abangan* tendencies towards observant Islam is still questionable: does he refer to an *abangan* generation becoming more orthodox or a secular Muslim from a *santri* background beginning to re-Islamise itself?

[82] See *Tempo*, 3 April 1993. See also Liddle, "The Islamic Turn," 624.

[83] Ibid.

[84] Julia Day Howell, "Sufism and the Indonesian Islamic Revivalism" *The Journal of Asian Studies* 60 no. 3 (Augustus 2001), 710.

[85] *Islam Jamaah* and *Ahmadiyah* were among groups considered deviant in Indonesia.

[86] Daud Ali, "Fenomena Sempalan Keagamaan di PTU: Sebuah Tantangan Bagi Pendidikan Agama Islam," in *Dinamika Pemikiran Islam di Perguruan Tinggi* (Jakarta:Logos, 1999), 254. Prof. Daud Ali was the head of Arif Rahman Hakim mosque of Universitas Indonesia, Jakarta and a senior lecturer at the Faculty of Law of UI.

[87] Kuntowijoyo, *Muslim Tanpa Masjid*, 133.

[88] Crouch, "Islam in Politics in Indonesia," 27.

[89] See Sidney Jones, "Indonesia: Violence and Radical Muslims" *ICG Indonesia Briefing* (10 October 2001).

[90] Martin van Bruinessen, "Genealogies of Islamic Radicalism in Post-Suharto Indonesia," *South East Asia Research*, 10 no. 2 (2002), 128.

[91] Widjiono Wasis, *Geger Talangsari: Serpihan Gerakan Darul Islam* (Jakarta:Balai Pustaka, 2001), 179.

[92] See Sidney Jones, "Recycling Militants in Indonesia: Darul Islam and the Australian Embassy Bombing" *ICG Asia Repost no. 92* (22 February 2005), 2.

[93] Ibid.

[94] "Tanya Jawab Estapeta Pemimpin NII dalam Darurat Perang," 14 September 2002.

[95] Jones, "The Recycling Militants in Indonesia," 3.

[96] See *Tempo*, 14 July 2002.

[97] Interview, Anonymous, Jakarta 4 March 2003.

[98] See *Tempo* 30 September 1978.

[99] In order to recruit new members, the NII approach was sometimes to kidnap the target and give indoctrination. For further details see "Jalan Pintas ke Surga, Katanya," *Tempo*, 14 July 2002.

[100] There is the NII's concept of *fai*, raising funds by attacking the enemies of Islam. However, what they call the enemies of Islam are not only non-Muslims but also fellow Muslims who are not members of the movement. For further details, see ICG report, "Al-Qaedah in Southeast Asia: the Case of the Ngruki Networks in Indonesia," *Indonesia Briefing* (8 August 2002), 8.

[101] See Tapol, *Indonesia: Muslims on Trial* (London: the Indonesian Human Rights Campaign, 1987), 91-92.

[102] Jones, "The Recycling Militants in Indonesia," 21.

[103] Ibid.

[104] ibid.

[105] ibid.

[106] Even though the elder generation of Indonesian Muslims were influenced by international events to some extent, this younger generation have started to take global inspiration to revitalise Islamic activism in Indonesia. In the past, Muhammadiyah, NU, and Persatuan Islam (Persis) were influenced by an intellectual interaction between Indonesian Muslims and Middle Eastern Muslim in the 20th century. See Martin van Bruinessen, "Global and Local in Indonesian Islam" *Southeast Asian Studies* 37 no. 2 (1999), 46-63.

[107] For further details of this issue see chapter III of this thesis.

[108] Azyumardi Azra, *Islam Reformis: Dinamika Intelektual dan Gerakan* (Jakarta: PT Raja Grafindo Persada, 1999), 46-47.

[109] Ibid., 57.

[110] Interview with Mustafa Kamal, Depok, 11 June 2003.

[111] Despite indirect influence from Arabic-translated books, some pioneers of Jemaah Tarbiyah had encountered Muslim Brothers' activists and lecturers in Saudi universities and disseminated their message to their Muslim counterparts in Indonesia.

[112] In fact, the decision to disengage from political and social realities by focussing on the development of personal piety was a decisive and significant moment that Jemaah Tarbiyah's activists often consider a stage of *kahfi*, or withdrawal preparatory to action. Interview with Rahmat Abdullah, Jakarta, 11 May 2003.

[113] Ibid.

[114] Liddle, "The Islamic Turn," 624.

[115] See Imam Thalkhah and Abdul Aziz, "Gerakan Islam Kontemporer di Indonesia, Sebuah Kajian Awal," in *Gerakan Islam Kontemporer di Indonesia* (Jakarta: Pustaka Firdaus, 1996), 17.

[116] Tim Peduli Tapol, *Fakta Diskriminasi Rezim Soeharto terhadap Umat Islam*, trans. Mohammad Thalib (Yogyakarta: Wihda Press, 1998), 22.

[117] See "Banyak Jalan Menuju Kehidupan Islami," *Suara Hidayatullah*, August 2000.

[118] Interview with Aus Hidayat, Depok, 15 May 2003.

[119] Interview with Sigit Susiantomo, Surabaya, 17 March 2003.

[120] See Chaidar S. Bamualim, "Radikalisme Agama dan Perubahan Sosial di DKI Jakarta" (Jakarta: Tim Peneliti Pusat Bahasa dan Budaya, 2000), 40.

[121] Ibid., 43.

[122] For further details about this group see Sidney Jones, "Indonesia Backgrounder: Why Salafism and Terrorism Mostly Don't Mix," *ICG Asia Report* no. 83 (13 September 2004).

[123] See the *Salafy Magazine* no. 30 (1999).

[124] See *Bulletin Al-Islam* no. 45 (2000).

[125] Sidney Jones, "Radical Islam in Central Asia: Responding to Hizb Ut-Tahrir" *ICG Asia Report*, no. 58 (30 June 2003). For further details also see Hendra Kurniawan, "Realitas Gerakan Hizbut Tahrir di Indonesia: Wacana Hegemonik dan Praksis Ideologi" (Master thesis, University of Indonesia, 2003).

[126] See *Jawapos*, 27 December 2004.

Chapter 2: Jemaah Tarbiyah and Islamisation in Indonesia

The long process of Islamisation[1] that planted its roots in the society of the Indonesian archipelago in the 14th century is by no means yet finished. It continues to bring about change and continuation, from conversion to re-islamisation.[2] After Islam gained its roots in Indonesia until now, all efforts of Islamisation carried out by its agents mainly have aimed to bring the followers of Islam closer to practices of orthodox Islam (reform).[3] Both traditionalists and modernist have been known for their role in carrying out the reform in different degree and approaches. This ongoing process has also manifested interesting and distinct phenomena through time, depending on the varying contexts of social and cultural change.

Over the centuries, Islam has played a major role, not only in shaping society but also in directing the course of Indonesian politics. The fact that Muslims are the majority in Indonesia is considered clear evidence of the importance of Islam. However, to what extent Islam has been adopted at the contemporary structural level is still debatable. In order to gain sufficient knowledge about its role, two distinct approaches: cultural and political, in the Islamisation process need to be presented.[4] While cultural approach tends to focus itself effort in Islamising the society, the political (structural) approach prefer to rely on structural and political power in carrying out its Islamisation agenda.[5]

Thus the emergence of Jemaah Tarbiyah in Indonesia is not an isolated phenomenon, but part of the general process of Islamisation. Through a detailed study of the model and approach of Jemaah Tarbiyah in furthering its *dakwah* or predication, we can discover the religious and political orientations of the movement, and in particular, the movement's view of the relationship between religion and the state in Indonesia. As part of an agenda of Islamisation in Indonesia, Jemaah Tarbiyah has devoted its energies to two kinds of reform: to cultivate those who are "already Muslims" and to reform the formal political structural system according to Islamic teachings.[6]

This chapter aims to analyse the strategy of Jemaah Tarbiyah in its efforts to Islamise Indonesia at the levels of society and the state. Since the issue of Islam-state relations is an important one in Indonesia, it deserves elaboration in this chapter. Through a detailed investigation of the movement, the author will argue that the Islamisation process by the *Tarbiyah* movement since the 1980s has brought cultural and political changes leading to demands that the state accommodate better the "ideals of Islam" (*cita-cita Islam*).

A. Islamising Society: Towards Orthodox Islam

In general, a cultural strategy aims to influence people's behaviour and views. It often uses an individual and moral approach to bring about change in society as a whole.[7] It was through such a cultural approach that Islam was first introduced, avoiding any confrontation with local beliefs. Accommodation through cultural dialogue becomes an alternative solution in minimising friction between the proponents of old beliefs and the preachers of the new religion.[8]

The spread of Islam from the Middle East, the Indian subcontinent and China, to Indonesia was a considerable process of conversion that has made Indonesia the largest Muslim country, while also accommodating local elements from previous religions. Islam in Indonesia has shown diversity in nature; indeed any effort to generalise about current Islamic phenomena throughout the Muslim world as homogenous would be misleading.

An analysis of new Islamic movements in relation to an ongoing process of Islamisation will increase awareness of local contributions, rather than overestimating international influences. Interestingly, almost all current new-style Islamic movements throughout the Islamic world share common inspirations, that is from Hasan al-Banna of the Muslim Brothers of Egypt or Mawlana Mawdudi of the *Jamaat Islami* of Pakistan but they are distinguished by their national contexts and experiences.[9]

Geographical, structural and cultural challenges contribute to the agenda and character of the new Islamic movements. It is more reasonable to speak of the Muslim Brothers-inspired movements in the context of their geographical domains, such as the Egyptian Muslim Brothers, the Syrian Muslim Brothers and the Indonesian Jemaah Tarbiyah Muslim Brothers rather than to depict these movements as a monolithic phenomenon of Muslim Brothers followers. Both the societal and structural processes of Islamisation are an important starting point in comprehending the character of this growing of Islamic activism, particularly Jemaah Tarbiyah, since it has transformed itself from a religious into a political movement.

The tension between Islam *Kafah*[10] and the accommodation of local beliefs, which occurs in many parts of the archipelago, has given rise to the emergence of religious movements under the banner of purification and perfection. At times this has become a prominent phenomenon among sections of Indonesian Muslims. These movements consider it necessary to carry out a process of religious rectification in order to eradicate local cultures and customs and to embrace a process of religious revitalisation by bringing Islam into political practices, in order to liberate Muslim politics from foreign, mainly Western domination.[11]

For many centuries, Islam in Indonesia has been embraced by its followers in different forms of expression and commitment. Initial converts, for instance, simply perceived Islam as a supplement to their old beliefs and rituals.[12] In the coastal part of Java, at least until the late 18th century, Islam attracted followers for economic and political reasons rather than doctrinal ones.[13] Some historians have argued that in the coastal ports of the archipelago there were to be found more committed Muslims than their fellow Muslims in the interior areas. However, it is too early to identify coastal Muslims as "more self-conscious about their religious identity" than the majority of the inhabitants of the interior.[14] Conflicts between coastal and inland Javanese states often occurred, but they were not necessarily triggered by religious issues. They often resulted from contesting economic priorities between the coast and the hinterlands.[15] It is still patently true that the Islamisation process in Indonesia was slow and a long time passed before Islam became recognised as the main religion.[16]

There are many approaches to examine the process of Islamisation in Indonesia.[17] First, the nature of the cultural approach of accommodating local beliefs led to a syncretic form of Islam. Islam developed to provide myriad detailed practices and rituals. However, the essence of Islam as prophetic revelation in the sense of requiring of its believers a total commitment and submission to the ultimate truth had been submerged. Such a total conversion was not the case in the initial Islamisation in Indonesia.[18] In this phase, becoming a Muslim was very simple, requiring the convert merely to accept Islam by declaring the profession of faith.

Second, the political and economic dimension of Islamisation in Indonesia informs us that increased trade in the coastal regions of the archipelago made Muslim traders the main international mercantile network.[19] The coastal courts controlling the trade routes and landfall for ships were chiefly interested in Islam in order to preserve their economic and political interests. In many cases the Islamisation of the coastal courts involved a change of religion, while the heads of kingdoms and the political structures remained unchanged.[20] The establishment of the Islamic kingdoms in Indonesia resulted from the process of adoption of Islam by the rulers, not from the imposition of foreign powers in the archipelago.[21] Or it was often the case that the people of a kingdom embraced Islam first, followed by their king. In order to secure his privilege the king would take an Islamic name, without firmly adhering to the doctrine of Islam.[22]

Third, in studying religious origins, the "authenticity" and "purity" of Islam in Indonesia has often come under question. Islam came to Indonesia by various routes, including by way of South Asia and not directly from the Middle East. It has been established that Indian and Persian customs and rituals had influenced Islam before it was transferred to Indonesia. In Indonesia, the concepts and practices of mysticism are considered to be mostly derived from non-Islamic sources. The roles of Sufi preachers were significant in this process of Islamisation since the thirteenth century.[23] For instance, the doctrine of the "Seven Stages" (*martabat tujuh*) and the "Perfect Being" (*insan kamil*) was adopted from Persian

Sufism and attracted many kings in the archipelago to embrace Islam because both systems assured privileged status for the rulers.[24]

However, considering the Middle East as the source of a "purer" Islam and condemning non-Middle Eastern variants as "inauthentic" lead to unfair judgments. Islam in Indonesia is seen by many reformist groups as being far from authentic or peripheral compared to Islam in the Middle East. The reality is that both the Middle East and beyond has played a significant role in spreading Islam and both have made their contributions in shaping broader Islamic civilisation.

Since the 16th century, the *Haramayn*, the two Arabian holy cities of Mecca and Medina, were centres of Islamic education where many great scholars and Sufi masters passed on their knowledge to their students. A large number of these great scholars and Sufi masters were not originally from the Middle East. They came from India or Persia and developed their religious authority in the *Haramayn*, attracting large numbers of students from throughout the Islamic world, including Indonesia. For instance, Sayyid Syibghat Allah Ibn Ruh Allah Jamal Al-Barwaji (d. 1606) was born in India. He travelled to the *Haramayn* and became influential as a leading reformer and great Sufi master. He became the focal point of an international network of learning in the *Haramayn*.[25] His two predecessors, Ahmad Al-Qusasyi (b. 1583) and Ibrahim al-Kurani (1614-1690) were among leading reformers in Mecca and Medina.[26]

In fact in this era, many non-Arabs developed religious networks and were recognised for their religious authority as a main reference for Muslims to study Islamic practices and knowledge. It was through such a network that the early reformist movements in the 17th and 18th century spread their influence throughout the Muslim world.[27] Syaikh Yusuf Al-Maqassari from South Sulawesi (b. 1626) and Abd Al-Rauf of Singkel (b. 1620) from Aceh were among prominent Muslim scholars from Indonesia who gained their religious authorisation from Ahmad Al-Qusyasyi and Ibrahim Al-Kurani.[28]

In order to gain sufficient insight into the types of Islamisation processes in bringing religious practices of Indonesian Muslims closer to Islamic orthodoxy, the following will be elaborated two approaches of Islamisation: accommodationist and purificationist. As we shall see later, Jemaah Tarbiyah has provided an alternative to the existing orientations, seeking the balance between accommodationists and purificationists. For summary see the following table.

Table 2: Models of Islamic Reform in Indonesian Religious Movements

	Accommodationist	Purificationist
Group	Traditionalists (Nahdlatul Ulama)	Modernists (Muhammadiyah) and Revivalist (Persis, *al-Irsyad*, Salafi Groups)
Ideas	Understanding the Qur'an and Hadith based on opinions of Shafi'i *madhhab*	Return to the Qur'an and Hadith; *non madhhab*.
Local cultural practices	Accommodation	Rejection
The role of Islam in politics	Substantialist (cultural)	Legal Formalist (political)

1. Accommodationist Reformism

We have seen how Islam has demonstrated its ability to penetrate Indonesian life in a peaceful manner and in natural ways.[29] The accommodative picture of Islam was not the only case in Java; most areas in the archipelago before the coming of the colonial powers and the emergence of more aggressive purification-oriented movements indicated similar trends.[30] It was later, after long interaction between the archipelago and the Middle East that orthodox Islam took root, influencing Indonesian Islam to observe religion as it was practised by the Prophet Muhammad and his companions in seventh century Saudi Arabia. The advance of technology in sea transportation and the easing of restrictions on the pilgrimage to Mecca enabled more Indonesian Muslims to visit the Middle East and to experience more of the practice of orthodox Islam.[31]

In addition, socio-economic changes in the archipelago in the first half of the nineteenth century resulted from the operation of large plantations and sugar mills and made it possible for rural farmers to send their children to the Middle East to be educated in a "purer" style of religion.[32] Those graduating from such Middle Eastern training contributed in changing the nature of Indonesian traditional religious education (*pesantren*) which has been widely known for its easy accommodation of local traditions and as the backbone of the traditionalist wing of Islam.[33] Muslims were now directed to observe Islamic teachings more comprehensively, such as regularly performing the daily prayers, fasting, paying *zakat* (Ar. *zakah*) and making the great pilgrimage of the Hajj.

These efforts to introduce more orthodox Islam did not immediately correspond with ideas of rigid purification but constituted a more gradual process. The traditionalist group transformed itself into an agent of reform, to draw a line between nominal and syncretic Muslims (*abangan*) and orthodox Muslims (*santri*). They started to observe regular prayers, fasting in the month of *Ramadhan* and making the great pilgrimage to Mecca. The old practices were still tolerated as long as they did not distort the essence of Islamic teachings.[34] In fact, the generations of Indonesian Muslims who returned from pilgrimage from the 17th until the 19th centuries, even though they promoted orthodox Islam as they had experienced it during their stay in the Middle East, remained non-confrontational towards local beliefs.[35] They returned to their homeland, were accorded the title of *kyai* (scholar) and set up Islamic boarding schools to instruct young men to practise some otherwise neglected aspects of Islamic teachings and to educate them about other classical knowledge of Islam.[36] Their courses contained study of Qur'anic exegesis, the Prophet's traditions, and Islamic Jurisprudences were written in special books called *Kitab Kuning* (Yellow Book) in both Arabic and Malay.

Although Nahdlatul Ulama (NU) was traditionalist, it nonetheless carried out a significant agenda of reform in Indonesia. NU was founded in 1926 by Hasyim Asyari (1875-1947) with the support of *kyai* networks and their religious schools, the *pesantren*. While requiring the application of orthodox Islam, they still carried out reform in gradual ways. This strategy was intended to avoid cultural and social disruption in society. According to the criticism by non accommodation-oriented movements, Muhammadiyah and Persis, this accommodation pattern often was often unable to prevail against existing practices. The opponents of gradual and slow Islamisation have blamed the traditionalist approach as being too tolerant of local customs and unaccepted practices (*bid'ah*).

According to M.C. Ricklefs, in practice, the Islamic teachers associated with the traditionalist groups often have more in common with rural *abangan* than with more urbanised modernist Muslims.[37] However, this is true only in the case of common association between *abangan* and traditionalist *santri* in the countryside; in the case of religious and political commitment there are sharp distinctions among them. The conflicts between the Communists and the *santri* community in the bloodsheds of 1948 and 1965 there was a strong cooperation between traditionalist and modernist *santri* to fight against the *abangan*. Generally speaking, the traditionalists have been unhappy to be associated with *abangan* practices and syncretism, since both traditionalist *santri* and *abangan* identities carry very different connotations and orientations in Indonesian society.[38]

Further analysis of traditionalist *santri-abangan* relationship and how traditionalist figures rejected the accusations of practicing syncretic practices, we can refer to Abdurahman Wahid's articles. Wahid is of the most prominent even controversial - traditionalist figures, the chairman of NU (1989-1998) and the third president of Indonesia (1999-2000). He proposed the concept of *pribumisasi Islam* (the indigenisation of Islam). *Pribumisasi* entails a cultural accommodation that proceeds in natural ways; it is a kind of reconciliation process in order to solve any conflict that might arise between religion and local culture. This indigenisation process is not designed merely to avoid resistance from local cultures but it aims to preserve the very existence of all cultures in the society. According to Wahid, the total identification of Islam with the Middle East has endangered the cultural roots of Indonesia and threatens the essence of Islam itself. Indigenisation also is required in religious interpretation; especially important is an awareness of local circumstances, law and justice.[39]

Abdurahman Wahid argues that *pribumisasi* is not a process of "Javanization" that will bring about syncretism. In formulating religious laws, for instance, an awareness of local cultures and customs can proceed without distorting the essence of Islamic law. It is because the principle of Islamic jurisprudence also provides the significant precept, *al-'adah mu'addalah*, "custom is made law." Muslims should be aware of prevailing circumstances and not simply impose their own agenda, and here the effort to formalise the implementation of *shariah* is included. Such formalisation, according to Wahid, relegates the substance of Islam itself to a lesser importance.[40]

Among the traditionalists, the concept of the common good that gives a higher priority to the welfare of the community (*maslahah*) is considered a main principle in dealing with broader issues in society and politics. In the political arena, NU has been known for its strong commitment to accommodation and compromise, a valuable quality of flexibility in dealing with the realities of Indonesian politics.[41] NU has tended to consider the reality of power as its main argument in order to enable its elites to gain influence in the political structure, instead of being strictly guided by ideological and religious positions in pursuing its Islamic goals.[42]

Nonetheless, in actual practice, the flexibility of NU in dealing with political and religious issues has been accompanied by a reluctance to develop cooperation with other Islamic groups and parties. NU's critics have focussed on the issue that NU has no barriers to cooperation with non-Muslims but hesitates to build solidarity with other Islamic groups, particularly with the modernists. The existence of different doctrines and schools (*madhahib*) has impeded Islamic groups from cooperating with one another. In many cases cooperation and coalition did occur at first, but was subsequently broken off.[43] The problem did not lie totally with the traditionalists but reflected the fragile nature of Islamic interest groups that were prone to disintegrate.

In fact, many of the younger generation of NU, particularly those who studied in the Middle East and were attracted to the practices of orthodox Islam, subsequently joined Jemaah Tarbiyah. Middle Eastern countries, such as Egypt, Saudi Arabia, Yemen, Jordan and Sudan, before known as the strongholds of traditionalist students coming from Indonesian *pesantren*, nowadays have become the backbone of Jemaah Tarbiyah caderisation.[44]

2. Purificationist Reformism

The traditionalists, then, have carried out an agenda of reform in order to bring the followers of Islam in Indonesia to practice orthodoxy. However, because of their accommodation to local customs, this has been mixed with non-Islamic teachings.[45] When great numbers of Indonesians were able to travel to Mecca to perform the pilgrimage of the *Hajj* and to study, access to the "purer Islam" of the Middle East opened up.[46] Newly returned pilgrims were not satisfied with what they saw as the incomplete process of Islamisation and the mixing of Islam with pre-Islamic local traditions at home. Consequently, they embarked on a further process of purification.

The purification-oriented reformists call for a return to the original foundations of Islamic teaching, the Qur'an and the Hadith (the Prophet's Traditions). In stark contrast to the methods of the accommodationists who had carried the agenda of reform in a slow and silent manner, the purification-style reformists often harshly criticised practices that they found in violation of "authentic" Islam. This group claimed that corrupt practices such as *bid'ah* (innovation), *khurafat* (mysticism) and *takhayul* (superstition) and other local practices caused a deterioration of the Muslim community. The tension between accommodationist reformists and purificationist reformists has regularly led to disputes and mutual criticism. In addition, the intrusion of Western traditions into Muslim countries, including Indonesia, has been perceived by purificationists as a major cause of the decline of Muslim civilization in Indonesia, since the nineteenth century, when colonial rule caused many indigenous states to lose their independence.[47]

It is understandable that the main idea of the purification movement is to free all religious practices from extraneous elements and to follow "original" Islam strictly.[48] Accordingly, not only religious practices and rituals must be in line with a purer source of Islam but worldly matters as well must be freed from non-Islamic influences, including Western traditions. The purification that aimed initially at internal reform within a particular community often developed into an attack on what was perceived as an external threat to Islam.[49] During colonial times, religious leaders returning from the Middle East often opposed the Dutch and their associated local civil court system. These *hajis* not only appeared as a new force to oppose local traditional *kyais* but also to de-legitimise alien elements in colonial society.[50] Nonetheless, some political purification-aimed reformists also chose to keep their distance from the established political system, realising that they were unable to change it. Others tried to work within the system in the hope that they might reform it after gaining solid support from the mass of the people.

In general, the purification-oriented movements do not show a common pattern in promoting the refinement of non-Islamic elements when they view the political problems of Muslims in the modern age. Some of them rigidly require religious and political practices to be totally free from things foreign, whilst other groups limit their actions to religious matters and openly accept local and modern influences in non-religious practices. It seems that the different orientations of these groups in responding to modern problems become the distinctive feature of revivalist and modernist groups respectively. While the revivalists tend to eliminate and remove all un-Islamic influences in religion, the modernists are more concerned with the restoration of neglected aspects of Islam as it was at the time of the Prophet, for the time being, downplay the rigid purification of alien elements that already exist within establishment Islam.

The purification movements draw their ideological and doctrinal references from prominent Muslim scholars and reformers in Saudi Arabia and Egypt. Chief among these are Abdullah Ibn Abd al-Wahab (1703-1791) who generated the core element of the revivalist group (uncompromising purificationist reformism) and Muhammad Abduh (1849-1905) who advocated the idea of modernism (accommodative purificationist reformism). Subsequently, Abduh's student, Rasyid Ridha (1865-1935) also played an important role in combining modernist and conservative orientations of Muslims. Both inspirations have greatly influenced the transformation of Islamic thought and the praxis of Indonesian Muslims since the late eighteenth-century.

a) Revivalism

This type of uncompromising purification-aimed reformism involves a strict application of the original sources of religious practice and worldly activity. The idea is to return to the practices as laid down by the Qur'an and the Prophet's Traditions. The term *kolot* (traditionalist) and *moderen* (modernist) has been used in distinguishing the authenticity of the respective Islamic practices. Traditionalist *santri* have often become the focus of criticism of revivalist *santri* because of their accommodation in carrying out Islamisation. In fact, the impatient nature of this movement towards establishment Islam by embarking on radical patterns of purification has created deep and painful conflicts between the purifiers and the adherents of the old practices.

In Indonesia, early in the twentieth century, it was local religious leaders in West Sumatra, influenced by the teachings of Abdul Wahab, who generated the primary impulse of uncompromising purification, both religious and political. Their efforts not only caused religious division between the *kaum muda* (younger group) and *kaum tua* (older group) of their day but also drew upon similar roots of earlier civil war in Sumatra (1821-1837). This confrontation had been played out between the forces of Islam and Minangkabau *adat* (custom) and its champions.[51] By launching an aggressive campaign of purification, Imam Bonjol and his Padri supporters tried to rid Islam of un-Islamic practices, such as cockfighting and gambling. They failed to defeat the adherents of *adat* because of Dutch armed intervention. One religious leader, Tuanku Nan Rintjeh felt that bare force was necessary to implant his tenets, under the rubric "to abolish all Minangkabau customs which were not sanctioned by al-Qur'an, with death as punishment for those who refuse to give their obedience."[52]

Another uncompromising purification-oriented movement is the Islamic Union, Persatuan Islam (Persis). Differing from its predecessors regarding the need to use force in promoting its agenda, Persis, which is influenced by Rashid Rida's ideas has declared itself the agent of purer Islam through education and predication. Founded by A. Hasan in Bandung in 1923, Persis developed into a cadre-type organization, which has worked for the establishment of a Muslim community strongly committed to meet "uncontaminated" Islamic obligations. Since it claims to be a cadre organization, Persis does not emphasise the expansion of membership and has tended to be exclusive in cultivating its cadres. However, it has produced a number of Islamic leaders and religious scholars who have become involved in national political activities in Indonesia. Among them are M. Natsir, Endang Syaifuddin Anshari, Isa Ansyari and many others.

Persis has striven to educate Muslims to abandon any practices not sanctioned in Islam, particularly those of traditionalist Muslims. In order to create a "backbone", Persis established their own *pesantren* in Java, such as in Bandung and in Bangil, East Java. Again, the confrontational method of revivalist-type movements such as Persis in disseminating their religious doctrines has given rise to frequent conflicts among adherents of different Islamic groups. Strong cadre-type operations have proved to be more successful than broader, slower mass-based movements.

In a new phase, the seminal Salafi groups that have developed since the early 1980s represent a more conservative revivalist spirit in Indonesia. They urge all Muslims to practise their Islam based on the example of the Prophet Muhammad, his companions, and the trusted medieval scholars of the 7th and 8th centuries, the *salafus-salih*. Similar to the purification-oriented reformists, the Salafi groups are stricter and more rigid in implementing their ideas. They do not use a modern type of mass organization, but limit their efforts to whatever has been prescribed by the Prophet and trusted scholars. The exclusive nature of this movement requires the establishment of an Islamic community and the maintenance of networks among them. Islamic real estate and housing projects are interesting new phenomena in Indonesia and are mainly dominated by this group, and other Muslims wishing to create an Islamic living environment.

While many younger members of Persis have been attracted to join Jemaah Tarbiyah due to its similar aims of promoting the return to the Qur'an and Hadith, most members of Salafi groups have been reluctant to embrace Jemaah Tarbiyah. After having studied deeply the Salafi doctrines, many have left Jemaah Tarbiyah since they considered it too diluted in practising Islam due to its political inclinations.[53]

b) Modernism

Some purification-oriented reformists in Indonesia, influenced by various streams of purification movements in Egypt, have adopted different approaches in promoting their agenda of Islamisation. One such modernist group, identified by its willingness to cooperate with the challenges of modern life, promotes the call for Muslims to return to the foundations of Islam, the Qur'an and the Hadith. Their attitudes are in the main more accommodative and their programs are implemented to different degrees, depending on local social and cultural responses. Strictly speaking, this kind of purification movement is marked by its inclination to receive modern developments in conformity with Islamic teachings.

Muhammadiyah, which was founded in 1912 in Yogyakarta, Central Java by K.H. Ahmad Dahlan is a typical reform movement. It strongly promotes the ideas of religious purification and prohibits various practices considered to have a basis in pre-Islamic culture, such as visiting graves for meditation and veneration, mysticism and all forms of polytheism, but it demands less purification in the social sphere and in politics. Muhammadiyah has insisted that Islam must be adapted to the requirements of modern life through the practice of *ijtihad*, a return to the Qur'an and the Tradition in the light of individual, rationalist interpretation.[54]

Whilst other purificationists have failed to gain mass support, particularly in rural areas, the flexibility of the new *ijtihad* applied by Muhammadiyah has enabled it to deal with changes in Indonesian society. As a result, the advances of the reformists have been made at the expense of the traditionalist Muslims.[55] This is mainly because Muhammadiyah has been able to provide social services and educational institutions for Muslims at the grassroots level. Since Muhammadiyah has focussed its activities on social and educational programs, many of the younger generation who are inclined toward political activities have little space to exercise their political interests within the organisation. In their search to meet these needs, they have found Jemaah Tarbiyah the best vehicle to develop their career in politics.[56]

3. The *Tarbiyah* Model: An Alternative Islamisation

The emergence of Jemaah Tarbiyah represents the process of synthesis between accommodation and purification-orientated reformism in Indonesia. The movement emerged when the traditionalist-modernist dichotomy had blurred. The younger generation of Indonesian Muslims has been uninterested in involvement in the doctrinal disputes of the traditionalist and modernist groups; instead they turned to new ideas coming from the Middle East for their inspiration.

Jemaah Tarbiyah is inspired by the Islamic thought of Hasan al-Banna (1906-1949), the founder of the organisation *Ikhwanul Muslimun*, the Muslim Brothers of Egypt. The political and ideological aspects of al-Banna's movement are well known and they have attracted the attention of scholars studying political Islam and the phenomenon of fundamentalism in the Muslim world. However, only a few observers have considered the religious and theological ideas of al-Banna, since most focus on the political and radical impact of his movement on newer fundamentalist groups.[57]

Although many studies have linked his ideas to revivalist figures, such as Abd al-Wahab and Jamal al-Din al-Afghani (1838-1897), al-Banna himself has never aspired to emulate them or mentioned their names in his writings and sermons. He was most influenced by Rashid Rida (1865-1935) whom he cites in his memoirs. Rida was a revivalist Salafi leader who was born in Syria and developed his intellectual career in Egypt. Al-Banna often attended Rida's gatherings and visited the Salafi bookstore where he could read Salafi books and discuss them with the store's owner, Muhibb al-Din al-Khatib, himself a Salafi scholar.[58] Al-Banna was more typical leader of a movement than an intellectual or scholarly figure.

In his memoirs, al-Banna himself often stressed the influence of his traditional Sufi teachers, masters of mysticism, and rarely talked about revivalist figures. During the establishment of his social movement, and even later when it developed a more political orientation, he aspired to the model of Sufi guidance and the fellowship. Yet he was also driven by the ideal of bringing Islamic practices in line with the fundamental sources of Islam, the Qur'an and the Hadith.[59] The establishment of the Muslim Brothers was an expression of his obsession to expand the spirit of the Sufi community into a broader context. He criticised the narrow interpretation of brotherhood applied by the Hasafi Sufi order, which he wanted to make its benefits and rules applicable to all Muslims. His long experience with the Hasafiyyah led him to reform certain aspects of Sufi practices that were, according to him, in violation of "purer" Islam.[60] In fact, he was a devout adherent of Sufism and there was no evidence throughout his life, until his assassination, that he had renounced his Sufi practices.[61]

On one hand, the Jemaah Tarbiyah movement is very much concerned with the idea of returning to the original sources of Islamic teachings, but on the other hand it is flexible in promoting its ideals. In these ideals not like the traditionalists who conform to cultural and local realities; Jemaah Tarbiyah prefers to promote a distinctly Islamic behaviour in society. For instance, while traditionalists do celebrate the pre-Islamic feast of the seventh month of a woman's pregnancy (*tujuh bulanan*) adapting it with Islamic prayers, Jemaah Tarbiyah tends to avoid this practice. However, compared to other supporters of purificationist movements, such as Persis or Muhammadiyah, Jemaah Tarbiyah is less strict but it is more concerned about promoting the role of Islam in politics.

In order to create strong cadres for the movement, Jemaah Tarbiyah emphasises the significance of cultivating "perfect character" (*muwassafat*) that must be thoroughly internalised.[62] Candidate members are not fully admitted as members of Jemaah Tarbiyah until they show the required personal commitment. The qualities that all cadres of Jemaah Tarbiyah must possess are: uncontaminated faith (*salim al-a'qidah*), right worship (*salim al-'ibadah*), perfect morals (*matin al-khulq*) an ability to work (*qadirun 'ala al-kasb*), wide knowledge (*muthaqqafah al-fikr*), a strong and healthy body (*qawiyy al-jism*), tenacity (*mujahidun li nafsih*), the capacity to demonstrate good management in all affairs (*munazzam fi shu'nih*), punctuality (*harisun 'ala waqtih*) and they must be useful to others (*nafi'un li ghayrih*).[63] In order to ensure that members do physical exercise and develop new expertise, for instance, they are given special assessments. They are obliged to take exercise twice a week and to read books outside their own specialisation.[64]

The special qualities of the cadres are derived from the main principles of al-Banna's teachings called *arkan al-bay'ah*, the principles of allegiance.[65] The training manuals of PKS describe at length the significance of holding to right faith and ask Muslims not to perform spiritual healings (Ar. *ruqyah*) unless using Qur'anic verses, not to be associated with jinn or to seek help from the souls of the deceased.[66] Regarding the issue of what Jemaah Tarbiyah calls the "right and uncontaminated faith" there is no mention of a need to fight against local cultures and the like. Even the case of innovation *(bid'ah)* or practices not ratified by Islam, Jemaah Tarbiyah follows al-Banna and tends to deal with them in a considerate manner. For instance, Al-Banna also tolerated the Sufi practice of *tawasul (Ar. tawassul,* the recitation of prayers requesting the mediation of the saints), which is considered an unlawful innovation by strictly purification-oriented reformists. Furthermore, al-Banna explained the way to deal with such variant practices among Muslims:

> Every innovation in religious matters that has no roots in Islam and follows only personal desire is unlawful. It must be eliminated by using the best of ways. Those ways must not trigger another unlawful innovation [i.e. a negative reaction] which is more dangerous that the original innovation itself.[67]

One Jemaah Tarbiyah activist, Muslikh Abdul Karim, who holds a doctorate from Ibn Saud University, Saudi Arabia, and who was schooled in the traditional *pesantren* of Langitan, in Tuban, East Java, explained his attitude towards the different opinions on practice between the traditionalists and the modernists in Indonesia.[68] He maintains his own traditional rituals, such as *tahlilan,*[69] even though this practice has become a sore point of criticism from both revivalist and modernist groups.

> When we were in Saudi Arabia, we established our own association that was neither too much NU nor Muhammadiyah. In King Saud University we used to perform *tahlilan* every Friday.[70]

In fact, both Jemaah Tarbiyah and the Muslim Brothers have similar opinions in responding to religious differences, such as in ritual and devotions. This has come about mainly because of the long involvement of the founder of the Muslim Brothers with a Sufi *tarekat*. (In Indonesia such practices are very much associated with traditionalist Islam.) And yet, in its earliest stage of development during the 1980s, Jemaah Tarbiyah inclined more to modernism than traditionalism, since most focal leaders of the movement were former active members of Islamic organizations, such as the Islamic University Students Association, Himpunan Mahasiswa Islam (HMI) and the Indonesian Islamic Students, Pelajar Islam Indonesia (PII). In addition, the influence of Saudi Arabia as a site of transmission of the ideas of the Muslim Brothers to Indonesians studying there has carried an indirect impact on revivalist and modernist views into Indonesia. What is not often discussed is the fact that activists of a traditionalist background are also in strength in the movement. They have had little public exposure because although they are culturally members of NU, they are not actively involved in it or its associated organizations.

My interviews with Jemaah Tarbiyah cadres and leaders reveal an important finding. There are significant numbers of NU background within PKS and this fact has not publicly recognised. The interviewees were specially selected figures occupying important positions in PKS, such as chairman, secretary and members of *shariah* Board, either on the Central Board of the Justice Party in Jakarta or in its provincial branches, such as East Java, West Sumatra, and South Sulawesi. About 36 persons were interviewed during 2003-2005. The religious background of respondents' families and their affiliation with traditionalist or modernist organizations can be summarised as follows: based on parents' religious affiliation, 19 out of 36 (53%) interviewees were from a traditionalist background and 12 out of 36 (33%) interviewees were from a modernist background. Only 5 out of 36 (14%) respondents come from a non-*santri* background (*abangan*).

When they were asked about their attachment to traditionalist or modernist organizations, 72% (26 persons) said they did not have association with either organization. Only 8% (3 respondents) and 19% (7 respondents) still identified themselves as part of traditionalist or modernist associations respectively, this being indicated by formal involvement or simply by self-identification. The tendency of PKS members to be reluctant to mention their previous association with traditionalist groups is mainly influenced by their goals to bring all Islamic forces into unity.[71] This is summarised in the following table.

Table 3: Traditionalist and Modernist Affiliation of PKS Committees

Background	Traditionalist		Modernist		Abangan		Non Affiliation	
Parent	19	53%	12	36%	5	14%	0	0%
Activist	3	8%	7	19%	0	0%	26	76%

Even though Jemaah Tarbiyah emerged within a revivalist milieu and has adopted the Muslim Brothers' model in implementing its agenda, it has not adopted all of their ideas. Jemaah Tarbiyah is more a reflection of the younger generation of Muslims who are trying to find alternative references to the established Muslim groups, modernist or traditionalist.

Jemaah Tarbiyah has tried to play a major role as an agent of reform and to function as a mediating force among the various streams of Muslims in Indonesia. It has been accommodative in promoting its ideals in order to gain support from communities of different religious expression and has downplayed the role of religious purification. In general, as long as there are Muslims who believe that Islam is a way encompassing all aspects of life, Jemaah Tarbiyah will accommodate them.[72]

Based on the Jemaah Tarbiyah agenda mentioned above in its effort of bringing together Islamic forces in Indonesia, more aggressive revivalist groups, in particular those of Salafi groups, have often accused the activists of Jemaah Tarbiyah of sacrificing their Islamic principles to promote their ideas and recruit their members, since they have always kept an eye on popular support. In contrast, Jemaah Tarbiyah has been seen by traditionalist groups to be too radical in implementing its ideas, in particular in its demand for the formalisation of Islamic law. Its attempted role in integrating all Islamic forces has placed the movement in an ambiguous position. It criticises both traditionalist and modernist practices from time to time, but it also tries to urge them to unite under its Islamic political Islam.

The distinctive character of Jemaah Tarbiyah, in comparison with mainstream Islam in Indonesia, is its strong individualistic pattern of Islamisation. In general, the process of Islamisation has followed two templates. Firstly, that of communal conversion in which Islam is adopted by a tribal group, by certain members of society or by the inhabitants of a village. This pattern of Islamisation provides sufficient space these newly converts to maintain their own cultural identities and group interests. Those espousing the new doctrine are mainly downplayed and submerged by the old.[73] Secondly, the template of individual conversion, in which new adherents accept not only the new religion but also a new cultural and ethnic identity. Individuals have to be ready to break off ties with their old society or group. The commitment to the new doctrine takes priority. These patterns of conversion lead to the possibility of alienation from the old group, association and even territory. The former type of Islamisation requires no "definite crossing of religious frontiers and the acceptance of new worship as useful supplements and not as substitutes."[74] The latter type entails a greater struggle for the reorientation of faith and a more meaningful change, in which individual consciousness plays a large part.[75] In this kind of individual Islamisation Jemaah Tarbiyah has relied on its strength and basis for caderisation.

Building on the individual pattern of Islamisation, Jemaah Tarbiyah has made strenuous efforts to cultivate and educate the commitment of individuals to Islam. The Tarbiyah model of Islamisation aims to call "existing Muslims" to embrace total Islam as an all-encompassing system (*shamil*). Islam is to be the only guidance for life (*minhaj al-hayah*) providing all the spiritual and worldly needs of human beings. It is law, civilization and culture, political system and governance. Muslims who follow the concepts of *tarbiyah* believe that there is no single matter remaining which is not under the rules of Islam. As the first caliph of Islam, Abu Bakar (d. 634) said, "if the robe for my camel has been lost, I will certainly find it in the Holy Book (the Qur'an)."[76]

During its early development as a new, underground group, Jemaah Tarbiyah had a very limited scope for spreading its ideas. Under the New Order regime, the movement's new orientation, mainly derived from foreign influences, might have raised more public suspicion than broad acceptance. The capability of the activists of the movement to disseminate their new ideas of Islam as encompassing the whole of life required an acceptance of universal Islam, rather than an ethnically or territorially -associated Islam. The individual call (*al-da'wah al-farziyyah*) gained tremendous ground, as is indicated by the Justice Party's political success during the 1999 and 2004 general elections. In both general elections, PKS gained about 1.4 million and 8.3 million supporters through the work of only 70,000 and 400,000 cadres respectively.[77] However, PKS's strategy of anti corruption and its campaign for social welfare also became attractions for voters during the 2004 general election.

The individual pattern of Islamisation, however, needs a long process which involves individuals and small groups. In contrast to older patterns of Islamic conversion, which for the most part was carried out by influential figures and professional teachers, including traders, saints and Sufis, in Jemaah Tarbiyah it is the students of reform minded religious teachers who have principally carried out the Jemaah Tarbiyah model of Islamisation. They have advanced predication and set up religious circles (*halaqah*) on university campuses. They have attracted many students and provided them with moral support and academic tutorials. A student who is interested in studying Islam in a "specific way" may be motivated to attend regular *halaqah*.[78]

Through the *halaqah*, new members are cultivated and their responsibility toward Islam is enhanced. They are not only encouraged to observe the obligatory duties as prescribed in the five principles of Islam, but also optional and recommended responsibilities, such as reading the Qur'an, pursuing religious knowledge, visiting their Muslim brothers and sisters so on. In this stage, members of *halaqah* are obliged to cultivate their religious capacities and devotions and to call other people, including their friends and families, to observe all religious obligations.[79] By attending regular *halaqah,* usually, once a week, the members are expected to observe all religious obligations in the right manner according to the Qur'an and Hadith.

In addition to ordinary students working as agents of Islamisation, there are ideologues as well trained in Islamic institutions either in the Middle-East or in other modern Islamic schools in Indonesia, such as the Pesantren Gontor in Ponorogo, East Java, Pesantren Maskumambang in Gresik, East Java, the Institute of Arabic and Islamic Studies of Ibn Saud University in Jakarta (LIPIA) and other State Institutes of Islamic Religion (IAIN). They are attracting large numbers of students, from the secular state universities, who are convinced of the effectiveness of *tarbiyah* as an alternative model in carrying out Islamisation in Indonesia. For them, *tarbiyah* is "truly a process of Islamisation that encourages deep changes in individuals in terms of morality, intellectuality and spirituality."[80]

B. Islamising the State: Towards a Pragmatic Approach

The structural approach of Islamisation tends to use a collective pattern, in which Islamic predication is mediated by the state. The structural change of the state, including its elites and apparatuses, enables its proponents to insist upon the implementation of Islamic teachings in society. Demands for structural change, however, make the government feel threatened, whether change is carried out in a gradual or a revolutionary way. Since the proponents of the structural approach believe that Islam must play a role within the state, they differ in regard to how best to pursue their goals. Does Islam need to be implemented through formal legislation, or it is enough to present it as a moral and inspirational source of the state's rules and legislation? In other words, as formulated by Dawam Raharjo, "how (are we) to promote Islamic ideas in a religiously democratic system that acknowledges the influence of religion in the state's affairs?"[81] Within these parameters, most Indonesian Muslim scholars have differed in defining the concept of structural Islamisation and its scope within a context of pluralism.

Historically, Islam has been understood and applied by Indonesians in both its political and cultural aspects in various stages. To struggle for Islam in society and the state, Muslim activists have used both cultural and political expressions, depending on social and political contexts. "Cultural Islam", as it was initiated by the generation of the 1960s and 1970s, by no means neglected the political consciousness of Muslims. The political aspirations of Indonesian Muslims, however, had to be expressed in terms of temporary and short-term goals by the means of a political party.[82] Against this it must be understood that Indonesian Muslims subscribe to the idea that there can be no ultimate separation between religion and society, though there may be many ways to implement this principle.[83]

Generally speaking, the political experiences of Muslims in the Middle East have taken three types of expression, secular, fundamentalist, and moderate. A secular orientation emphasises the need to completely differentiate the state and religious affairs; in contrast, the fundamentalist approach considers that Islam and the state are inseparable. This position requires its followers to establish an Islamic state. The moderate stance seeks to compromise between secular and fundamentalist goals. In the case of Indonesia, a secular orientation, which promotes the total separation of religion and the state, has been not prominent. Similarly, a fundamentalist orientation, even though gaining momentum, has received little support. In general, Indonesian Muslims hold moderate attitudes towards the status of religion in the state. The main debate has been around the question of whether Indonesia should be ruled according to Islamic law or Islam is to be considered one source of laws and allow other sources of legislation than Islam. The debate has taken place between the group who understands Islam as a political ideology (the legal-formalist position) and those who consider it as merely a moral force in politics (the substantialist). Even though in the 1950s, all Islamic parties demanded the implementation of some aspects of *shariah*, their aspirations were channelled through democratic ways.

Therefore, the struggle to create an Indonesian Islamic state by particular groups promoting radical action has failed, while any efforts by Muslim activists to control political directions has been crushed by the regime of Soeharto's New Order. The political expression of Muslims is no longer directed to a struggle for the establishment of an Islamic state, but rather it has given priority, explicitly or implicitly, to "colouring" the existing government with Islam. For the proponents of political Islam, their struggle mainly aims to promote some aspects of Islamic law to be accommodated within the national laws.[84]

Yet, in order to neutralise the influence of the forces of political Islam among Indonesians since the late 1980s, the New Order has also actively supported Islamisation at the structural and societal level. The establishment of the Association of Muslim Intellectuals in Indonesia, Ikatan Cendekiawan Muslim Indonesia (ICMI) in 1990, led by B.J. Habibie, a close associate and minister of Soeharto, succeeded in placing its cadres in strategic positions, including some ministerial posts, which under the Soeharto regime had been seen as the fruits of new Muslim Middle class groups in the process of social mobilization.[85] However, the phenomenon of ICMI also represents the success of the regime in monopolising power and co-opting Islamic forces in Indonesia. It was an "instrument designed and used by President Soeharto for his own purposes."[86]

At the very least, the role of Muslims within the system during that regime had the effect of increasing the development of Islam at the grassroots level and in some areas of state structure.[87]

Corresponding with the two streams of cultural and political orientation in Indonesian Islam, there are two typologies for explaining Muslim views. The political Islam group calls for a legal and formal approach and the cultural group promotes a substantialist approach. Apart from these two, there is an emerging tendency in political Islam to play a mediating role between formal-legalistic and substantialist strategies, regarded as pragmatic. Here the role of Jemaah Tarbiyah in shaping the political praxis of PKS is the phenomenon to be addressed.

1. The Legal Formalists

The legal formalist group views Islam not merely as a religion that consists of ritual and worship and a source of ideology; it is the main ideology. For this group, the establishment of a political party based on Islamic ideology is important. The group struggles for the recognition of Islamic law and tries to safeguard the implementation of *shariah* as the all-embracing way of life through the organs of the state.

Two common ways to promote the legal formalist strategy are channelled either through the establishment of an Islamic state or through struggle within the political system. The former demands revolutionary change and may result in radical changes in the existing regime that are not based on the Islamic principles. However Islamic groups are supposed by radical groups to comply with the people's expectations and lead to revolution or contra- state movements.[88] This approach requires that Islam must be politicised.[89] In the case of Indonesia, the regime has been quick to handle such Islamic state-aimed movements harshly. As well, the obstacles in creating an Islamic state through revolution and confrontation have come not only from the ruling system but predominantly from Indonesian Muslims themselves.

A political approach that focuses on struggle through the establishment of a legal political party, even though it is not free from government intrusion, at least provides the possibility of achieving its goals. The hostility of the regime towards organised Islam during the New Order period contributed to reducing the survival of Islamic parties in the long term. The only Islamic party that might have survived at that time was forced to follow the regime's interests. The supporters of Islamic political Islam found themselves not only increasingly oppressed by the regime but they also increasingly isolated from the Indonesian people. However, the situation changed after the fall of the New Order in 1998, resulting in the emergence of a remarkable number of new Islamic parties. This political party approach believes that Islam is a practical religion, offering guidance in political, social, economic and international affairs.[90] In order to promote the ideas of Islam, politics indeed needs to be "spiritualised."[91]

It seems that current Islamic parties in Indonesia are quite aware of the social, political, and cultural dynamics of their country. Parties promote most Islamic aspirations in modest and moderate ways in order to gain public support. They understand well that political change in Indonesia happens only through the accommodation of political groups and the majority support of the Indonesian people. Any effort to impose an Islamic orientation without considering social and political contexts not only will fail but also will surely meet with great resistance from the people. This has been proved by the fact that Islamic parties that devoted to the formalisation of *shariah* in Indonesia performed poorly during the 1999 and 2004 general elections.

2. Substantialists

The substantialist group, on the other hand, supports secularism, believing that Islam is not an ideology. Any effort to make Islam a political ideology will result in the relegation of Islam to the sidelines and neutralise specific values of the religion itself. An ideology that results from human thought and truth is subject to the contexts of time and space, whilst Islam as a divinely revealed religion is far from human limitation.[92] For this group, the establishment of an Islamic party is not necessary, because in political matters, they believe Muslims may derive various ideologies from many sources, including Islam.

Nurcholish Madjid, Abdurahman Wahid, and many proponents of cultural Islam are the champions of the substantialist movement. Rather than trying to implement Islamic laws that are derived from certain religious traditions, they prefer to formulate the substance of Islamic teachings and laws into general principles. For instance, Madjid asserted that Islamic ideals are indeed in line with humanity in general. Islam provides the values of inclusiveness, pluralism, and tolerance.[93] Religion, in its original message, refrains from seeking to force or impose an exclusive political and social system on its adherents, which opens up for discrimination against others. Another prominent figure from this group is Dawam Rahardjo. According to Rahardjo, instead of promoting a legal formal approach, Muslims should uphold the values and the essence of Islamic teachings on liberation and justice. These two principles are the key to a true understanding of the message of Islam, and the Indonesian political system and law should reflect these principles.[94]

Abdurahman Wahid advocates the idea of substance and essence rather than symbols and formalisation by instituting the "de-confessionalisation" of Islam from Indonesian political discourse. According to him, Muslims should not demand an Islamic state because it would be impossible for one to exist. It opens up the possibility of further violation of non-Muslims' human rights because it would affect the status of non-Muslims and regard them as second-class citizens.[95] The discourse of "de-confession" promoted by Wahid does not aim to support the establishment of a totally secular state in Indonesia, but rather it is his strategy to accommodate Indonesian Islam within the context of pluralism, even though Islam is the majority religion of Indonesian citizens.

The mainstream discourse on Islam and state relations in Indonesia has never gone beyond the boundaries of a moderate stance. The proponents of liberal Islam, according to some Muslims in Indonesia, have gone far beyond Islam in promoting their substantialist ideas. The leading Liberal Islamic Network, Jaringan Islam Liberal (JIL) does not really represent the face of secularism. This is because the major role of Islam in politics and governmental affairs can still be accommodated, without following a formal legalist direction. Ulil Abshar Abdalla is the chair of JIL. He is known to be a supporter of secular and liberal ideas. He recognises the historical fact that Islam as lived out by the Prophet Muhammad contained a large measure of political experience and practice. However, Abdallah does not agree that Indonesian Muslims should follow totally the political practices of the Prophet and his companions. What is needed is a new understanding of the political example of the Prophet so that this can then be applied to Indonesian realities and circumstances.[96]

In short, while JIL members strongly opposes the idea of imposing an organic relationship on Islam and the state, they still tolerate a degree of religious influence within the state. They insist, too, that all religions, not just Islam, should be treated equally before the law.[97] Based on the experiences described above, Jemaah Tarbiyah realised that to participate in Indonesian politics it needed to develop a pragmatic approach.

3. The Pragmatic Approach

It appears that the phenomenon of Jemaah Tarbiyah and its political party, PKS, represents a kind of synthesis between legal formalist and substantialist inclinations. The political expression of PKS has shown a more pragmatic approach in which it has tried to steer a course between the demand for the formal acknowledgment of Islam and the substantialist issue. In fact, Jemaah Tarbiyah, with its revivalist experience in its role as a religious movement has transformed itself into a political party which is very much aware of the need to use political vehicles in a way which is likely to allow compromise with the existing system.

a) Relations between Jemaah Tarbiyah and PKS

In general, the establishment of a political party became an urgent decision for Jemaah Tarbiyah in order to Islamise the national structure. However, by forming a political party, Jemaah Tarbiyah, which had previously organised its activities in covert ways to avoid the regime's oppression, was transformed into a legal institution. In 1998, during the early days of its establishment, the Justice Party (PK) functioned to carry out its mission as a "vehicle" to interact with society and the state in legal ways.[98] The first priority for Jemaah Tarbiyah activists after establishing the party was to formulate the relationship between the movement and party.

Even though in the early stages of its establishment, not all members of Jemaah Tarbiyah had chosen to channel their activities into a political party, some of them preferring to establish non-political organizations instead, all members finally accepted the decision after the majority of activists decided to form a political party through an internal referendum in 1998. Like it or not, they have had to follow the result of consultation and referendum among the core cadres of Jemaah Tarbiyah. Furthermore, the obligation for members to support the establishment of a political party has strengthened the principal tenet of the movement that says "*al-jama'ah hiya al-hizb wa al-hizb huwa al-jama'ah*", which means "the movement is the party and the party is the movement." This tenet emphasizes the unity of religious and political association in which there is no distinction between the party and movement.[99] The term *jemaah* (Ar. *al-jama'ah*, movement) is used when a religious movement is unlikely to carry out its mission in legal ways because of the political repression of the regime. In addition, the term *hizb* (Ar. *al-hizb*, political party) is used when the regime has lifted all political restrictions to allow all segments of society, including religious movements, to promote their ideas in legal and structural ways.[100]

At this stage, Jemaah Tarbiyah and the Justice Party are united as one institution, each synonymous of the other. Before the setting up of the party, individuals who interacted within the networks of Jemaah Tarbiyah were responsible for all recruitment and training activities. Thus, after the establishment of PK, all members of Jemaah Tarbiyah automatically became members of PK and all religious training and activities were taken over by PK, now PKS.[101] The leaders of Jemaah Tarbiyah were accommodated in an institution of the party called *Majelis Syura* (the Consultative Board) and all members of Jemaah Tarbiyah must vote for PK.[102]

The concept of *sirriyyah al-tanzim wa alamiyyah al-da'wah*, meaning "the structural of organization is secret and the predication is open" was only valid before the establishment of a formal political party.[103] Most members of Jemaah Tarbiyah believed that during the repressive era of the regime, keeping the structural organization of the movement and its coordinators were unavoidable, but when the regime promoted openness and freedom of expression, the secret nature of the movement was no longer necessary. The formal organization of PKS has been considered the formal form of Jemaah Tarbiyah movement itself.[104]

However, nowadays the term "Jemaah Tarbiyah" is still used by Indonesian Muslims to refer activists of PKS.

There is also a group of Jemaah Tarbiyah that has not agreed about the total transformation of the movement into a political party. They have preferred to consider the party as no more than the political wing of Jemaah Tarbiyah.[105] However, the opinion of this group is peripheral since most members of Jemaah Tarbiyah have accepted the existence of the political party as a manifestation of the movement. For those who had not admitted the existence of political party, were excluded from Jemaah Tarbiyah memberships.

So the establishment of the political party in 1998 was a momentous event for Jemaah Tarbiyah. There was broader political change in that year, and Jemaah Tarbiyah was able to benefit from the new situation and to form itself into an open organization. For years involved in secret activities, it finally found the momentum to appear as a legal political party. The PK then transformed itself into PKS, and was immediately promoted to represent the mission of Jemaah Tarbiyah in developing a strong social capital and a basis for supporting the political ideas of the movement.[106]

b) Political Realities and Religious Ideals

However, besides its pragmatic attitude in politics in promoting the agenda of Islamisation, PKS still envisions promoting Islamic ideas in Indonesia. It has faced obstacles in its involvement in political activity. Yet the solid and loyal cadres, who are the result of an intensive individual process of Islamisation through regular *tarbiyah* training, have enabled the movement to develop the party. Conflict and friction within the party so far has been easily resolved, since it is strongly supported by core activists of Jemaah Tarbiyah who have no vested interests in conflict.

However, since PKS has become a political party of considerable size, accommodating some non-Jemaah Tarbiyah cadres as well, dispute is likely to occur. So, to what extent is the party able to maintain its religious aspirations and make compromises with political realities and challenges in Indonesia? Dilemma often occurs between accommodating the militant cadres' demands and those of pragmatic political players. This conflict of interests among PKS members has manifested itself in decisions that to some extent have showed inconsistency. The following discussion will show how doctrines of Jemaah Tarbiyah have provided guidelines for its cadres involved on the political stage in Indonesia.

Many observers and scholars of Indonesian politics have wondered about the attitude of the new party towards the existing system. The question is often raised in academic debates about the phenomena of Islamic activism in politics, "are Islamists ideological or pragmatic?"[107] However, as is common in political games, the involvement of religious movements in political activities by integrating with the existing political system will usually entail a degree of political compromise.[108] The experience of PKS offers many examples of how the party has diluted its ideology to conform to political realities. However, while there are central principles that serve to guide activists, the conflict between idealism and pragmatism remains widely discussed in Indonesian politics.

The principle of "to interact but not to dilute" (*yakhtalituna walakinna yatamayyazun*) has encouraged activists of Jemaah Tarbiyah to socialise with others beyond the movement.[109] This principle has no clear-cut direction other than to advise the cadres to maintain their Islamic distinctions and not be contaminated by existing corrupt practices. The challenge to be involved in social and political affairs was prescribed by the Prophet Muhammad in his saying: "the one who interacts with others and is patient is better than the one who does not interact with people and shows his intolerance."[110] The risks of being co-opted by the system are accepted by Islamists, and they still believe that neglecting political activities is much worse.[111]

The flexibility of PKS in conforming to the ideology of the social and political realities of Indonesia is based on the consideration that involvement within politics should not trespass the limits of Islamic teachings or *shariah* but it also should not strictly restrain the political creativities of activists.[112] In elaborating this concept, a member of the legislation of PKS, Zulkieflimansyah, told a story that gives a lesson in keeping the balance between holding the ideology and compromising with political realities.

> A knowledge seeker came to a grand teacher asking him to teach him wisdom. The teacher taught him nothing but asked him to look around his temple while he held a lamp. The only thing that he remembered from his teacher was not to let the lamp go out. With care he kept it on and went around the temple. He then went to his teacher saying that he had finished his job and gave the lighted lamp back to him. Immediately his teacher asked his opinion about the library in the temple. The wisdom seeker was surprised because he had not even looked at the library, so busy was he with keeping the lamp alive. Finally, he repeated his job and focussed on observing the details of the library and all the other places within the temple. He proudly went back to his teacher informing him of his observations. The grand teacher asked, "Where is my lamp?" The poor student was shocked because he had left it somewhere while he was busy observing the building.[113]

The pragmatic inclination of the party is also supported by the application of principles of Islamic jurisprudence and a strong encouragement to practice *ijtihad* in responding to issues that are not clearly prescribed by the Qur'an and the Hadith. Among these famous principles are the concepts of *maslahat* (Ar. *al-maslahah*, the common good), *akhaffud durarain* (Ar. *akhaf al-durrarayn*, choosing the lesser of two evils) and *ma la yudraku kulluh laa yutraku kulluh* (something that cannot be wholly attain does not mean it can be left out totally). These principles have made a great contribution towards the exercise of political pragmatism, as in the case of NU, which has used just such jurisprudential principles to justify its political decisions.[114] The following are some precepts adopted by PKS in justifying its political decisions:[115]

First, in order to decide among favourable options, *Jemaah Tabiyah* activists must consider these formulas (1) giving priority to something definite rather than something uncertain, (2) giving priority to something that has great benefit rather than small, (3) giving priority to communal interests rather than to the individual, (4) giving priority to permanent benefit rather than temporary, (5) giving priority to essential and fundamental issues rather than the superficial and symbolic and (6) giving priority to something that affects the future rather than the present.

Second, in order to choose among harmful consequences, the precepts are (1) avoiding further harm, (2) eradicating all harmful actions (3) not using destructive means to avoid harmful things, (4) choosing something that is less harmful and (5) choosing something harmful that affects particular interests rather than the general good.

Lastly, in order to choose among mixed favourable and harmful conditions, the precepts are as follows (1) giving priority to prevent destruction rather than taking benefit, (2) small destruction is tolerable in order to gain a large benefit, (3) temporary destruction is acceptable in order to gain continuous benefit and (4) giving priority to assured benefit, regardless of uncertain negative impacts.

These jurisprudential precepts are often applied by the party to justify its political decisions that to some extent have no consistency with its main doctrinal ideas. For instance, the case of appointing a woman as a president is a problematic issue for many Muslims. During the Indonesian presidential elections of 1999, the Justice Party had no alternative but to support Abdurahman Wahid for president. Even though most figures of the Justice Party disagreed with Wahid's religious ideas, the party supported Wahid instead of Megawati in order to minimise further harmful conditions for Muslims. Wahid was the candidate of the Central Axis (*Poros Tengah*) supported by Muslim groups. In addition, doctrinal issues related to the prohibition on a woman becoming a president became a decisive consideration. The Justice Party itself still held the opinion that a president must be man.[116]

However, after one and a half years of enjoying the position of president, Abdurahman Wahid was forced to leave, due to an impeachment process by the Peoples Consultative Assembly (MPR). The Justice Party and its cadres were among the protesters who urged Wahid to step down. Nonetheless, after Megawati replaced Wahid, the Justice Party gave support to her and downplayed its opposition towards a woman president.[117] Jurisprudential precepts and political considerations were used to justify this pragmatic decision. Supporting Megawati was less harmful than maintaining Wahid in power, which might cause further damage for Muslims. Indeed, not all constituents have agreed on this issue, asking responsibility for those who elected her. As was stated in *Syariahonline.com*, a website run by activists of PKS:

> Any decision to propose a woman as a president must have risks and consequences. The appointment of Megawati as the Indonesian president, intentionally or accidentally, would carry consequences for those who elected her.[118]

In short, the nature of Indonesian politics has necessitated that PKS follows a realistic, pragmatic approach to deal with all issues. This is because both radical and secular inclinations in promoting Islam in Indonesia would not find favour with the Indonesian people. Down-to-earth approaches become an unavoidable option in order for political parties to survive. In its religious activities Jemaah Tarbiyah has shown its accommodative ways in promoting its ideas. In addition, the history of Jemaah Tarbiyah in responding the New Order regime's oppression also has indicated its well-prepared strategy of avoiding conflict and confrontation with the regime, while keeping the spirit of reform, instead of revolution and confrontation. The following chapter will give a detailed analysis of how Jemaah Tarbiyah was able to flourish within a hostile environment of the New Order period.

ENDNOTES

[1] In this regard "Islamisation" means the effort to call people to adhere to Islamic teachings. To some extent, Islamisation also has been understood as a process of conversion. But since the process of religious conversion has rarely involved total conversion, Islam in Indonesia is still perceived as being far from Islamic orthodoxy and pietism. For some Muslims, Islam is not only understood as a religion of ritual but also as a system of thought and a way of life. Islam requires its adherents to embrace total Islam (*Islam Kafah*).

[2] Re-islamisation is the process to make a nominal Muslim into a devout one.

[3] Reform in an Islamic context is different from reformism within Christian traditions. Islamic reform (Ar. *al-Islah*) aims to return Islam to its original message since some various misinterpretations and distortions had occurred. See John L. Esposito, ed. *The Exford Encyclopedia of the Modern Islamic World Vol. 2* (New York: Oxford University Press, 1995), 242. In this chapter Islamic reform in Indonesia is defined as the efforts to bring Muslims to embrace Islamic orthodoxy.

[4] As suggested by Snouck Hurgronje Islam in Indonesia has been categorised as religious and political Harry J. Benda, "Christian Snouck Hurgronje and the Foundations of Dutch Islamic Policy in Indonesia," *The Journal of Modern History* 30 no. 4 (December 1958), 341-342.

[5] For instance through various interactions involving religious, economic and political factors, not only ordinary people were attracted to Islam but many local elites and royal families of the Indonesian kingdoms embraced Islam as their religion. Marriages between a Muslim preacher and a daughter of a royal house assisted the process. Or at times, the lower orders would embrace Islam first and their masters later. See M.C. Ricklefs, *A History of Modern Indonesia since C. 1200* (Hampshire: Palgrave, 2001), 3-17, R. Jones, "Ten Conversion Myths From Indonesia," in *Conversion to Islam* (New York: Holmes and Meier, 1979), 158, and Paul B. Means, "The Religion Background of Indonesian Nationalism," *Church History* 16 no. 4 (December 1947), 238.

[6] Mahfudz Sidiq, "Peran Serta Da'wah dalam Politik" (Paper presented at the Square House Building, University of New South Wales, 9 August 2002).

[7] See Kuntowijoya, *Muslim Tanpa Masjid* (Bandung:Mizan, 2001), 118-119.

[8] Bassam Tibbi, *Islam and the Cultural Accommodation of Social Change,* trans. Clare Krojzl (San Francisco: Westview Press, 1991), 8-9.

[9] John L. Esposito and John O. Voll, Islam *and Democracy* (New York: Oxford University Press, 1996), 8.

[10] This term has been widely used by Islamist groups in Indonesia to indicate their commitment to struggle for Islam. *Kafah* (Ar. *Kaffah*) means a full submission in embracing Islam. The Qur'an II: 208 says, "O you who have believed, enter into Islam completely [and perfectly] and do not follow the footsteps of Satan. Indeed, he is to you a clear enemy."

[11] Tibi, *Islam and the Cultural Accommodation,*125-126.

[12] B.J.O Schrieke, *Indonesian Sociological Studies I* (Den Hag and Bandung: Van Hoeve, 1995), 38.

[13] Ricklefs, "Islamisation of Java" in *Conversion to Islam,* 105.

[14] M.C. Ricklefs, "Islamization in Java" in *Islam in Asia II* (Boulder: Westview Press, 1984), 12.

[15] Ibid.

[16] C.A.O. Van Nieuwenhuijze, *Aspects of Islam in Post-Colonial Indonesia* (Bandung: Van Hoeve Ltd, 1958), 35.

[17] For details about theories of Islamisation in Indonesia see Azyumardi Azra, *Jaringan Global dan Lokal Islam Nusantara* (Bandung: Mizan, 2002), 24-36.

[18] Azra, *Jaringan Global dan Lokal Islam Nusantara,* 20.

[19] Ibid., 31.

[20] R. Jones, "Ten Conversions of Myths from Indonesia," in *Conversion to Islam*, 158.

[21] Ibid.

[22] Ibid.

[23] Azra, *Jaringan Global dan Lokal Islam Nusantara,* 33.

[24] A.H. Johns, "Islam in Southeast Asia: Problems of Perspective," in *Readings on Islam in Southeast Asia* (Singapore: Institute of Southeast Asian Studies, 1985), 20-24.

[25] Azra, *Jaringan Global dan Lokal Islam,* 69.

[26] Ibid. 98-99.

[27] Bruinessen, "Global and Local in Indonesian Islam," 46-63.

[28] Azra, *Jaringan Global dan Lokal Islam,* 98-99.

[29] Nieuwenhuijze, *Aspects of Islam in Post-Colonial Indonesia,* 35-36.

[30] Ibid.

[31] See Clifford Geertz, *Islam Observed Religious Development in Morocco and Indonesia* (Chicago and London: University of Chicago Press, 1968), 66.

[32] Abdurahman Wahid, "Islam, the State, and Development in Indonesia," in *Islam in South and South-East Asia* (New Delhi: Ajanta Publications, 1985), 85.

[33] Ibid.

[34] See Abdurahman Wahid, "Pribumisasi Islam" in *Islam Indonesia Menatap Masa Depan* (Jakarta: P3EM, 1989), 82.

[35] Bruinessen, "Global and Local in Indonesian Islam," 46-63.

[36] See Geertz, *Islam Observed Religious Development in Morocco and Indonesia,* 67.

[37] Ricklefs, "Islamization in Java" in *Islam in Asia II,* 14.

[38] See Wahid, "Pribumisasi Islam," 82.

[39] Ibid., 83.

[40] Ibid.

[41] Allan A. Samson, "Islam and Politics in Indonesia" (Ph.D. diss., University of California, 1972), 2.

[42] Ibid.

[43] The coalition among Indonesian Muslims in 1999 within the Middle Axis group (*Kelompok Poros Tengah*) to propose Abdurahman Wahid from NU as president Indonesia has been considered by Muslims as the beginning of integration among Islamic forces, however it ceased when Wahid was forced to leave his position by his Muslim allies.

[44] See "Ulil Abshar: NU Akan Mengalami Penggundulan Generasi," *Media Indonesia Online*, 30 April 2005.

[45] James L. Peacock, *Muslim Puritans: Reformist Psychology in Southeast Asian Islam* (University of Berkeley: California Press, 1978), 18.

[46] Ibid.

[47] Bruinessen, "Global and Local in Indonesian Islam," 46-63.

[48] Azyumardi Azra, *Islam Reformis:Dinamika Intelektual dan Gerakan*, (Jakarta: Rajagrafindo Persada, 1999), 46.

[49] Christine Dobbin, "Islamic Revivalism in Minangkabau at the Turn of the Nineteenth Century," *Modern Asian Studies* 8 no. 3 (1974), 319.

[50] Bruinessen, "Global and local in Indonesian Islam," 46-63.

[51] Dobbin, "Islamic Revivalism in Minangkabau at the Turn of the Nineteenth Century," 319.

[52] Ibid., 335.

[53] Interview, anonymous, Jakarta, 14 March 2003.

[54] Ricklefs, "Islamisation of Java" in *Conversion to Islam*, 122.

[55] Ibid., 123

[56] See Azyumardi Azra, "Fenomena Hidayat Nurwahid dan Politik Islam," *Media Indonesia*, 11 October 2004.

[57] Among books about religious and social movement aspects of the Muslim Brothers are Ishak Musa Husaini, *The Moslem Brethren: The Greatest of Modern Islamic Movements,* (Westport: Hyperion Press, 1956), Richard P. Mitchell, *The Society of the Muslim Brothers* (New York: Oxford University Press, 1993), and Bryjar Lia, *The Society of Muslim Brothers in Egypt: The Rise of Islamic Mass Movement 1928-1942* (Reading: Ithaca Press, 1998).

[58] Husaini, *The Moslem Brethren*, 7.

[59] Hasan al-Banna, *Memoar Hasan Al-Banna*, trans. Salafuddin Abu Sayyid and Hawin Mustadho (Solo: Era Intermedia, 2004), 227.

[60] Ibid., 46.

[61] See Ibrahim M. Abu Rabi, *Intellectual Origins of Islamic Resurgence in the Modern Arab World* (Albany: State of New York Press, 1996), 69.

[62] Tim Departemen Kaderisasi DPP PK Sejahtera, *Manajemen Tarbiyah Anggota Pemula* (Jakarta:DPP Partai Keadilan Sejahtera, 2003), 3-4.

[63] Ibid.

[64] Interview, anonymous, Jakarta, 24 March 2003.

[65] See Hasan al-Banna, *Risalah Pergerakan 2*, trans. Anis Matta (Solo: Era Intermedia, 2001), 161-175.

[66] Tim Departemen Kaderisasi DPP PK Sejahtera, *Manajemen Tarbiyah*, 6.

[67] Al-Banna, *Risalah Pergerakan 2*, 164.

[68] Muslikh Abdul Karim is currently member of *Shariah* Council of the Central Board of the Prosperous Justice Party (2004-2009).

[69] *Tahlilan* is the repetitive recitation of the *shahadah* or some such phrase of prayer performed in a group often for a recently deceased person. According to the revivalists and modernists it has no foundation in Islam and is considered an unlawful innovation in worship.

[70] Interview with Muslikh Abdul Karim, Depok, 9 September 2003.

[71] Interview with Nurmahmudi Ismail, Depok, 8 May 2003.

[72] M. Arlansyah Tandjung, "Tarbiyah, Perjalanan dan Harapan," in *Tarbiyah Berkelanjutan* (Jakarta: Pustaka Tarbiatuna, 2003), 18.
[73] Nehemia Levtzion, "Comparative Study of Islamisation," in *Conversion to Islam* (New York: Holmes and Meier, 1979), 19.
[74] Ibid. See also A.D. Nock, *Conversion: the Old and the New in Religion from Alexander the Great to Augustine of Hippo* (New York: the Oxford University Press, 1961), 7.
[75] Ibid.
[76] Salim Segaf Al-Jufri, forward to *Politik Da'wah Partai Keadilan*, by Syamsul Balda, Abu Ridha, and Untung Wahono (Jakarta:DPP Partai Keadilan, 2000), 6.
[77] See PKS Online, 1 Juni 2005.
[78] See Tim Departemen Kaderisasi DPP PK Sejahtera, *Manajemen Tarbiyah*, 12-14.
[79] See Heddy Shri Ahimsa Putra, "Ramadhan di Kampus, PNDI, dan Safari Ramadhan: Beberapa Pola Islamasasi di Masa Order Baru" in *Agama Spiritualisme dalam Dinamika Ekonomi Politik* (Surakarta: Universitas Muhammadiyah Surakarta, 2001), 12.
[80] See Tandjung, *Tarbiyah Perjalanan dan Harapan*, 12.
[81] See Dawam Raharjo, *Islam dan Transformasi Budaya* (Yogyakarta: PT Dana Bhakti Prima Yasa, 2002), 200
[82] Syafi'i Anwar, *Pemikiran dan Aksi Islam Indonesia: Sebuah Kajian Politik Tentang Cendekiawan Muslim Order Baru* (Jakarta: Paramadina, 1995), 136.
[83] Ibid.
[84] B.J. Boland, *The Struggle for Islam in Indonesia* (The Hague: Martinus Nijhoff, 1971), 116-118.
[85] Taufiq Abdullah, "The Formation of a New Paradigm: A Sketch on Contemporary Islamic Discourse" in *Toward New Paradigm: Recent Developments in Indonesia Islamic Thought* (Tempe: Arizona State Univesity, 1996), 56.
[86] William Liddle, "The Islamic Turn in Indonesia: A Political Explanation," *The Journal of Asian Studies* 55 no. 3 (August 1996), 615.
[87] Robert W. Hefner, "Islamizing Java? Religion and Politics in Rural East Java," *Journal of Asian Studies* 46 no. 3 (August 1987), 533-554.
[88] James P. Castori, ed., *Introduction to Islam in the Political Process* (London: Cambridge University Press, 1983), 5.
[89] Ibid.
[90] Ibid., 3-4
[91] Ibid.
[92] Nurcholish Madjid, "Cita-Cita Politik Kita", in *Aspirasi Umat Islam di Indonesia* (Jakarta:Leppenas, 1983), 4.
[93] Ibid.
[94] Dawam Rahardjo, "Umat Islam dan Pembaharuan Teologi" in *Aspirasi Umat Islam*, 118.
[95] Mark R. Woodward, "Conversation with Abdurahman Wahid," in *Toward New Paradigm*, 147.
[96] Ulil Abshar Abdallah, "Muhammad Nabi dan Politikus", *Media Indonesia*, 04 May 2004.
[97] Ibid.
[98] See Mahfudz Sidiq, *Dakwah & Tarbiyah di Era Jahriyah Jamahiriyah* (Jakarta: Pustaka Tarbiatuna, 2002), 15.
[99] See Syamsul Balda, Abu Ridha, and Untung Wahono, *Politik Da'wah Partai Keadilan*, (Jakarta:DPP Partai Keadilan, 2000), 57.
[100] Ibid.
[101] Interview with Ahmad Shidik, Padang, 19 June 2003.
[102] Ibid.
[103] Mahfudz Sidiq, *KAMMI dan Pergulatan Reformasi: Kiprah Politik Aktifis Dakwah Kampus dalam Perjuangan Demokratisasi di Tengah Gelombang Krisis Nasional Multidimensi* (Solo:Intermedia, 2003), 84.
[104] Interview with Rafqinal, Padang, 24 June 2003.
[105] See an article entitled "Jamaah Partai, Partai Jamaah," *pkswatch.blogspot.com,* 26 October 2005.

[106] Ibid.

[107] See Martin Kramer, ed., *The Islamism Debate* (Ramat Aviv: Tel Aviv University, 1997), 51-85.

[108] A study of the failure of political Islam by Olivier Roy is a good account of how political parties have mainly been co-opted by the system and diluted of Islamic aspirations. See Olivier Roy, *The Failure of Political Islam*, trans. Carol Volk (Massachusetts: Harvard University Press, 1994).

[109] Tandjung, *Tarbiyah Perjalanan dan Harapan*, 18.

[110] Ibid.

[111] Interview with Rofi' Munawar, Surabaya, 7 March 2003.

[112] Cahyadi Takariawan, *Rekayasa Masa Depan Menuju Kemenangan Dakwah Islam* (Jakarta:Pustaka Tarbiatuna, 2003), 65

[113] Interview with Zulkieflimansyah, Canberra, 30 August 2004.

[114] For further details about the application of these concepts see Greg Fealy and Greg Barton, ed., *Nahdlatul Ulama, Traditional Islam and Modernity in Indonesia* (Clayton: Monash Asia Institute, 1996), 35.

[115] See Takariawan, *Rekayasa Masa Depan Menuju Kemenangan Dakwah Islam*, 66-68.

[116] Discussions of this issue are elaborated in detail in *Syariahonline.com* which strictly opposes a female president. The religious consultation on the web is organized mainly by members of the Central Board of Justice Party.

[117] See Ali Said Damanik, *Fenomena Partai Keadilan: Transformasi 20 Tahun Gerakan Tarbiyah di Indonesia* (Bandung: Teraju, 2002), 296-304.

[118] *Syariahonline.com*, 01 January 2003.

Chapter 3: Flourishing in A hostile Political Environment

In retrospect, the era of the 1970s and 1980s is considered by many former activists of Islamic groups as a most difficult and challenging time. Within the university campuses, signs of distrust and grievance towards Soeharto's New Order regime were very common. The regime's restrictions on the students' involvement in political activities and on the use of the campus as a free space to criticise the government caused considerable disillusionment among them. In their eyes, the regime was a tyrant similar to the Pharaoh of Egypt.[1]

In similar way radical activities carried out by some sections of Indonesian Muslim groups outside campus were met with uncompromising measures on the part of the government. Such heavy-handed responses resulted in spontaneous reactions of violence and destruction by some radical groups. Many other oppositional groups were suppressed and their activists jailed. The regime did not hesitate to use armed force in handling civil dissent at the grassroots level.[2] President Soeharto firmly stated that "groups that were greatly influenced by their respective ideologies [tried] to impose their will on other groups, and if necessary, we must take up arms."[3] Confrontation between particular Muslim groups and the regime apparatus was unavoidable.

In fact, since the late 1970s many Islamic activities organised by various groups mushroomed in the secular campuses. They were mainly identified with exclusiveness and developed small religious circles, attracting many students. They focussed their religious activities on cultivating personal piety and devotion. These Islamic circles usually provided students with a strict set of behavioural rules, observing the *halal* and *haram* regulation and promoting a familiar and reassuring Islamic identity.[4] They perceived themselves to be the carriers of "true" Islam whilst viewing other students as not committed Muslims. They practised Islamic teachings strictly and sought to avoid acts prohibited by Islam. They were eager to draw a sharp line between themselves and other Muslim students; to a great extent they were too quick to cast blame on anything that they considered was "un-Islamic" in nature.

Jemaah Tarbiyah grew out of this situation. Instead of directly opposing the regime through physical confrontation or by raising harsh criticism in public, Jemaah Tarbiyah developed its activities by strengthening religious belief and encouraging the basic religious obligations. How could this movement survive during oppression in the 1980s and regroup to establish a political party during the era of political participation in 1998? Why did it not actively respond to the regime's oppression with violence?

In fact, the success of Jemaah Tarbiyah in transforming itself into a reputable political party has been interpreted in various ways. Not a few activists from other movements during the time of oppression accused Jemaah Tarbiyah of being infiltrated and orchestrated by government intelligence officers.[5] Was it for ideological reasons or due to co-optation by the regime that induced members of Jemaah Tarbiyah to keep silent when some radical Islamic movements, such as Negara Islam Indonesia-associated groups, increasingly mounted direct confrontation?

This chapter analyses the factors behind the success of Jemaah Tarbiyah in consolidating its cadres during the period of the regime's oppression. There are three reasons contributing to its success. First, Jemaah Tarbiyah had learned from the bitter experiences of Islamic oppositional movements, in which direct confrontation resulted in oppression or even liquidation. There are three categories or groups that suffered this suppression: the Islamic state-aimed movements, the ranks of resentful modernist groups and the anti-*Asas Tunggal*[6] movements. Second, the commitment of Jemaah Tarbiyah to keep its approach of Islamic reform, instead of revolution and violence, led it to firmly uphold its commitment to a gradual and longer agenda. The fruit of this approach is that many of the younger generation of Muslims coming from oppositional groups finally joined Jemaah Tarbiyah. Third, political openings in the early 1990s and the collapse of Soeharto in 1998 opened more space for Jemaah Tarbiyah to express its ideas and establish its political party.

A. Learning from the Earlier Experiences of Muslim Opposition Groups

In general, Muslim resistance toward successive regimes in Indonesia had been driven by various motives and factors, such as the notion of the establishment of an Islamic state, political exclusion, or the rejection of certain of the government policies. Thus, the factors responsible for triggering Muslim opposition were not always ideological but economic and political as well. Major resistance in Indonesia has been represented by a particular group, chiefly the modernists, who act from disenchantment with the regime.

In fact, Islam had occasionally served as an ideological opposition to the established Pancasila state ideology and endangered the stability of the government. The seeds of conflict were between the most powerful forces in Indonesia, the army and Islam, in which suspicion and distrust widely existed.[7] The army was most concerned about the latent threat of political Islam. Despite the cultural roots of hostility, in which Javanese (*abangan*) figures dominated the army, the main reason for the army's hostility to Islamic forces was the ability of Muslim activists to win loyal support among those who strictly observed the teachings of Islam. With their strong social basis, the army worried that Muslim activists harboured a secret agenda to establish an Islamic state.[8]

Many policies issued by the army-backed government were widely received by Muslims as designed to restrain the role of Islam in society and politics. The proposed marriage legislation in 1973, giving authority to Kantor Catatan Sipil (the Civil Registration Office) to register marriages and the draft of *Aliran Kepercayaan* legislation in 1978 regarding mystical belief, which put Javanese mysticism on the same level as the five officially recognised religions, were perceived by some Muslims as evidence of the increasingly secular orientation of the regime. This was further considered to de-legitimise the role of Islam in society and politics.[9] However, Muslim activists never lost the resolve to challenge government policies which seemed inimical to Islam teachings. Any policies perceived to undermine the role of Islam in society and the state have always faced great pressures. Extra-parliamentary force, such as demonstrations, became an alternative to force the regime to postpone such proposals, since the United Development Party, Partai Persatuan Pembangunan (PPP) at that time was considered incapable of voicing the interests of the Muslim community.

Opposition and resistance against the state had taken various forms of expression, such as violence, harsh criticism and civil disobedience. These were mainly driven by the ideal of an Islamic state, demanding a radical shift in the state from a secular to a purely Islamic one. Other groups demanded that the regime accommodate former activists from Masyumi into political activities. Still others merely wanted the state to acknowledge their specific character and identity, manifested in their organizational ideologies and that this need not be challenge or de-legitimise the national ideology of Pancasila.

In addition, the timing and targeting of repression have also been important factors in encouraging either confrontation or conformity. In studying types of contention in Egypt, Mohammad M. Hafez and Quintan Wiktorowicz classify the timing when repression is applied as either pre-emptive or reactive.[10] Repression is pre-emptive when it is applied before the opposition movement has had a chance to arrange and assemble disparate supporters and sympathizers around a common goal. Repression is reactive when it is applied in the rising phase of the protest cycle - that is, after activists have gained organisational momentum. Hafez and Wiktorowicz also classify the targeting of repression into two patterns, selective when repression simply targets the leaders and core activists of the movement and indiscriminate when it expands to include supporters, sympathisers and even ordinary citizens suspected of involvement in the movement. Pre-emptive and selective repression will discourage violent conflict on collective actions, while reactive and indiscriminate repression is likely to encourage reactive response and confrontation.[11]

1. The Notion of an Islamic State

Modern Islamic state-motivated rebellions have fought long periods of resistance against the secular Indonesian state, dating from the declaration of the Islamic State of Indonesia, Negara Islam Indonesia (NII) in 1949 up to the present. The rebellions have been represented by various groups and factions, but originated with the movement called Darul Islam (DI) led by Kartosuwiryo in West Java. In the contemporary Indonesian Islam discourse DI and NII are distinguished by the fact that the former represent the old Islamic state-aimed movement led by Kartosuwiryo in the 1950s, while the latter refers to the continuation of DI that has been supported by a younger generation, who had not experienced rebellion. However, the government, particularly the military, has used the name NII to label any groups who struggle for an Islamic state in Indonesia, without considering the diversity of movements.

A subsequent formation, Negara Islam Indonesia (NII) that was proclaimed on 9 August 1949 in Malangbong, Garut, West Java, gained wide support in West Java and beyond. Two strong Islamic rebellions in South Sulawesi (1952-1965) and Aceh, led by Kahar Muzakkar and Daud Beureuh (1953-1962) respectively, supported the struggle towards the establishment of an Islamic state under the leadership of Kartosuwiryo in Java.

Even though the Indonesian central government successfully curbed the initial rebellions and captured most of the leaders and forced them to sign a declaration of allegiance to the state on 1 August 1962, some splinter groups of DI have continued to develop in the regions. Many DI members considered that those who signed the declaration of allegiance had betrayed their leaders. They regrouped and continued their struggle in clandestine ways. Some of them still genuinely believe in Darul Islam doctrines, whilst others are merely orchestrated by Indonesian intelligence.

By the 1970s, some former members of DI had regrouped themselves. They were then supported by Indonesian intelligence under a mission of Special Operation, *Operasi Khusus* (OPSUS). The head of Opsus, Ali Murtopo, was in charge of reactivating the old DI to help the government defend the country from the threat of resurgent communist groups.[12] The intelligence involvement in reactivating DI and its interest in discrediting the image of the Islamic parties contributed to accelerating the violence perpetrated by a group called Komando Jihad.[13] In 1981, Imran bin Muhammad Zein hijacked a Garuda Airlines aircraft, killing all passengers. Following the Tanjung Priok riots in 1984 in North Jakarta in which several hundred Muslims were shot dead by the military, on 21 January 1985, an explosion damaged stupas of the newly restored Buddhist temple of Borobudur in Central Java, while yet other groups associated with Komando Jihad were involved in the bombing of Bank Central Asia in Jakarta and several Christian institutions in East Java.[14] The connections between state intelligence and Komando Jihad have never been denied. Two former advisers of Ali Moertopo, Harry Tjan Silalahi and Jusuf Wanandi, admitted this but claimed that most recruits had misused their mandate.[15] However, general opinion among Indonesians, including military figures, reportedly acknowledged the link.[16]

In general, NII associated groups do not recognise the existence of the Republic of Indonesia because it is not ruled by Islamic law. In their eyes, since Indonesia is not an Islamic state, it has inevitably drifted into moral, economic and political deterioration. These groups argue that the Republic of Indonesia needs to adopt an Islamic system.[17] Muslims who currently live in an un-Islamic state, according to them, do not need to obey state laws that are not derived from the Qur'an and Hadith. In fact, many NII members have been involved in criminal activities, such as robbery and assassination.

On the other hand, in responding to further development of NII groups, the New Order regime applied firm and uncompromising measures, marking indiscriminate targets. Like the communist groups in Indonesia, the Islamic state-motivated groups were considered a serious threat since they intended to replace the national ideology of Pancasila with Islam. They used its power to hit not only at the leaders and core activists but includes all supporters, sympathizers and ordinary people suspected of being involvement in radical movements.

Some state reactions seemed extreme. For instance, the regime suppressed an *usrah* group in Purwakarta in 1983. Most of its members were ordinary farmers and traders in the village and unlikely to pose any significant threat to the regime. The regime accused this group of secretly criticising their program to implement the national ideology of Pancasila and of having links with NII, so many the *usrah* members were raided and sentenced to jail. They were accused of carrying out subversive activity to establish an Islamic state in Indonesia.[18]

However, since NII still clung firmly to its utopian vision of establishing an Islamic state, it remained the target of regime oppression. The regime justified its suppression of all utopian groups and demolished them after an *usrah* group in Lampung, led by Warsidi, clashed with local army and government officers, causing many casualties on both sides in 1989. Warsidi's followers were part of the Ngruki network of Surakarta, Central Java, under leadership of the charismatic cleric, Abdullah Sungkar. Sungkar had transferred his allegiance to NII in 1976, and subsequently the Pesantren Ngruki became a stronghold of NII.[19]

Even though the regime's indiscriminate targeting of NII received criticism from many Muslim leaders and some members of the Indonesian parliament in 1981, the government continued to launch operations. The head of Supreme Military Operations Command for Security and Order, Panglima Komando Pemulihan Keamanan dan Ketertiban (Pangkopkamtib), Admiral Soedomo, reminded the critics not to underestimate the government's resolve to crush subversive groups, since their existence endangered the stability of Indonesia and, Soedomo claimed, they did not represent Islam.[20]

According to the activists, the regime deliberately pushed Muslims into a corner by raising the issue of Kommando Jihad mentioned above. Some Muslims in politics, such as the PPP, believed the motives behind exaggerating the issue of Komando Jihad was to tarnish the image of the Islamic parties and link them with terrorist action in the public mind.[21] By means of this tactic, PPP suffered and lost much of its popular sympathy during the general elections (1982 and 1987) since many cases of Islamic radicalisation always accelerated before elections.[22]

The most effective way used by the regime to destroy Islamic subversive groups was by intelligence operations that aimed to break the spirit of resistance among their members and to discredit them in the eyes of mainstream Islam. These allegedly radical groups were provoked into responding violently to the regime's policies, when the military could easily crush them by arresting their core activists and supporters. These kinds of operations caused many death and casualties.

Reports of actions by Komando Jihad that periodically prevailed in parts of Sumatra in the 1970s and in Java in the 1980s were common and were generally believed be the work of Indonesian intelligence. Instead of providing the catalyst for a major Muslim uprising, they became a serious embarrassment to the rest of the Muslim community.[23] However, the fact remained that intelligence operations through DI revivals succeeded in trapping many sympathisers and imprisoning them.[24]

2. Political Exclusion

The Masyumi group represents another type of faction of Muslim resistance and opposition. Instead of being driven by the ideology of an Islamic state, Masyumi's resistance was the result of political exclusion by the New Order regime, an exclusion which has made the heirs of Masyumi compelled to continue to oppose government policies. They sought to destabilise the Soeharto regime in order to force structural change to provide them with political accommodation. The regime restricted former Masyumi leaders from being involved in national politics and the officially sanctioned new political party, the Indonesian Muslim Party, Partai Muslimin Indonesia (PMI) established in 1968 made a poor performance in the 1971 general elections. Thus a strategy of opposition and confrontation became the alternative to regain political credibility and influence among Indonesian Muslims.

The main reason for the regime, and particularly for most army leaders, to restrain the re-entry of the Masyum elite into national politics was the involvement of some Masyumi leaders in the 1958-1961 regional rebellion in Sumatra in the name of the Revolutionary Government of the Republic of Indonesia, Pemerintah Revolusioner Republik Indonesia (PRRI). Even though Masyumi did not officially endorse the PRRI rebellion, its three top leaders, Mohammad Natsir, Syafruddin Prawiranegara and Burhanuddin Harahap did join the rebellion. In addition, the Javanese faction within the military's high ranks who was suspicious of *santri* (mostly non-Javanese figures) remained strong and influential.[25]

Similarly, the good rapprochement between the New Order and the Chinese, as well as certain Christian figures, further broadened discontent among former activists of Masyumi who had organised themselves into the mass organisation called the Indonesian Council for Islamic Predication, Dewan Dakwah Islamiyah Indonesia (DDII). They accused the regime of implementing a policy of politically excluding Muslims and favouring to non-Muslims. At the grass roots level, a process of conversion of some nominal Muslims to Christianity had strengthened the sense of insecurity among Muslims about the missionary activity of Christian.[26] Criticism was raised in almost all Friday mosque sermons and at public gatherings (*pengajian*) organised by DDII preachers, asking the government to stop Christian missionary activities. In order to avert further conflict between the Christian and Muslim communities, the government barred DDII from newly converted communities in South Central Java.[27] In fact, the government responded to Muslim pressure for an end to Christian missionary activities by issuing a decree restricting foreign aid for religious purposes and prohibiting attempts to convert anyone from other religious faiths.[28]

The spirit of resistance expressed by Masyumi group however was not limited to religious slogans, but was extended in scope by involving support from non-religious figures. For instance, in 1980, some former Masyumi leaders joined the petition of the Group of the Fifty (*Kelompok Petisi 50*) criticising the government's announcement of intent to suppress oppositional forces in Indonesia. To strengthen their power to destabilise the regime, veterans of Masyumi sought secular as well as religious alliances. Nonetheless, Masyumi's disillusionment with the regime was mainly expressed in non-violent ways, using spoken and written media. Their resistance usually faded when the regime became ready to accommodate their political interests.

Because the criticism of the former activists of Masyumi had persisted and circulated through religious sermons and gatherings since the 1970s, the regime began to regulate all religious gatherings and to prohibit the raising of political issues during the Friday sermons. Military officers were under order to take necessary action whenever violations of this regulation occurred, and such violations would bring about prosecution or a sentence to military detention. Many Muslim preachers suffered from this restriction and some were sentenced to jail for years. Many hard-liner preachers were banned altogether from delivering sermons in mosques. Members of the Islamic Preachers Corps, Korp Muballigh Islam (KMI) an organization founded by a former leader of Masyumi, Syafruddin Prawiranegara, were known for their harsh terms in criticising the government. Mawardi Noer, Abdul Qadir Djaelani, A.M. Fatwah, and Tony Ardi were among members of KMI who were sentenced to jail for years.[29]

In contrast to the NII group, this group of political discontent, represented by activists of DDII, did not demand the establishment of an Islamic state. However, since their existence posed a threat to the regime, it did not hesitate to repress them. DDII consisted of many elements, ranging from moderate to radical figures, and it often received the indirect impact of its activists' radical actions. DDII was often associated with hardline groups. For instance, many members of NII were activists of the DDII. Despite their position as Darul Islam leaders, both Abdullah Sungkar and Abu Bakar Ba'asyir were members of DDII committees in Central Java.[30] The loose membership of DDII permitted any Muslims to join as long as they shared the same ideas on political Islam.

But it remains a fact that the regime succeeded in silencing all openly active oppositional movements. With a combination of reactive and pre-emptive action, it was able to repress its political rivals even before they were able to organise vital organizations. Not only did Islamic state-oriented movements experience bad treatment, but also many activists of DDII and KMI suffered from the regime's severity. Professor Oetsman al-Hamidy, an ex-military figure and a rector of Higher Education for Islamic Predication, Pendidikan Tinggi Dakwah Islam (PTDI) was 72 years old when he was sentenced to jail for a harsh sermon attacking the government. He stated during the trial.

> Now, in 1985 public criticism of the government by a Muslim preacher is considered to be a subversive action. Its perpetrator is threatened to jail for life. It is very frightening.[31]

The pre-emptive approach of the regime also resulted in restrictions on all political Islam-oriented groups who expressed their struggle within the legal system. Even Muhammadiyah, "long considered the most secularly inclined of the Islamic groups" expressed its pain about the unfair attitude of the government.[32] In its official newspaper, *Mertju Suar* dated 4 April 1968, it stated its frustration with the regime's attitude towards Islam

> Mr. President! We will support you and we will do our best so that you will succeed in your mission, although we know that we will be continuously slandered as followers of Darul Islam, anti-Pancasila, and so on. In fact, we do not expect that you will have much confidence in our [Muslim] leaders because it has been widely publicised through the [Christian] mass media that the Muslims are a hindrance to national

development and modernization, and that the Muslims are merely disseminators of magic amulets and the like.[33]

However, the government's policies toward these groups of political discontent differed from those of NII. The regime still applied selective targeting in containing their resistance. Leading figures and core activists of modernist groups usually became subject to the regime's suppression, while many sympathizers and followers were still able to carry out their activities, as long as they did not openly attack the regime. In short, the government's obsession to control all political rivalries did not end along with the decline of radical groups and the demise of political discontent. The regime continued to ensure its control of all individuals and mass activities to follow the Sole Principle of Pancasila.

3. Anti *Asas Tunggal* (the Sole Principle)

By imposing the idea of a collective ideology, the regime created an authoritative and legitimising identity with Pancasila as the Sole of Principle (*Asas Tunggal*). The regime decided that Pancasila, as the only authorised ideology in Indonesia, would force all the people's activities to be in accordance with its spirit. Even more, the regime seemed to be intending to impose Pancasila as a standard of personal and communal values for its citizens, replacing the role of religion. As a result, immediate resistance came from Muslim communities who regarded Islam as their chosen way of life.

The regime made it known that any other ideologies were considered subversive by the government and were to be monitored and contained. Thus, in the regime's eyes, there was no discrimination between Islamic groups and communists, since both ideologies were seen as rivals to the official ideology. Conversely, Pancasila, particularly within its first principle of "Belief in One God", was understood by the regime as implying an indirect warning that not only communist ideology but also Islam was unacceptable.[34] However, not only Muslim organisations opposed this government initiative but many Christian, Catholic, Hindu and Buddhist groups conveyed the same concern - that each had its own a basis of conformity and loyalty to its own religion, while at the same time being good guardians of Pancasila.[35] Among broader social and mass organizations, the Muslim organizations mostly rejected the government's proposal, though finally they came to accepting it with caution.

Muslim student and youth organizations formed a special group of Muslim resistance. They rejected the implementation of "Sole Principle" imposed on all mass organizations by the government. These groups wanted the government to accommodate other ideologies that might be incorporated within exclusively religious organizations, as long as they were not in violation of the ideology of the state. The status of Pancasila as the fundamental basic value for society and nation was indisputable, even among Muslim communities. Yet serious problems would arise if the government forced all mass organizations to replace their own basic identities and values with Pancasila.[36]

However, though the government still tried to impose their Sole Principle some organizations persisted in practising their own lines of thought. The government banned organizations that did not conform to government policy. A Muslim student organization called The Islamic Student Association-the Protector Committee of the Organization, Himpunan Mahasiswa Indonesia-Majelis Penyelamat Organisasi (HMI MPO) and a high school student association, Indonesian Islamic Students, Pelajar Islam Indonesia (PII) were among the more stubborn guardians of Islamic rather than the New Order ideology.[37]

In 1983 a National Congress of HMI was held in Medan, through the Junior Minister of Youth and Sport Affairs, Abdul Ghafur (a former chairman of HMI, Jakarta branch) the government pushed the organization to endorse Pancasila as the Sole Principle. At that time, new legislation regulating mass organizations had not yet been issued and was still in the process of endorsement by the legislative body.[38] In responding to the government's intervention, the participants of the congress split into two factions. The first faction wanted to comply with the government in order to avoid political oppression; a second faction tried to oppose the government's interference and postponed taking a position on the issue until the relevant bill was formalised. However, after committee meetings that claimed to represent the interests of the organisation, held in Ciloto, West Java, 1-7 April 1985, the committee issued a statement expressing HMI's approval of the regulation to enforce Pancasila as the Sole Principle of all mass organizations. The decision of HMI to adopt Pancasila as its ideological basis was ratified through the 1986 National Congress of HMI in Padang.

This acceptance of Pancasila by HMI Central Board resulted in criticism from other HMI branches in the provinces and at the district level. On 15 March 1986 in Jakarta some activists of HMI who opposed the decision of the Central Board of HMI established a counter organization, named Council to Save the Organization, Majelis Penyelamat Organisasi (MPO) and Eggi Sudjana was elected as the chairman. This new council claimed to protect the spirit of HMI and accused the pro-Pancasila group, based in Diponegoro, Jakarta, of deviating from their true ideals. Consequently, the chairmen of HMI branches that supported the establishment of HMI MPO were expelled and replaced by committees favourable to HMI's Central Committee. In contrast, HMI MPO declared itself a rival to the official HMI and held a congress to de-legitimate the existence of the former committees. In so doing, not only had HMI MPO split from the Central Committee but it had also transformed itself into a radical and militant movement opposing the regime's policies.

Another aggressive group opposed to the government policy regarding the "Sole Principle" was PII. PII was established in 1947 in Yogyakarta, and initially aimed to bridge the gap between students in *pesantren* and public schools.[39] However, in its development, PII turned to represent an organisational wing of the modernist political party, Masyumi. This was because since the 1960s, in particular after the banning of Masyumi, many of its former activists wanted to use PII as an alternative vehicle to preserve the Masyumi spirit among students and to continue the struggle to oppose the regime. However, PII itself went into decline, mainly after the government had implemented its policy of the Sole Principle of Pancasila and prevented all social and youth organizations from maintaining affiliations with political parties. When the government issued the *Asas Tunggal* policy, PII immediately rejected the use of Pancasila as the basis of its organization. PII was outlawed and its activities came under strict surveillance by the regime. As a result PII began to run its activities in secret, as an underground movement.

While heavy-handed policies were applied in response to NII activities, and to some extent also applied to politically discontented groups of the modernist factions, less firm measures were directed at the opponents of *Asas Tunggal*. The pre-emptive and selective measures applied by the regime were mainly directed at Islamic youth associations (HMI MPO and PII) to limit their influence within student movements. Even though, the regime did not physically oppress members of both organisations but their activities were under total surveillance. In fact, after the mid 1980s, there were two focuses of the New Order intelligence and security operations: Islamic communities and student movements as well as the labour movements.[40]

The government's total control of its citizens was achieved by the success of the regime in applying constant surveillance over civic space.[41] This surveillance was aimed at detecting any signs of opposition that might undermine the regime's authority. The tight supervision almost destroyed all underground resistance groups. The regime also began to encourage its people to engage in self-censorship and awareness, for intelligence officers might be anywhere at any time, watching all activities.[42] A Jemaah Tarbiyah activist described the situation

> In the eyes of the regime, we served as potent challenges and it kept us under surveillance. Certainly, the situation was dreadful as there was no way to escape from this surveillance.[43]

The government's restraint on political activities and censorship of Islamic predication had inadvertently stimulated *dakwah* activities on the university campuses. Because the regime's prohibition on delivering religious sermons containing political issues, many activists found that campus predication was the only safe way to preserve the idea of political Islam. However, surveillance over campus mosques also occurred because of the regime's suspicion of student political activities. Campus mosques were no longer safe places for oppositional groups. An activist of the University of Indonesia and the Arif Rahman Hakim Mosque in Jakarta believed that intelligence officers monitored the mosque and had planted "wiretap devices" (*alat penyadap*).[44]

In general, all activities, social or religious, private or public, had to be endorsed by stamped letters from relevant authorities.[45] As a result of the state's monitoring of Friday and public sermons (*ceramah agama*) many activists started to indicate their resistance on using pamphlet and circulating anonymous letters. But the power of the regime to control its people was enormous. No matter how secret or disciplined the group might be in conducting its activities, if it dealt with political or sensitive issues, it could not escape government surveillance. Many underground activities were detected and raided. The capture of *usrah* activists associated with Darul Islam in the mid 1980s in Cental Java, for example, proved that the regime was easily able to identify and locate its opponents.

The regime's indiscriminate targeting of rivals prompted many activists to change their strategy. The *usrah* model applied by the Muslim Brothers in Egypt became an alternative way for Islamic groups to avoid confrontation with the regime. Hence, Jemaah Tarbiyah, committed to working for the spirit of reform within the system, emerged in the mid 1980s.

B. Committing to the Ideology of Reform

The study of state oppression and the Muslim response in Indonesia reveals a clear relation between the regime's oppression and Muslims' confrontational reaction. During the New Order, the regime's political suppression of Muslims was exercised to different degrees. The regime distinguished between tolerated and non-tolerated actions, and its measures vis-a-vis resistance groups varied. The regime handled them with armed force, intimidation and imprisonment, close surveillance and co-optation. Muslims response also played through a spectrum of resistance, from violent activity to civil disobedience or loyal opposition.

However, the repressive policies of the regime also became a determining factor of social movements in calculating their actions. Repression greatly increased the cost of collective action. In the case of Jemaah Tarbiyah, the strict surveillance of the regime over their citizens reduced the movement's capability to expand its material and organisational resources. In their lack of feasible means to oppose the regime, the activists began to avoid confrontation and to detach themselves from involvement with radical groups. Commitment to a strategy of reform within the system became the viable alternative. They devoted their activities to studying basic and practical Islam.[46] Nonetheless, this change in strategy from confrontation to predication did not take place in a vacuum. It was a younger generation of Indonesian Muslims who introduced this strategy in order to keep the ideals of the movement alive. They were young Indonesian Muslims who had graduated from universities in Saudi Arabia since the mid 1980s.

The arrival home of those Middle Eastern graduates who had had direct contact with prominent activists of the Muslim Brothers in Saudi Arabia energised student religious commitment and affirmed their non-political activities at some universities in Indonesia. To transfer the ideas of Hasan al-Banna to Muslim students, they established Islamic circles (*halaqah*) on the campuses. They did not support the regime's "Sole Principle" but countered it by studying and practising Islam in a way that could indirectly challenge the stance of the regime.[47] By embracing the concept of total Islam, in time they succeeded in planting Islamic ideology among Jemaah Tarbiyah cadres, without direct physical confrontation with the ruling power.

The non-revolutionary approach of Jemaah Tarbiyah also attracted many student activists from Islamic resistance groups. In this sense, Jemaah Tarbiyah did not represent a resistance movement, as some authors have described it.[48] Rather, Jemaah Tarbiyah persuaded oppositional groups to leave unproductive confrontation and to focus on cultivating cadres and enhancing their understanding of Islam. This resulted in some of the young generation of NII-associated groups, the Masyumi network and the Islamic student movements (HMI MPO and PII) changing their orientation and converted to the Muslim Brothers-influenced movement. Through their interaction with Jemaah Tarbiyah, these other activists were able to soften their radical orientation in championing Islam and to channel it into a more organised form that would have a long term impact.

It was the case that after the arrest of certain NII activists in the mid 1980s and the escape of some of its leaders to Malaysia, recruitment to NII declined. Many Muslim youths and students, who in the past had been interested in NII, shifted their allegiance to Jemaah Tarbiyah. This was chiefly brought about by the influence of Hilmi Aminuddin, head of the Consultative Board of PKS, who was also the son of a prominent Darul Islam figure, Danu Muhammad.[49] It caused some NII activists to accuse Aminuddin of damaging the growth of NII, particularly among the Indonesian students and the youth.[50]

Aminuddin himself denied his involvement with NII. Instead, he introduced a new strategy to preserve the *dakwah* during the era of oppression. However, Umar Abduh made the claim that Hilmi Aminuddin was the Foreign Minister of Darul Islam during the leadership of Adah Jaelani in 1980s.[51] He was arrested and held in military detention without trial in 1984 but was released in the same year. He went to a Middle Eastern country to continue his study, where he met with activists of the Muslim Brothers.[52] It seems that Abduh's claim about Aminuddin's role in DI is questionable, since he had never joined NII. He was imprisoned because he was found in possession of and had distributed a confidential government document containing an intelligence report, which was intended to discredit Islamic groups.[53] What is more, formal documents released by the government and media coverage regarding the issue of DI and Komando Jihad, for instance, did not mention a figure named Hilmi Aminuddin.[54]

So there is insufficient evidence of Aminuddin's involvement with DI or NII. Even though his father was a DI leader, Aminuddin denied any relationship with either DI or NII activities. He said, "He was my biological father but not my ideological one." The Jemaah Tarbiyah's stance towards radical groups in Indonesia is very strict. It will not recruit any cadres who belong to NII, because this could cause future problems for the movement.[55]

Similarly, the "family of the Crescent and Stars" (Masyumi) have gone through significant changes. Since the 1950s and 1960s its leaders have focussed their activities almost entirely on the political sphere and neglected the development of the social and intellectual aspects of Islam, including predication. The ban on Masyumi and the marginalisation of political Islam by the regime encouraged the younger generation of Masyumi to be concerned with Islamic thought and predication. The ideas of the Muslim Brothers and Islamic revival have become major issues for them.[56] It was M. Natsir, president of DDII and a former leader of Masyumi, who opened up opportunities for Indonesian Muslims to interact with the ideas of the Muslim Brothers of Egypt. Natsir himself was known to have established close contact with Muslim Brothers activists.[57]

DDII is one of the channels of recruitment for Jemaah Tarbiyah. Initial contact with *ikhwan* (member of the Muslim Brothers), or Muslim Brothers' ideas through publications and books have enabled the activists of DDII to join Jemaah Tarbiyah. It is not clear, however, just when DDII activists made their initial contacts with the Muslim Brothers. In fact, several years before 1960, a number of Masyumi leaders had studied in Cairo. Even Hamka, a prominent modernist leader, although only on a brief visit to Egypt, became familiar with the Muslim Brothers' literature and used the Qur'anic exegesis written by Sayyid Qutb *Fi> Z}ila>l al-Qur'an* as the main reference for his famous Qur'anic interpretation, *Tafsir al-Azhar*. He regularly urged Indonesians to read the works of Muslim thinkers such as Sayyid Qutb. Among those Indonesians who had interacted with Qutb were Muhammad Rashidi, the former first Minister of Religious affairs, Kahir Muzakkir, the founder of Sunan Kali Jaga University and Professor Fuad Fachruddin.[58] They were the pioneers who brought the ideas and thought of the Muslim Brothers to Indonesia.

The government's policy of restricting students' political activities in the 1980s helped Jemaah Tarbiyah to expand its influence on the campuses. Since preachers from outside had to be endorsed before being permitted to give lectures in the university, hardline preachers were refused permission to deliver sermons in the mosque-based universities or at religious gatherings held by students. Being restricted in public spaces, Muslim students focused their activities on private and small spaces, such as the prayer room situated in their faculty or department. Feeling the lack of Islamic preachers, Muslim student activists started to support predications by creating more cadres to serve as trainers in Islamic circles. Even though not supported by competent preachers, the *tarbiyah* model, of self-sustaining cadres, helped to accelerate a massive Islamic predication within campuses.

As a result, DDII has not been entirely able to consolidate the followers of Masyumi or to gain the attention of the broader Muslim community. Newly established Islamic parties associated with Masyumi gained poor results in the 1999 and 2004 general elections. Even more so, the Crescent Star Party, Partai Bulan Bintang (PBB) the only party to be formally recognised as representing the Masyumi "family", did not reach the electoral entry threshold in the 2004 general elections. In contrast, many successors of Masyumi have joined with PKS and even become leading figures within the party. Abu Ridha, for instance, the Middle Eastern graduate sponsored by DDII, is a famous figure within PKS inner circles and is considered to be the first DDII cadre to initiate and to activate a *dakwah* program following the Muslim Brothers model. Many of the younger generation of DDII, such as Daud Rasyid,[59] Mashadi,[60] and Didin Hafiddudin[61] followed the same path as Ridha, while Jemaah Tarbiyah has developed into an independent organization no longer dependent on DDII as its patron. In the University of Indonesia, for instance, since the establishment of the Arif Rahman Hakim Mosque in 1968, its committees developed close contacts with Masyumi figures, particularly in the matter of finding preachers for Friday sermons and other gatherings. However, after the 1990s, it has not relied on DDII support because of the Jemaah Tarbiyah-associated missionary body, Lembaga Dakwah Khairu Ummah (LDKU), which has proved able to take over DDII functions.[62]

Within the Islamic student organizations, HMI MPO and PII also contributed cadres for the consolidation of the initial movement of Jemaah Tarbiyah. After HMI MPO developed as an illegal organization, most of its training programs and activities were carried out in secret and were underground in nature. The spirit of anti-*Asas Tunggal* enabled many of its activists to interact with other resistance groups and made it more radical in its orientation. It developed good relations with DDII figures, so that many funds coming from Middle Eastern donations were channelled by DDII and allocated to HMI MPO.

In addition, the informal activities developed by some members of HMI MPO which were focussed on cultivating good Muslim character, rather than developing their political sympathies, encouraged them to incorporate new Islamic ideas from the Middle East. Many members of HMI MPO seemed to prefer Hasan Al-Banna's teaching, besides the knowledge of other modernist thinkers, such as that of Jamaluddin al-Afghani, Muhammad Abduh and Rashid

Ridha.⁶³ Because of that it is understandable that some members of HMI MPO joined PKS rather than other Islamic parties.⁶⁴ This is the case with former chairman of HMI MPO, Tamsil Linrung, who became a member of parliament for PKS. Other HMI activists were elected as PKS members of parliament (2004-2009), such as Abdul Hakim, Nasir Djamil, Nursanita Nasution and Suswono, while many others have occupied positions of leadership in PKS, especially in the Province of Yogyakarta, which has become a stronghold of HMI MPO.

Similarly, after PII opposed the policy of Pancasila as Sole Principle in 1985, its activities were monitored and restricted by the government. In 1987, PII was formally banned. In order to maintain the recruitment of members and to promote Islam as the basis of ideology, under the leadership of Mutammimul Ula, its chairman from 1983-1986, PII introduced the training of cadres. This was adopted from the Muslim Brothers' model of *usrah,* after Ula attended leadership training held by the International Islamic Federation of Student Organization (IIFSO) in Malaysia.

Under heavy repression by the regime, *usrah* was found to be the most effective model for PII in transforming its ideas and recruiting new members. It was Mutammimul Ula who also persuaded his members to join Jemaah Tarbiyah. He himself formally joined Jemaah Tarbiyah after his chairmanship of PII expired. He met with a Jemaah Tarbiyah activist, Zainal Muttaqien, in Hartono Marjono's house.⁶⁵ When Jemaah Tarbiyah announced the establishment of its political party, the Justice Party, Mutammimul Ula was one of the founders. He was elected a member of parliament (1999-2004) and was re-elected (2004-2009) by PKS. Other members of PII who have been elected as members of parliament (2004-2005) are Abdi Sumaithi, Aboe Bakar, Hidayat Nurwahid, Luthfi Hasan Ishaaq, Makmur Hasanuddin, Refrizal, Wahyudin Munawir and Zuber Safawi.

The reason why Jemaah Tarbiyah was able to maintain its survival under the oppression of the Soeharto regime was its faith in the idea of Islamic reform, developed through a process of continuous cultivation, or *tarbiyah*. Jemaah Tarbiyah activists believed that Islamic reform should follow evolutionary, not revolutionary steps. The movement requires its activists to believe that the only way to promote the ideas of Islam at the level of society and the state is through a difficult struggle that offers definite results (s}a'bun wa tha>bit) a long process that preserve the original ideology (ta}>wil wa as}>il) and a slow change that guarantees success (ba>t}i' wa ma'mun).⁶⁶ According to this approach, any response to the regime's oppression must not be through confrontation, but rather through predication and internal cultivation.⁶⁷

It was the deliberate strategy so that Jemaah Tarbiyah's activists both avoided radical confrontation with the regime and kept its activists away from the regime's targets of oppression. Confrontation and resistance of the regime's power were replaced by a resolve to enhance the spiritual and religious qualities of Muslims through mental training.[68] As a result, since its emergence in Indonesia in the mid 1980s, no activist from Jemaah Tarbiyah occupying a central position in PKS has been jailed.[69]

This strategy of passive resistance focussed on the individual cultivation of spirituality and character has had two side effects. Firstly, it implicitly opposes the ideological hegemony of the regime and secondly it reduces further radicalisation among Muslims, particularly the youth. Jemaah Tarbiyah applied this strategy to preserve the very existence of the movement. Through education and predication, they believed that some day all Indonesian Muslims would accept Islam as their whole way of life, even though they might at first feel alien to the true teachings of Islam. For instance, in 1982 the Ministry of Education issued a decree forbidding female students from wearing head-scarves at schools. Many female cadres of Jemaah Tarbiyah in high schools were not allowed to attend class or even female students at ITB were not allowed to attend practical work or examinations.[70] Some Muslim organizations raised protest against the school policy and demanded the lifting of the prohibition on girl students wearing the scarves. Most activists of Jemaah Tarbiyah kept calm and did not go on the streets in protest because they were confident that when the time came, people would accept their way of dressing. Finally on 16 February 1991 the Minister of Education and Religious Affairs signed a decree which allowed female students wearing head scarves at schools.[71] Hidayat further explained:

> At that time we did not want direct confrontation with the government. We just needed to encourage our cadres to adopt Islamic thinking and practice.[72]

In addition, efforts made by the activists of Jemaah Tarbiyah to strengthen their personal spiritual practices and religious knowledge served as a protection from infiltration or influence from radical groups. The success of Jemaah Tarbiyah in recruiting cadres during the 1980s and 1990s not only expanded its membership but also reduced the number of radical groups on the campuses. The presence of Jemaah Tarbiyah provided an alternative, more productive way of struggling for Islam. When an extremist understanding of Islam had prevailed on the campuses and Rahmat Abdullah, one of the pioneers of Jemaah Tarbiyah, was very concerned.

> In the 1980s there were many students who dropped out of university because of their rigid and extreme understanding of Islam. They considered that what they learned at university made no contribution towards the development of Islam. The English language was perceived as the language of the infidels and architecture was in violation of the Prophet Muhammad. There was a *hadith* saying that whoever built a two-storey building would be crushed by the angels. As a result of these

excesses, many Muslim students became too lazy to study, turned to a kind of escapism and even refused to wear the gifts of shoes that were bought by their parents.[73]

Abdullah further elaborated his concern

> This issue was very naïve, but was exactly as it happened at that time. Here Jemaah Tarbiyah functioned as a bridge between hardline and soft line orientations. If we did not think of saving them from that situation, the *dakwah* of Islam would be blamed for their role in hampering the national development program of Indonesia. We started to give them sensible arguments to change their orientations. Their resistance towards the regime was accumulative and reached the situation where they even rejected wearing clothes that were associated with the regime, such as *batik* shirts and dress coats. Such was the repressive attitude of the regime towards Islamic groups and they reacted to its repression in radical ways and with physical confrontation.[74]

However, the success of Jemaah Tarbiyah in avoiding the regime's oppression appeared suspicious to other Islamic movements in the 1980s. There were indications of Jemaah Tarbiyah's rapprochement with the regime. First, it was suspicious that most of Jemaah Tarbiyah activists remained beyond the reach of oppression and intimidation. The Islamic Youth Movement (Gerakan Pemuda Islam-GPI) a militant youth group previously affiliated to Masyumi, for instance, accused Jemaah Tarbiyah of playing a role in the capture of hundreds of suspected militants in 2003. "It was not understandable that within a short time, the National Intelligence Bureau of Indonesia caught three thousand militant figures," said one of activists from GPI.[75] The role of Suripto, a former member of the National Intelligence Bureau, in supporting the establishment of PK, strengthened such allegations. Suripto was a former staff of the National Intelligent Bureau in 1967-1970. Second, LDKU, an Islamic missionary program affiliated with PKS, used the house of Soeharto's son, Bambang Trihatmodjo, in Menteng, Jakarta.[76] So it was argued that Jemaah Tarbiyah received funding from the Soeharto family.

The evidence tells a different story and the allegations seem to be the misunderstanding of Jemaah Tarbiyah by other Islamic groups of the 1980s, many of which mostly failed to survive under the heavy-handed measures of the regime. Suripto himself has intensively interacted with activists of Jemaah Tarbiyah since the 1980s.[77] In 1990 he represented Indonesian Muslim community to send humanitarian assistance to Bosnia. Since then Suripto who was an activist of the socialist movement during his study in Padjajaran University in 1964 became closer to Muslim activists.[78] In addition, since the 1990s, many activists of Jemaah Tarbiyah who graduated from the State

Universities, mainly from University of Indonesia in Jakarta have become professional staffs in the Bimantara, a national business group managed by Soeharto's family. Preachers from LDKU often have been invited to deliver sermons and lectures in Bimantara mosque in Jakarta.[79] Even though the activists of Jemaah Tarbiyah did not suffer from intimidation and torture, they were kept under surveillance by intelligence officers.

> We were so careful not to let the regime demolish our *dakwah* activities. We also suffered from the restrictions, as did most Islamic movements, but we did not react aggressively. To be honest, we were unable to contact and communicate with other activist groups because of tight surveillance from the regime.[80]

Jemaah Tarbiyah developed a strategy to keep its activists from making contact with radical groups. The event of the "one million" gathering in 2000 held at the National Monument of Jakarta when a NII activist, Alchaidar, declared in his speech the urgency to establish an Islamic state in Indonesia became a sensitive issue among members of Jemaah Tarbiyah. Earlier, through PK, they had supported such action but after Alchaidar's speech, PK immediately withdrew its support, declaring that Alchaidar had no relationship with PK.[81] All efforts were aimed at the survival of PK's political struggle

> Our group is immune from radical activities and groups because we strictly avoid them. Before, we had personal contact with them but then we finally realised that we had a different agenda and orientation. We left them and kept our distance because the regime apparatus launched its operations without compromise. When many Muslim activists from a particular group were arrested during training sessions in Puncak, West Java, we did not get arrested, even though we held similar training there. We always emphasise the need to protect our movement from radical influences. Rather than recruiting cadres with radical backgrounds, it is better to train and educate ordinary people with no Islamic knowledge at all.[82]

This long process of educating the people to understand Islam has proved to be the best way for Jemaah Tarbiyah to carry out a gradual process of Islamisation in Indonesia. Any impatience to Islamise Indonesian society and the state will only lead to destruction. A clear conviction, such as "we have a step by step strategy in carrying out our ideas" has distinguished Jemaah Tarbiyah from radical groups in Indonesia.[83]

However, the ideology of Islamic reform was not the only reason for Jemaah Tarbiyah to confine its activities to religious and non-political activities. Social movement theory emphasises that political constraint and opportunity also compel a movement to avoid confrontation.[84] Since the regime had tightened its grip over all civil society groups, any effort to oppose the government policies was risky. The decision of Jemaah Tarbiyah not to take part in demonstrations against government policy was influenced by this condition to a certain extent.

C. Political Opening and the Regime's Collapse

There are two political events that brought a significant change in Jemaah Tarbiyah's development. Firstly, political openness (*keterbukaan*) initiated by Soeharto's regime in the early 1990s resulted in the accommodation of Muslim oppositional groups. Nonetheless, Islamic state motivated-groups were still unlikely to be integrated within the Indonesian political system because of their rejection of participation in a non-Islamic system. Secondly, the collapse of the Soeharto regime in 1998 opened up more opportunities for Islamic groups to publicly advertise their existence. Even those who opposed the implementation of Pancasila as Sole Principle were still allowed to form organizations based on their respective ideologies. Islamic ideology, then, has reappeared within political and social discourse in the form of the freedom to establish political parties based upon it.

The willingness of the Soeharto regime to accommodate Muslims from the politically marginalised groups can be viewed from two perspectives. Firstly, Soeharto designed political openness in order to fulfil his own agenda to secure his power and protect his interests, including those of his family. The Association of Indonesian Muslim Intellectuals, Ikatan Cendikiawan Muslim Indonesia (ICMI) was created to accommodate Islamic forces and to compel them to conform to the regime's agenda.[85] Secondly, the growing Indonesian middle class group came from Muslim backgrounds that changed state-society interaction so that the regime would make significant concessions for them.[86] The process of *santrinisation* within middle class ranks and the professionals impressed the regime, since these new Muslim intellectuals were in fact different form earlier ones.[87]

Internal conflict within the regime itself was another reason for Soeharto to open up political opportunities for Muslims. In permitting political openings, he did not mean to introduce a fully democratic system in his time. Nonetheless, a loosening of the censorship of the press, the release of certain dissidents and the toleration of political protests, demonstrations and criticism signified the era of *keterbukaan*.[88] In fact, Muslim activists and groups mainly benefited from these opportunities to create rapprochement with the government; whilst the regime needed to include Muslim powers under Soeharto's supervision, since serious division between Soeharto and active or retired ABRI officers loyal to L.B. Murdani brought some kind of disability to the regime's power.

It seemed however that only Islamic groups, which downplayed their orientation of political Islam were able to welcome the regime's political openness. Other groups that maintained their call for the establishment of an Islamic state remained excluded. Finally, many Muslim activists who previously rejected the idea of *Asas Tunggal* subsequently supported the regime's inclusion policy.[89]

The shift in the regime's attitude, which began in the early 1990s, had to some extent reduced the oppression and surveillance over Islamic organizations and illegal underground activities. State and Islam relations were no longer viewed in terms of suspicion and hostility. The cultural and historical roots of conflict, as suggested by Allan S. Samson,[90] immediately dispersed. This era was signified by a new relationship between the State and Islam. Instead of following a pattern of oppression, resistance and co-optation, it offered a new momentum for Muslim groups to express their political identities and orientations. For instance, the authorised party still allowed some members of HMI MPO and PII to carry out their activities, as long as they did not display their organization's banner in public areas. Formerly they had faced military oppression and dispersal.[91] In addition, in 1993 President Soeharto formally launched a national program to support the dissemination of short Islamic training (*Pesantren Kilat*) for students at the elementary, high school and university levels.[92] State officials in the provinces and at the district level formally supported this policy.[93]

Lastly, the economic crisis experienced by Indonesia in the mid 1990s, which brought about the collapse of the Soeharto regime in 1998, changed every prediction about the fate of politics in Indonesia. Soeharto had to step down, but he did not ensure that his successor could continue his mission and more importantly, protect him and his family. In fact, B.J.Habibie, his vice president, who became the next president, was only able to hold power for less than two years. This was because of a huge demand by the public for a "genuine" general election that finally resulted in formation of the 1999-2004 parliament members who elected Abdurahman Wahid, who was not favourable to Soeharto as a president.

Soeharto's resignation in 1998 led groups in Indonesia to freely express their political and religious identities within the democratic system. When during the New Order's governance most Islamic resistance movements showed an enthusiasm to destabilise the power of the regime and even to replace the existing rule, after the ruin of the regime, political Islam groups started to participate in national events. These new political events have since opened up the possibility for further participation and cooperation between Muslim groups and the government.

The only Muslim groups that did not benefit from this political opening were some that originally represented counter state movements. They could not integrate with the government agenda, since their doctrines required the whole nature of the Indonesian state to be Islamic. Because Indonesia is not an Islamic state but a secular one, they could not participate in the political processes unless all became Islamic. When Jemaah Tarbiyah organised its members and formed a political party, other Islamic groups such as Hizbut Tahrir and Salafi groups also started to establish formal mass organizations. Non-violent NII groups also reinstated their existence to struggle for the implementation of *shariah* in Indonesia and in local regions, for instance, the Council for Indonesian Fighters, Majelis Mujahidin Indonesia (MMI) and the Committee for the Preparation and Upholding of Islamic Law, Komite Persiapan Penegakan Syariah Islam (KPPSI) were founded in Central Java and South Sulawesi respectively. Other violence oriented movements, such as NII and JI suffered from political change and became the targets of Indonesian intelligence operations for combating terrorism.

Furthermore, the era of political openness since the 1990s and the fall of the Soeharto regime in 1998 offered more opportunity to alter the tone of relationships between the state and Islamic forces. Suspicion and hostility in the most powerful elements in Indonesia, such as the regime, the army and Islam, reached an understanding that lifted political constraints on Muslims. Jemaah Tarbiyah also benefited from the change from political constraint to the political inclusion of Muslims.

The commitment of Jemaah Tarbiyah to maintain its reform and gradual approach to the struggle for Islam has gained momentum. The establishment of the Justice Party with its Islamic ideology is its only means for manifesting its belief and ideas about Islam and for testing them in a challenging political game. The reform approach is mainly supported by activists coming from the university campuses. In the next chapter we will discuss the internal significance of these campus activists within PKS.

ENDNOTES

[1] Interview, anonymous, Jakarta, 12 March 2003.

[2] See "Beragam Jalan Menempuh Dunia," *Tempo*, 3 April 1993.

[3] Guy J. Pauker, "Indonesia in 1980: Regime Fatigue?" *Asian Survey* 21 no. 2 (Feb, 1981), 241.

[4] R. William Liddle, "Media Dakwah Scriptualism: One Form Islamic of Political Thought and Action in New Order Indonesia" in *Toward a New Paradigm: Recent Developments in Indonesian Islamic Thought* (Tempe: Arizona State University, 1996), 344.

[5] For details see *Dewan Rakyat*, October 2003.

[6] *Asas Tunggal*, the Sole of Principle, is a part of the regime's policy to impose the state's ideology to its citizens.

[7] Allan A. Samson, "Army and Islam in Indonesia," *Pacific Affairs* 44 no. 4 (Winter, 1971-1972), 545.

[8] Pauker, "Indonesia in 1980: Regime Fatigue?" 241

[9] Robert W. Hefner, "Islam, State, and Civil Society: ICMI and the Struggle for the Indonesian Middle Class," *Indonesia* 56 (October 1993), 3.

[10] See Mohammed M. Hafez and Quintan Wiktorowicz, "Violence as Contention in the Egyptian Islamic Movement," in *Islamic Activity: a Social Movement Theory Approach* (Bloomington and Indianapolis: Indiana University Press, 2004), 68.

[11] Ibid.

[12] See *Tempo*, 30 September 1978.

[13] For further details of radical actions in Indonesia during the New Order regime, see Candra June Santosa, "Modernization, Utopia and the Rise of Islamic Radicalism in Indonesia" (Ph.D. diss., Boston University, 1996). See also Harold Crouch, "Islam in Politics in Indonesia," in *Politics, Diplomacy and Islam: Four Case Studies* (Canberra: The Australian National University, 1986), 27.

[14] See Sidney Jones, "Al-Qaedah in Southeast Asia: the Case of the 'Ngruki Network' in Indonesia" (Corrected on 10 January 2003)," *Asia Briefing* no. 20, 8 August 2002, 15.

[15] David Jenkins, *Suharto and His General: Indonesian Military Politics 1975-1983* (Ithaca: Cornel Modern Indonesian Project, 1984), 57.

[16] Ibid.

[17] Umar Abduh, *Pesantren AL-Zaitun Sesat? Investigasi Mega Proyek dalam Gerakan NII* (Jakarta:Darul Falah, 2001), 32.

[18] See Tim Peduli Tapol, *Fakta Diskriminasi Rezim Soeharto terhadap Umat Islam*, trans. Mohammad Thalib (Yogyakarta: Wihda Press, 1988), 149.

[19] Umar Abduh, "Konspirasi Gerakan Islam & Militer di Indonesia" (Jakarta: Cedsos, 2003), 83.

[20] Yusuf Hasyim, a member of Indonesian parliament from PPP was vocal in criticising government actions toward the radical Islamic groups. See *Suara Karya*, 21 April 1981 and *Kompas*, 21 April 1981.

[21] Crouch, "Islam and Politics in Indonesia," 27.

[22] Ibid., 15.

[23] Sidney R. Jones, "It Can't Happen Here: A Post-Khomeini Look at Indonesian Islam," *Asian Survey* 20 no. 3 (March 1980), 315.

[24] *Tempo*, 30 September 1978.

[25] Samson, "Army and Islam in Indonesia," 547.

[26] After the Communist Party abortive coup on 30 September 1965 a great numbers of former members of the Indonesia Communist Party converted to Christianity. See B.J. Bolland, *The Struggle of Islam in Modern Indonesia* (The Hague: Martinus Nijhoff, 1971), 232-233.

[27] This restriction was lifted when Soeharto began to accommodate Muslim interests in the 1990s. See Robert W. Hefner, *Civil Islam: Muslims and Democratisation in Indonesia* (Princeton and Oxford: Princeton University Press, 2000), 109.

[28] See Jones, "It Can't Happen Here," 318.

[29] See Tim Peduli Tapol, *Fakta Diskriminasi Rezim Seoharto,* 94-112.

[30] Abdullah Sungkar was a former chairman of DDII branch, Surakarta in 1970s.

[31] See Tim Peduli Tapol, *Fakta Diskriminasi Rezim Seoharto,* 91.

[32] Samson, "Islam in Indonesian Politics," 1014.

[33] Ibid., 1015.

[34] Pauker, "Indonesia in 1980: Regime Fatigue?" 232-244.

[35] Faishal Ismail, "Pancasila as the Sole Basis for all Political Parties and for all Mass Organizations; an Account of Muslim's Responses," *Studia Islamika* 3 no. 4 (1996), 31.

[36] M. Rusli Karim, *HMI MPO dalam Kemelut Modernisasi Politik di Indonesia* (Bandung:Mizan, 1997), 129.

[37] The socialist oriented movement, Gerakan Pemuda Marhaenis, also rejected the imposition of the Sole Principle. See Karim, *HMI MPO dalam Kemelut Modernisasi Politik di Indonesia,* 127.

[38] Ibid.

[39] See "Sejarah Kebangkitan dan Perkembangan PII," *PelajarIslam.or.id*.

[40] Richard Tanter, "The Totalitarian Ambition: Intelligence and Security Agencies in Indonesia" in *State and Civil Society in Indonesia* (Clayton: Monas University, 1990), 250.

[41] Merlyna Lim, "Cyber-Civic Space in Indonesia: From Panopticon to Pandemonium?" *IDPR* 24 no. 4 (2002), 386.

[42] Ibid., 388.

[43] Interview, Hilmi Aminuddin, Jakarta, 23 December 2003.

[44] Interview, anonymous, Jakarta, 24 March 2003.

[45] Lim, "Cyber-Civic Space in Indonesia," 367.

[46] Interview with Aus Hidayat, Depok, 13 May 2003.

47 Interview with Sigit Susiantomo, Surabaya, 17 March 2003.

48 The book by Andi Rahmat and Mukhammad Najib, *Gerakan Perlawanan dari Masjid Kampus* (Surakarta: Purimedia, 2001) and Ali Said Damanik, *Fenomena Partai Keadilan:Transformasi 20 Tahun Gerakan Tarbiyah di Indonesia* (Bandung, Mizan, 2002) emphasise the role of Jemaah Tarbiyah as a resistance group towards the regime.

49 See Umar Abduh, *Al-Zaitun Gate: Investigasi Mengungkap Misteri Dajjan Indonesia Membangun Negara Impian Iblis* (Jakarta: LPDI, 2002), 29.

50 Interview, anonymous, Depok, 11 June 2003.

51 See Abduh, *Al-Zaitun Gate*, 29.

52 Ibid

53 Interview with Hilmi Aminuddin, Jakarta, 23 December 2003.

54 See "Kliping Komando Jihad," *Pusat Sejarah ABRI*, 1978-1980.

55 Interview with Rahmat Abdullah, Jakarta, 11 May 2003.

56 Martin van Bruinessen, "Geneologies of Islamic Radicalism in post-Suharto Indonesia," *South East Asia Research* 10 no. 2 (2002), 125.

57 Interview with Ahmad Mudzafar Jufri, Surabaya, 17 March 2003.

58 See Fred R. von der Mehden, *Two Worlds of Islam: Interaction between Southeast Asia and the Middle East* (Gainesville: the University Press of Florida, 1993), 88.

59 He is the Al-Azhar -graduate who strongly opposes Nurcholish Madjid's ideas of Islamic renewal.

60 He is a Member of Parliament from PK (1999-2004) and former secretary of M. Roem, a leader of Masyumi.

61 He was a DDII activist who was nominated by PK to be a candidate for Indonesian President during the 1999 General Election.

62 M. Rasyidi was Chief Imam (*imam besar*) of the Arif Rahman Mosque in the 1990s. He was given the opportunity to deliver the first Friday sermon when the mosque was formally opened to the public. See Y. Setyo Hadi (ed), *Masjid Kampus Untuk Umat & Bangsa* (Jakarta: Masjid ARH UI and LKB – Nusantara, 2000), 23.

63 Karim, *HMI MPO dalam Kemelut Modernisasi Politik di Indonesia*, 141.

64 See Syahrul Effendi D. "Dimana HMI Berada dan Mau Kemana?" *Portal Perjuangan HMI MPO*, 25 January 2005 or see http://www.hminews.com.

65 Interview with Mutammimul Ula, Jakarta, 16 June 2003.

66 See Muhammad Sa'id, "Tarbiyah Suatu Kemestian," in *Tarbiyah Berkelanjutan* (Jakarta: Pustaka Tarbiatuna, 2003), 45-52.

67 Interview with Sigit Susiantomo, Surabaya, 17 March 2003.

68 Bruinessen, "Geneologies of Islamic Radicalism in Post-Suharto Indonesia," 132.

69 Interview with Aus Hidayat, Depok, 13 Mei 2003.

70 Rifki Rosyad, "A Quest for True Islam: A Study of the Islamic Resurgence Movements among the Youth in Bandung, Indonesia" (Master thesis, the Australian National University, 1995), 91.

71 Ibid.

72 Interview with Aus Hidayat, Depok, 13 Mei 2003.

73 Interview with Rahmat Abdullah, Jakarta, 11 Mei 2003.

74 *Ibid*

75 See "Dinas Rahasia Susupi PKS," *Dewan Rakyat*, 1 October 2003, 19. *Dewan Rakyat* is monthly magazine published by former activists of HMI and PII, such as Ferry Mursyidan Baldan, AM. Fatwa, Eggi Sudjana.

76 See "Cikal Bakal PKS," *Dewan Rakyat*, 21.

77 See "Sosok Yang Jadi Sorotan," *Saksi*, 31 December 2003, 75-76.

78 Ibid.

79 Interview, anonymous, Jakarta, 24 May 2003.

80 Interview with Budi Darmawan, Canberra, 24 May 2004.

81 See Irfan. S. Awwas (ed), *Dialog Internet: Aksi Sejuta Ummat dan Issu Negara Islam* (Yogyakarta: Wihda Press, 2000), 65.

[82] Interview with Rahmat Abdullah, Jakarta, 11 May 2003.

[83] See Hilmi Aminuddin, *Strategi Dakwah Gerakan Islam* (Jakarta: Pustaka Tarbiatuna, 2003), 144.

[84] See Doug McAdam, et.al., ed., *Comparative Perspectives on Social Movements: Political Opportunities, Mobilizing Structures, and Cultural Framings* (Cambridge: Cambridge University Press, 1996), 42-48.

[85] R. William Liddle, "The Islamic Turn in Indonesia: a Political Explanation," *The Journal of Asian Studies* 55 vol. 3 (August 1996), 615.

[86] Hefner, "Islam, State, and Civil Society," 24.

[87] Ibid., 26

[88] Jacques Bertrand, "False Starts, Succession Crises, and Regime Transition: Flirting with Openness in Indonesia," *Pacific Affairs* 69 no. 3 (Autumn, 1996), 325.

[89] Andi Rahmat and Mukhammad Najib, *Gerakan Perlawanan dari Masjid Kampus* (Surakarta: Purimedia, 2001), 65. See also and Mahfudz Sidiq, *KAMMI dan Pergulatan Reformasi : Kiprah Politik Aktivis Dakwah Kampus dalam Perjuangan Demokratisasi di tengah Krisis Nasional Multidimensi* (Solo: Era Intermedia, 2003), 66.

[90] Samson, "Army and Islam in Indonesia," 547.

[91] Karim, *HMI MPO dalam Kemelut Modernisasi Politik di Indonesia*, 147.

[92] Before Islamic trainings, such *Pesantren Kilat*, were under surveillance of the regime apparatus but then since the 1990s they were used by the regime to win the support of Muslims. See V.S. Naipaul, *Beyond Belief: Islamic Excursions Among the Converted Peoples* (London: Little, Brown and Company, 1998), 9.

[93] See Yon Machmudi, *Partai Keadilan Sejahtera: Wajah Baru Islam Politik Indonesia* (Bandung: Harakatuna Publishing, 2005), 55.

Chapter 4: Patterns of controlling Institutions: from campus to state

> Indeed, the victory of Islam is due to the success of the *ummah*. The success of the *ummah* rests on its youth of good character and morality - Anonymous Muslim scholar.[1]

The important status of university students in Indonesian society has encouraged political and religious groups to establish their influence upon them. For students, being involved in political activities has provided them with political careers in return. Realising this, the focus of Jemaah Tarbiyah, since the beginning, has been to attract students in prestigious secular campuses since they offer the greatest opportunities in terms of vertical and horizontal mobilization.[2] For activists of Jemaah Tarbiyah, students are their greatest assets in the duty of the Islamisation of Indonesia and for the victory of Islam.

Most activists of Jemaah Tarbiyah who were elected members of the Indonesian national parliament representing the Prosperous Justice Party in the 2004 general elections hail from secular campuses. During their study life, members of Jemaah Tarbiyah in the 1990s were able to control student governments and other intra campus organisations. Their role reached its peak of significance when they succeeded in mobilising huge demonstrations involving thousands of students from various campuses to topple Soeharto in 1998. How has Jemaah Tarbiyah been able to control the campuses and use campus predication to serve its interests? Does success on campus also bring the same victory for Jemaah Tarbiyah in controlling and influencing the Indonesian state?

This chapter attempts to analyse the significance of the secular universities as strongholds of Jemaah Tarbiyah in providing political cadres for its party, PKS. The presence of the campus Islam activists who have dominated the membership and leadership of PKS have had a significant influence over PKS politics. They have contributed to making its political policies pragmatic. Their experience during their involvement in student senates and other intra-campus organisations since the 1990s, in particular their interaction with different cohort groups can account for this realistic approach.

A. The Decline of Student Organisations

The 1960s was an era of high student mobilisation. The key body was the Indonesian Student Action Union, Kesatuan Aksi Mahasiswa Indonesia (KAMI), established on 25 October 1965, supported by student organizations and endorsed by the Minister of Higher Education and Science, Dr. Syarif Thayeb. KAMI succeeded in uniting student elements in the struggle against the Communist party and its sympathisers.³ The good rapprochement between the military and campus organs, such as the Minister of Higher Education and Science, rectors, lectures and students, resulted in the cooptation of student activists. Inevitably, the student activists of the 1960s lost their significance as agents of change. Their spirit of struggle declined after they succeeded in overthrowing the regime of first President Sukarno. During the period of consolidation of Soeharto's New Order which followed, some students chose to return to campus whilst others continued their political careers and joined the government.⁴ The student movement of 1966 became a core component of the New Order regime and figures of historical memory commemorated by associations of the "generation of 1966".⁵

The extra-campus organizations which had previously supported KAMI showed their ineffectiveness after they regrouped under the supervision of the New Order regime.⁶ In July 1970, through an initiative of the government, most extra-campus organizations such as HMI, GPI, PMII, GMKI, Pemuda Anshor and other organisations under the auspices of the ruling party, Golkar (Golongan Karya) led by Abdul Ghafur formed a committee for the preparation of an umbrella youth organisation. In 23 July 1973 the Committee of Indonesian National Youth, Komite Nasional Pemuda Indonesia (KNPI) was set up to organise all extra-campus organizations with government assistance.⁷

However, student activists of intra campus organizations began to evaluate their role in voicing the interests of the people in general. The Student Council, Dewan Mahasiswa (Dema) began to re-activate their function of criticising the government's policies. Since the mid-1970s, Dema succeeded in replacing the role of extra-campus organizations and received firm recognition among students,⁸ which allowed Dema to become an arena for Muslim and Leftist activists to gain influence over students.

The most influential Dema at the level of national politics were those of the Indonesia University (UI) and the Bandung Institute of Technology (ITB). In its meeting on 1-5 November 1973, Dema UI stressed its commitment to give voice to the people's aspirations. This led Dema UI to play an active role in criticising the government.⁹ The case of Malari in 1974, abbreviated from *Malapetaka Lima Belas January* or the Tragedy of January Fifteenth, signalled the increasingly critical attitudes of students towards the government. The Malari incident was a reflection of the students' frustration with the regime's economic policies which had allowed extensive foreign involvement in Indonesia's economic affairs, causing an unprecedented riot that resulted in the destruction of over a thousand of Japanese vehicles and foreign-owned buildings. Immediately after the incident, the government issued a decree (SK No. 28/U/1974) through the Ministry of Education and Culture to block the influence of the Student Councils. It required all students to attain formal approval from university rectors in order to hold gatherings on campus and to coordinate all activities outside campus through KNPI.[10]

Another important issue for student activists in the 1970s was the statement by a national student consortium of Student Councils in Bandung made in October 1977, which demanded the application of Indonesia's Constitution and Pancasila in a pure and consistent manner (*murni dan konsekuen*) and called for the People's Consultative Assembly (MPR) to hold a Special Session (*Sidang Istimewa*) to ask President Soeharto to account for the abuse of Pancasila.[11] Student willingness to criticise and mobilise against Soeharto gathered momentum. In Bandung, the Bandung Institute of Technology's Student Council issued what they called as "the White Book of the 1978 Student Struggle" accusing Soeharto of abusing his power and deviating from the Constitution and Pancasila.

As widespread unrest developed among student activists, the government issued a decree, the Normalization of Campus Life, *Normalisasi Kehidupan Kampus* (NKK) in April 1978 to limit students' rights of expression, assembly and association which led to another policy of the Coordinating Body for Student Affairs, *Badan Koordinasi Kampus* (BKK). The Minister of Education, Daoed Joesoef, issued a statement directing students to be involved only in activities related to student welfare (i.e. educational facilities and material and spiritual well-being), student interests (arts, sports, journalism, outdoor recreation and campus community pursuits) and student thought and reasoning (study clubs and seminars).[12] The policy of NKK/BKK was effective in ending student involvement in political issues. Subsequently, in 1984 the government issued the policy of "Sole Principle" (*Asas Tunggal*) that was perceived mainly by Muslim activists as aimed at breaking the ties of the Islamic extra-campus organizations and the Islamic parties with students on campuses.[13] Under these conditions the activities of both extra- and intra -student organisations indeed declined.[14]

Muslim student activists also indicated their reluctance to join Islamic parties after the government forced the only Islamic party, the Development Unity Party, Partai Persatuan Pembangunan (PPP) to use Pancasila as its political basis in 1984. In general, the attitude of Muslim students in responding to the policies of the New Order varied. Nurmahmudi Ismail, a former activist of Jemaah Tarbiyah at the Bogor Institute of Agriculture, Institut Pertanian Bogor (IPB) and ex-president of the Justice Party, described two orientations in students' responses to the government co-optation in the mid 1980s. A first group still believed that there was a need to struggle for the sake of Islam through the political party system, even though the party was under the control of the government at the time. A second group felt deeply disillusioned with the party and could not see any good intentions whatsoever in the Muslim activists who joined the PPP. According to this second group, they were no different from government puppets. The Jemaah Tarbiyah activists, as represented by Nurhmahmudi Ismail, were counted among those who were doubtful the role of PPP. From 1987 they began to express their disenchantment by not voting in the general elections.[15] Ismail further stated

> I was one of those who were disenchanted with the PPP. I decided not to vote during the general elections, and most of us chose this way.[16]

Throughout the Soeharto era, the regime gradually reduced the influence and political role of student organizations and pushed them to focus on academic activities. Soeharto attempted to control student activism and broke its ties with its political patrons. Instead, the regime gave an opportunity to the ruling party, Golkar, to establish its political influence in the campuses. Thus it was that during the reign of Soeharto that many students resolved to devote their time to studying and to turn away from political activities.

Nonetheless, political reasons aside, ideological and religious factors became important for students for action in student organizations. The decline of extra-campus organisations after the implementation of NKK/BKK in 1978 caused a rise in religious student activities. The emergence of the Islamic study groups was also coincidental with the emergence of Christian and Leftist student movements in campuses. The Christian organisation at UI, Persekutuan Oikumene Univiersitas Indonesia (POSA UI), established in 1981, was able to organise its congregations at the faculty and university level. The Leftist-oriented students also developed similar study clubs. They were in competition for the control of student governing bodies and other strategic intra-student organizations within campuses. They were often involved in clashes, collaboration and even in agreements for sharing power within student activities. This resembled Realpolitik in the broadest sense, because they had to resort to all kinds of practical politics for their own interests.[17] In fact, their combination of religious activities and political experiments on campus would come to be considered important preparation in developing their political careers in the future.

B. The Rise of Campus Predication

In order to gain insight into Indonesian student activism with a developing interest in Islam, it is helpful to consider Azyumardi Azra's categorisation of three orientations.[18] The first of these are students of high religious and spiritual inquiry. They consider the Islamic circles on campus, the *halaqah* as suitable to their spiritual needs. They attend regular meetings organised by senior students and are able to develop close contacts with one another and consider themselves and their fellow Muslims as one family. There is a practice of sharing material goods and a sense of security in these newly Islamic environments. Spirituality, piety, the regular observance of Islamic duties, solidarity and togetherness are the features that draw students to join these circles.[19] New students coming from remote areas or villages who have no family in the city feel that these kinds of activities help them to find friends. Since their involvement within the group is highly motivated by religious needs and security, friendships become easier to build.[20]

Their interactions with the group are not confined to attending to their own religious needs; they are soon also challenged to spread the ideas they have gained to their fellow Muslims on campus. They do not limit their activities to the mosque but often meet in the small prayer rooms located in the faculties and departments within the universities. They ask their friends to observe the daily prayers while on campus and invite them to join their religious circles. Topics for discussion are not only religious but are often related to students' academic needs. For instance, they feel encouraged when facing assignments and examinations since these are also considered to be tasks that will be rewarded by God.

A second group of students are those of Muslim upbringing who are more inclined towards Leftist associations. They are not necessarily from families with a Communist background; rather the majority have been raised in devout Muslim families. Like the first group, who tend to be affiliated with religious activities of a different orientation from their parents, this group has begun to distance itself from formal religious activities. It is more interested in activities such as the People's Democratic Party, Partai Rakyat Demokrat established in 1994. Both first and second type of students signify the emergence of a new trend in which the children of faithful Indonesian Muslims no longer follow their parents in their approach to religion.[21]

The last group of students are those who are similar to the first category but prefer to gain organisational and political experience, rather than spiritual accomplishments. They join the Islamic organizations that have established branches in their campuses, such as HMI, PMII, and PII because they also provide political opportunities for the future. Through connections with their mentors, they often find jobs more easily. This type of student wants to develop both an understanding of Islam and organisational skills. However, we might state generally that most Islamic campus organizations focus their activities on organisational and political advancements; they are unable to fulfil students' interests in spiritual dimensions.

Students who have not been satisfied with the extra-campus organisations have sought alternatives to fulfil their spiritual needs and finally join the first group. Since the existing Islamic organisations on campus have been unable to respond to all the spiritual needs of some students, the *halaqah* groups have been able to gain an advantage.

The *halaqah* groups, later on known as *Kelompok Tarbiyah* (*Tarbiyah* Group) or Jemaah Tarbiyah, have advanced a more organised *dakwah* to attract students. Through their campus predication, the most successful Islamisation processes on secular campuses have taken place since the 1990s. The prestigious state universities of Java, such as the Bandung Institute of Technology (ITB), University of Indonesia (UI), Gadja Madah University (UGM), Bogor Institute of Agriculture (IPB), Airlangga University (Unair) and the Sepuluh November Institute of Technology (ITS) have become strongholds of Jemaah Tarbiyah.

Those who have sought remedies against profane activities have found that the idea of a total Islam as an all-encompassing way of life meets their spiritual demands. In so far as their campus activities and lives had alienated them from religious practice, they felt themselves distanced from the benefits of religious guidance. They have compensated for this by involving themselves in Islamic predication. Through predication activities they have developed a sense of brotherhood and solidarity that they believe they could not find in other groups. One activist of Jemaah Tarbiyah told of his memory during his initial contact with this group

> I felt secure and at peace when I gathered together with members of Jemaah Tarbiyah. The feeling of brotherhood, caring and togetherness which was developed among the *ikhwa>n* made me feel at home.[22]

In addition, the political ambition of HMI, PMII and other student organisations to gain influence were perceived by Muslim activists as merely set to achieve a short-term goal. They were more interested in power and access into the bureaucracy after graduating from university rather than inspired by the spirit of *dakwah*. Many Muslim students viewed the involvement of HMI alumni within the system ineffective, since they did not bring any change to colour the system with Islamic ideas – in other words, they had been co-opted by the regime.[23]

Thus the dynamics within the state universities became an important reason for Jemaah Tarbiyah activists to introduce their Islamic ideas. Students of the prestigious institutions were seen to have more potential to bring about social and political change in Indonesia, and efforts to cultivate the seeds of activism on the campuses were believed to be the fastest ways to bring about change in the society.[24] In contrast, the campaign of Islamic renewal, which is more favourable to secular ideas, only draws a limited following in secular campuses. While the secular campuses have proved to be fertile soil to receive the seeds of non-liberal Islam, religious campuses, such as the State Institute of Islamic Religion (IAIN) predominantly support the ideas of the renewal associated movements led by intellectuals, such as Nurcholish Madjid.[25]

The explanation for the prevalence of Islamist groups in the secular campuses and their scarcity on the IAIN lies in the gap between secular and Islamic educational institutions. There have been schisms between these two tertiary sectors, in which students from the secular universities tend to underestimate the qualities of students from the IAIN. In return, students from the IAIN often consider their counterparts in the secular universities ignorant about Islam. Islamic student organisations, such as HMI, PMII and IMM, which are supposed to bridge the gap, cannot perform well since they are not able to reconcile their own differences in terms of religious and political orientations. Many Muslim students are critical of the division between traditionalists and modernists, for example.

The Jemaah Tarbiyah is one of the few groups which have been able to channel students' interests in religious activities, and in fact their *dakwah* has helped create this Islamic intensity. Its focus on *dakwah* has enabled Jemaah Tarbiyah to recruit new cadres who are not interested in politics. In the 1980s, after the implementation of NKK/BKK, students kept themselves at a distance from the political parties and were more interested in taking part in discussions of academic issues and the basics of Islam. The growing development of the activism of the Campus Predication, *Aktifis Dakwah Kampus* (ADK) under the Body of Islamic Campus Predication, Lembaga Dakwah Kampus (LDK) that expanded its network throughout the secular campuses in Java and the Outer Islands strengthened the role of students in *dakwah* activities.

Islamic student movements in the secular universities were also a major component of the demonstrations which brought down Soeharto. They organised themselves into a front, the Indonesian Student Action Muslim Union, Kesatuan Aksi Mahasiswa Islam Indonesia (KAMMI). Along with other Student Executive Bodies from secular universities in Java they poured on to the streets to launch strikes against the regime. How could KAMMI and other elements of campus predication, mainly members of Jemaah Tarbiyah, organise huge demonstrations and establish their networks throughout the secular universities in Indonesia? These actions were not merely the result of spontaneous reaction but of a long-term process of caderisation within the campuses. They had a long history before they emerged as a huge and organised power to challenge the existence of a crumbling regime.[26]

1. Introducing Islam on Campus: the Role of Imaduddin

Imaduddin Abdurahhim, a lecturer at The Bandung Institute of Technology (ITB) is an important figure who deserves our consideration. He is from a Modernist background; his father was a prominent leader of Masyumi in Sumatra who graduated from al-Azhar University, Cairo. Imaddudin founded the Institute for the Struggler of *Dakwah*, Lembaga Mujahid Dakwah (LMD) in 1973, and through the LMD many students from non-religious universities attended his "mental training sessions" and finally developed *dakwah* programs of their own on their campuses.[27] Indeed, the alumni of LMD became key activists in many universities.

Imaduddin had been a Muslim activist while still a student at ITB, when he was involved with the Islamic Students Association (HMI). It was he who proposed the establishment of ITB's mosque, the Salman al-Farisi, named after an important figure from the stories of the Prophet Muhammad's companions. The first president of Indonesia, Soekarno, gave the mosque its name. Imaduddin, an engineer by training, was appointed as secretary of the committee of the project.

In 1963 Imaduddin went to the USA to pursue his studies towards a master's degree at the University of Iowa. During his stay there he became involved with international Islamic propagation, making contact with other Muslim students from various countries.[28] His Islamic orientation and his vision of struggle became more international in scope.[29] It was also in the USA that he established his first contact with Muslim Brothers who were students in the university. Imaduddin developed this contact until he finally became a member of Muslim Students Association (MSA) of the USA and Canada.

After his return home to Indonesia in 1966 he was appointed chairman of the Central Board of Islamic Education and Propagation (PB LDMI, Lembaga Dakwah Mahasiswa Islam) a campus missionary institution under HMI. Through LDMI Imaduddin became close to Nurcholish Madjid, then chairman of HMI. During the time Imaduddin was chairman of LDMI he was sent to attend an international seminar organised by the International Islamic Federation of Student Organizations (IIFSO), which finally led him to be elected secretary-general of this organization. Now he enjoyed interaction with Muslim leaders from around the world.[30]

Imaduddin set up propagation training or Latihan Mujahid Dakwah (Training for Islamic Propagators) at the Salman Mosque of ITB in 1973 after a visit to Malaysia, which lasted two years. In Malaysia, besides working under the Ministry of Education to prepare the conversion of a certain polytechnic institution into a university, he helped to activate the Young Muslim Organization (ABIM) for the propagation of Islam. His presence in Malaysia influenced the dynamics of the Islamic activities of many organizations, particularly ABIM, so that even Anwar Ibrahim himself, as chairman of ABIM, considered Imaduddin as his teacher.[31] Imaduddin's aim was to use mosques not just as places of worship but also as centres to educate young Muslims who might be hoped to become leaders in the future.[32] The training attracted many students, not only from ITB but also from other universities in Java and Sumatra. The first training even involved student activists from the cosmopolitan centres of Jakarta and Yogyakarta.[33] In fact, the Salman mosque of ITB subsequently became a centre for the training of Muslim activists in the secular universities.

Imaduddin's growing popularity among students and his rising criticism of the government led the New Order regime to increasingly scrutinise his activities.[34] He not only maintained a close relationship with DDII activists but also made outspoken attacks on the personality of Soeharto and his family. He even accused Soeharto and his family of accumulating wealth taken from the people. In his eyes, Indonesia was full of injustice and ruled by an authoritarian president.[35] As a result, in 1978 he was charged with propagating anti-Pancasila ideas and seeking to overthrow the regime. Finally, he was sentenced to jail for 2 years.[36]

Imaduddin admitted that his vision of Islam was not only influenced by the literature of the Muslim Brothers leaders in Egypt but also Abdul A'la al-Maududi of Pakistan.[37] While Imaduddin succeeded in establishing the LMD, he did not carry out any *usrah* activities within the formal structure of his organization. When he was sentenced to jail, his cadres ceased the struggle. Nonetheless, it is important to note that his moral training sessions and the LMD are reportedly acknowledged by Muslim activists to be the forerunners of the campus *dakwah* model, spreading from ITB to numerous other campuses in Indonesia.[38] His monumental training handbook, *Kuliah Tauhid* (Lectures on Religion) became a major reference and was circulated in almost all of the campuses in Java and in some in Sumatra, Kalimantan and the Eastern parts of Indonesia.[39] In Jakarta, many alumni of LMD returned to their campuses and established Islamic study groups. In UI they introduced various programs in each faculty under different names, such as the Integrated Study of Islam, Integratif Studi Tentang Islam (ISTI) in the faculty of economics, the Integrated Islamic Study, Studi Islam Terpadu (SIT) in the Faculty of Letters and the Forum of Study of Fundamental Islam, Forum Studi Dasar Islam (Fondasi) in the Faculty of Science.[40]

In 1979, not long after his detention, the Studi Islam Intensif (SII) was established and *halaqah* were formed as alternative activities replacing the LMD.[41] At the same time, the involvement of the large student associations such HMI, PII and many others on the campuses were restricted by the government after through the policy of NKK/BKK. Since the 1980s, initial efforts by SII at ITB coincided with the creation of other Islamic circles and study clubs, including the Muslim Brothers-influenced Jemaah Tarbiyah. Better-structured materials of the Muslim Brothers were introduced to students, emphasising the need to develop individual morality and piety.[42]

Many alumni of LMD who had already established their Islamic activities in some secular universities embraced Jemaah Tarbiyah and implemented more structured teachings from Hasan al-Banna.[43] They learned these systematic teachings of the Muslim Brothers under guidance of Middle East graduates. Some pioneers of Jemaah Tarbiyah who had graduated from Saudi Arabia, such as Hilmi Aminuddin and Abu Ridha helped to introduce the ideas of Hasan al-Banna in ITB, UI and IPB. They focussed on Islamic predication by maximising the use of prayer rooms and organised other activities for students and staff. They were known among students as *aktifis mushallah,* or prayer room activists.

2. Prayer Room Activists: Typical Jemaah Tarbiyah Cadres

It is something of a paradox that the government's restraining of political *dakwah* activities in Indonesian society at large inadvertently inflated *dakwah* activities on the campuses. Since any political *dakwah* conducted through the Friday prayers and public sermons was monitored and restricted by the Soeharto regime, many Muslim activists found that *dakwah* on campus was the safest way to preserve their struggle for Islam.[44] In most cases, all social and religious activities, private or public, had to be endorsed by stamped letters from authorised agents of the regime.[45] These authorised parties, including the rector, dean and members of a special committee for Islamic activities in the university consistently monitored students' activities. For instance, the authorised party on campus required that students submit the names of preachers before permission was given for guest lectures or sermons. The rector of the university was indirectly responsible for endorsing or rejecting any preachers from outside campuses and preachers of radical or hardline orientation would not be permitted to deliver sermons in the university-based mosques or at any religious gatherings held by students. As a result of the state's monitoring of public prayers and sermons (*pengajian*), Muslim students preferred to use their own prayer rooms to attract students to perform the daily regular prayers.

Since the public space for propagating Islam was restricted, students read printed materials and circulated them to their fellow students in secret. In fact, from the 1970s onwards, the circulation of translated books written by Muslim Brothers activists has been remarkable: hundreds of Muslim Brothers books were translated to Indonesian. In the early emergence of Jemaah Tarbiyah in the mid 1980s the works of Sayyid Qutb and Sayyid Hawwa became alternative books for cadres because they were seen as providing a new spirit of Islamic activism.

The implementation of the government policy of "normalisation" of campus life, *Normalisasi Kehidupan Kampus* (NKK) in 1979 and the ensuing tight surveillance of student activities by the rector and deans of faculties weakened the political activism of students. In addition, the policy of the "Sole Principle" of Pancasila in 1984 imposed by the government had an impact on the ability of extra-campus organizations to build connections with students. Having realised that any resistance towards the regime was futile and easily contained, Muslim students in the 1980s focussed their activities on Islamic predication, putting aside political and social issues for the moment. For that reason, study clubs, rather than demonstrations and public orations (*mimbar bebas*) attracted students, and small circles were preferable to large gatherings. Thus the *tarbiyah* model of the Muslim

Patterns of controlling Institutions: from campus to state

Brothers became an alternative for students in conducting *dakwah* as well as preserving idealism within the campuses.[46]

In order to survive in these circumstances, the Jemaah Tarbiyah activists carried out their *dakwah* by establishing *halaqah* that focussed on practical issues. They were not alone in choosing this course of action, fearing government scrutiny at a time when the regime did not hesitate to crush political resistance, particularly from Islamic organizations. Many Muslim student activists who did not agree with the government's imposition of the *Asas Tunggal* set up massive networks of Islamic circles on the campuses that limited their programs of study of basic and practical Islam.

Having been exiled from public space, and in order to develop their ability to resist the government, activists carried out religious training secretly in small and private spaces. They did not use the campus mosques, choosing rather the modest prayer rooms located at the level of faculty or department[47] or conducting their activities in university rented accommodation around the campuses.

Aware of the lack of appropriate preachers for handling the increase in the Islamic circles, Muslim student activists started to build programs aimed at creating more cadres to serve as trainers. Even though these were not supported by professional preachers, the *Tarbiyah* model of self-sustaining cadres helped to accelerate a massive Islamic predication within the campuses.[48] Students were awakened to their responsibilities and started to search for long-term solutions for the prosperity of Islam.

Through independent training that did not rely on preachers from outside campus, Jemaah Tarbiyah has been able to provide more cadres, better acquainted with religious terms and doctrines, to assume more initiative in religious activities. They have been able to produce their own qualified preachers who are not only able to lead the religious circles but who are also confident in delivering sermons in public gatherings, including the Friday prayers. Equipped with their non-religious expertise as well, they are well received by those who take pride in the status of the secular universities. At the Arif Rahman Hakim Mosque of the University of Indonesia, for instance, from the 1970s until the mid-1980s, most of the Friday sermons were delivered by DDII preachers, but since the early-1990s, many Jemaah Tarbiyah's activists have been able to replace them.

It has become evident that these *Mushallah* activists not only target the penetration of religious institutions by controlling the religious education section (*Kerohanian Islam*, Rohis) at the university and faculty level and by establishing the Forum for Islamic Studies, Forum Studi Islam (FSI) within the faculties, but they have also started to gain influence over politically oriented campus organizations. They won control of Student Senates, Senat Mahasiswa(SM) and established the intra-campus student movement, KAMMI. Such organs within student politics have contributed to strengthening the political role of Jemaah Tarbiyah in student affairs and in national politics.

a) Forum Studi Islam (FSI)

If Imaduddin placed explicit emphasis on the rejection of Pancasila as an un-Islamic ideology, the Jemaah Tarbiyah activists avoided talking about such issues. In the Bogor Institute of Agriculture (IPB) during the 1980s, for example, Jemaah Tarbiyah established the religious section, *Kerohanian Islam* (Rohis) that trained Muslim students in an understanding of the most fundamental Islamic teachings and practices. Activists of Rohis on campus also played a significant role in assisting certain lecturers with courses on Islam. Through these tutorials on religion they were further able to set up their networks of Islamic circles.[49]

The non-political nature of the Jemaah Tarbiyah training and meeting circles has attracted wide attention among students. However, its apolitical attitude at that time by no means passed without criticism. Many other Muslim student activists severely criticised the government repression of students and Muslim activists, while accusing members of Jemaah Tarbiyah of lacking the courage to stand up for the truth before the tyrants.[50]

As has been suggested by van Bruinessen, Jemaah Tarbiyah, despite its important role in building individual good character, also manifested an inner rejection of the Pancasila state and of un-Islamic practices in modern Indonesia.[51] However, Jemaah Tarbiyah did not reject the state existence of Pancasila but carried this spirit of rejection against the imposition of it as the "Sole Principle" upon all political parties and mass organizations as well.[52] It must also be said here that Jemaah Tarbiyah's disagreement with government policy was not merely the rejection of Pancasila. What Jemaah Tarbiyah really disagreed with was the policy of the government of disregarding other ideologies that were perceived to be in contradiction with Pancasila. Of course, the regime had its own interpretation of Pancasila, which it sought to enforce. The Soeharto regime never ceased to try to impose its self legitimising understanding of Pancasila onto the broader context of Indonesian society at large.[53]

Since the 1990s the members of Jemaah Tarbiyah have expanded their influence by penetrating and controlling formal Muslim student activities within the campuses. They have been able to make good their existence through the establishment of autonomous activities under the supervision of the deans of faculty. In turn, they were authorised by faculty and to carry out Islamic activities. For instance, they organised celebrations of the Prophet Muhammad's birth, collected funds for charities and set up new Islamic circles as well. In the Faculties of Humanities and Medical Science at the University of Indonesia they established the Forum for Islamic Studies and Practices, Forum Amal dan Studi

Islam (Formasi) and the Forum for Islamic Studies, Forum Studi Islam (FSI) respectively. In almost all faculties of state universities they founded similar forums under the generic name of the Forum of Islamic Studies. Since then, religious activities have developed and won wide influence among students.[54]

The existence of these faculty based organizations within the universities has attracted new students to join their programs in numbers. Beginning at the freshman year, the members of the FIS successfully provided alternative Islamic training sessions. These take a form similar to that of the traditional Islamic boarding schools (*pesantren*), while they may differ in terms of length of study and the way in which course contents are presented. Although most training sessions are held during the weekends and campus holidays, they are always sited in interesting venues, such in the villas of the mountain resort of Puncak, West Java. Such training appeals to new students who are happy to spend their holidays in recreation and enhancing their religious knowledge and practice.

The expansion of FIS in the faculties has necessitated the establishment of a broader organization to manage all Islamic organisations under the umbrella of one body at university level, the Campus Predication Institute, Lembaga Dakwah Kampus (LDK), particularly to respond to the need for broader activities, aimed to build contacts with various bodies of student predication on other campuses. At UI, Nuansa Islam Campus (Salam) was founded in 1997. At IPB and ITB, activists of Jemaah Tarbiyah who were involved in the Forum for Islamic Studies coordinated their activities through the organisation called the Council for Mosque Cultivation, Dewan Kemakmuran Masjid (DKM) al-Hurriyah, established in 1997 and the Family of Islamic Students, Keluarga Mahasiswa Islam (Gamais) ITB, established in 1991 respectively. At UGM the Shalahuddin Congregation (*Jamaah Shalahuddin*) has become a significant organisation affiliated with Jemaah Tarbiyah. Thus, activists of Jemaah Tarbiyah who organised themselves in LDK have begun to participate in a broader network of inter-campus predication, the Forum for Coordination of Campus Predication, Forum Silaturahmi Lembaga Dakwah Kampus (FSLDK).

FSLDK held its first national conference 1986, which aimed to coordinate and unify Islamic campus predication at various universities in Indonesia.[55] As an umbrella of campus predication throughout the universities, FSLDK became an important organ through which Muslim activists could disseminate their ideas.[56] For instance, after the Eighth Conference of FSLD in Makassar, South Sulewesi in 1993 the book written by a scholar of Hizbut Tahrir, Taqiyuddin an-Nabhani (1909-1977) entitled *Kitab Mafahim*, became a standard text read by activists of LDK in many universities.[57] However, since the book was introduced through an elite top-down process, it could not last for long. In its Tenth Conference in Malang in 1998, Jemaah Tarbiyah activists were able to take control the leadership of FSLDK.[58]

Since the activists of Jemaah Tarbiyah do not dominate all Islamic campus activities, a number of conflicts with different movements have often arisen. We need to examine how splits and competition among new Islamic movements operate in the process of recruitment of new members. The conflict involves three main groups, the Jemaah Tarbiyah, the Salafi group and Hizbut Tahrir. As stated by Ismail Yusanto, a spokesperson of Hibut Tahrir Indonesia (HTI) Islamic movements in Gadjah Mada University (UGM), for instance, have maintained a long rivalry for the control of the intra-campus organisations. When a particular movement has gained control over students in an institution, they would not invite in preachers other than their own. For instance, since the early 1990s, Yusanto has been given no opportunity to lecture to student gatherings. But more recently, after Jemaah Tarbiyah established its political party in 1998, he was often called on to give Islamic lectures in UGM because pragmatic members of Jemaah Tarbiyah have created the opportunity for Hizbut Tahrir in UGM to consolidate with them.[59]

In Surabaya, where three state secular universities operate, before the establishment of PK, most Islamic activities had been organised by Jemaah Tarbiyah activists. However, after the involvement of their members in politics, Salafi groups and Hizbut Tahrir have started to put down roots and have managed to lessen the role of Jemaah Tarbiyah in campus predication.[60] As before, many of the younger generation of Muslim students criticised HMI for its political inclinations and its competition to win political careers, now many students in campuses also have begun to criticise the obvious political inclinations of Jemaah Tarbiyah. *Halaqah* have been fuelled with a rhetoric that aims to defend the political decisions of PKS.[61]

However, for those students who are politically minded, memberships of Jemaah Tarbiyah brings opportunities to follow a political path that might lead them to occupy positions of leadership in PKS, or even to be elected members of parliament. In fact, many former student activists of Jemaah Tarbiyah have now been elected members at the district and national levels.

b) Senat Mahasiswa (SM)

Besides the Forum for Islamic Study, another set of important campus organizations currently under the control of Jemaah Tarbiyah is the Student Senate, *Senat Mahasiswa* (SM) of the secular state universities, which has become the Student Executive Body, *Badan Eksekutif Mahasiswa* (BEM). This body comprises the central leadership of students, organising and managing activities at the campus level that may involve student executive bodies at the faculty level in turn.

The Student Executive Body is very much influenced by the dynamics of national politics, in so far as it leads students to be directly involved in political action.

Its leadership is very important for certain students with aspirations of further political progress. It influences national politics, and the activists themselves, in the political games of the Indonesian leadership configurations. For this reason, there is competition to take over the leadership of this body, not only by the students, but the government also tries to exert its influence upon it. In fact, the elections of this body always entail political consequences at the level of campus and of the state.

The control exerted by the regime over campus life has succeeded in diminishing students' political and social activism and has led them to focus on academic activities and special interest study groups. Demonstrations against the development of the Kedung Ombo reservoir in 1989, for instance, was initiated by a study group that organised themselves under a committee of *Kelompok Solidaritas Korban Pembangunan Waduk Kedung Ombo* (Group in Solidarity with the Victims of the Kedung Ombo Reservoir Development).[62]

In 1990 the Minister of Education proposed a new form of student government called The Student Senate, Senat Mahasiswa (SM) under the control of the university rector. However, most student activists perceived this body as part of the regime's intervention on student activism. The rector's intrusive role within the activities of SM led students to organise their protests through ad hoc action committees, rather than using the formal organisation of the student senate.

Even though it no longer had a significant influence on national issues, the student senate was still an important organ of impact on internal student issues. Rivalry among activists of Islamist, Leftist, Nationalist and Christian fronts often occurred over recruitment and to secure their positions in SM. In the Faculty of Letters of the University of Indonesia (now the Humanities) during the 1990s, for example, activists of Jemaah Tarbiyah were prevented by the head of the student senate of the Faculty from forming an intra-campus organisation. This was because the committees of the senate were predominantly Leftists.[63] In fact, the Faculty of Humanities, UI, was a Leftist stronghold.[64] In order to be able to establish an Islamic organisation there, Jemaah Tarbiyah activists turned to working with other nationalists to run for the annual student senate elections.

When their candidate was elected by a decent majority, the activists of Jemaah Tarbiyah were allowed to establish an organisation on campus. In 1990 the Forum for Islamic Implementation and Study (Formasi) was formally established in the Faculty of Humanities of UI. In 1993, activists of Jemaah Tarbiyah, through Formasi, participated in the student elections and succeeded in placing their cadre as head of the student senate. Mustafa Kamal was elected as the head of SM and became the first Jemaah Tarbiyah cadre to hold such a position and in other faculties, a number of activists of Jemaah Tarbiyah were also elected as heads of the student senates. In 1994 a cadre of Jemaah Tarbiyah,

Zulkieflimansyah, was elected as the head of the student senate of UI, securing the highest position of the student senate at the university level.[65] Subsequently, most student senates of prestigious secular state universities such as ITB, IPB, UGM and many others have come under the control of Jemaah Tarbiyah.

The success of Jemaah Tarbiyah in securing positions in the student senates at the levels of faculty and university in certain prestigious universities forced nationalist and Leftist students to become marginalised. In 1996 the Forum for Communication of Student Senates in Jakarta, Forum Komunikasi Senat Mahasiswa Jakarta (FKSMJ) was established as a counter against the domination of Jemaah Tarbiyah activists. The aim of this organisation is to oppose formal organisations within campuses which prevent students from involvement in grassroots issues. This forum chiefly represents the student senates of the private universities, because of Jemaah Tarbiyah domination of the state universities.[66]

During the demonstrations in 1998 to topple Soeharto, when most of heads of student senates from state universities such as UI, IAIN Syahid, UGM, Unila,[67] Unair,[68] Unibraw,[69] IPB and ITB joined KAMMI to launch a huge demonstration in the Al-Azhar Mosque of Jakarta on 10 April 1998, members of FKSMJ were absent.[70]

c) Kesatuan Aksi Mahasiswa Muslim Indonesia (KAMMI)

Through intensive communication among campus predication activists in 1998, the activists of Jemaah Tarbiyah were able to establish an intercampus organization that played a significant role in the demonstrations calling for the resignation of President Soeharto. The Indonesian Muslim Student Action Union (KAMMI) was established in 29 March 1998 after activists of student Islamic predication held a tenth intercampus meeting under the Forum for the Coordination of Campus Predication Institution, Forum Silaturahmi Lembaga Dakwah Kampus (FSLDK) in Malang, East Java.

The decision to establish an intercampus organization was not formally endorsed at the FSLDK national conference in Malang, but certain members proposed it after the meeting closed. The coordinator of the centre for communication, region I, of FSLDK (Sumatra, West Java and DKI Jakarta), Mohammad Basyumi, issued a press release stating that KAMMI was not representative of FSLDK but an individual initiative.[71] The founding of KAMMI was announced by the head of LDK of the Muhammadiyah Malang University (UMM), not by the coordinator of national FSLDK. It seems that the rejection by some members of FSLDK was triggered by the fact that activists of Jemaah Tarbiyah had led the way to the establishment of KAMMI. Even though FSLDK has been dominated by Jemaah Tarbiyah, activists of FSLDK have represented various streams of Islamic groups, but in small numbers.[72] In fact, *mushallah* activists affiliated with Jemaah Tarbiyah have dominated the memberships of FSLDK.

At the level of student organisation, KAMMI has offered an alternative Islamic student networking that bridges the gap between the religious and secular campuses in Indonesia. Before the establishment of KAMMI in 1998, the absence of Islamic extra-campus organizations within the secular campuses led Muslim student activists to organise their activities independently. They developed contacts with some secular universities and did not attempt to engage with activists from Islamic higher education institutions. This fact that Islamist groups have developed on secular campuses but have few roots in the IAIN is the result of the absence of extra-campus organizations. KAMMI has represented a new Islamic student organization that was expected to take the initiative in developing closer relations with the Muslim activists of Islamic institutions. The former chairman of KAMMI, Fahri Hamzah, explained the three important tasks of KAMMI

> First, it would conduct networking in campus mosques throughout Indonesia. Second, the group would elicit support from Indonesian students who were studying outside of the country, in order to rally international support. Large Indonesian student populations in Germany and Japan in particular produced quite active KAMMI branches. Third, it would attempt to forge connections with other groups, including the students of rural Islamic boarding schools – traditionally an extremely important source of political power in Indonesia.[73]

In general, KAMMI has tended towards a centrist stance on issues related to student and Muslim affairs. For instance, when the Reformation movement in Indonesia had just began in May 1998, many student movements openly demanded the resignation of Soeharto. KAMMI, through its chairman, Fahri Hamzah took a softer line. Hamzah asserted that "if Soeharto changes and comes to the forefront of reform, it is not impossible that we would support him."[74] For KAMMI, the critical dimension of reform was not merely change of regime but rather moral, political and legal reform of the total system.[75] However, when the huge wave of students and national leaders, including Amien Rais, demanding Soeharto's resignation gained momentum, KAMMI supported the majority stance.

The following example also demonstrates KAMMI's middle position in responding to issues of political and religious controversy and of how KAMMI tried to place itself as a moral guard between radical action and moderation. On March 1999, when many Islamic groups, including PK, PBB, PPP and other Islamic organisations in Yogyakarta marched in the streets to condemn the tragedy of Ambon, which had caused the death of many Muslims, and to call for *jihad* to protect their fellow Muslims, KAMMI as an organization was absent.[76] Even though most of its members joined the march, the organization did not come to an agreement to show its formal support for any *jihad* that involved military action. Instead, KAMMI initiated a rehabilitation team to support the Muslim refugees by providing essential supplies.[77]

Since most KAMMI activists are also members of Jemaah Tarbiyah, their relations with PKS are obvious. In many cases, even though it claims to be an independent organisation,[78] KAMMI serves as the student wing of PKS. It also provides opportunities for its activists to pursue political careers. Most former chairmen of KAMMI hold important positions of leadership in PKS and some have even been elected members of the national parliament. Fahri Hamzah, the first chairman of KAMMI and Andi Rahmad, his successor, have been PKS representatives in the national parliament (2004-2009) whilst Haryo Setyoko, a general secretary became a deputy general secretary of the Central Board of PKS (2000-2005).

Nonetheless, KAMMI does not always try to follow the policy of PKS. In responding to the issue of the government's hike in oil prices in 2004, KAMMI displayed a different opinion. In the beginning, PKS through its representative in the national parliament opposed government policy, considering that the negative impacts on the little people were bigger than the benefits.[79] During the *Rapat Paripurna* (general meeting) between DPR and the government on 14 March 2004, PKS withdrew its previous decision to oppose the government's proposal.[80] One of the members of PKS, Nursanita Nasution even blatantly stated that PKS would have never accept a policy to raise the oil prices for the people.[81]

However PKS then changed its stance. After a long and heavy discussion in parliament, PKS dropped its decision and supported the proposal of the government, with some notes that the government was required to ensure that compensation funds for petro-fuels (*Bahan Bakar Minyak*, BBM) should be directed towards reducing the economic burdens of the people. In addition, PKS demanded that the government take strict measures to solve big coruption cases.[82] In contrast, KAMMI took a different direction and continued to pressure the government through demonstrations. KAMMI expressed its disappointment towards PKS for its ambiguity in supporting the people's interests. KAMMI complained to PKS during the DPR meeting discussing the issue of oil prices and carried in a free-range chicken as a symbolic gift, in the hope that PKS would not act "chicken" (*ayam sayur*).[83]

Jemaah Tarbiyah activists had drawn public attention to the condition of the Indonesian people after the resignation of Soeharto in 1998. Cadres of Jemaah Tarbiyah who were the heads of university student senates and Islamic intra-campus organisations, together with the activists in KAMMI, had launched demonstrations to topple Soeharto. They also collaborated with other student groups in guarding the agenda of the political reformation of Indonesia. However, the cooperation between Islamist groups and other student groups did not last long after most members of KAMMI and its affiliates showed their support of

B.J Habibie to replace Soeharto, whereas nationalist and Leftist student groups rejected him.

In the event, the end of the Soeharto regime changed the orientation of student activism. Students have started to re-establish their connections with political parties and have opened up their political opportunities, while many parties make intensive approaches to student activists. The secular campuses have become more dynamic in terms of competition and rivalry among various religious and political interests, in order to secure important positions within the student governing bodies. The success of the activists of Jemaah Tarbiyah in securing central leaderships of student senates has strengthened the role of the secular campuses as a source of political caderisation. Rama Pratama, a former head of the Student Executive Body of UI and Fahri Hamzah, a former chairman of the Indonesian Muslim Student Action Union (KAMMI) were among the leaders of a huge demonstration against Soeharto in 1998, and have subsequently been elected members of the legislature of the Prosperous Justice Party.

C. Campus Islam as a Source of Political Recruitment

The popularity of Jemaah Tarbiyah in the state universities is the result of its intensive and massive *dakwah* predication. In contrast to Martin van Bruinessen's suggestion that most of its activists are enrolled in the faculties of science and technology, the core activists of Jemaah Tarbiyah are dominated by students from the Humanities and Social Sciences, as well as from Islamic studies.[84] The first triumph of Jemaah Tarbiyah on campus was its success in winning the general student elections in the Faculty of Humanites, the University of Indonesia in 1993 when Mustafa Kamal, now the Member of Parliament for PKS (2004-2009) was elected head of the student senate. The following year, Zulkieflimansyah, an economics student, was elected head of the student senate at the university level in UI. Zulkieflimansyah's successors were Kamaruddin, Selamat Nurdin and Rama Pratama. Both Kamaruddin and Nurdin were students in the Faculty of Political Science whilst Pratama was from the Faculty of Economics. As a general principle, in order to secure the position of student senate at level of faculty and university, the candidate must win thousands of student votes. It is a mark of the success of Islamic predication by Jemaah Tarbiyah activists in the Faculties of Humanities and Political Science in recruiting members that enabled them to win the elections.

In addition, pioneers of Islamic predication in UI who have also gone on to occupy important positions on the PKS national committees, some of them being elected as members of legislatures, also graduated from the Faculties of Social Science and the Humanities. Among them are Yusuf Supendi, Al-Muzammil Yusuf and Mahfudz Sidiq. They have become influential figures in the current PKS leadership (2005-2010). Sidiq is the chairman of the PKS faction in the national parliament and former head of department of caderisation. Caderisation is the most important department in the committee of PKS because of its vital role in ensuring the recruitment process within both Jemaah Tarbiyah and PKS. Yusuf was the first president of PKS (2003). Both vice chairmen of the PKS faction in the national parliament of DPR RI, Fahri Hamzah and Zulkielfimansyah, graduated from the Faculty of Economics.

The general trend within the Islamic parties and parties of Muslim constituents shows that most cadres of DPR RI (2004-2009) come from the secular universities rather than Islamic institutions. The percentages are as follows. PPP - among 58 members, 34 persons (59%) graduated from secular universities and 21 persons (36%) graduated from Islamic institutions. PKB - among 52 members, 28 persons (54%) graduated from secular universities and 22 persons (42%) graduated from Islamic institutions. PKS has the same figures - among 45 members, 23 persons (51%) are from secular universities and 18 persons (40%) are from Islamic institutions. For PAN, PBB and PBR, the percentage of secular university graduates is even more significant. Secular university graduates for PAN, PBR and PBB are 43 persons (83%), 11 persons (85%) and 9 persons (75%) respectively, while Islamic university graduates are 6 (11%), 0 (0%) and 3 (25%). The role of the secular universities as sources of political candidates is still unshakeable. Overall, the percentages of members of the national parliament for the above six parties who graduated from secular universities and Islamic higher education institutions are 64% (148 persons) and 30% (70 persons) respectively, while the remaining 6% (14 persons) are high school graduates.

Table 4: Educational Background of Members of DRR RI (2004-2009)

Education	PPP		PKB		PAN		PKS		PBR		PBB	
PTU[85]	34	59%	28	54%	43	83%	23	51%	11	85%	9	75%
PTA[86]	21	36%	22	42%	6	11%	18	40%	0	0%	3	25%
High School	3	5%	2	4%	3	6%	4	9%	2	15%	0	0%
Total	58	100%	52	100%	52	100%	45	100%	13	100%	12	100%

The transformation of Jemaah Tarbiyah from an informal religious movement into the open political party, PKS, brought significant changes in the composition of its membership, its strategy and style of leadership. While the first Jemaah Tarbiyah activists were represented by the PK, further development manifested itself in PKS. In addition, activists coming from secular campuses and representing FSI, KAMMI and SM have contributed to the political directions of PKS. In order to broaden its appeal, PKS has transformed its Islamic aspirations into a more realistic agenda. The rich experience of its activists from campus milieus has helped PKS to negotiate with the political realities of Indonesia. The distinctively different modes of performance between PK and PKS are proof evidence of the way in which activists of Jemaah Tarbiyah have prepared themselves to be involved within the grey areas of politics that are totally removed from religious ideals. As a result the split has often occurred within activists of PKS rather than PK. Many cases in some regions in Indonesia have proved this trend. For instance, in Depok, West Java, a member of legislative from PKS, Saleh Martapermana, allied himself with the party rival, Badrul Kamal during the district election in 2005 and PKS already chose Nurmahmudi Ismail as its own candidate.[87] He was sacked as a member of the District Parliament (DPRD II) in June 2006.[88]

In general, the activists of campus Islam within the formation of the PKS leadership have demonstrated moderate views in responding to the position of Islam vis-à-vis the state and the struggle for Islamic ideals. Their experience within student politics and government in the past has helped them to position themselves in responding to national issues of pluralism and diversity. Based on their experience on campus they are divided into three streams: the generations of the Forum Studi Islam, of student senate and of KAMMI respectively. My observations on the distinctive performances of PK and PKS indicate the significance of these activists of campus Islam.

The character of the militant cadres of Jemaah Tarbiyah may be seen in PK profiles. Most activists of PK directly experienced the political constraint and hostility of the Soeharto regime during the 1980s. Observing PK's seven representatives in DPR between 1999-2004, it appears that most of its cadres were of the first stratum of Jemaah Tarbiyah, mainly former activists of the Forum for Islamic Studies on campus, such as Irwan Prayitno, Yusuf Supendi and Zirlyrosa Jamil, and of the modernist student organizations (PII) such as Mashadi and Mutammimul Ula. There were also cadres from a traditionalist background, such as Nurmahmudi Ismail and Roqib Abdul Kadir.

In contrast, the configuration of the elite of PKS is represented by more moderate figures, the generation of the 1990s, who have not encountered political repression. They began their political activities during an era of political openness, since the 1990s. Their attitudes towards national issues and pluralism are more open. They are not only able to maintain good communication with other groups, including non-Islamic organizations, but they are also more pragmatic in their approach towards politics and *dakwah*. More former activists of intra-campus organizations are remarkably accommodated in DPR. Figures such as Mahfudz Sidiq, Al Muzammil Yusuf, Untung Wahono, Nursanita Nasution, RB Suryama, Chairul Anwar, Agus Purnomo, Andi Salahuddin and Idris Lutfi were leading activists of Forum Studi Islam in the 1980s, whilst other new comers are mainly former activists of Student Executive Bodies and KAMMI in the 1990s, such as Zulkieflimansyah, Mustafa Kamal, Rama Pratama, Fahri Hamzah and Andi Rahmat.

The composition of the general membership is another issue. PK owed its main support to its core cadres and their families. There was little influence over non-*santri* families in society. Their main strongholds were the regions where Islamic parties of the past, particularly Masyumi, had gained support and enjoyed its triumphs. These are West Java, DKI Jakarta and certain parts of Sumatra. At the level of leadership, the main players were ideologists and the intelligentsia. Yet in the mean time, PKS has broadened its appeal to garner popular support. Another grouping, not core cadres, but mainly of the pious middle class and urban poor have given tremendous support. PKS now reflects different kinds of social affiliations. While the pious middle class can also be accepted within differently constituted elite circles, the urban poor have become the main constituents of PKS. This is because many former campus activists have begun to "colour" the political directions of PKS. Their participation in student politics has served to enrich PKS's strategies in promoting the party to the Indonesian public in general.

A lack of financial and facility support was once the common picture of PK. It used Islamic institutions and mosques to which its cadres were affiliated to run the party. It also used cadres' houses as party offices in many areas. The public who attended its political campaigns in the 1999 general elections were in the main ideologically in tune with the ideas of Jemaah Tarbiyah. Female participants wore the headscarf and rarely came from lay, or non-observant, households. On the other hand, the campaigns of PKS were far more attractive. They rented convention halls in hotels and avoided using the mosques. In terms of financial support, PKS is far more prosperous than PK. Many of the elite, public figures and other high-placed members of society have attended its campaigns. Even more surprising, people with no interest in religion, including certain actresses, have lent their support. In Surabaya, women prostitutes from surrounding localities in the city attended the PKS campaigns.[89]

In keeping with its policy of Islamisation, Jemaah Tarbiyah made strict Islamic demands through PK, so that its interests as an Islamic party were heard loudly in the 1999 elections. Although PK was ready to join with a non-religious party, the National Mandate Party, Partai Amanah Nasional (PAN), its motivation for this was more for the fact that the chairman of PAN, Amien Rais was so well known as a Muslim leader and activist. In contrast, PKS tends to show its non-religious orientation by favouring professional organizations and in its demands for economic, political and social reform. Its Islamic values are presented as much as possible within activities that are closer to the day-to-day lives of the people. For PKS, the implementation of *shariah* laws need not necessarily be proposed through its campaigns or by a call for the upholding of the *shariah* by the government. It is more important to make an effort to urge people in general about the importance of the *shariah* and for them to implement it in their daily lives with full understanding and consciousness. (A further discussion of this issue will be given in Chapter VII.)

Since the secular campuses in Indonesia are still considered as to be backbones of PKS caderisation, it seems they will continue to play a significant role in the future. Their ability to control almost all strategic positions of the student bodies is certainly an inspiration of the possibility of reaching their goal to Islamise government. However, the external challenges of the social, cultural and political realities of Indonesia compel them to play in accommodative ways to promote their ideas of Islamisation. They have often demonstrated a readiness to negotiate to secure their position on a structural level in order to exert an influence on the state. Interestingly, all of these accommodative approaches within religious and political activities find their justification in the teachings and ideas of Hasan al-Bana, the founder of the Muslim Brothers in Egypt. Thus, the relation of Jemaah Tarbiyah of Indonesia and the Muslim Brothers of Egypt will be elaborated in our next chapter.

ENDNOTES

[1] Quoted from Mahfudz Sidiq, *Risalah Dakwah Tulabiyah: Kajian Komprehensif Manhaj Dakwah Tarbiyah di Kalangan Pelajar dan Mahasiswa* (Jakarta: Pustaka Tarbiatuna, 2002), 13.

[2] Sidiq, *Risalah Dakwah Tulabiyah,* 3.

[3] The extra-campus organizations that comprised KAMMI were HMI, GMNI, SEMMI, SOMAL, PELMASI, and MAPANTJAS. See Arbi Sanit, "Gerakan Mahasiswa 1970-1973: Pecahnya Bulan Madu Politik," in *Penakluk Rezim Orde Baru Gerakan Mahasiswa '98* (Pustaka Sinar Harapan:Jakarta, 1999), 45.

[4] See Abdul Mun'im DZ, "Gerakan Mahasiswa 1966 di Tengah Pertarungan Politik Elit," in *Penakluk Rezim Orde Baru,* 41.

[5] Edward Aspinall, "Political Opposition and the Transition from the Authoritarian Rule: the Case of Indonesia" (Ph.D., diss., the Australian National University, 2000), 160.

[6] Generally student organisations are divided into intra- and extra- campus organisations. Intra-campus refers to student organisations established in campuses with no organisational links with other organisations off campus, while the extra-campus groups have their own offices outside campus but also establish branches on campus.

[7] See Arbi Sanit, "Gerakan Mahasiswa 1970-1973", 48.

[8] Ibid.

[9] Ibid., 52-53.

[10] See Richard Gordon Kraince, "The Role of Islamic Student Activists in Divergent Movements for Reform during Indonesia's Transition from Authoritarian Rule, 1998-2001" (Ph.D. diss., Ohio University: 2003), 89.

[11] Ibid., 91

[12] Ibid., 96.

[13] Interview with Nurmahmudi Ismail, Depok, 8 May 2003. See also Harold Crouch, "Islam and Politics in Indonesia," in Politics, Diplomacy and Islam: Four Case Studies (Canberra: the Australian National University, 1986), 21.

[14] Irene H. Gayatri, "Arah Baru Perlawanan Gerakan Mahasiswa 1989-1993," in *Penakluk Rezim Orde Baru,* 65.

[15] Ibid.

[16] Ibid.

[17] Interview with Mustafa Kamal, Jakarta, 23 December 2005.

[18] Azyumardi Azra, "Kelompok Sempalan di Kalangan Mahasiswa PTU: Anatomi Sosio Historis" in *Dinamika Pemikiran Islam di Perguruan Tinggi: Wacana tentang Pendidikan Agama Islam* (Jakarta: Logos, 1999), 224.

[19] Interview with Muhammad Irwan, Surabaya, 12 March 2003.

[20] Ibid.

[21] See "Comparing Islamic Leftist and Rightist," *The Jakarta Post,* 21 September 2002.

[22] Interview with Muhammad Arif, Padang, 19 June 2003.

[23] Mahfudz Sidiq, *KAMMI dan Pergulatan Reformasi:Kiprah Politik Aktifis Dakwah Kampus dalam Perjuangan Demokratisasi di Tengah Gelombang Krisis Nasional Multidimensi* (Solo: Era Intermedia, 2003), 72

[24] Jemaah Tarbiyah activists believe that in order to be successful in carrying on the *dakwah*, the support of qualified cadres is crucial. See Ahmad Satori Ismail, *Tarbiyah dan Perubahan Sosial* (Jakarta: Pustaka Tarbiatuna, 2003), 9.

[25] Azra, "Kelompok Sempalan di Kalangan Mahasiswa PTU," 224.

[26] See Sidiq, *KAMMI dan Pergulatan Reformasi*, 113.

[27] Interview with Marfendi, Padang, 23 June 2003.

[28] *Ulumul Qur'an* 2 no. V (1994), 86-94. For further details also see *Gatra*, 7 October 1995.

[29] V.S. Naipaul, *Among the Believers: an Islamic Journey* (New York: Vintage Book, 1982), 373.

[30] Nurhayati, Djamas "Gerakan Kaum Muda Islam Masjid Salman" in *Gerakan Islam Kontemporer di Indonesia* (Jakarta: Ikapi, 1996), 265. Djamas suspected that Imaduddin's first interaction with MB ideas was during the time that he was actively involved in the International Islamic Federation of Student Organizations (IIFSO). However, long before he held a high position in the IIFSO, Imaduddin was active in Islamic propagation during his first departure in 1963 to the US where he made contact with the Muslim Student Association (MSA), the Muslim Brothers-influenced student movement in the USA. See *Muslim Executive and Expatriate Newsletter* 3 no. 1 (2000). See www.islamic-path.org.

[31] *Ulumul Qur'an* 2 no. V (1994), 86-94.

[32] *Muslim Executive and Expatriate Newsletter* 3 no. 1 (2000).

[33] Ibid.

[34] Naipaul, *Among the Believers*, 363.

[35] Ibid. 377.

[36] Ibid., 364.

[37] Ibid., 374.

[38] ITB was considered as centre for Islamic revival and accused by the government of being a source of Islamic radicalism during the 1970s and 1980s.

[39] Interview with Mustafa Kamal, Depok, 11 June 2003.

[40] Sidiq, *KAMMI dan Pergulatan Reformasi*, 71.

[41] Djamas "Gerakan Kaum Muda Islam Masjid Salman," 265

[42] Interview with Abu Ridha, Jakarta, 11 October 2003.

[43] Ibid.

[44] Although the bans on lectures and radio programs against the aims of the state were repealed in 1978 and there was a change towards the "normalisation" of the people and religion in that year, this regulation was used as a new stage in the surveillance of the activities of *dakwah Islam*. However, as long as religious activities did not turn into political criticism or agitation against the regime, they were allowed to be held.

[45] Merlyna Lim, "Cyber-Civic Space in Indonesia: From Panopticon to Pandemonium?" *IDPR* 24 no. 4 (2002), 367.

[46] See Sidiq, *KAMMI dan Pergulatan Reformasi*, 113.

[47] The moving of the University of Indonesia (UI) in 1987 from Jakarta to Depok near Bogor, for instance, represented the government's aim to prevent students from engaging in dissident political activities by weakening the role of the Dewan Mahahiswa as centres. Instead, the activities were rolled back into the faculties because of the distance of one faculty from another.

[48] Sidiq, *KAMMI dan Pergulatan Reformasi*, 113.

[49] Interview with Nurmahmudi Ismail, Depok, 8 May 2003.

[50] Interview, anonymous, Depok, 9 May 2003.

[51] Martin van Bruinessen, "Genealogies of Islamic Radicalism in Post-Suharto Indonesia", *South East Asia Research* 10 no. 2 (2002), 133.

[52] Hidayat Nurwahid, the former President of PKS and the Chairperson of MPR RI emphasized that in the 1980s he did not reject Pancasila but he opposed the imposition of the Sole of Principle. See *Tempo*, 19-25 June 2006.

[53] See Ramage Douglas, *Politics in Indonesia: Democracy, Islam and the Ideology of Tolerance* (New York, Routledge, 1995), 24-31.
[54] See Abdul Aziz, "Meraih Kesempatan dalam Situasi Mengambang: Studi Kasus Kelompok Keagamaan Mahasiswa Univesitas Indonesia," *Penamas* no. 20 (1995), 3.
[55] See Rifki Rosyad, "A Quest for True Islam: A Study of the Islamic Resurgence Movements among the Youth in Bandung, Indonesia" (Master thesis, the Australian National University, 1995), 56.
[56] See Ismail Yusanto, "LDK: Antara Visi, Misi dan Realitas Sejarah Perkembangannya," *www.fsldk.20m.com*.
[57] See "Banyak Jalan Menuju Kehidupan Islami," *Suara Hidayatullah*, August 2000.
[58] Ibid.
[59] Interview with Ismail Yusanto, Canberrra, August 2004.
[60] Interview, anonymous, Surabaya, 24 May 2005.
[61] Interview, anonymous, Surabaya, 12 March 2003.
[62] Edward Aspinall, "Students and the Military: Regime Friction and Civilian Dissent in the Late Suharto Period," *Indonesia* 59 (April 1995), 32.
[63] Interview with Mustafa Kamal, Jakarta, 13 December 2005.
[64] Ibid.
[65] Ibid.
[66] See *Kontan Online*, 16 November 1998.
[67] University of Lampung, Sumatra.
[68] University of Airlangga, Surabaya, East Java.
[69] University of Brawijaya, Malang, East Java
[70] Muridan S. Widjojo and Moch. Nurhasim, "Organisasi Gerakan Mahasiswa 1998: Upaya Rekonstruksi," in *Penakluk Rezim Orde Baru*, 366.
[71] Sidiq, *KAMMI dan Pergulatan Reformasi*, 104-105.
[72] Interview, anonymous, Jakarta, 23 May 2003.
[73] See Kraince, "The Role of Islamic Student Activists," 169-170.
[74] Ibid., 183
[75] Ibid., 184
[76] Ibid., 238
[77] Ibid., 240
[78] See "Profile Kesatuan Aksi Mahasiswa Muslim Indonesia," *Kammi.or.id*.
[79] See a press release issued by FPKS, 4 Maret 2004
[80] See a press release issued by FPKS, 15 Maret 2004.
[81] *Keadilan Online*, 18 Maret 2005.
[82] See press release of PKS, 21 Maret 2005
[83] See "*Tertunda, Pencarian Dana Kompensasi BBM*," *Kompas*, 8 March 2005.
[84] Martin van Bruinessen, "Post-Suharto Muslim Engagements with Civil Society and Democratisation," in *Indonesia in Transition: Rethinking 'Civil Society', 'Religion', and 'Crisis,'* (Yogyakarta: Pustaka Pelajar, 2004), 52.
[85] *Perguruan Tinggi Umum* or Secular University
[86] Perguruan Tinggi Agama or Islamic Higher Education
[87] See "PKS Ancam Recall Anggotanya," *Jawa Pos*, 17 April 2005.
[88] See "Anggota DPRD Depok dari PKS Dipecat," *Kompas*, 6 June 2006.
[89] See "Belasan PSK Hadiri Kampanye PKS," *Jawa Pos*, 18 March 2004.

Chapter 5: Indonesian and Egyptian Brothers

In the early morning before dawn, a congregation of prayer gathered in the Mosque of Arif Rahman Hakim, on the campus of the University Indonesia in Central Jakarta. After the obligatory dawn prayers were done, the congregation started to recite *dhikr,* another collection of prayers - something that would never happen in a mosque associated with modernist Muslim groups. It was like the prayers regularly recited together by members of Nahdatul Ulama but it differed in its content. This particular collection is called *al-ma'thurat,* compiled by Hasan al-Banna, the founder of the Society of Muslim Brothers in Egypt.[1]

Dhikr, or *wadifah* is well-known among followers of the Sufi mystical orders, the *tariqah,* which are the preserve of traditionalist Muslims in Indonesia. In the Sufi tradition there are three central institutions: *murshid* (the teacher), *salik* (the student) and *suluk* (the ritual). A student of the *tariqah* has to follow his master and practise a specific ritual, or *dhikr,* and the student's submission to his master is identified by his commitment to practice *dhikr.* Currently, the *suluk al-ma'thurat* of Hasan al-Banna has become popular; the members of an Islamic group called Darut Tauhid in Bandung, led by a young charismatic leader, Abdullah Gymnastiar, also practise *al-ma'thurat.*[2] It is undeniable that the Muslim Brothers have had a significant influence in Indonesia. Uniquely, the respect given to the master and the adoption of his practice and ideas does not necessarily to lead to organisational and hierarchical links within the Sufi tradition. Each new group may develop into an autonomous order and maintain its own agenda. This is the case of the Muslim Brothers in Indonesia.

The Society of the Muslim Brothers (*al-Ikhwan al-Muslimun*) is the most phenomenal group among Islamic movements in the world because of the movement's ability to expand its ideas and influence worldwide. Even though in its country of origin, Egypt, the Society has faced harsh political repression that limits its growth as a significant political force, it has, by contrast, grown quickly in other parts of the Muslim world. Indonesia, as the largest Muslim country, is not immune from this phenomenon. This chapter tries to analyse the relationship between the Egyptian Society of Muslim Brothers and Jemaah Tarbiyah in Indonesia. I will argue that ideologically and religiously both movements have an obvious connection. The influence of Sufism and political constraints encountered by the central movement in Egypt have shaped the nature of organisational interaction with its international offshoots. Indonesia provides a case study of this process.

This chapter also explores the local role of Indonesian Muslims in accommodating international influences and combining these to shape the face of Jemaah Tarbiyah. Rather than viewing the phenomenon of Jemaah Tarbiyah in Indonesia as a monolithic movement, it is better to focus on different religious orientations and social groups which make up its membership. In doing so, the heterogenous nature of the movement will become more evident. For the purpose of analysis, I categorise the membership of Jemaah Tarbiyah into three main variants: revivalist, modernist and traditionalist.[3]

A. Basic Organisational Principles of Jemaah Tarbiyah

Tarbiyah is an Arabic word and meaning "education." In the present specific context, this term has been used to name a particular movement, *Harakah Islamiyah* (Islamic Movement) in Indonesia that has developed a process in understanding Islam called *Tarbiyah*. It is also known interchangeably as Jemaah Tarbiyah (the Society of Tarbiyah) or Gerakan Tarbiyah (the Tarbiyah Movement). Jemaah Tarbiyah developed its influence among students in the state secular universities, in campuses in Java and in various universities in the Outer Islands, such as Sumatra, Sulawesi, Maluku and Kalimantan.

The Jemaah Tarbiyah focuses its activities on Islamic predication through *tarbiyah* activities. *Tarbiyah* refers to a practice of spiritual supervision carried out by a spiritual leader of a Sufi group, the *murshid*. *Tarbiyah* aims to cultivate and enhance the spiritual quality of pupils under the guidance of their teacher. This term was adopted by Hasan al-Banna, not only for spiritual enhancement but it was also developed as way to transfer Islamic knowledge and other skills needed by his followers.[4] *Tarbiyah* was manifested in small religious circles, or *usrah*, which al-Banna considered to be an essential tool in guiding Muslims to live better in accordance with the teachings of Islam.[5] This is why, from the beginning, Jemaah Tarbiyah has focussed its programs on cultivating theology (*tawhid*), moral issues (*akhlaq*) and thought (*fikrah*) in the process of gaining popularity among students who have become disillusioned with the politics of their times.

According to this group, Indonesian Muslims in general are "ignorant" about Islam (*al-jahl 'an al-islam*) and they need to be educated through specific *tarbiyah* training.[6] In order to strengthen the relationships among its members, *tarbiyah* employs the following programs: *usrah* (family), *katibah* (gatherings of *usrah*), *rihlah* (recreation), *mukhayyam* (camping expeditions), *daurah* (intellectual training and Islamic workshops), *nadwah* (seminars) and *muktamar* (international seminars). These activities are held regularly and involve most of the members.

Jemaah Tarbiyah developed since the mid-1980s through small study groups in campuses, called *halaqah*.[7] *Halaqah* literally means "circle" or more specifically refers to a small religious gathering in which a teacher sits surrounded by 5-10 students. In practice, the term *halaqah* has the same meaning as *usrah*, "family." However, for political reasons, *halaqah* is more widely known among the members of Jemaah Tarbiyah and is often distinguished from *usrah*. During the mid-1980s the Indonesian government often referred to certain radical movements in Indonesia that were associated with violent activities by the term *usrah*, therefore Jemaah Tarbiyah avoided its use,[8] preferring instead terms like *halaqah* or *liqa*, "meeting".[9] As was explained by Hidayat Nurwahid, a former chairman of PKS and the Chairman of MPR RI, the term *usrah* had negative connotations since it was used to refer to subversive groups.[10] Certain other figures of PKS have also distinguished themselves from the *usrah* groups of the 1980s

> The ones who name their groups "usrah" indeed were groups of the so-called Islamic State of Indonesia, Negara Islam Indonesia (NII) and the Indonesian Islamic Army, Tentara Islam Indonesia (TII). We have no association with them.[11]

It is plausible that the *usrah* model was widely applied by a more radical Islam during the 1980s, since it was an effective method of disseminating ideas, establishing secret religious clubs, particularly during the years of political suppression of Islamic movements which posed an ideological challenge to the regime[12].

However, *usrah*, both in Muslim Brothers and the Jemaah Tarbiyah texts, is specifically considered to be the central means of conducting Islamic predication and education. In establishing a small "family" unit, solidarity and a sense of togetherness among members are developed. In addition, through this organised training, it is hoped that members will know (*ta'aruf*), understand (*tafahum*)) and support (*tafa'ul*) one another.[13] In a practical sense, the *tarbiyah* model was and is still regarded by proponents of the society of the Muslim Brothers as an ideal method to develop direct interaction among members that enables the process of changing individual thought and behaviour in keeping with the group's ideals.[14]

Through *tarbiyah*, it is believed that close and strong relations between members and leaders, as well as among members, grow. A senior member usually acts as mentor (*murabbi*) with the important duties of training and disciplining junior members. This kind of religious circle has proved itself to be a good medium for indoctrination and the dissemination of the group's ideals to Islamise the individual, family, community and the state.[15] Jemaah Tarbiyah focuses on establishing models of individual morality, of ideal family life, of strong community and of functional institutions, all of which should be in line with the teachings of Islam.

B. Intellectual and Religious Connections

The nature of the Egyptian Muslim Brothers as an international movement is apparent in its wide spread beyond Egypt. Research findings on the Society published in the early 1950s presented important analysis of the spread of Muslim Brothers-associated movements throughout the Middle East and wider Asia. Richard P. Mitchell indicated the existence of brothers in Syria, Palestine and other parts of the Middle East, while an Egyptian scholar, Ishak Musa Husaini also pointed out the tendency of the movement to organise international networks around the world.[16] Today, the society of Muslim Brothers is among the most influential groups in the Arab world and other Muslim countries.

Many supporters of the Muslim Brothers themselves acknowledge the existence of their movement throughout the world, in more than seventy countries in the Middle East, Asia, Europe and the United States.[17] Most local offshoots are committed to its central figures and doctrines but retain their own administrations and organizations. Therefore, the influence and existence of the Muslim Brothers in Indonesia is not an isolated phenomenon.

According to Hilmi Aminuddin, head of the Consultative Council of PKS (2004-2009) the adoption of a model with reference to the Muslim Brothers is an effort to institutionalise the unity of faith (*aqidah*) and thought (*fikrah*); in this, the name of the movement is not important.[18] Some Muslim Brothers-associated movements take the form of legal political parties, such as in Jordan, Yemen and Indonesia, while many others have formed more social organizations. In the case of Indonesia, a Muslim Brothers scholar based in Qatar, Yusuf Qardawi has stated in one of its books that the Jemaah Tarbiyah-backed party is part of the Muslim Brothers mission in Egypt.[19] However, the community of Jemaah Tarbiyah itself has never claimed organisational links with the Muslim Brothers. Hidayat Nurwahid, a former president of PKS said, "we don't want to claim be identical to the Muslim Brothers because this movement is so great. We are afraid to claim it as it may jeopardise the image of the Muslim Brothers. We just work for the sake of Islam."[20]

Nevertheless, although the members of the Jemaah Tarbiyah do not explicitly claim to be a part of the Muslim Brothers, their way in conducting Islamic training and their religious orientation are similar.[21] Nor do they try to deny their association with the Muslim Brothers. According to Rahmat Abdullah, not all organizations affiliated with Muslim Brothers use the formal name of *al-Ikhwan al-Muslimun*, for the name does not mean anything if they do not comply with the genuine character of the Muslim Brothers. On the other hand, there are many associations that prefer to name themselves something else, even while the essence of their struggle is the same.[22] For Abdullah, the name is not important, what matter is the essence of the organization, which must be in accordance with the movement's ideals.[23]

As the Muslim Brothers are not recognized, indeed are repressed by the government of Egypt, the movement has turned to spreading its international network.[24] In 1954, under the regime of Gamal Abd al-Nasir, hundreds of Muslim Brothers activists were jailed, its six leaders were executed and finally it was outlawed.[25] Nasir continued to suppress Muslim Brothers activities, to arrest thousands of people and hundreds were sentenced and tortured. Three leading activists, including Sayyid Qutb, were hanged in Cairo in 1966. In 1971, when Anwar Sadat came to power he released the Brothers from jail. But fearing similar repression by the Sadat regime, many activists left Egypt. In fact, in 1982, Sadat repeated what his predecessor had done to the Muslim Brothers. He ordered the arrest of hundreds of its members and its leaders.[26]

It was through certain activists of the Muslim Brothers who found asylum in Saudi Arabia and Western countries that an international organisation developed. Muhammad Qutb fled to Saudi Arabia while Sa'id Ramadhan went to Switzerland. Mustafa Masyhur, after his release in 1971, went to Germany and organised international representatives for the Muslim Brothers in exile.[27] In 1996, Masyhur was elected as supreme leader of the Muslim Brothers in Egypt. All of the local offshoots, either in the Middle East, Europe, United States or Asia are theoretically under Egyptian leadership.[28] However, in practice they develop autonomous agendas depending on their local social, political and cultural conditions.

Moreover, observing the models employed to spread their ideas, which are predominantly similar to those of the Muslim Brothers in Egypt, it appears that Jemaah Tarbiyah has emphasised its international and global orientation rather than local interests. Its adoption of the Muslim Brothers ideas and religious practices make it distinct from existing Islamic organizations and groups in Indonesia. The frequent use of Arabic words, (instead of English or even local languages) in the fields of politics, economics and daily activities are some indication of its distinctiveness. These terms, such as *siyasah* (politics), *musharakah* (cooperation), *hizb* (party), *iqtisad* (economics), *ma'ishah* (income) and *rabat* (benefit) are common. The most popular term used by Jemaah Tarbiyah is *ikhwan* (brothers) which has two forms, *ikhwan* (brothers) and *akhawat* (sisters).[29]

So international influences on Jemaah Tarbiyah have been evident, though they have not entirely overridden local dynamics. Of course, the international dimension is more apparent than the local when we consider the distinct ideas of the movement. A careful study of the intellectual formation of Jemaah Tarbiyah reveals a process of adoption of new ideas quite different from current trends in existing Islamic parties and organizations in Indonesia.

Nonetheless, the ability to accommodate an international idea and to combine it with its Indonesian context has made Jemaah Tarbiyah far from a totally foreign movement. It has not broken its connections with older traditions. Often accommodation is made of some traditional religious practice in order to maintain links with mass organisations such as Nahdlatul Ulama (NU) and Muhammadiyah. Muslikh Abdul Karim, an activist of Jemaah Tarbiyah who spent years attending religious trainings at the traditional NU *Pesantren* of Langitan, East Java and gained his doctoral degree in theology from the University of King Abdul Aziz, Saudi Arabia, described his attitude toward his previous association, NU

> When we came to Saudi Arabia we were different from our fellow Indonesian Muslims. In Saudi Arabia, most students are either sponsored by M. Natsir of DDII or M. Syaikhu of NU. Such students keep their own religious identity. Those who were affiliated with NU stay with NU members. We did not do such thing. We were about fifteen students, and we had left our identities behind [NU or Muhammadiyah] because we took them off at the Jakarta airport. We were sponsored by the Institute of Arabic and Islamic Studies of Ibnu Saud [LIPIA] in Jakarta. We decided not to identify ourselves either with NU or Muhammadiyah. But we still practised our traditions as NU members.[30]

However, it was not only Jemaah Tarbiyah that was influenced by the Muslim Brothers movement; other Islamic movements during 1980s also had connections either directly or indirectly with them. This influence was mostly received through printed media and organizational relations and there were also some individuals who built direct connections with the Muslim Brothers leaders. For example, the Malaysian Youth of Islam, Angkatan Belia Islam Malaysia (ABIM) was the best channel in the dissemination of Muslim Brothers' ideas through its relations with international Muslim youth organizations. Some Indonesian youth organizations, such as HMI and PII attended an international meeting organised by ABIM.[31] Bruinessen has argued that ABIM served as a trans-national agent connecting HMI with the Muslim Brothers and the Pakistani Jamaat Islami; however, the role of Indonesian figures such as Imaduddin, a lecturer in the Institute of Technology, Bandung, in transmitting Muslim Brothers' ideas to ABIM in the 1980s is another example. Imaduddin became the mentor of ABIM during his visit in Malaysia. Then, in 1983, the leader of PII, Mutammimul Ula, attended an international workshop held by IIFSO in Malaysia, where he was attracted to the *usrah* model and tried to apply it in Indonesia when he returned.[32]

The simplest way to see the connections between the Egyptian and Indonesian Brothers is by analysing the nature of the movement and the social and political circumstances in Egypt, from which the central movement grew. Our first analysis deals with the model of Sufi leadership which - albeit not totally - has been adopted by the society.[33] The second focus is on the political constraints faced by the movement in its home country. We will then consider the question of how the relationship developed with Indonesia and ask: how independent are the offshoots?

We will see that although both the Egyptian and Indonesian Brothers are intellectually and ideologically connected, they have developed autonomous relations in which the branches are not tightly in step with the central movement's agenda. Since the central movement does not operate directly through top-down or vertical relations on practical issues, and while local dynamics surrounding the movements play a significant role, new movements under international influence display a heterogeneity in nature.

The most appropriate way to describe these connections is by framing them within a theory of Sufi links and networks. This is because the founder of the Muslim Brothers himself, Hasan al-Banna, grew up within Sufi traditions. The common use of terms by members of the Muslim Brothers in Egypt and Jemaah Tarbiyah in Indonesia, such as *murshid* (guide), *ikhwan*, and *wazifah* (*dhikr*, the remembrance of God) are derived directly from Sufi traditions. Similarly, *tarbiyah* itself was deliberately applied by al-Banna out of admiration for the Sufi teaching model. Thus the nature of the Muslim Brothers leadership has reflected the very basic nature of Sufi organization, while the tenure of *murshid* is a lifetime appointment[34].

For centuries, the Sufi orders have proven their power, spreading far and wide from their original places of birth. The principles of Sufi organization, beyond the central leaders and their structural and intellectual connections, are maintained in order to preserve the originality of the teachings and genealogies; but they do not necessarily espouse a shared agenda. Therefore, the Muslim Brothers' international offshoots are local expressions that rightly follow the socio-political and religious dynamics of their countries

> We tried to adopt the ideas of *ikhwan,* but not precisely as in Egypt or Syria. We saw that the *ikhwan's* ideas on Islam were genuine and up to date that suited to a modern movement. But their application in Indonesia has conformed to Indonesian circumstances.[35]

So as a Sufi-influenced movement, the Muslim Brothers enjoy spiritual and intellectual connections among their members that are not confined by territory. In the earlier stages of development, the embryos of the Muslim Brothers tended to carry out their activity following Sufi models. They avoided involvement in any political activites which might endanger or jeopardise the movement's existence. The teacher-pupil learning model was applied to recruit members and to develop commitment. As the followers reached a certain level within the membership, they were requested to practise certain formulas of prayer and ritual. They were also required to attend regular weekly meetings in order to receive supervision and guidance in the rituals and codes of conduct. These meetings (*halaqah*) ensured the process of supervision between the teacher and his followers.

However, the mixture between spirituality and political activism developed by the Muslim Brothers has driven the branches to be involved in the political processes in their own countries. When the movement grows to a significant size, it may appear to be a political institution in struggling for its ideals, in turn reforming the government of the day in accordance with its Islamic principles.

In the case of the Muslim Brothers in Egypt and Indonesia, the latter are autonomous from the central leadership of the movement in Egypt. It is reasonable that the offshoots do not try to associate with the central movement in dealing with their domestic affairs, while still preserving the transmission of ideas.

It is not odd among the Sufi orders that branches outside the central order disassociate themselves from the patron merely for reasons of security. For instance, during the 19th century, the Sanusiyyah order in Indonesia changed its name to the Idrisiyyah order in order to avoid confrontation with the Dutch colonial government.[36] The former order had been known for its fiercely anti-colonial attitude in Africa, its home territory, whilst in the case of Indonesia such an affiliation would have put its existence in jeopardy. The Indonesian form of the Sanusiyyah order became more cooperative with the colonial regime than its patron in the Africa. However, both orders still maintain their connections in terms of their spiritual network.

In addition, the political constraints experienced by the Muslim Brothers in Egypt have influenced the nature of its relations with the offshoots outside Egypt. The strict surveillance maintained over their veterans and leaders has meant that they are not able to set up proper communications with their offshoots. They struggle in facing government restrictions and experience great difficulty in maintaining their survival in Egypt. Whilst many young cadres have been sentenced to jail, the government has kept the older leaders under domestic surveillance and has restricted their contact with the outside. Therefore, rather than appearing as a political party, the Muslim Brothers in Egypt have worked intensively to provide social services, thus strengthening the role of the movement in society.

Undoubtedly, the limited access to leaders open to their followers, and particularly foreigners, has weakened the society of the Muslim Brothers. It has not been possible for them to think of spreading their influence outside Egypt, nor to structurally organise the branches according to central orders. Nonetheless, the position of the Egyptian Muslim Brothers vis-a-vis their fellow Muslims internationally is still very important. Their spiritual leadership is respected around the world. The General Guide in Egypt serves as a spiritual supervisor who no longer actively instructs his orders to broaden the membership. He plays the role of a wise consultant, the same role that is usually enjoyed by the *murshid* in almost all Sufi orders. The international assistance of a *murshid 'am*, also known as the *muraqib 'am* (supervisor) functions to supervise members' behaviour in accordance with the original teachings of the Muslim Brothers.

C. Transmission

How has the international movement of the Muslim Brothers penetrated Indonesia and how has it been manifested within Jemaah Tarbiyah? In order to gain a better understanding of the role of the central movement in the Middle East, and in turn how the local players regarded the Muslim Brothers and its ideas, and how they were influenced, we need to elaborate the process of transmission of Muslim Brothers' ideas into Indonesia.

The development of the Muslim Brothers beyond home territory is clear evidence that the movement is a transnational phenomenon. Advances in communication technology have enabled the messages and ideas of the society to be easily received by other Muslims. This can happen through Internet facilities and other media. However, as a religious movement that still believes in the significance of conventional transmission through human encounter, all processes of transferring Islamic knowledge and religious authority still rely on direct interaction. Thus it is better to seek the personal framework of diffusion and processes of emulation in which religious movements and events of the Middle East may encourage similar processes in other countries.

A very general definition of diffusion is a communication process with a source that sends a message through a channel to a receiver.[37] In describing the process of transmission of the Egyptian Brothers' influence on fellow Muslims in Indonesia we need to consider precisely the source of the message, the channels and the actors.

1. Roots of the Jemaah Tarbiyah Movement

The role of the reference country in transmitting religious and political influences is highly significant. The fact that the Middle East was the birthplace of Islam guarantees its central role as a source of religious authority. Moreover, the strategic position of the Middle East, particularly Saudi Arabia, in providing services for the study of Islam and the yearly international religious pilgrimage of the Hajj strengthens its credentials as the safeguard and true example of Islamic practice and inspiration. Every religious manifestation from these regions is highly esteemed by fellow Muslims outside Arabia, particularly in our case, Indonesia. In fact, there has been close contact and a mutual relationship between Indonesia and the countries of the Middle East for centuries.

Historically, Mecca was the centre of Islamic religious education for Indonesian students. From the 17th through the 19th centuries, many prominent religious leaders and scholars in Indonesia studied under the supervision of the great *ulama* in Mecca.[38] Large numbers of Indonesians, either formally or informally, visited for the purpose of pursuing religious knowledge. In some cases, they went initially only to perform the pilgrimage, but afterwards stayed on for some period of time to learn from the great Meccan scholars. As the numbers of pilgrims to the holy city increased over the centuries, so the numbers of Indonesian students in Mecca grew.

In contrast, Cairo in those early centuries was not a place of interest for Indonesians. Most students coming to the Middle East were motivated by religious goal, and Egypt was less well known in that regard. It was after the emergence of the Reformist movement led by Muhammad Abduh in the early years of the 20th century that the role of Egypt as a source of religious learning and political ideas for Muslims increased. But still, in terms of numbers, Indonesian students in Egypt were never more than those in Saudi Arabia.

In 1902, a report from the Egyptian government revealed that among 645 foreign students at al-Azhar University, only about seven were Indonesians.[39] Other information supplied by Abaza about Indonesian students in Cairo shows that in the middle of the 19th century, a Javanese dormitory (*riwaq Jawi*) in Cairo housed only 11 Javanese.[40] However, in 1871 seven students from Indonesia were still in residence, briefly, and not long afterwards they moved out of the dormitory.[41]

By the middle of the 1920s, as a result of the Modernist movement in Egypt, the motivation of Indonesian students shifted from the religious to the political and ideological, and the centre of Islamic education too shifted from Mecca to Cairo. Students in Mecca only attended classes in religious subjects; in contrast, in Cairo, according to the historian William Roff, they could benefit from the lively political and intellectual dynamics of Egyptian society of the time.[42] After their study at Egyptian universities they were expected to return home to become political figures of influence.[43] Thus Egypt subsequently served as the preferred destination in terms of acquiring educational and political experience for Indonesian Muslims. Because of the high reputation of Al-Azhar University and its scholars, many Indonesian Muslims received their degrees from universities in Egypt.

The fact that the influential modernist figure, Muhammad Abduh, was a prominent scholar who became Rector of al-Azhar, as well as Grand Mufti, meant that most Indonesian students who studied in Egypt took their inspiration from him. His modernist ideas spread rapidly throughout the Indonesian archipelago. In Java, in 1912, his pupils established the Islamic organization of Muhammadiyah. Although Ahmad Dahlan, the founder of the organization, did not himself graduate from Cairo, he studied modernist thought during his stay in Mecca under the supervision of a great Mecca scholar, Ahmad Khatib, a follower of Abduh. Khatib was of Indonesian descent, hailing from the Minangkabau region of Sumatra. Many other religious activists, particularly in

Java and Sumatra, received their religious training in Egypt. Accordingly, upon their arrival back home, they carried the modernist ideas of Abduh, and certain books on religion, to be taught in their schools.[44]

On the whole, however, relations between Egyptian and Indonesian Muslims were more noticeable after Indonesian political independence in 1945. Owing to the longstanding intellectual and religious connections between the two countries, the Egyptian government was the first to acknowledge the independence of Indonesia. During the national revolution to defend independence, in 1947 some Indonesian delegations including Syahrir and Agus Salim were assigned to meet the chairman of the Society of the Muslim Brothers, Hasan al-Banna on an Indonesian government mission to thank to him and the Egyptian people for their support.[45] Alongside political developments, in this era, the impact of Egyptian modernist Islam upon Indonesian society was seen in the development of Islamic schools into fully modern educational institutions.

Syahrir accompanied by other Indonesian delegations met with the General Guide of the Muslim Brothers, Hasan al-Banna, in Cairo in 1947.[46]

Furthermore, the numbers of Indonesians studying in Egypt fluctuated during the stage from immediately post-Indonesian independence until the late 1950s and was the result of domestic conflicts and civil strife in defending the nation from the aggression of the Dutch. In 1953 only about 80 students studied in Cairo. However, from the mid-1960s to the mid-1970s when Indonesian political conditions had become more stable and economic progress had improved many Indonesians went to Egypt to further their studies.[47]

H. Agus Salim, the chairman of Indonesian delegation and H.M. Rasyidi in discussion with Hasan al-Banna in Cairo in 1947.[48]

Regarding the increase in Indonesian students in Egypt after the 1970s, Abaza saw this as an indirect result of an intensive process of Islamisation that prevailed in Indonesian society at the time.[49] She found that the process of Islamisation increased the ratio of devoted Muslims (*santri*) in the relevant levels of society and the administration who encouraged the Indonesian government to send its students to Egypt. Drawing on Hefner's findings about the Islamisation process that took place in East Java since the 1970s, she argued that what happened in a particular region of the province of East Java was clear evidence to explain the trend of increased numbers of Indonesian students attending the Egyptian universities.[50]

However, Abaza failed to explain the fact that most students who studied in Egypt were not newly devout *santri*s, the product of the process of Islamisation and *santrinization*. Rather they came from families of a strong Islamic background and had already passed through the Islamic educational traditions of the *pesantren*, since it was only candidates who had strong basis in Islamic studies and had demonstrated an ability in memorizing the Qur'an who could be admitted to the Egyptian universities, particularly al-Azhar in Cairo. They studied there on Egyptian scholarships or with private financial support from their parents. Even more frequent were students receiving financial support from mosques and charitable institutions in Egypt. It is highly unlikely such students were the product of any short-term Islamisation process; they must have gone through long training in Islamic institutions in Indonesia.

In fact, the Islamisation process in some areas of Indonesia was initiated by government agents, in particular the ruling party, Golongan Karya (Golkar). It was aimed to serve the government's short-term political interests in controlling the Islamic community. The government support of Islamic activities attempted to attract Indonesian Muslims and in particular to take over the role of Islamic predication from local and independent religious leaders who were mostly associated with opposition political parties. The government initiated many Islamic activities and construction projects, such as activating missionary programs (*dakwah*) and building mosques and Islamic institutions. However, during this era, rather than encouraging students of religion to study in the Middle Eastern countries, the government preferred to send its students to study in the West, such as in Canada or America. More than 200 graduate students, mainly from the State Islamic Religion Institute, Institute Agama Islam Negeri (IAIN) were sent by the Department of Religion to prestigious universities in the West, while only 50 students were sent to al-Azhar or other institutions in the Middle East to pursue undergraduate degrees in Islamic studies.[51]

It appears that the increase in Indonesian students in Cairo during the 1980s was more the result of economic progress in the Middle East, the so-called the rise of "Petro-Islam" that made possible a rise in the numbers of scholarships provided by the Egyptian government.[52] In addition, there were political changes in Indonesia, in which the New Order regime attempted to push aside politically oriented Muslims. A feeling of disillusionment towards the government inclined many young Muslims to study in Egypt in order to avoid further repression.[53] The influence of M. Natsir in building contact with Middle Eastern leaders and organizations also succeeded in bringing more Indonesians to study in the Middle East. In 1982-1983 there were 415 students and in 1993 this increased significantly to 1000.[54] The current figure of Indonesian students in Egypt in 2005 is 2.700.[55]

In short, Indonesia-Middle East relations have had an impact on religious and intellectual developments. In general, we can say that the influence of the Middle East mediated by Indonesian students graduating from Middle Eastern universities stimulated the dynamics of Islam in Indonesia. This influence is best described in terms of three different generations.[56] The first generation of Middle East-graduates were students during the late Dutch colonial era. They were divided into two further groups: the Mecca network, associated with the traditionalists and the Cairo network favoured by the modernists. Both the Mecca and Cairo groups then established two outstanding but different Islamic organizations, Nahdlatul Ulama and Muhammadiyah, each with its own distinctive membership in Indonesia. The second generation was the post-Independence generation, identical in their orientation to Islamic liberal and rational thought. The rationalist movement, initiated by Harun Nasution and followed by other liberal figures such as Abdurrahman Wahid, signified a different phase in Indonesian Islam. The third generation was that of the 1970s and 1980s, who were attracted to fundamentalist ideas. The ideas of Sayyid Qutb and the society of the Muslim Brothers influenced them most.

An interesting observation reported by Dawam Rahardjo during two short visits to Egypt confirmed this changing orientation in different generations of Indonesian students there. In the 1970s he visited Cairo and witnessed that the renewal ideas of Nurcholish Madjid were not accepted and rather harshly criticised by students.[57] On his second visit in November 1999 he observed a different phenomenon, when students were more open towards the ideas of renewal Islam and less attracted to fundamentalist dogma. Interestingly, he also predicted the emergence of political representation by various Indonesian Muslim groups. He was so impressed with what he perceived as the wide acceptance by students towards the establishment of the National Mandate Party, *Partai Amanat National* (PAN) initiated by the modernists and then followed by other Muslim-represented parties.[58] He further elaborated

> What attracted my mind was the establishment of political parties. The National Mandate Party (PAN) in fact gained much support because of the existence of Muhammadiyah members among students. The National Awakening Party (PKB) also existed. It meant that students from NU started to study in Cairo and al-Azhar. Usually, students who had graduated from NU's *pesantren* prefer to study at the University of Medina, even though Saudi Arabia is the stronghold of the Wahabi movement. What was most interesting was the strong support of students for the Justice Party (PK) which indicated that the influence of Salafiyah and fundamentalism was still strong enough.[59]

However, Rahardjo's favourable impression of the remarkable presence of modernist students in Cairo did not last long. In fact, the composition of Indonesian students in Egypt has changed since the 1980s. It was understandable that during the 1970s and 1980s resistance to the ideas of renewal Islam represented the dominant face of Indonesian students in Egypt. This was because modernist groups, mainly students sent by DDII, were attracted to the ideas of Sayyid Qutb. However, since the 1990s, as was witnessed by Rahardjo, students were more receptive toward the renewal movement, but still Islamist views gained popularity. Polls for the 1999 and 2004 general elections held in the Indonesian Embassy in Egypt showed the interesting phenomenon that the PKS

Party won a majority, followed by PKB, whilst PAN performed poorly. Therefore, the generation of Islamist-oriented groups, mainly represented by PKS, had strong roots among students in Egypt since the late 1990s.[60]

The dynamics of the socio-cultural milieu of Egypt is a major factor in generating influential students who have contributed to religious and political discourse after their return home to Indonesia. Egypt, and in particular, Cairo is one of the central Islamic civilisations, where the struggle between traditionalism and modernism has taken place more dynamically than in other parts of the Islamic world, including Saudi Arabia.[61] The dominant role of the Wahabi doctrine formally adopted by the Kingdom of Saudi Arabia has not allowed space for religious or political disagreement.

However, since the mid-1990s, religious and socio-political movements imported from the Saudi patrons have tremendously influenced Indonesian Islamic discourses. How has the shift of influence from Egypt to Saudi occurred? Despite the fact that the numbers of Indonesian students in Egypt have continuously increased, contemporary Islam in Indonesia is characterised predominantly by the emergence of movements built on strong relations with Saudi patrons. The mushrooming of radical groups in Indonesia, such as FPI, Laskar Jihad and MMI are evidence of connections with Saudi Arabia networks. It should also be noted that the initial contact between Indonesian students and Egyptian Muslim Brothers occurred in Arabia - not in Egypt, where the movement was born. The role of Mecca and Medina, called the *Haramayn* (the Two Holy Cities) as sites for the transmission of new religious ideas to Indonesia has increased once more. The main reason for this shift in the source of religious influence lies in efforts conducted by the Saudi government to become an influential leader among Muslim countries.

The emergence of Saudi Arabia as a petrol-dollar power in the 1970s and the success of the Iranian revolution were key points in this development. Supported by economic progress, the Saudis tried to establish influence in Muslim countries, among them the Muslims of Southeast Asia, while at the same time making efforts to halt any spread of the Iranian Shi'ite ideology to other Muslim areas. The Iranian Revolution contested the fundamental issue of the legitimacy of the Saud monarchy. The long historical theological dispute between Shiite and Sunnite doctrines is another reason why Saudi Arabia wanted to eliminate the threat of the Iranian Shi'ism.[62]

Since the 1980s, the Saudi government has expanded its role in sponsoring religious activities by establishing and building Islamic centres and educational institutions. It established the International Islamic Relief Organization (IIRO) that has made efforts to spread the message of Islam in the Islamic world. What is more, the cachet of Saudi Arabia as the guardian of the Two Holy Cities has not been confined to the non-Arab Muslim countries but has also expanded into

Egypt itself, though renowned for the religious prestige of al-Azhar. Thus, when the Egyptian government suppressed many veterans of the Muslim Brothers, the Saudi government provided them with refuge.[63] In the 1980s, for instance, the Saudis and Arab Muslim Brothers established a cooperation in which the Muslim Brothers agreed not to operate in Saudi Arabia but to serve as Saudi agents in determining organizations and individuals fit to receive Saudi financial assistance.[64] However, this was broken off during the Gulf War in the 1990s, when most activists of the Muslim Brothers criticised the Kingdom of Saudi Arabia for requesting military assistance from Western countries. Since that date, the kingdom of Saudi Arabia has limited the access of the Muslim Brothers, which also has had a great impact on their activities in the Holy Cities of Arabia, including efforts to develop cadres among Indonesian students.[65]

The following sub-sections will discuss how Indonesian Muslims have played a role in transmitting Muslim Brothers principles to Indonesia, initially mediated through educational institutions in Saudi Arabia and through other means.

2. Channels

The era of 1980s and 1990s signified the encounter of Indonesian Muslims with new transnational movements. Contemporary Islamic movements in this period have been generally identified by their connections with movements in the Middle East. For instance, in the mid-1980s the Muslim Brothers influenced Indonesian Islam through printed media and through personal interaction.[66] At the same time, another Middle East based organization, Hizbut Tahrir, also began to expand its influence and attracted many young Muslims.[67] The Salafi group that developed since the 1990s represents a still later wave of international movement. Salafism was brought home by Indonesian students from Saudi Arabia and was also mediated through the encounter of Indonesian students with Salafi lecturers in a Saudi-sponsored institution in Jakarta, the Arabic and Islamic Education Institute of Ibnu Saud, Lembaga Ilmu Pengetahuan Arab dan Islam (LIPIA) in Jakarta.[68] This institution was built around the end of 1980 and became the main source of Salafi leaders in Indonesia.[69]

It was not only the Salafi group that benefited from the establishment of LIPIA, since Jemaah Tarbiyah was also able to recruit cadres from this institution, many of its students coming from both traditionalist and modernist *pesantren* in Java and the Outer Islands. In the early 1990s, a split developed among lecturers who belonged to the purist Salafi movement and those who were influenced by the Muslim Brothers. The competition between the two groups also occurred among students. It seemed that the influence of the Muslim Brothers increasingly developed so much as to move the Salafi rivals to discourage their followers from attending the institution, to avoiding the political dominance of the Muslim Brothers-influenced Jemaah Tarbiyah movement.[70]

What make the ideas of the Muslim Brothers so readily accepted by the generation of Muslims of the 1980s in Indonesia are their practical ideas and their moderation. The practical character of the society lies in its gradual reform of Muslim society by promoting economic, social and political solutions for Muslim disadvantage. The moderation of the movement can be seen in its attitudes towards "re-Islamising" society

> The modern and scientific approach of the Muslim Brothers scholars in Saudi attracted us, particular in organising a movement. Currently we can see that most literature about Islamic *dakwah* and movements has been dominated by the writings of the *ikhwa>n*.[71]

Furthermore, there is a deeply spiritual dimension within the Muslim Brothers movement that has enabled it to integrate with Indonesian Muslims since, for many centuries, Indonesia has been renowned as a centre of Islamic spirituality.[72] The richness of the Muslim Brothers in dealing with the inner dimension of Islamic teachings, in particular the issue of purifying the soul and the heart, has attracted Indonesian Muslims who are familiar with Sufi principles. For instance, activists of the Muslim Brothers emphasise the significance of a purified heart and a total submission to God in order to revive Islamic civilisation.[73] Further details about the place of the Sufi aspects of the Muslim Brothers' teachings will be discussed in chapter VI.

So how precisely did the initial contact between the Egyptian Muslim Brothers and Indonesian Muslims take place? Generally speaking, two channels mediate the process of religious transmission: contact through direct or indirect interaction that involves two parties (the parent movement and its offshoots). There are two kinds of channels: media (one-way communication) which tends to be imitative, and interpersonal contact (two-way communication) which is of an interactive nature. The interactive form means that both the sender and receiver assume an active role, so that the spread of ideas takes place through interpersonal relations, whilst the imitative form means that the source of the idea takes no active part, but rather the receiver imitates the idea through indirect contact.[74]

The theory of interpersonal contact is the best tool to demonstrate the relationship between the Egyptian and Indonesian Muslim Brothers. This is because the transmission of knowledge and the adoption of religious practices in Islamic history stress the significance of direct contact. It is also understandable that the Sufi nature of the Muslim Brothers would develop this kind of interaction. However, we cannot deny the role of current more advanced information systems in transmitting ideas. In the case of the transfer of the religious authority of the Muslim Brothers, however direct contact has been considered the only authoritative way of passing on the chain of religious legitimacy.

The transmission of the Muslim Brothers' influence into Indonesia took place in two stages. First, it was absorbed by Indonesian Muslims through the print media, mainly Arabic books translated into Indonesian since the mid-1970s. Second, the Middle East graduates who had had direct contact with the source of ideas returned to their home country to disseminate them further to their fellow Muslims. Those Indonesians already familiar with the Muslim Brothers' ideas at home easily welcomed the calls of the Middle Eastern graduates. Furthermore, the graduates supplemented the new ideas with the mode of establishment of the movement itself, borrowing the Muslim Brothers' training and organisational hardware as well.

a) Direct Contact

My analysis will focus on the process of interaction between Indonesian students abroad, as well as Indonesian Muslims at home, and the senders of ideas. Direct contact between the Muslim Brothers activists and Indonesian students takes two different forms: personal and formal communication. However, we stress that it is only through personal and intensive contact between the receiver and sender of the ideas can the transfer of religious knowledge and practice be spiritually valid.

The structure of *halaqah* permits an intensive and deep contact between the teacher *(murabbi)* and the students *(mutarabbi)*, usually in the form of an informal meeting between the *murabbi* and 5-10 pupils. Of course, the teacher takes the role of the transmitter of ideas and the pupils are the receivers. In initial contact, the role of Indonesian students was crucial as actors *(murabbi)* in the transmission process to Indonesia. As the first generation of Indonesian students abroad, it was they who would select, interpret and disseminate the ideas.

In Saudi Arabia during the 1980s, the establishment of initial *halaqah* outstripped those of Egypt. The strict surveillance of the Egyptian government limited the possibility for Indonesian students in Egypt to participate in Muslim Brothers' *usrah* meetings. Moreover, the very functioning of *usrah* was unlikely to continue in Egypt whilst in Saudi, the establishment of *halaqah* enabling a direct transmission of ideas did not face any significant challenges from the government.[75]

In Egypt, however, it is unlikely that members of the Muslim Brothers conducted *halaqah* to any great extent. In the absence of personal interaction between the Egyptian Brothers and Indonesian students, transmission of the movement could not occur. The students succeeded in importing ideas from abroad but failed to set up any movement. Regarding this fact, Rahmat Abdullah described his teacher's experience in Egypt during the 1970s. When his teacher returned from Egypt he brought more interesting ideas for carrying out *dakwah* but he did not initiate a Muslim Brothers movement

> In 1973, my teacher, *Kyai* Baqir Said, went to Egypt to study at al-Azhar University. He was an active and enthusiastic figure, particularly in the struggle for the sake of Islam. Nonetheless, he could not answer when he was asked how he would formulise his struggle in a productive way. Yet his interaction with the leaders of the *ikhwan* for about 5 years during his study at al-Azhar changed his thoughts about Islam. He returned to Indonesia with a new orientation influenced by the Muslim Brothers ideas.[76]

It is for this reason that the Indonesian graduates of Egyptian universities did not have a significant influence on the establishment of and the early development of the Jemaah Tarbiyah movement in Indonesia. Most Jemaah Tarbiyah cadres graduated from Egyptian universities after they had interacted with Muslim Brothers ideas in Indonesia beforehand.[77]

During the 1950s, at M. Natsir's request, the Egyptian government gave 90 scholarships to Indonesian students.[78] They were more attracted to the Muslim Brothers' ideas than the movement per se; moreover, Egyptian politics did not allow for explicit campaigning by the Brothers as a movement. As was told by Surahman Hidayat, a PhD graduate from al-Azhar University and the chairman of the *Shariah* Council of the central board of PKS, "most veterans of the Muslim Brothers were not allowed to publicly deliver their message and it was very difficult to make sure that a preacher actually was an activist of the Muslim Brothers."[79]

Another and less important contact was through formal interaction within academic encounters. Some Indonesian students attended religious public gatherings led by Muslim Brothers activists but these were not specifically designated as Brothers activities. They were set up for a general audience, and it was only incidental that the speakers came under the Brothers' organization. While close intellectual contact with the Egyptian Brothers was not developed within a framework of strong and intimate relations between students and the mentor, yet face to face contact remained one of the important channels in transferring ideas. In fact, the early ideologues of the Jemaah Tarbiyah, such as Hilmi Aminuddin and Abu Ridha, who were well versed in Muslim Brothers' teachings and who developed intellectual and spiritual relations with them have not come through the Egyptian connections but from the Saudi channels.

Since many veterans of the Muslim Brothers were involved in academic activities and education in Saudi Arabia and the regime before the 1990s was favourable to them, they were likely to convey the *ikhwan's* ideas to the students in their classes. They also received more respect for their academic writings, particularly on subjects of religious studies. Muhammad Qutb[80] himself had been among the prominent leaders of the Muslim Brothers in Egypt who fled to Saudi and taught in a Saudi university. He was also responsible for preparing the contents of the Saudi elementary schools curriculum. Only students who were personally attracted to these teachers would seek closer contact. Afterwards, informal meetings would be set up. And so the process of initiation to the Muslim Brothers movement would begin to take place.[81]

The interaction of Indonesian students with ideas of the Muslim Brothers in Saudi Arabia persuaded them of the importance of a multi-dimensional struggle for Islam. Islam was not confined within a practice nor narrowed into political activism. It encompasses all political, economic, social and cultural dimensions of the human being. As Abu Ridha said

> When I first arrived in Riyadh I had no idea about Islamic thought. I read an Arabic newspaper called *al-Mujtama'* that elaborated the significance of Islamic ideas in daily life. In addition, I attended many seminars delivered by prominent scholars of the Muslim Brothers, such as Yusuf Qaradawi, Said Hawwa and Fathi Yakan. I became aware about Islam and its relation to the political, social and economic aspects of life. I felt compelled to translate articles and books from Arabic to Indonesian. I developed my new profession by transferring these new ideas to Indonesia.[82]

b) Media

Since the 1980s many books from the Middle East have been translated into Indonesian, among them works written by Muslim Brotherhood scholars of Egypt, such as Sayyid Qutb and Hassan al-Banna, and Jamaat-I Islami scholars of Pakistan such as Mawdudi.[83] For example, the article *Diskusi Buku Agama* [84] (A Discussion of Religious Books) (Tempo, 1987) noticed that 12 books by Qutb and 3 books by al-Banna were translated to Indonesian during the four years between 1982-1986, while *Buku Islam Sejak 1945* [85] (Islamic Books Since 1945) counted 14 books by Maududi and 8 books by al-Banna.[86] Surprisingly, in more recent times many new publishers have been established and among the new books released since 1980-1996, according to my survey, there were about 130 titles written by Muslim Brothers' scholars, which were translated into Indonesian. Since 1998, the beginning of the post-Soeharto or Reformation era, it is no exaggeration to say that hundreds of books about the Muslim Brothers' thought and history have been printed and have enjoyed popular acclaim.

It is interesting that there has been a significant shift in terms of topics between books published in the 1970s-1980s and those of the 1990s and after. Before the 1990s most of the Muslim Brothers books translated into Indonesian dealt with the question of confronting Islamic ideals with non-Islamic ways of life but since then, they typically consist of more structured fundamental ideas of Hasan al-Banna, the socio-political history of his movement, and the messages of its leaders.[87]

These changes of topic in the translated books from the 1970s to the 1990s indicate the desire of Jemaah Tarbiyah to comprehensively adopt the ideas of the Muslim Brothers in all their aspects. The increasing appearance of manuals and training books related to the Muslim Brothers also helps Jemaah Tarbiyah to tighten its ideological and doctrinal links to the Brothers.

In the post Soeharto era a great deal of Islamic publishing has focussed on Muslim Brothers material. Thousands of copies have been printed and have become best-sellers. For example, Era Intermedia Publishers, established in 1998, has published *al-Ma'thurat* (al-Banna's collection of daily prayers) and *Risalah Pergerakan* (a collection of al-Banna's sermons and lectures) and sold more than 60,000 and 30,000 copies respectively.[88] Its success in publishing the Muslim Brothers' books has expanded Era Intermedia's business. In 2002 it was able to build a permanent office in Surakarta, Central Java, and started to publish more general books, though still related to Islamic topics. It seems that the Jemaah Tarbiyah networks throughout the outer regions of Indonesia have contributed a great deal in distributing books and have become its important trusted agents.

In addition, there is a wide availability of sources about the Muslim Brothers' ideas and their model in carrying out *dakwah* in contemporary times which is easily accessed through the Internet. In fact, the advanced technology of the Internet has provided most access for "beginners" to understand more about the Muslim Brothers. One well known website is www.ummah.org.uk/ikhwan/. However, this indirect contact is not regarded by the *ikhwa>n* as a reliable tool to transfer the ideas of the movement; direct contact in transferring the knowledge and religious practices, such prayer recitations of Hasan al-Banna and so on, is crucial. We should stress that the persons who transmit and introduce the movement to Indonesian Muslims are indeed important figures in the process of adoption and adaptation of the new movement. Direct oral transmission remains the preferred mode of disseminating religious knowledge, so that each *murabbi* grants his *mutarabbi* a kind of *ijazah, or* licence, as in the Sufi tradition which then permits him to set up another circle.

3. Actors and Ideologues

Another of the crucial elements in the process of diffusion is the actor who "selects, interprets and in turn disseminates."[89] In terms of channelling transnational ideas and movements, the figures who have extensive overseas contacts and who participate in building the network of co-operation are important. They serve as intermediaries and as receivers in the diffusion process as well.[90] When we study the religious and educational backgrounds of its pioneers, it is obvious that the members of the Jemaah Tarbiyah not only take the activists of the society the Muslim Brothers as their inspiration but also consider them as their mentors, through whom direct contact with the central movement in the Middle East takes place.

Strictly speaking, there are at least three important ideologues who have played a significant role in transferring and disseminating the ideas among young Muslims in Indonesia. They are Hilmi Aminuddin, Abu Ridha and Rahmat Abdullah. Hilmi Aminuddin is an influential figure in Jemaah Tarbiyah and currently chairman of the Consultative Assembly of PKS, who in the mid 1980s established initial contact with the Muslim Brothers during his study in Saudi Arabia. Hilmi himself was raised within a traditionalist background. He graduated from the NU Pesantren of Tebuireng in Jombang, East Java in 1958 and had close relations with "stakeholders" of the *pesantren*, in particular Abdul Kholiq Hasyim, son of the great NU leader, Hasyim Asyari (1875-1947). In the late 1970s he went to Saudi Arabia to study.[91]

Another among Jemaah Tarbiyah activists is Abu Ridha (nickname of Abdi Sumaiti). He is a former activist of the Dewan Dakwah Islam Indonesia (DDII) (Committee for Islamic Missions in Indonesia) who graduated from Madinah University. His father owned a traditionalist *pesantren* in Banten that was affiliated with Masyumi. He followed Islamic education from the elementary level into university. In 1978 he went to Saudi Arabia to study at the University Imam Ibn Saud of Riyadh. In the early 1980s he returned to Indonesia and became a lecturer at the Agriculture Institute of Bogor, Institute Pertanian Bogor (IPB) and often gave Islamic lectures at the Institute of Technology Bandung, Institut Teknologi Bandung (ITB). He is the first figure to introduce Muslim Brother's ideas to both of these prestigious universities.

In addition, Rahmat Abdullah is also a leading figure in Jemaah Tarbiyah. His reputation is widely acknowledged and has even been considered to be *Shaikh al-Tarbiyyah* (the Grand Teacher of Jemaah Tarbiyah).[92] Abdullah's parents were from a NU family but he preferred to join Masyumi. Abdullah himself was actively involved in PII. He did not graduate from the Middle East, his formal education was mainly in a traditional *pesantren* affiliated to Masyumi, Pondok Pesantren Salafiyah Asy-Syafi'iyah in Jakarta. He was introduced to the Muslim Brothers' ideas through his teacher, Kyai Bagir Said, who belonged to a prominent NU family in South Jakarta. Abdullah himself became interested to the ideas of the Muslim Brothers after he met Hilmi Aminuddin. In order to spread his ideas among students he established a boarding school called Rumah Pendidikan Islam Darut Tarbiyah (the Islamic Educational House of Darut Tarbiyah) in Jakarta. Through this institution many students from the University of Indonesia (UI) were drawn to attend his lectures and Islamic training sessions.[93]

If before the 1980s Indonesian Muslims, students in particular, only read the literature of the Muslim Brothers, after the arrival home of the Middle East graduates they were able to interact directly with its activists.[94] One of the discussion groups in the universities consulted by van Bruinessen in his research labelled itself "Muslim Brothers, and claimed to be the Indonesian branch of the Brothers in Egypt".[95] After the 1980s and 1990s more Middle East graduates returned to Indonesia to strengthen the life of Jemaah Tarbiyah. Among these were Salim Segaf Aljufri, Abdul Hasib and Abdul Raqib.

One of the distinct characteristics of the Indonesian Brothers in contrast to the "old" brothers in Egypt is apparent in the composition of the membership. Despite sharing common ideas developed by the founder, Hasan al-Banna, the Indonesian Brothers are distinct in terms of their religious and social backgrounds. Given the fact that the encounter between both parties takes place chiefly through academic and intellectual relations, the nature of the Jemaah Tarbiyah in Indonesia is also characterised by intellectual and academic inclinations. This trend is also supported by the fact that the transmission of the Muslim Brothers, both as a collection of particular ideas and as a movement, has been channelled by a mainstream and moderate type of activist.[96]

An examination of the backgrounds of Jemaah Tarbiyah activists, particularly the elite and key figures, reveals an obvious connection of the individuals with wider existing Islamic groups. Many key ideologues of Jemaah Tarbiyah are from NU families which have had some form of association with Masyumi and DDII. Since Masyumi, and particularly DDII is considered as a modernist group, it is understandable that the emergence of Jemaah Tarbiyah and Justice Party has been seen as part of modernist history. It is also due to early students in state universities who responded to the Muslim Brothers' ideas were largely from the modernist activist associations HMI and PII. They are not merely lay members but are active in the formal structural organization.

Despite the predominant traditionalist and modernist composition of the membership of Jemaah Tarbiyah, few hardliners coming from Islamic dissent groups have also entered the movement. Many of the young generation of Dewan Dakwah Islam Indonesia and Darul Islam-oriented groups have attended Jemaah Tarbiyah training, and have since changed their orientation to follow the ideas of the Muslim Brothers.

For the Jemaah Tarbiyah activists, such fellow Muslims who have transcended their old connections and have come to hold a new understanding about Islam in Indonesia (as conveyed in the training) are called "already educated Muslims" (*Muslim tertarbiyah*). While they still interact with their old associations, they display no fanatical stand toward their parents' organisational associations and are keen to undermine the old religious doctrines only if the latter are in contradiction with Jemaah Tarbiyah ideas.[97] Their continuing interaction with their old organizations has the aim of influencing these in order to support their new ideas and in particular to support the idea of political Islam.

The important role of actors in transmitting religious ideas is characterised by their movement from their original place to a foreign one, from Indonesia to Saudi Arabia, and their return to Indonesia to disseminate the new ideas they have gained from abroad. This process Peter Mandaville has called "travelling theory", in which not only human beings but also ideas travel from place to another.[98] Through extensive travel, however, an idea will lose its radical edge. Or an idea can take on a new critical consciousness, both in itself and in influencing other ideas after undergoing travel.[99] The case of the transmission of Muslim Brothers' ideas to Indonesian Muslims channelled through Saudi Arabia as the meeting point has also brought about change and revision. Traditionalist Indonesian students have received the Muslim Brothers' ideas mixed with the revivalist doctrine of Saudi Arabia. They disseminated this new religious synthesis to Indonesian students in the state universities which had been in the first stage dominated by modernist activists.[100]

Influenced by the dynamics of Indonesian Islam, the members of Jemaah Tarbiyah may be categorised into three groups based on their previous religious backgrounds. Thus the face of Jemaah Tarbiyah, including its political party, the PKS, is distinguished by the religious background of its members - revivalist, modernist and traditionalist. In fact, PKS is neither a traditionalist nor a modernist movement but it might resemble Muhammadiyah, NU, or even Persis.[101]

a) Revivalist Brothers

The Indonesian *ikhwan* of a revivalist background are in general more enthusiastic in conducting religious "purification" and more rigid in interpreting religious doctrines. Because of previous religious affiliations, they stem predominantly from the Indonesian rigid purification-oriented movement, Persatuan Islam (Persis) and the hardline branch of DDII. Some of them have also gone through lengthy training in Salafi doctrines either in the Saudi universities or their associates. The activists associated with this sub-group are keen to single out their movement from other existing Islamic organizations in Indonesia. Their involvement within the formation of the initial Jemaah Tarbiyah has led the movement towards more restricted and exclusive operations. They prefer to develop militant cadres over spreading their influence into the broader society.

Organisationally, though they share the ideal of religious "purification" with DDII, they have less commitment to its agenda. They may interact intensively with the DDII activists and support their programs. However, they have not been reluctant to withdraw their support when they have found that they have been used for the political interests of a certain figure or another of DDII. In the 1990s, for example, Jemaah Tarbiyah followers broke off their cooperation with the DDII-established movement, the Islamic Committee for Islamic World Solidarity, Komite Solidaritas Dunia Islam (KISDI) led by Ahmad Soemargono.

The committee had become a political vehicle for Soemargono in developing ties with certain military figures.

A subsequent event in 1998 triggered the movement to publicly break relations with DDII. The claim of the Moon and Star Party, Partai Bulan Bintang (PBB) to be the only recognised party for the "family" of Masyumi led directly to Jemaah Tarbiyah establishing its own political party, the Justice Party. Actually, the revivalist *ikhwan* wanted to maintain the relationship with DDII, but again political events cut the links. Rather than advancing such relations, political issues during the 1999 general elections campaign sharpened the conflict between the two camps. Uniquely, the Jemaah Tarbiyah members appointed their cadre from a NU background, Nurmahmudi Ismail, as first party president.

Finally, the acquaintance of the revivalist *ikhwan* with ideas of purification made them promote the agenda of preserving a "purer" Islam rather than expanding the movement. The creation of more solid and dedicated cadres became more important than drawing loose popular support. In the case of East Java, Jemaah Tarbiyah's failure to gain support among the people has been mainly due to a lack of involvement by traditionalist figures and leaders. Most PKS leading figures in this province have been dominated by activists of a revivalist group, in particular Persis. The former chairman of the East Java Provincial Board of PKS, Rofi' Munawwar is a committee member of DDII and Muhammadiyah in East Java. Similarly, the vice chairman of the Provincial *Shariah* Board was Hud Abdullah Musa (d. 2001) the head of a prominent *pesantren* of Persis in Bangil.[102] Musa finished studies at the University of Baghdad, Irak in 1976 and continued at Karachi University in Pakistan. During his stay in Pakistan he developed close contact with Dr. Ramadhan al-Buti, a son in law of Hasan al-Banna.[103] In addition, despite his popularity among Persis followers, he also delivered regular lectures for Muslim students of state universities in Surabaya. In fact, many of Jemaah Tarbiyah's training programs to provide an adequate knowledge of Islam for its cadres in East Java are conducted in the Pesantren Bangil.

b) Modernist Brothers

Even though modernist *ikhwan* have not dominated the membership of Jemaah Tarbiyah (since the more active and vocal pioneers of modernism have been mostly attached to modernist groups), members of Jemaah Tarbiyah are also renowned as heirs of modernism. In addition, many activists are former leaders of modernist student associations, such as the Muslim Students' Association, Himpunan Mahasiswa Islam (HMI) and the Indonesian Muslim Students, Pelajar Islam Indonesia (PII).

Undoubtedly, before the establishment of its political party in 1998, Jemaah Tarbiyah had developed close contact with modernist figures, so that the activists have been more familiar with modernist elites than with traditionalist leaders.

They were able to communicate more easily with M. Natsir, Anwar Haryono, Hussein Umar, Amien Rais and other figures from modernist organizations. They regularly attended religious gatherings in DDII or Muhammadiyah offices rather than meetings with Abdurahman Wahid or NU gatherings.

At the national congress of Lembaga Dakwah Kampus (LDK) the Campus Predication Association, held in 2000 and attended by almost all Muslim student representatives throughout Indonesia, Amien Rais was invited to be a keynote speaker. In order to capture his audience's attention he told about his acquaintance with the Muslim Brothers in Egypt

> I stayed in Egypt and learned many things from activists of the Muslim Brothers. I am very familiar with the society of the Muslim Brothers, from A to Z. I met with its *murshid am* (General Guide), Umar Tilimsani. I also met other prominent leaders of *ikhwan* in Cairo, such as Mustafa Masyhur, Abbas as-Sisi and Jamal Yusuf. They were known for their devotion, knowledge and humility.[104]

However, the relationship of Indonesian *ikhwan* with modernist figures does not automatically guarantee their support of modernist organizations in political games. Even though the second president of PKS, Hidayat Nurwahid was a committee member of Muhammadiyah and his General Secretary, Anis Matta was also raised in the Muhammadiyah tradition, the party backed Amien Rais - in the event, too late in the 2004 Indonesia presidential elections. Rais' electoral failure was due to the reluctance of some members of the Majelis Syura to support him, even though after long debate in the Majelis Syura meeting on 1 July 2004 the decision to support of Rais had come out. However, this did not help him, since such "political support" contained no obligation that the members should give him their vote.[105] In fact, the recommendation to support Rais was ambiguous in real political terms because the activists of PKS were not allowed to be members of presidential campaign teams for any candidate.[106] Instead, some of PKS leaders preferred Wiranto, a retired general, and his running mate, Shalahuddin Wahid, a member of the NU committee.

c) Traditionalist Brothers

In terms of cultural and religious orientation, it is the activists of the Jemaah Tarbiyah from a traditionalist background that predominate in the movement. Yet this does not necessarily mean that they have been associated with traditionalist organizations, such as NU. Most of the influential figures of the movement, such as Rahmat Abdullah, Hilmi Aminuddin, and Abu Ridha indeed have a traditionalist background - but they stem from the traditionalist wing of the modernist political party, Masyumi. They are not well connected with the mainstream leaders within NU and may even tend to be critical of the proponents of traditionalism. However, they also do not conceive the existence of the modernist organization as more significant than any others. These traditionalist *ikhwan* may well out number the modernists but they are less politically active.

This group is more interested in the spiritual aspects of Jemaah Tarbiyah and less in political and organisational issues. They are very much involved in expanding the membership of the movement (albeit with little public recognition) and represent the largest group within the movement. The current expansion of PKS in the 2004 general elections in regions once the strongholds of traditionalist organizations indicates their considerable contribution to the party, and this can only be expected to increase in the future. In fact, many of the younger generation of NU who have studied in both secular and Islamic universities in the Middle East countries such Egypt, Saudi Arabia, Yemen and Sudan have given their support to PKS. Voting in these countries, Indonesian students gave the Party their absentee votes, this political event indicating significant support from traditionalist brothers within the Jemaah Tarbiyah. Indeed, it may be predicted that for the next decades, the modernist face of PKS will no longer be dominant and is likely to be replaced by the traditionalists.

However, the relationship between PKS and NU is not close as it is with Muhammadiyah. This is because traditionalist *ikhwan* have not maintained their connections with NU leaders after joining Jemaah Tarbiyah. The case of Nurmahmudi Ismail is an example of tension between Jemaah Tarbiyah and the traditionalist group. From 1998 to 2002, under the leadership of Nurmahmudi Ismail, an activist of the Jemaah Tarbiyah with an NU background, the Justice Party enjoyed good rapport with the president of Indonesia, Abdurahman Wahid, who is also of NU. Nurmahmudi was appointed Minister of Forestry and Plantation in 1999. On many occasions, Wahid introduced him as a NU cadre to a number of *pesantren,* which they visited together. However, the relationship with Wahid was not to last for long. Nurmahmudi was fired from office because Wahid did not find in him a required degree of loyalty when thousands of Justice Party members launched demonstrations demanding Wahid's resignation. However, he was able to develop good relations with the local branch of NU in Depok, East Java. In June 2005, he ran for election to mayor in the district of Depok. He took a NU committee member of the local branch, Yuyun Wirasaputra as his running mate as vice mayor. Wirasaputra was formally supported by the NU committees of Depok,[107] while the reason for support for Nurmahmudi was the fact that many NU cadres were active in PKS.[108]

Other influential figures of Jemaah Tarbiyah of NU background are Abdur Raqib (a former member of national parliament for PK), Surahman Hidayat (head of the Syariah Council of PKS), Abdul Aziz Arbi (member of the national parliament of PKS), Agus Purnomo (member of the national parliament of PKS), Zulkieflimansyah (member of the national parliament of PKS) and Seniman Latif (member of the national parliament of PKS).

To conclude, even though Jemaah Tarbiyah has been greatly influenced by the Muslim Brothers in Egypt, it has developed into an autonomous movement different from the central movement. The adoption of Muslim Brothers' ideas by Indonesian students who studied in Saudi Arabia in the 1980s has produced the interesting phenomenon of a new movement which is a combination of international and local experience. Indonesian Muslims from various backgrounds (revivalist, modernist and traditionalist) have contributed to domesticating the international face of the Muslim Brothers into the more Indonesian Jemaah Tarbiyah. Jemaah Tarbiyah has not tried to remove the influence of the Muslim Brothers; instead, its activists have sought to return to the original ideas of Hasan al-Banna as for guidance in their involvement in politics.

ENDNOTES

[1] I joined the dawn prayers and enjoyed the recitation afterwards, on 14 May 2003.

[2] See *Tempo*, 3 April 1993.

[3] *Ikhwan* ('brothers' in Arabic) is simply used to identify the members of the Society of Muslim Brothers. In daily social interaction, since they refer to themselves and their fellow members as *ikhwan*.

[4] Hasan al-Banna, *Memoar Hasan Al-Banna Untuk Dakwah dan Para Dainya,* trans. Salafuddin Abu Sayyid and Hawin Murtadho (Solo: Era Intermedia, 2004), 46

[5] See "Profesional dari Mujahid Kampus" *Hidayatullah,* April 2000.

[6] The term *"jahl"* (*al-jahl*) produces the further term *jahiliyah* (*al-jahiliyyah*) which was used by Sayyid Qutb, but here it has different emphasis, for the Jemaah Tabiyah it elicits the response to "educate or preach" while for Qutb it meant to judge other Muslims as infidels.

[7] A leader or mentor of an *usrah* is called a *murabbi* (trainer) and members of the *usrah* are called *mutarabbi* (pupil). A *murabbi* has to set a good example for the members while *mutarabbi* has to follow what *murabbi* orders.

[8] Activists of the Jemaah Tarbiyah always emphasise that their groups differ from other *usrah* groups of the 1980s. Interview with Mahfudz Sidiq, Sydney, 13 August 2002.

[9] Islamic student associations such as HMI MPO (Himpunan Mahasiswa Islam – Majelis Penyelamat Organisasi) and PII (Pelajar Islam Indonesia) began to implement *usrah* as part of their *dakwah* strategy in opposing the *Asas Tunggal*. Some more radical groups, including NII also used *usrah*. These groups were often mixed and it was not easy to distinguish between them. Interview with Mustafa Kamal, Jakarta, 11 Juni 2003.

[10] *Sriwijaya Post*, 9 November 2002.

[11] Interview with Aus Hidayat, Depok, 15 May 2003.

[12] Azyumardi Azra distinguishes between *usrah*, which has developed international networks such as Jemaah Tarbiyah, Hizbut Tahrir and the Salafiyah and those *usrah* which were influenced by local elements, such as Negara Islam Indonesia. See his article "Kelompok Sempalan di Kalangan Mahasiswa PTU: Anatomi Sosio Historis" in *Dinamika Pemikiran Islam di Perguruan Tinggi* (Jakarta: Logos Wacana Ilmu, 1999), 226.

[13] Hassan Al-Banna, *Usrah dan Da'wah* (Kuala Lumpur: Ikhwan Agency, 1979), 4.

[14] Ali Abdul Halim Mahmud, *Perangkat-Perangkat Tarbiyah Ikhwanul Muslimin*, trans. Wahid Ahmadi, et.al. (Solo: Era Intermedia, 1999), 21. The same explanation regarding *"tarbiyah"* has been presented by Irwan Prayitno, a parliament member of PKS, in his book, *Tarbiyah Islamiyah Harakiyah* (Jakarta: Pustaka Tarbiatuna, 2001).

[15] See Martin Van Bruinessen, "Genealogies of Islamic Radicalism in Post-Suharto Indonesia," *South East Asia Research* 10 no. 2 (2002), 132.

[16] See Richard Mitchell, *The Society of the Muslim Brothers* (New York and Oxford: Oxford University Press, 1993), 173; see also Ishak Musa Husaini, *The Moslem Brethren: The Greatest of Modern Islamic Movements* (Westport: Hyperion Press, 1986), 73.

[17] See http://www.meta-religion.com/Extremism/Islamic_extremism/muslim_brotherhood.htm.

[18] See Hilmi Aminuddin, *Strategi Dakwah Gerakan Islam* (Jakarta: Pustaka Tarbiatuna, 2003), 149.

[19] His statement in Indonesian is the following, "*di samping itu juga berdiri Partai Keadilan yang merupakan perpanjangan tangan dari gerakan Ikhwanul Muslimin Mesir...*" For further details see Yusuf Qardhawi, *Umat Islam Menyongsong Abad 21*, trans. Yogi Prana Izza and Ahsan Takwim (Solo: Era Intermedia, 2001), 92.

[20] *Republika*, 3 September 2000.

[21] See "Ikhwanul Musliminnya Indonesia?" *Sabili*, 1 Agustus 2001.

[22] As stated by Rahmat Abdullah, a senior member of Jemaah Tarbiyah in his interview in *Hidayatullah*, August 2001.

[23] Ibid. In his statement in *Hidayatullah*, Rahmat emphasized the important of Islamic conduct and deeds in accord with the essence of the Muslim Brothers, rather than any similarity in name. He implicitly stated that although PK did not use the Moslem Brotherhood name, it did not mean that PK did not share the same vision and agenda with them.

[24] Aminuddin, *Strategi Dakwah Gerakan Islam*, 149.

[25] Barry Rubin, *Islamic Fundamentalism in Egyptian Politics* (New York: Palgrave Macmillan, 2002), 12-13.

[26] Ibid., 21.

[27] See "Catatan Wafatnya Mustafa Masyhur," *EraMuslim.com*, 15 November 2002

[28] Olivier Roy, *The Failure of Political Islam*, trans. Carol Volk (Massachusetts: Harvard University Press, 1994), 110.

[29] The term *ikhwan*, is not new but Jemaah Tarbiyah has made efforts to promote its use among Indonesian Muslims who are more familiar with the term "*sahabat*." According to Mustafa Kamal, a member of Indonesian national parliament from PKS (2004-2009), adopting *ikhwan* initially was aimed to strengthen the solidarity and brotherhood, while subsequently it developed a more specific meaning, referring to members of Jemaah Tarbiyah. Interview with Mustafa Kamal, Depok, 11 June 2003.

[30] Interview with Muslikh Abdul Karim, Depok, 9 September 2003.

[31] See Bruinessen, "Genealogies of Islamic Radicalism," 133.

[32] Interview with Mutammimul Ula, Jakarta, 16 June 2003.

[33] Further details on how the Muslim Brothers adopted the model of Sufi leadership and Sufi terminology will be elaborated in chapter VI.

[34] Brynjar Lia, *The Society of the Muslim Brothers in Egypt: the Rise of an Islamic Mass Movement 1928-1942* (Readings: Ithaca Press, 1998), 9.

[35] Interview with Ahmad Mudzafar Jufri, Surabaya, 17 March 2003.

[36] This Sufi order now has developed its influence among Indonesian Muslims in Sukabumi, West Java.

[37] Anders Uhlin, "Indonesian Democracy Discourses in a Global Context. The Trans-national Diffusion of Democratic Ideas," Working Paper 83, The Centre of Southeast Asian Studies Monash University (1993), 8.

[38] Further detailed information about the Indonesian Islamic scholars during the 17th until the 19th century, see Azyumardi Azra, *Jaringan Global dan Lokal Islam Nusantara* (Bandung: Mizan, 2002), 102.

[39] Bayard Dodge, *Al-Azhar: A Millenium of Muslim Learning* (Washington DC: the Middle East Institute, 1961), 177.

[40] She quotes from Ali Mubarak, an historian from Egypt see Mona Abaza, *Islamic Education: Perception and Exchanges Indonesian Students in Cairo* (Paris: Cahier Archipel, 1994), 99.

[41] See Azyumardi Azra, "Melacak Pengaruh dan Pergeseran Orientasi Tamatan Cairo," *Studia Islamika* 2 no. 3 (1995), 207.

[42] It was in Cairo that Malay students (from both Indonesia and Malaysia) were exposed into overt political discussion on the concepts of Pan-Islamism, Pan-Malayanism and anti-colonial nationalism. See William R. Roff, *The Origins of Malay Nationalism* (Kuala Lumpur: Universiti Malaya, 1980), 89.

[43] Dodge, *Al-Azhar: A Millenium of Muslim Learning*, 177.

[44] Fred R. von der Mehden, *Two Worlds of Islam: Interaction between Southeast Asia and the Middle East* (Gainesville: the University Press of Florida, 1993), 14.

[45] According to some information the society of the Muslim Brothers played a significant role in lobbying the government in favour of Indonesian independence. See M. Zein Hassan, *Diplomasi Revolusi Indonesia*

di Luar Negeri: Perjuangan Pemuda/Mahasiswa Indonesia di Timur Tengah. (Jakarta: Bulan Bintang, 1980), 220.

[46] Ibid., 227

[47] Mona Abaza, *Islamic Education: Perception and Exchanges Indonesian Students in Cairo* (Paris: Cahier Archipel, 1994), 99.

[48] Ibid., 220.

[49] Ibid.

[50] See ethnography report of Robert W. Hefner, "Islamising Java? Religion and Politics in Rural East Java," *Journal of Asian Studies* 46 no. 3 (Augustus, 1987), 533-554.

[51] See "Barat atau Timur; Tetap Islam," *Tempo*, 3 April 1993.

[52] Azra, "Melacak Pengaruh dan Pergeseran," 200.

[53] Ibid., 227.

[54] Abaza, *Islamic Education*, 99,.

[55] See "Mahasiswa RI di Mesir Mencapai Rekor Terbanyak," *Gatra*, 5 November 2005.

[56] Abaza, *Islamic Education*, 99.

[57] M. Dawam Rahardjo, foreword to *Islam Garda Depan: Mosaik Pemikiran Islam Timur Tengah* by M. Aunul Abied Shah, ed. (Bandung: Mizan, 2001), 28.

[58] Ibid.

[59] Ibid.

[60] In the 1999 general elections the total votes for PK, PKB, PAN, PBB and PPP were 566, 289, 286, 176 and 127 respectively. In the 2004 general elections PKS gained 1,126 voters whilst PKB and PAN gained 278 and 175. Interestingly, the cadres of PKS itself only reached 500 students and many students coming from NU and Muhammadiyah background in fact chose PKS. Other polling held at the embassies of Indonesia in the Middle East showed the same phenomenon, see article "Nomor Wahid di Negeri Orang," *Gatra*, 10 April 2004

[61] Rahardjo, foreword to *Islam Garda Depan*, 27.

[62] Roy, *The Failure of Political Islam*, 116.

[63] Interview with Ahmad Mudzafar Jufri, Surabaya, 17 March 2003.

[64] Roy, *The Failure of Political Islam*, 117.

[65] Interview with Ahmad Mudzafar Jufri, Surabaya, 17 March 2003.

[66] See Salahuddin, "Menelusuri Kelompok Sempalan," *Detik.com*, 10 January 2001.

[67] See Sidney Jones, "Radical Islam in Central Asia: Responding to Hizbut-Tahrir," *ICG Asia Report* no. 58, (30 June 2003).

[68] See Salahuddin, " Menelusuri Kelompok Sempalan," *Detik.com*, 10 January 2001.

[69] Sidney Jones, "Indonesia Backgrounder: Why Salafism and Terrorism Mostly Don't Mix," *ICG Asia Report* no. 83 (13 September 2004), 8.

[70] Ibid.

[71] Interview with Ahmad Mudzafar Jufri, Surabaya, 17 March 2003.

[72] Hasan Al-Banna embraced the Sufi orders in Egypt. It is likely that the influences of Sufism also contributed to shape the character of the movement, such as the rituals and models of *dakwah*. But if Sufi movements usually do not pay much concern to political issues, the Muslim Brothers regard political struggle as one of their ways of re-islamising society.

[73] For further material on the Muslim Brothers curriculum that have been adopted by Jemaah Tarbiyah, see Ummu Yasmin, *Materi Tarbiyah: Panduan Kurikulum bagi Da'i dan Murabbi* (Solo: Media Insani, 2002).

[74] Uhlin, "Indonesian Democracy Discourses," 8.

[75] Interview with Ahmad Mudzafar Jufri, Surabaya, 17 March 2003.

[76] Interview with Rahmat Abdullah, Jakarta, 11 May 2003.

[77] Muhammad Imdadun, "Tansmisi Gerakan Revivalisme Islam Timur Tengah ke Indonesia 1980-2002: Studi Atas Gerakan Tarbiyah dan Hizbut Tahrir Indonesia," (Master's thesis, University of Indonesia, 2003), 105.

[78] The scholarship program provided by the Nasser regime was given via Masyumi, under the leadership of M. Natsir. This program aimed to calm the anger of Muslim activists in Indonesia after the capture of many Muslim Brothers in the 1950s. Masyumi had been renowned for its criticism of the bad treatment of many Brothers members by Egypt. See Ibid.

[79] Ibid.

[80] Muhammad Qutb was a prominent leader of the Muslim Brothers in Egypt. He was more moderate than his brother, Sayyid Qutb.

[81] Interview with Abu Ridha, Jakarta, 11 October 2003.

[82] Ibid.

[83] The 1980s also witnessed a growth in the publishing of Islamic books on Shi'ism, Sufism and certain Western books. For further details on this, see Azyumardi Azra, *Islam Reformis:Dinamika Intelektual dan Gerakan* (Jakarta: Raja Grafindo, 1999), 215.

[84] Tim Tempo, *Diskusi Buku Agama* (Jakarta: Tempo, 1987).

[85] See Pusat Informasi Islam, *Buku Islam Sejak 1945* (Jakarta: Yayasan Masagung, 1988).

[86] See Azra, *Islam Reformis*, 215.

[87] To mention publications in different eras, the books *Keadilan dalam Islam* (Justice in Islam) and *Petunjuk Jalan* (A Guide Along the Path) by Sayyid Qutb were published during the 1970s and 1980s while *Risalah Pergerakaan Ikhwanul Muslimin* (Collection of Messages) by Hasan al-Banna, *Perangkat Tarbiyah Ikhwanul Muslimin* (Elements of Tarbiyah for the Muslim Brothers), *100 Pelajaran dari Para Pemimpin Ikhwanul Muslimin* (One Hundred Lessons from Leaders of The Muslim Brothers) are best examples of translated books during the 1990s and afterwards.

[88] For more details on publishing, see www.eraintermedia.com.

[89] Uhlin, "Indonesian Democracy Discourses."

[90] Ibid.

[91] Interview with Hilmi Aminuddin, Jakarta, 23 December 2003.

[92] See "Syaikhut Tarbiyah, KH Rahmat Abdullah: Ikhwanul Muslimin Inspirasi Gerakan Tarbiyah," *Hidayatullah*, August 2001.

[93] Interview with Rahmat Abdullah, Jakarta, 11 May 2003.

[94] *Detik.com*, 10 January 2001.

[95] Bruinessen, "Genealogies of Islamic Radicalism," 133.

[96] Interview with Sholeh Drehem, Surabaya, 13 March 2003.

[97] Ibid.

[98] See Peter Mandaville, *Transnational Muslim Politics: Reimagining the Umma* (London and New York: Routledge, 2001), 85.

[99] Ibid.

[100] However, the generation Indonesian students at universities who have joined since 1990s and afterward mostly came from traditionalist backgrounds.

[101] Quoted in full, Hilmi Aminuddin said "*PKS itu bukan Masyumi bukan pula NU atau Muhammadiyah. Tetapi benar karakter PKS kadang serupa dengan ormas-ormas seperti NU, Muhammadiyah dan Persis.*" (Interview, 23 December 2003).

[102] See "Tegar Juga Ayah yang Sabar," www.PK-Sejahtera.org, 01 Oktober 2001.

[103] Ibid.

[104] See "Transkrip Pidato Dr. Amien Rais di FSLDK Nasional XI di Universitas Indonesia," *Ukhuwa.or.id*, 2000.

[105] See Press Release PKS, 1 July 2004.

[106] Ibid.

[107] See "PCNU Depok Deklarasikan Dukung Nurmahmudi," *PKS Online*, 10 June 2005.

[108] Ibid.

Chapter 6: The sufi influences: in Pursuit of an Islamised Indonesia

Before the formation of their political party, few observers would have predicted that the Jemaah Tarbiyah activists would turn to a pragmatic role in the politics of Indonesia. For PKS that grew out of a religious movement influenced by the Muslim Brothers of Egypt (which has had the reputation as a fundamentalist movement) such pragmatism in politics is quite surprising. Hamid Basyaib, at the website of the Liberal Islam Network (Jaringan Islam Liberal-JIL) praises the success of PKS in the 2004 general elections but emphasises a possible dilemma facing a party based on religious ideology. According to Basyaib, PKS should decide whether to follow either a pragmatic or an inflexible approach toward politics. In Basyaib's view, the structure of a party that is headed by a Consultative Board (Majelis Syura) is likely to inflexible.[1]

The reality has been contrary to expectations. After PKS gained its success in the 2004 general elections, it decided to join a coalition with nationalist parties in forming government under the leadership of Susilo Bambang Yudhoyono. When, in 2005, the government raised oil prices, a move that drew fierce protest from the public and caused some members of PKS to demand that the party leave the coalition, PKS would not withdraw its support.[2] Instead of adopting a hardline stance, PKS has softened its "religious aspirations" in order to move with the political realities of Indonesia. What are the grounds for such a practical decision?

It is interesting to note that since most important decisions of the party are taken through the mechanism of the consultative board (Majelis Syura), whose members are senior activists of Jemaah Tarbiyah upholding the teachings of Hasan al-Banna, political decisions of PKS have reflected the stance of Jemaah Tarbiyah in general. I argue that, quite apart from political obstacles from the ruling regimes experienced by Islamic parties and the socio-political circumstances of Indonesia, it is the teachings of the Muslim Brothers themselves that account for this "realistic" approach.[3] Learning from the experience of the past, a member of parliament for PKS stated, "If Masyumi was eager to confront any obstacle and even sacrificed itself for the sake of upholding its idealism, PKS would not; instead, we attempt to find a different way."[4] In fact, such moderation finds its justification in the Muslim Brothers' ideas.

This chapter attempts to analyse the influence of the Sufi dimension within the Muslim Brothers that has contributed to determine the political praxis of PKS. Strictly speaking, PKS activists always insist upon the importance of upholding the two fundamental sources of Islam (the Qur'an and Hadith) and the teachings of al-Banna. In dealing with political and social issues, they attempt to broaden their call to all of the Indonesian Muslim communities to encompass all religious orientations, particularly the traditionalist elements of Indonesian Islam.[5] This is keeping in mind the stages in building an Islamic society and state introduced by al-Banna, which have been adopted PKS, namely to adopt a gradualist approach in promoting their Islamic aspirations.

A. Sufi Influences

The general and "superficial picture" of PKS is that is dominated by modernist characters. In contrast, my study has discovered that there are significant numbers of activists from a traditionalist background in PKS and what is more, the pioneers of Jemaah Tarbiyah were children of traditionalist families. Since most of the modernist Muslim activists during the early development of the movement had previously been activists in their own organizations, while the traditionalists were merely ordinary members or maintained only cultural connections with traditionalist organisations, the face of Jemaah Tarbiyah bears the features of a modernist derived purification movement, rather than of any traditionalist stamp.

However, when studying the political praxis of PKS and the religious attitudes of its members in responding to jurisprudential issues, it becomes apparent that PKS has adopted a traditionalist approach. This pragmatic and accommodative stance of PKS in dealing with politics can be seen to derive from the teachings of Hasan al-Banna which give high priority to the unity of the Muslim community. Al-Banna himself developed these ideas from Sufi doctrines.

Since adolescence al-Banna had firmly embraced mystical practices and doctrines, so that from the beginning of his organisational career, Sufism exerted a significant impact on his thoughts.[6] He immersed himself deeply in the practices of the order of the Hasafiyyah for more than 20 years and remained involved with Sufism in a special way for most of his life.[7] There is no evidence in his writings that it ever ceased to influence him.[8] Thus the Sufi dimension shaped the deepest foundations of the Muslim Brothers movement, directing it to follow a natural and gradual process of social and political change.

This is one of the more neglected aspects of the history of the Muslim Brothers, overlooked both by researchers and by followers of the Brothers themselves. Studies of the movement so far place emphasis on its political activities and its role in spreading religious radicalisation. The Muslim Brothers are known more as radicals and a threat than for their moderate and gradual agenda in achieving their goals. Christina Phelps Harris, for instance, stresses the most influential experience of al-Banna's life as his father's fundamentalist Hanbalite orientation[9] in which "al-Banna was steeped from his earliest childhood in the puritan teachings of Ibn Hanbal."[10]

However, the direct effect of returning to al-Banna's original thought has meant that for PKS, all religious orientations must be accommodated. Intellectual and religious disputes will inevitably arise — yet the idea of purification itself opposes such inclusiveness. The question must be posed: does the need to return to the original message of the Muslim Brothers' movement require the adoption of the religious inclinations of its founder, or just its political ideas and organisational model? It seems indeed that the adoption of al-Banna's ideas is not confined to the area of politics. The earliest intellectual formation and development of Jemaah Tarbiyah started with the impulse to consider Islam as an alternative to the national ideology of the state. The totality of Islam and its comprehensive nature has since become the main discourse within Jemaah Tarbiyah circles. The influence of al-Banna on Jemaah Tarbiyah remains broad; it can be traced in the ideas, doctrines and organisational instruments of the movement.[11]

1. Heterogeneity of Jemaah Tarbiyah

Writings on specific religious questions, such as Islamic Jurisprudence (*fiqh*) by Jemaah Tarbiyah activists are rare. This indicates wide variation among the activists in their acquisition of religious knowledge and a tolerance of differing opinions. Most of their books are devoted to awakening individual religious awareness and not to compliance with particular issues in jurisprudential precepts. For the latter, they rely on Middle Eastern scholars. The books of Yusuf Qaradawi, for example, have become the most consulted reference for Jemaah Tarbiyah members. The general principle of Jemaah Tarbiyah in dealing with doctrinal issues is to avoid disputes and to seek a common understanding among Muslims, based on a deep grounding in the Qur'an and Hadith. Accordingly, the practices of particular aspects of Islamic jurisprudence depend on the individual religious backgrounds of those concerned.

The degree of rigidity in observance among Jemaah Tarbiyah members varies from one individual to another and in my observation, religious books written by the activists carry few details on the practices or doctrines of any particular school of jurisprudence.[12] Regarding disagreements over doctrine and practice, recourse is made to the rulings of the four orthodox schools, the Hanafi (689-759), Maliki (711-796), Shafii (767-820) and Hanbali (781-856). Jemaah Tarbiyah encourages its cadres to seek reference from authoritative sources. As long as the practices have strong bases in the two fundamental legitimate sources of the Qur'an and Hadith they are tolerated, regardless of possible quibbles over detail. The movement gives free choice to its members to consider the opinions of scholars of different schools. Tolerance in these matters aims to maintain unity among Muslims and to avoid any view that might be introduced by a new sect or belong to a particular group in society.[13] The distinctive character about this movement is its commitment above all to the totality of Islam encompassing all aspects of human life. Religious awareness is considered more important than religious difference

> To become educators on whom people rely for answers about religious questions without creating doubts and disintegration within the community. Attempting to revive the spirit of tolerance, in responding to Islamic jurisprudential disputes, is motivated by a spirit to find a common ground for the sake of uniting the *ummah*.[14]

A seminal book on the theme of preserving the heritage of Hasan al-Banna, entitled *Strategi Dakwah Gerakan Islam* (the Dakwah Strategy of the Islamic Movement) was written by Hilmi Aminuddin, currently head of the Consultative Assembly (Majelis Syura) of PKS. Aminuddin is one of the figures who made initial contact with Muslim Brothers' ideas during his studies in Saudi Arabia. He states the need to "preserve the originality of *dakwah*" (*muhafazah 'ala asalah al-da'wah*) by relying on three issues - originality of faith, worship and prayer, and ideas.[15] These three, however, must not promote a rigid purification or bring blame upon others for practising a "contaminated" form of religion. Although he took Islamic studies in Saudi Arabia, Hilmi Aminuddin is an heir to traditionalist inclinations, having spent many years earlier studying at the Pesantren of Tebuireng in Jombang, East Java, the renowned city of religious boarding schools of a traditionalist reputation.[16]

In fact, attendance at the Jemaah Tarbiyah *halaqah* or a religious meeting does not assure an advanced level of knowledge in any particular area of Islamic jurisprudence or theology. The role of the weekly meetings is only to raise religious awareness and to equip those attending in the broader concepts of Islam. The subjects taught in *halaqah* are very general and simple, far from an expert knowledge of Islam and its heritage.[17] In order to fill the shortfall in Islamic knowledge for its cadres the movement set up religious institutions, called *ma'had* (Ar. *al-ma'had*). In the absence of *ma'had* in areas where there are large numbers of new Jemaah Tarbiyah recruits, members are encouraged to attend other existing reliable Islamic institutions. In Jakarta, the role of the Institute of Islamic and Arabic Studies, Lembaga Ilmu Pengetahuan Islam dan Arab (LIPIA) affiliated with the Imam Ibn Saud University in Saudi Arabia to provide Islamic knowledge among both modernist and traditionalist students coming from a variety of *pesantren* throughout Indonesia has been very significant.

It is interesting to note that the heterogeneity within Jemaah Tarbiyah and the efforts of PKS to bridge the gap between traditionalist and modernist camps in Indonesia have drawn some suspicion from NU and Muhammadiyah. For NU activists, PKS is not only considered to represent the modernists but is also labelled the party of neo-Wahabis or Salafis.[18] This accusation has its basis on the general call of PKS activists to return to the Qur'an and Hadith and the trustworthy founding generation of scholars (*al-salaf al-salih*).[19] For some Muhammadiyah members, particularly the youth, PKS is an alternative and indeed makes more common sense in terms of political ideology. However, the older generation of Muhammadiyah activists still consider PKS not only a political party but also a religious movement subscribing to an ideology different from Muhammadiyah.[20] At the elite level, for both NU and Muhammadiyah PKS is a rival, since it promotes different political and ideological affiliations.

Among the Salafi groups, PKS is considered to have deviated from the true teachings of *al-salaf al-salih* and has often been accused of entertaining religious innovation (*bid'ah*).[21] This accusation is caused by the image of the "problematic figure" of Hasan al-Banna who drew his ideas from both Salafi and Sufi traditions alike. For the followers of "pure" Salafism, Hasan al-Banna was not committed to the doctrines of Salafism. Those ideas unacceptable to Salafi groups were in the main related to practices adopted from the writings of the medieval scholars; al-Ash'ari (d. 935) and al-Ghazali (d.1111).[22] Most Salafi groups do not accept these scholars, whilst al-Banna was very familiar with their writings and practices.[23]

In the 1990s, the once good relations between Salafi groups and Jemaah Tarbiyah in Indonesia were broken because of disappointment among Salafi followers with the decision of PKS to enter politics – Salafis reject practical politics.[24] It seemed that the reason was not only internal friction in Indonesia but rather international friction in responding to the Gulf War in 1990, when the Muslim Brothers gave their support to Iraq instead of Saudi Arab as the backbone of Salafism.[25] In Indonesia, the financial support offered to Jemaah Tarbiyah activities by Saudi Arabia declined after the Gulf War.

2. Turning into Traditionalists

Having realised the need to include traditionalist groups, which have significant numbers of followers in Indonesia, and yet to preserve the originality of the movement, Jemaah Tarbiyah has felt the need to return to the authentic model established by the founder of the Muslim Brothers, Hasan al-Banna. One of the many books written by Jemaah Tarbiyah activists, *Strategi Dakwah Gerakan Islam,* mentioned above, advocates the need to go back to the original texts written by al-Banna.[26] It is recommended that the Arabic versions be read in order to gain a full understanding of his ideas and mission.[27] Whilst other prominent figures such as Sayyid Qutb are widely emulated by contemporary Islamic movements throughout the world, Jemaah Tarbiyah has limited access only to his renowned Qur'an exegesis, *Fi Dilal al-Qur'an* (In the Shade of the Qur'an). Qutb's more radical works are not promoted. Instead, the influence of al-Banna is incalculable and most books written by Jemaah Tarbiyah activists refer to him.[28]

Efforts to preserve the originality of the movement employing the initial methods of al-Banna have led to other theological and doctrinal consequences. Al-Banna's traditionalist and Sufi orientations have greatly influenced the practices of the Muslim Brothers. Undoubtedly, members of Jemaah Tarbiyah brought up in the modernist traditions of Indonesia meet confusion in al-Banna's intellectual heritage. However, those already within Jemaah Tarbiyah and familiar with al-Banna's ideas have tolerance towards the practices of Sufism, as long as they are based in Islam. Sufism that upholds a valid Islamic morality and is derived from Islamic sources is allowable.[29]

However, the spirit of bringing the movement into accordance with the Qur'an and Hadith remains the main agenda. All efforts towards this end are carried out in a gradual and consensual manner, not to create tensions in society. For Jemaah Tarbiyah, a long-term predication is the only and best option and Jemaah Tarbiyah programs have started to accommodate traditionalist elements since its decision to be involved in the political arena.

Activists of Jemaah Tarbiyah have been well aware that esoteric Sufi teachings have had strong roots in Indonesian Islam for many centuries. Greater political Islamism, which would undermine spirituality, would cause alienation from mainstream Islam, in particular from NU. Instead of criticising the role of Sufism in the process of the Islamisation of Indonesia, the famed nine saints (*walisongo*) from the history of Java are considered by Jemaah Tarbiyah to be local pioneers of Islamic movements.[30]

On the other hand, the teachings of al-Banna are responsible for the "pragmatic approach" of PKS to politics. It was al-Banna who often advocated a "middle way" and was keen to avoid religious conflict in order to maintain social harmony. This "middle" inclination was also typical of al-Ash'ari and al-Ghazali, al-Banna's inspirations. PKS activists are quite aware that adopting al-Banna's ideas has led them to accommodation in politics. Ahmad Firman Yusuf, a former head of the Central Board of PK (1999-2004) says that "most Muslim activists have viewed the ideas of the Muslim Brothers as too tolerant and flexible in upholding the *shariah*. Al-Banna based his opinions on the concept of benefit in *dakwah* (*maslahah al-da'wah*). However, besides his "tolerant attitude" in *dakwah*, his opinions always have justification in the principles of *shariah*."[31] For instance, the decision to be involved in a secular system was widely criticised by many Muslim activists since this involvement meant to acknowledge secular and infidel rule that is in violation of the message of the Qur'an.[32] Within al-Banna's understanding of *maslahah*, involvement in a secular system is preferable if it prevents harm and beings benefit, even though that benefit may only be relative.[33]

This attitude sets Jemaah Tarbiyah apart from other Islamic groups, who prefer to make clear cut distinctions between what is allowable (*al-halal*) and unallowable (*al-haram*). Such tolerance of the secular system is influenced by Sufi teachings. As has been suggested by Michael Gilsenan, the political importance of the Sufi orders has been characterised by their inclination to serve as mediators and peacemakers in a system in which dispute has been only one element in the constant tension born out of a need for security.[34] The Sufi orders cut across the ties of geography, kinship and tribal affiliation, forming a framework for a broader set of social relations and political cohesion.[35]

Hasan al-Banna was "a schoolteacher with a background of individual and family religious studies and a modern oriented education."[36] He was not a typically deep thinker, such as Jamal al-Din al-Afghani, Muhammad Abduh or other reformist figures; rather he was a charismatic leader who was able to pave the way for the establishment of a viable and effective Islamic movement. What makes him distinct from scholars before and during his time, despite his success as a propagandist and leader of a movement, was that he never undertook advanced religious studies. He graduated from a secular university, Darul Ulum University in Cairo, specialising in educational training. He was more concerned with bringing people from different sects together and avoiding doctrinal disputes.[37] His training in mysticism (*tasawwuf*), which he received within the regime of the Hasafiyyah Shadziliyyah order, moulded his entire personality. However, his inclination toward Sufism, which had made itself felt since childhood, was not purely otherworldly; it did not prevent him from being actively concerned with concrete social issues and activities.[38]

Initially, the Muslim Brothers was a socio-religious movement which aimed at restoring the spiritual and social dimensions of Egyptian Muslims, while at the time challenging the influence of Christian missionaries in Egypt.[39] Overwhelmed by the political and social problems of his nation under the impact of Western civilisation, al-Banna felt that Egyptian society had departed from the gaols of its faith; therefore, returning society into the guidance of Islam became the main goal of the Muslim Brothers.[40] The movement expanded its role to engage in a struggle to "liberate" Egypt and the Arab world from foreign occupation and domination. Since it offered a reform-based Islamic framework against a corrupted society and government, it gained popularity and support from the humbler rural and urban societies of Egypt. Even more, albeit not organisationally controlled, the Muslim Brothers expanded their influence and attracted large numbers of Muslims throughout the world, including the Indonesian offshoot.[41]

Thus Hasan al-Banna tried to accommodate a wide range of Islamic orientations, conceiving his initial movement as (1) a Salafi movement (*dakwah salafiyyah*) to reject any actions contrary to the Qur'an and the *Sunnah*; (2) a Sunni path (*tariqah sunniyyah*) that inclines it to practise the Prophet's way of life; (3) a Sufi truth (*haqiqah sufiyyah*) that emphasises virtue and purity; (4) a political organization (*hay'ah siyasiyyah*) that calls for political change from within; (5) an athletic group (*jama'ah riyadiyyah*) that stresses the significance of physical exercise; (6) a cultural and scientific body (*rabitah 'ilmiyyah thaqafiyyah*) that seeks to enhance the knowledge of its members and others about Islam; (7) an economic enterprise (*shirkah iqtisadiyyah*) that calls upon its members to gain economic power and ensure its distribution; and (8) a social ideal (*jama'ah ijtima'iyyah*) that is committed to solve the malaise of society.[42]

It was Hasan al-Banna who laid the basic foundations of the doctrines that combined Sufism, which focuses on the spiritual and mental development of the individual, and social activism, which encourages its adherents to be involved with people.[43] Al-Banna himself saw no contradiction between Sufism's ethical and spiritual goals and his own social praxis.[44] In the end, he acknowledged that the final shape of the Muslim Brothers resulted from the intellectual and social evolution of his own Sufi affiliation with the Hasafiyya*h* order.[45] Interestingly, this order was led by his close spiritual friend, Ahmad Syukri, whom he transferred to the Muslim Brothers branch in Ismailiyah and then chose as his deputy in Cairo.[46]

Through his deep involvement with the Hasafiyyah order, al-Banna also paved the way for reform in Sufi doctrines which benefited their organizations as prospective religious and social movements. The structure of his own movement is very much based on Sufi concepts and terms. Even though he did not attribute it to any particular order (*tariqah*), the usages and practices of Sufism are found in the organisational terms of the Muslim Brothers. He called his followers *al-ikhwan* (brothers) and assumed the title of *murshid* (supervisor). He used the Sufi term *bay'ah* (oath) to initiate new members and obliged them to practise his compilation of *wirid* and *wazifah* (prayers). The mutual feelings developed among members also show a profound Sufi inclination, signified by such terms as brotherhood (*ukhuwwah*) and family (*usrah*).[47]

Al-ikhwan (brothers) indicates the specific type of mutual friendship among the members of a Sufi order; in its strictest sense, the term *al-ikhwan* refers to members of the same Sufi line, for instance, those of the Naqsyabandiyyah, Tijaniyyah, Qadiriyyah, and so forth. There is mutual obligation as well: a member of a *tariqah*, (*al-ikhwan*) may travel through distant regions, accepting hospitality along the way from local brothers. The *ikhwan* code guarantees the traveller will find shelter or food within the order.[48]

From the beginning, the Muslim Brothers did not aim to single themselves out from broader Egyptian society. Instead of identifying his followers as a tightly knit or closed group like the *tarekat* (Ar. *tariqah*), Hasan al-Banna preferred to name his organisation *al-ikhwan al-muslimun* (Muslim Brothers).[49] He did not want to deal with religious disputes arising among members of different Sufi orders or to limit his call to a narrow element of society. His organization had to address all levels of the broader society, based on three fundamentals –

knowledge (*al-'ilm*), education (*al-tarbiyyah*) and striving (*al-jihad*). However, he provided the opportunity for those who wanted to go through the special training of the brotherhoods to do so.[50] In the long run, however, the Muslim Brothers could not escape from an exclusivist orientation; indeed it developed into a group quite set apart from community at large.

Murshid (General Guide) is the title of the supreme leader of a Sufi order and the title taken by the head of the Muslim Brothers. It literally means "the one who gives spiritual guidance to his pupils" (*murid*). Within the Sufi tradition, the *murshid,* or *sheikh* is capable of bringing his pupils into a closer relation to God. He is "an inspired man to whose eyes the mysteries of the hidden are revealed, because he sees with the light of God and knows what thoughts and confusion are in man's hearts."[51] The uppermost thing in Sufi practice is to find a good guide on whom followers may rely totally. The pupils should follow the instructions of the guide without reservation.[52]

Most importantly for al-Banna, the choice of Sufi custom and the stress on the religious bond between the leader and the led reinforced the significance of personal authority within the Muslim Brothers. Al-Banna was able to revise the requirement of absolute obedience to the teacher into more flexible relations by emphasising the need for students to maintain their own freedom of thinking. He still required the sincere observation of the obligatory prayers *(salah),* the liturgies *(dhikr)* and ethics *(akhlaq).*[53] He based his leadership on his charismatic authority but also confined it within the framework of a bureaucratic and hierarchical organization.[54] Furthermore, he emphasised that not all of the instructions of the *murshid* should be followed, particularly in dealing with non-religious matters. In one of his "twenty principles and guidelines for followers of the Muslim Brothers" he explained:

> The opinion of the leader or his deputy regarding issues that are not clearly ruled out in the text and may attract possible interpretation but serve the public interest (*maslahah*) may be applied as long as the statement does not contradict *shariah* principles. However, it may change depending on the changing of conditions, time and local tradition. Principally, worship requires a total surrender without considering the meaning, but non-worship activities should be examined as to their meanings and goals.[55]

Nevertheless, al- Banna maintained the style of *murshid* leadership in running his society of the Muslim Brothers to a certain extent. He was a charismatic leader, since none of his companions was able to challenge his leadership. As General Guide of the Brothers, he demanded the loyalty of his followers and held "the power in his own hands and personally directed the program and the policies of his organization."[56] His personal characteristics and outstanding intellectual attainment were evident from the respect he was given. Even those who knew him personally, though had never belonged to the Muslim Brothers, acknowledged his personal qualities

> Al-Banna had three outstanding qualifications for leadership. He had an extraordinary amount of personal charm and magnetism; he was a most eloquent speaker, with a degree of oratorical power that moved his audiences deeply; and he possessed an unusually good command of his native tongue. In the Arabic-speaking world, any man with the ability to express himself fluently in excellent Arabic is highly appreciated and respected.[57]

However, it is because of his Sufi style of leadership that many writers on the Muslim Brothers have criticised his leadership: it was not democratic in nature. For instance, Zakariyya Sulayman Bayumi contended that the autocratic style of Hasan al-Banna and lack of democracy in the Muslim Brothers were serious defects in the organization.[58] Furthermore, a number of leftist Egyptian historians, such as Rif'at al-Said[59] and Tariq al-Bisri[60] accused the movement of representing the opponents of the democratic forces because of its alignment with the "autocratic" and "fascist" forces of the palace.[61] This leadership style has also drawn criticism of Jemaah Tarbiyah in Indonesia. It is accused of being too focussed on the relationship of the *murabbi* (mentor) towards his *mutarabbi* (student) in which the student should obey whatever the mentor has instructed. The process of conveying knowledge is often seen as indoctrination. Even the case of marriage among *halaqah* members, the *murabbi* has a significant role in determining the marriage process. The relationship between *murabbi* and *mutarabbi* also depends to a large extent on the character of the *murabbi*, who may be flexible or strict.[62]

Another term borrowed from the *tariqah* and applied by al-Banna is *bay'ah*, the oath taken by the seeker of mystical wisdom to abide by the organization's rules and guidelines. Strictly speaking, none of the Sufi orders accept new members of the *tariqah* without the swearing of this covenant. Only those to have taken the vow of allegiance to the leader of the order are allowed to begin practising the rituals. Before taking the oath, the candidate should make sincere repentance before God and renounce his or her past sins.[63] The new student places his hand in the hand of the *murshid* and the *murshid* administers the covenant that he or she accepts the *murshid* as his or her guide.[64] It should be noted that each Sufi order has its own particular details and ways of proceeding in performing the ceremony of covenant taking.

The first members of the Muslim Brothers swore their allegiance to the *murshid* al-Banna himself. They were six labourers working in the British Company of the Suez Canal, and were seeking a guide able to improve their spiritual and social conditions. Even though it has not been clearly described for posterity, the event of the covenant taking by these ordinary people indicates the strong relations between leader and led.[65] It explicitly shows the Sufi code, when laymen surrendered themselves and all their possessions - blood, soul and coin, to express their adherence to an honourable spiritual Guide.[66] Since that moment, al-Banna fulfilled his dream to become a respected Guide and teacher (*murshid* and *mu'allim*) and guided his followers accordingly.[67] He also successfully reformed the absolute dependence of students upon their teacher into the concept of solidarity and brotherhood among the members, under the banner of the Muslim Brothers, in which the *murshid* was included.

In the case of PKS, cadres are expected to make allegiance to the party, just as are cadres of Jemaah Tarbiyah. Since the Majelis Syura occupies the highest status in the party leadership, all committee members of the party should obey and exercise decisions issued by it. The Majelis Syura is also charged to elect the members of central board committees and to formulate all strategies of the party. Members of Majelis Syura are appointed through internal elections held by the central board of the party. It represents senior members of Jemaah Tarbiyah from the provincial branches, and some scholars and social leaders. Candidates of Majelis Syura must hold at least the level of *ahli* (expert) in the party. The membership of the party is divided into three levels: sympathizers or *pemula* (beginners) and *muda* (the young); core cadres of *madya* (intermediate), *dewasa* (mature) and *ahli* (expert) status, and *purna* (advanced), and *luar biasa* (extraordinary) which are based on merit. When the members of Majelis Syura are formally elected, they are obliged to swear allegiance to the party.[68]

To realise commonality and the sharing of aims rather than a single-focussed loyalty, al-Banna revised the concept and practice of attachment to the *murshid* (*rabitah murshid*) to the attachment to fellow students (*rabitah muridin*). When the *rabit}ah murshid* is undertaken as a practice in certain other Sufi orders, students are instructed to visualise their master and sense his presence within their hearts. Al-Banna's newly devised *rabitah* however involved a process of communal visualisation among fellow students.[69] Thus the *rabitah,* understood as a special spiritual relation, was not monopolised by the master but was shared by all members. In practising *rabitah,* the Brothers were to visualise their fellow members' faces and try to feel spiritual contact with them (even those with whom they had no acquaintance). Then the following prayer was recited

> O Allah, indeed you know that our hearts have gathered for the sake of your love, met for the purpose of obedience, united under your mission and promised to uphold your path. O Allah! Strengthen our relations, endure our passion, and give us your light that never reduces to a glimmer! Widen our hearts with full faith and the beauty of submission

and revive them with your knowledge. Show me the way of *jihad*. Surely, you are the best Guide and Helper.[70]

Recognising the Sufi aspects of al-Banna's teachings, it is understandable that some members of PKS have begun to acknowledge the practice of Sufism within Islam. A practical example of this is the forging of close contact between the PKS branches of West and Central Java with leaders of the Sufi orders, the Tarekat Syahadatain and Tarekat Rifa'iyyah of those provinces. The leaders of both of these *tarekat* have welcomed the PKS campaigns and have readily introduced the PKS to their members in the 2004 general elections.[71]

Furthermore, efforts to appreciate non-modernist elements of Islam by committee members of PKS have developed, not only in certain regions, but in many others as well. In the area of Islamic knowledge and thought there has been a similar trend. The publishing of books in great numbers dealing with Sufi subjects by PKS-associated publishers indicates the movement's increasing inclination to extend its membership among Muslims of a traditionalist background. The Rabbani Press which was so well known in the mid-1980s for publishing political materials by the Muslim Brothers has moved to concern itself with issues of the "purification of the heart," a central theme in Sufi traditions. It has published many books written by al-Ghazali (1058-1111), re-edited by the Muslim Brothers scholar, Sayyid Hawwa on the classic *Ihya Ulumuddin* (The Revival of the Religious Sciences) and other Sufi subjects. However, the categorical rejection of Sufism among modernist groups in Indonesia makes some activists of PKS inclined to use the term, *tazkiyyah al-nafs* (purification of heart) than "Sufism." In dealing with the subject of the love of God, Hidayat Nurwahid, former president of PKS and currently Chairperson of the People's Consultative Assembly, Majelis Permusyawaratan Rakyat (MPR, 2004-2005) avoids the use of the term "*tasawwuf*": "The love of God (*al-hub Ila Allah*) is a central and fundamental topic in theology and within the purified soul.".[72]

So to summarise all of the above, in comparison with their modernist predecessors, the activists of PKS of today value the practice of Sufism. In translating the ideas of al-Banna, they are far more permissive of Sufism than the "real" proponents of purification movements, such as Muhammadiyah or Persis. A heated issue in Sufism, and one stridently rejected by modernist groups, is the subject of *tawassul* (prayer for mediation). Whilst the reformist groups emphasise prayer as direct communication with God, the traditionalists allow room for mediation between humankind and the Creator. This mediation is believed to be carried out by the four great companions of the Prophet and deceased local saints. Al-Banna himself discussed this question of mediation at some length in his book, *Majmu'a al-Rasail* (Collected Writings), first translated into Indonesian by *Media Dakwah* in 1983 and recently again by the PKS-associated Era Intermedia in 2002. However, since *Media Dakwah* has been influenced by modernist and even puritan ideas, it interpreted the issue of *tawassul*, as addressed by Hasan al-Banna, as a denial of its validity. Era Intermedia, on the other hand, considers it to be a disputed issue that may be tolerated.[73]

The Sufi influences bringing PKS to a pragmatic and flexible approach in promoting its objectives can be seen in the way in which members of Jemaah Tarbiyah has formulated its strategy of Islamising the state. The following steps, as given by Cahyadi Takariawan in his book *Rekayasa Masa Depan Menuju Kemenangan Dakwah Islam,* [74] are an elaboration of al-Banna's emphasis on the need to initiate *dakwah* from individual, to family and to society. A society that is motivated and familiar with the teachings of Islam will automatically determine the nature of the state.[75]

B. Steps to Islamise the State

Jemaah Tarbiyah was originally a purely religious movement but it has remained by no means without political motives in the long term. My study of its fundamental doctrines and principles of operation reveals that since the very beginning, Jemaah Tarbiyah has had a systematic and clear political orientation, even if it had not then been put into practice. Mahfudz Sidiq, a student activist of Jemaah Tarbiyah in the 1980s and currently the head of the PKS faction in DPR RI illustrated the political nature of the movement

> When I joined Jemaah Tarbiyah in the mid 1980s, we had no aim to establish a political party. However, the main discourse was to develop a framework for Islam that included politics. In those socio-political conditions, Islam was considered as the antithesis of existing Indonesian political practice. Islam provides an alternative, but not necessarily a political party.[76]

In fact, not all cadres of Jemaah Tarbiyah initially supported the establishment of the political party in 1998. A survey circulated among 6000 cadres asking whether Jemaah Tarbiyah should establish a party or a mass organization produced surprising results. About 68% of respondents supported the establishment of a party, 27% of respondents preferred to form a mass organization and the remainder wanted Jemaah Tarbiyah kept to be as an informal movement.[77] Many members of PKS committees whom I interviewed revealed that they initially did not support the setting up of the party and would have preferred a mass organization.[78] One of the reasons in favour of forming a political party was in order to not provoke confrontation with the mainstream Islamic mass organizations: NU, Muhammadiyah, and Persis.[79] However, only Muhammadiyah and Persis members in the grassroots level felt close to PKS; members of NU were then still reluctant to join.

It was the growing student interest in politics that pushed Jemaah Tarbiyah towards taking a more politically explicit role. Through their political experiences within the campuses, the members of Jemaah Tarbiyah have been able to play a significant role in responding to political events outside. They have organised protests against the government on issues that varied from religious demands, such as the issue of women's head covering, to the more politically focussed, such as demanding that President Soeharto step down.

The unique character of Jemaah Tarbiyah lies in its attitude to *dakwah* and politics. In general, the group makes no distinction between the two. As a political party, the religious agenda of PKS is much more closely intertwined with its politics rather than is the case with other parties. Through the political party, huge public gatherings (*tabligh akbar*) are organised, combining both religious and political issues. Furthermore, most of the political activities are self-funded through professional arrangements of religious charities. Members of the party are obliged to pay religious dues, *zakat*,[80] *infaq*[81] and *shadaqah*[82] regularly to the party. Other Islamic parties like PKB, PPP and PBB, for instance, also use the religious services of NU for supporting party candidates, but not in such an integrated way as PKS. PKB has not organised the regular religious gatherings (*pengajian*) or the collection of donations as extensively as PKS has done.

Since there is no separation of the religious and the political in the party, the activists of the PKS prefer to consider it merely an extension of the field of *dakwah*. They distinguish their party from others in Indonesia by calling it *Partai Dakwah* (the *Dakwah* Party). So even though it is a political organ, it carries out the holy duty of *dakwah* within the broadest context. In order to manage and organise its constituents throughout the archipelago, PKS has divided Indonesia into four *dakwah* territories, or *Wilayah Dakwah* (Wilda). These are Wilda I for Sumatra, Wilda II for DKI Jakarta, Banten, West Java and Kalimantan, Wilda III for Central Jawa, Sulawesi and Papua, and Wilda IV for the East Java, West Nusa Tenggara and East Nusa Tenggara.[83] Each Wilda head is expected to appear as a religious and political figure among the people of the regions.

The principle of integrating religious and political activities is not an unusual one for PKS. They believe that Islam is an integral system guiding human beings to win prosperity on earth and in the hereafter. Prosperity itself can be achieved by individual and collective efforts to develop spiritual qualities for the triumph of Islam. The party should function as a vehicle to meet the needs of the people in attaining material and spiritual prosperity.[84]

In order to accomplish the mission of the *dakwah* party, *dakwah* should be managed in a professional way and follow a strategy, which is termed the *shiyasah al-da'wah* (the politics of predication). The effectiveness of the *dakwah* programme lies in its contribution to political, cultural and religious changes in society as well as within the state. Such changes are needed to ensure that society and the state are always under the guidance of the teachings of Islam.

The writings of the Jemaah Tarbiyah activists focus mainly on the issue of the "politics of *dakwah*." *Dakwah* must be carried out systematically, following well-prepared steps and phases that have been set by the movement. *Dakwah* cadres are not only required to convey religious messages to the wider members of society but they are also supposed to form "literate and educated groups" who clearly understand the essence of being Muslim and who will act in accordance with the goals and missions determined by the *dakwah* initiators. In general, steps to Islamise the state by the Jemaah Tarbiyah are best described in four stages. These phases are standard guidelines for all active members of the movement in order for it to achieve its long-term goal of the "Islamisation" of Indonesia.

1. Creating Strong Cadres

The first stage in creating cadres in Jemaah Tarbiyah is through special training, initially informal, with an emphasis on ideological internalisation. A strong cadre base is vital to achieve the movement's goals. It is through individuals who have internalised the teachings of Islam that a further process of Islamisation in all its aspects is likely. The slogan that Jemaah Tarbiyah espouses is derived from a saying of a prominent leader of the Muslim Brothers, Hasan al-Hudaibi, "uphold Islam in your heart, and it will grow strong within your society."[85]

Yet the phase of "ideology building" among new members (*mihwar tanzim*) is not an easy one.[86] This stage best describes the condition of Jemaah Tarbiyah during its initial development in Indonesia during the New Order. Most activists experienced difficulty in maintaining communications and contact with others. They could not easily liaise with their fellow members, since the government was suspicious of any movements they saw as threatening the stability of the nation. Jemaah Tarbiyah members were forced to maintain secrecy and to avoid contact with other Muslims.

The pioneers of Jemaah Tarbiyah newly returned from their studies in the Saudi universities, however, succeeded in establishing contact with fellow Muslim student activists on the Indonesian campuses. Since the mid-1980s they have been able to train many cadres, the majority from university backgrounds. The reason to target students in the secular universities as the backbone of the movement was prompted by the fact that such students were more open to new ideas that were different from traditionalist and modernist orientations. These students were not deeply rooted in the Islamic traditions of their parents, and the campus milieus loosened their attachment to any previous religious affiliations. New ideas brought back by the Saudi graduates and introduced into

Tarbiyah provided an alternative vehicle for young Muslim activists to struggle for Islam.[87]

The success of Jemaah Tarbiyah in generating strong cadres has also provided a strong base for PKS. PKS is the only real cadre party in Indonesia. Their strength of character has been evident in some of their activities involving thousands of participants. For instance, they often prove that they can hold demonstrations and stage political campaigns of mass participation without violence or anarchic behaviour.[88] Numerically, too, the solidity of mass support for PKS is the result of a long process of *Tarbiyah* training since the 1980s. *Tarbiyah* training has created thousands of cadres with strong ideology, so that the movement has become widespread throughout the Indonesian archipelago.[89]

The dynamics of *halaqah*, influenced by Sufi patron-client relations, differs from the methods of caderisation of other Islamic student groups, such PMII,[90] HMI and PII. During the cadre phase, members are requested to make selective recruitment through the *halaqah*. A successful *halaqah* is one which continues to grow and constantly generates more groups of *halaqah*. However, the essence of *halaqah* is not a matter of the recruitment of cadres in terms of numbers alone; careful consideration must also be given to cadres' qualities and expertise.[91] For instance, the religious and educational backgrounds of prospective cadres are important considerations as to whether or not to include them in the movement. Candidate cadres with a high level of education who hold vital positions in the work place or in society are more favourable than those who have only basic schooling. In addition, those who have been involved with terrorist organisations are to be excluded, since it is Jemaah Tarbiyah's policy not to recruit or even make contact with them.[92] It actively discourages its members from communicating with such groups for any purpose, including business activity and social interaction.[93]

The chief concern is to selectively enlist potential cadres who will guarantee the movement's interests in the future. Because of the secret nature of the recruitment process in the past, when Jemaah Tarbiyah was under surveillance from the regime, many members segregated themselves from wider society. However, when the regime's surveillance was lifted and there was more freedom to express ideas, the model of secret recruitment changed. Now, under the banner of PKS, all recruitment is open to the public. Members of *halaqah* are allowed to invite non-members, including non-Muslims, to attend *halaqah*. These non-member guests are usually asked to share their own knowledge and expertise with the members.[94]

Cadres formed in the first phase commit themselves to uphold the movement's ideals. The Jemaah Tarbiyah doctrine of Islam as an all encompassing system of life, as formulated by Hasan al-Banna, becomes their guideline.[95] Though they may have come from different religious backgrounds or social affiliations, they are expected to subvert these to the movement's mission. The movement requires their adherence and observance, and in order to join Jemaah Tarbiyah the cadre needs to take an oath of allegiance (*bay'ah*).[96]

According to the PK database of 1999, since the establishment of Jemaah Tarbiyah activities in the 1980s, about 30,000 cadres, mostly student and university alumni, have joined the campaign for the party in the 1999 general elections. The party gained about 1,436,565 votes. It claims that during the 2004 general elections, numbers of active members of PKS reached more than 300,000 full time workers for the party.[97] Furthermore, the increase in the numbers of cadres has had an impact on the party's performance in the general elections of 2004, even though external factors, such as campaign programmes that have allied the party with the urban grassroots, have also played a part in this success.

2. Socialising the Ideas

The members of Jemaah Tarbiyah recognise that significant changes towards a more "Islamic" society cannot be built solely on cadres; the movement must also muster mass support.[98] Needless to say, they also maintain that the process of Islamising Indonesian society and the state must be gained through gradual and non-violent ways. Creating committed cadres is simply the first step in influencing the masses.

Thus Jemaah Tarbiyah is well aware of the need for interacting with and influencing broader sections of society. Once the strong cadres have been formed, the group moves to the second phase of its strategy, preparing to socialise its ideas and aims to the people in general. This stage is called "the phase of socialization" (*mihwar sha'bi*) in which popular acceptance is sought. If the first stage emphasises building the character of cadres, this second stage moves forward to examine to what extent *Tarbiyah* ideas will be accepted or rejected. Cadres are expected to present as exemplars to all people from various backgrounds. If earlier they have considered non-members of the movement as "others," they are now required to display a common interest with all of society. It is crucial that they develop the skills of good communication.

At the same time, cadres are still required to recruit new members so far as possible. Activists introduce the movement's aims to members of the elite and to prominent figures in society. The role of such figures becomes an important consideration. For instance, in the past, Nurcholish Madjid received harsh criticism from many activists of Jemaah Tarbiyah. A sharp debate between Nurcholish Madjid and Daud Rasyid (of Jemaah Tarbiyah) in 1992 resulted in a strong rejection of the ideas of Madjid among Jemaah Tarbiyah members. Others of Jemaah Tarbiyah, such as Abu Ridha, Hidayat Nurwahid and Didin Hafiduddin also joined in the attack on Madjid. Interestingly, relations between Madjid and Jemaah Tarbiyah improved, in particular after Madjid was invited by the Justice Party to be a keynote speaker during the opening ceremony of its National Meeting (*Musyawarah Nasional*) in 2000. Madjid himself, in order to draw the interest of Islamic parties (since he intended to stand as a presidential candidate in 2004) affirmed he did not mean by the slogan "Islam Yes, Islamic Party No!" to reject the existence of an "Islamic party" per se. On the contrary, he admitted that his earlier rejection of an "Islamic party" during the 1970s was prompted by his criticism, as a young Muslim, of the then Islamic parties that were mostly corrupt.[99] Jemaah Tarbiyah activists were able to accept Madjid's change of attitude as normal when referred to the example of one of the founders of Islamic jurisprudence, Muhammad Ibn Idris Al-Shafi'i (d. 820) who held both *al-qawl al-qadim* (the old opinion) and *al-qawl al-jadid* (the new opinion) to make new ruling.[100]

Social services and community assistance have become the movement's chief instruments in attracting the masses. In this, it is supported not only by its core cadres but also by outsiders sympathetic to its objectives. It has also subsequently established a number of non-governmental organizations (NGO) that focus on social, educational and cultural activities. It has established a number of educational and religious institutions to support the process of recruitment from various levels of society, such as the educational tutoring centre of Nurul Fikri in 1984, the Islamic higher education of al-Hikmah in 1987, the Islamic missionary institute of Khairu Ummah in 1989 and the contemporary Islamic and social studies of Sidik in 1992.

The Nurul Fikri Foundation has helped high school students to enter university, training them to successfully answer the entry tests. Besides its secular subjects, the foundation also has provided students with religious instruction and encouraged them to support Islamic activities on campus once they have gained admission. Many alumni of the foundation have become student activists affiliated with PKS.

The Islamic higher education institution of al-Hikmah was set up to prepare university students in Islamic subjects. Initially it was a type of traditionalist educational centre, founded by Haji Hasan. It was Hasan's son, Abdul Hasib, who graduated in Saudi Arabia in 1987 who developed it into a formal institution. Abdul Hasib is currently a member of the Consultative Board of PKS. Students from secular universities in Jakarta, such as UI, IKIP and Trisakti University, have attended evening classes in al-Hikmah. It has been responsible for many activists of Jemaah Tarbiyah establishing similar institutions in other regions where secular campuses also exist.[101]

The Khairu Ummah foundation is a predication institute (*lembaga dakwah*) established by some senior members of Jemaah Tarbiyah. It aims to provide preachers and Friday lecturers for campuses and community mosques in Jakarta. It also sends preachers to give lectures in Islamic training organised by Muslim students and other Islamic gatherings in commercial offices and business centres. Activists of Khairu Ummah also often serve audiences outside Jakarta and other areas outside Java.[102]

Abu Ridha, Al-Muzammil Yusuf and Habib Abu Bakar al-Habsyi established the Study and Information for Contemporary Islamic World, Studi dan Informasi Dunia Islam Kontemporer (SIDIK).[103] This centre aims to provide social and political studies for members of Jemaah Tarbiyah. Through SIDIK, news of events in the Islamic world have been passed on to students in universities and Islamic communities as well, through printed media, audiovisual material and seminars. SIDIK also contributed to political analysis in preparing for the establishment of PK in 1998.

3. Forming a Political Party

Jemaah Tarbiyah continues to enter political institutions. This is the "stage of political penetration" (*mihwar mu'assasi*) in which it introduces political education and training to its cadres, even though they have known from the beginning that the movement makes no hard and fast distinction between religion and politics. The problem was once that they did not previously know whether the movement would transform itself into a political party or a religious mass organization, such as NU and Muhammadiyah.

The application of this third stage is again a further elaboration of a concept of al-Banna to exert political influence on the existing government. Even though al-Banna did not recommend establishing a party, the concept of Islam as a universal and complete system encompassing all aspects of human life has been translated by Jemaah Tarbiyah activists as a reason to participate in the political process through a political party. Al-Banna himself said that Islam is a combination of inseparables: state and nation, rulers and people, morality and strength, love and equity, civilization and constitution, knowledge and justice, income and natural resources, effort and wealth, *jihad* and *dakwah*, and army and knowledge.[104]

Since then many activists who had previously devoted their energies to religious training and *dakwah* activities have become keen to be involved in political issues. Jemaah Tarbiyah activists on campus in the 1990s became more familiar with day-to-day student concerns, ranging from labour issues to national political problems, alongside their previous religious interests. Of course, their involvement in political activities has not been achieved without preparation. Eep Saifullah Fatah, a former Islamic activist at the University of Indonesia, reports that in 1994 the Jemaah Tarbiyah cadres began to run political training in tandem with the regular religious programs. According to Fatah, the training aimed to raise the political awareness of the members and prepared the way for the next step of "Islamisation." A number of prominent political scholars and experts, such as Arbi Sanit and Deliar Noer were invited to give lectures.[105] Jemaah Tarbiyah activists then not only read books on Islamic subjects but began to read more widely into politics, sociology and philosophy.

The process of "Islamisation" for Jemaah Tarbiyah is not limited to the *dakwah* programs but includes a highly structured progression in expertise. When the cadres have successfully passed through the first stage, they proceed to the next. The success of their political experiments on the campuses has prompted them to find a more explicit political vehicle to achieve the movement's goals. The activists of Jemaah Tarbiyah are expected to play a role as politicians. The politicians of PKS should be able to present themselves as professional and clean figures in the People's Representative Assembly (DPR). They should be able to restore the bad image of some politicians and demonstrate a high standard of personal morality. In addition, the political party serves as a vehicle to further influence the policies of the government by drafting policies of a more apparent Islamic nature.[106]

The establishment of Partai Keadilan in 1998 indicated that the stage of political penetration had begun. Nonetheless, at this stage cadres were still permitted to join other political parties of similar vision and ideology.[107] The reason was that *dakwah* should not be confined to any one political institution.[108] But some Jemaah Tarbiyah figures maintained that cadres could only possibly join social missions or professional organizations, and not another political party, as the group had already established its own.[109] As it turned out, few members of the Jemaah Tarbiyah actually gave their allegiance to parties other than their own. This was because Jemaah Tarbiyah considered PK as the only political party for their activists.

4. Penetrating the State

After the stage of political participation, cadres are encouraged to enter the state bureaucracy and to bring about changes in policy toward more Islamic goals. If the stage of building a political institution allows the movement to bring its cadres into the legislative body of the state, the next stage is more practically aimed of placing cadres in government organs. This is called "the era of the state" (*mihwar dawli*).[110] The movement has no ambition to foment revolution or to take power but rather to exert influence through the active participation of its best cadres in cabinet and other governmental positions.

The commitment of the movement to abide by constitutional law is without question. It believes that the only way to bring change is through natural and constitutional means, in which the people and the state organs freely accept it. Of course, "change" here is the transformation of the state towards becoming more Islamic in nature. Does this stage entail the establishment of an Islamic state?

In general, both the ideals of Jemaah Tarbiyah and its political vehicle, PKS are on common ground about the nature of the state. The state and its leaders merely carry out their duties to God, in whom resides ultimate authority. The state should not violate the rules of God or pass laws that are in contradiction with the laws of God. In addition, the role of the leaders of the state should be solely to provide the people's necessities. The task of the state for PKS activists is

> Reforming it to be a "truly Islamic state" so that it will serve the interests of the people and function as a servant of the people for their sake and welfare.[111]

It appears so far that for PKS, the question of a formal Islamic state is not part of its political platform. A truly "Islamic" state need not necessarily be an Islamic state by name but should represent the Islamic virtues, such as accountability, love and care, justice, modesty and probity in spending funds.[112] However, this does not mean that the party rejects the idea of an Islamic state altogether. Some members of PKS still envision an Islamic state of some form or another. Some still insist that "if not an Islamic state, then what kind of state do Muslims need?"[113] This issue is likely to be a major obstacle against PKS' expansion of its political influence in the future; there is real suspicion and a sense of threat that has developed among non-Muslim groups and other sections of the Indonesian people.

In order to bridge the disjunction between their Islamic ideals and political realities, some activists of PKS are prepared to compromise the idea of an Islamic state by stating that as long as the state realises universal virtues and functions to meet the needs of the people, such a state may be considered to be Islamic.[114] The chairman of PKS, Tifatul Sembiring has insisted that the Republic of Indonesia is the final form of the state for Indonesians.[115] The possible synthesis between small members of Jemaah Tarbiyah's insistence on a formal Islamic state and PKS's realistic approach of Islamisation needs further experiment in Indonesia's consolidated system of democracy. The contribution of all groups and communities that make up the nation must be considered.

By carefully following its steps in Islamising society and the state, Jemaah Tarbiyah and its political party have developed confidence in achieving their ideals. If the ideologues of Jemaah Tarbiyah have succeeded in solving the theological disputes over the issue of politics and Muslims' involvement in an un-Islamic system, their solutions to internal obstacles in accepting democracy should reach the same outcome. Their argument in accepting democracy is very simple.

> If we define democracy as the sovereignty of the people whilst all of the *umat Islam* are hostile to democracy and politics, we, as the majority of citizens will loose the opportunity to rule our country and we will let

the country be ruled by others. We have to use democracy to reclaim our power.[116]

The political actions of PKS are based on the premise that there is no shortcut to achieving its distant objectives.[117] These must be attained through the disciplining of cadres and a gradual transformation of society. And democracy has provided the way to achieve this goal.[118] Similarly, the pragmatic and flexible approach of PKS in the arena of practical politics is evident in its stance towards the implementation of *shariah* law in Indonesia. This is a further issue that is subject to scrutiny and fierce debate among Indonesian Muslim scholars and politicians.

ENDNOTES

[1] See Hamid Basyaib, "Dilemma Partai Agama," *Islamlib.com*, 19 April 2004.

[2] An internal survey conducted by PKS in Jakarta and Yogyakarta reports that 62% of supporters were upset with the party's position and 75% of members believe that supporting the government costs the party a lot. See "Survey PKS Yogya: Citra PKS Turun Gara-Gara Dukung SBY," *Tempointeraktif.com*, 24 November 2005.

[3] In this case, Oliver Roy seems to attribute it as the failure of political Islam, however in contrast I prefer to see it from a different perspective. The domestication of universal Islam represents the success of an Islamic movement in adapting itself to political realities and making its Islamic agenda more practical, for its survival. See Olivier Roy, *The Failure of Political Islam*, (Cambridge: Harvard University Press, 1994)

[4] Interview with Muttammimul Ula, Jakarta, 16 June 2003.

[5] Based on the author's observations during field research (February 2003- January 2004) Jemaah Tarbiyah has struggled to maintain its intellectual origins with the founder of the Muslim Brothers, Hasan al-Banna.

[6] In his writings al-Banna repeatedly used Sufi terms. There is no evidence to support the claim that he embraced the strict practices of Hanbali Sufism; rather, he demonstrated a thorough acquaintance with the classical doctrines of al-Ghazali and other Syafi'ite scholars. For further details of the biography of al-Banna see Hasan al-Banna, *Memoar Hasan al-Banna*, trans. Salahuddin Abu Sayyid and Hawin Mustadho (Solo: Era Intermedia, 2000).

[7] Richard Mitchell, *The Society of Muslim Brothers* (London: Oxford University Press, 1969), 3.

[8] Ibrahim M. Abu-Rabi, *Intellectual Origins of Islamic Resurgence in the Modern Arab World* (Albany: State University of New York Press, 1996), 68-69.

[9] The Hanbalite School of Jurisprudence is known for its strict implementation of Islamic teachings.

[10] Christina Phelps Harris, *Nationalism and Revolution in Egypt: the Role of the Muslim Brotherhood* (The Hague: Hoover Institution Publication, 1964), 143.

[11] See Ali Said Damanik, *Fenomena Partai Keadilan: Transformasi 20 Tahun Gerakan Tarbiyah di Indonesia* (Bandung: Mizan, 2002), 109.

[12] The firm Pustaka Tarbiatuna has published many original writings of the Jemaah Tarbiyah activists. These deal predominantly with practical *dakwah* issues and organization rather than religious issues. There are many publishers, such as Era Intermedia of Solo in Central Java and Rabbani Press of Jakarta, that are allegedly associated with this group but they mainly publish translated books from the Middle East and the Egyptian Muslim Brothers. The work of an influential Muslim Brothers figure, Yusuf Qaradawi, on Islamic jurisprudence has become the main reference. Qaradawi tries to position himself among moderate scholars in dealing with questions of differences in Islamic jurisprudence.

[13] Aminuddin, *Strategi Dakwah Gerakan Islam*, (Jakarta: Pustaka Tarbiatuna, 200), 141.

[14] Aminuddin, *Strategi Dakwah Gerakan Islami*, 143.

[15] Ibid.

[16] Interview with Hilmi Aminuddin, Jakarta, 23 December 2003.

[17] Tim Departemen Kaderisasi Partai Keadilan Sejahtera, *Manajemen Tarbiyah Anggota Pemula* (Jakarta: DPP Partai Keadilan, 2003), 57.

[18] See Rizqon Khamami, "Kebangkitan Neo-Wahabisme," *Duta Masyarakat*, 16 August 2005.

[19] Ibid.

[20] See "Kader Muhammadiyah Tergiur 'Rumah Yang Lain'" *Suara-Muhammadiyah.or.id*, 5 October 2005. Within Muhammadiyah, and in particular among the older activists, there have been worries about PKS members taking over Muhammadiyah branches and activities in the strongholds of Muhammadiyah, such as West Sumatra. See Abdul Munir Mulkhan, "Sendang Ayu: Pergulatan Muhammadiyah di Kaki Bukit Barisan," *Suara-Muhammadiyah.or.id*, 2 January 2006.

[21] The charge was circulated by the so-called "pure" Salafis in order to preserve the original teachings of *salafus salih* and it excluded those who did not follow in the way which their predecessors had understood. For more detailed allegations, see www.salafy.or.id under the title *Membongkar Pikiran Hasan al-Banna* (Revealing Hasan al-Banna's Thought). The article was translated from the Arabic version written by Shaikh Ayyid ash-Shamary, *Turkah Hasan al-Banna wa Ahamul Warithin*, (Saudi: Maktabah as-Sabab, 2003). See also "Historical Development of Methodologies al-Ikhwan al-Muslimeen and Their Effect and Influence upon Contemporary Salafee Dawah," *Salafi Publication* (March 2003).

[22] Both Abu al-Hasan al-Ash'ari and Abu Hamid al-Ghazali are main references for traditionalist in terms of theology and Sufism respectively.

[23] See Hasan al-Banna, *Risalah Pergerakan Al-Ikhwanul Muslimin 2*, tran. Anis Matta et.al. (Solo: Era Intermedia, 2001), 234-238.

[24] See "Gerakan Islam Kontemporer: Sebuah Sketsa tentang Gerakan Salafi dan Laskar Jihad di Jogyakarta," *www.lkis.org/islam_kontemporer.php*.

[25] See Roy, *The Failure of Political Islam*, 121.

[26] Aminuddin, *Strategi Dakwah Gerakan Islam*, 142.

[27] Ibid.

[28] Three important books written by leading figures of the Jemaah Tarbiyah and the committee of PKS, *Strategi Dakwah Gerakan Islam* (the *Dakwah* Strategy of the Islamic Movement) by Hilmi Aminuddin, *Negara dan Cita-Cita Politik* (the State and Political Ideals) by Abu Ridha, and *Rekayasa Masa Depan Menuju Kemenangan Dakwah Islam* (the Engineering of Future towards the Triumph of Islamic *Dakwah*) by Cahyadi Takariawan are filled with quotations from Hasan al-Banna; there is no mention of Sayyid Qutb.

[29] See Ainur Rofiq Tamhid Foreword to Syekh Abdur Rahman Abdul Khaliq, *Penyimpangan-Penyimpangan Tasawuf*, trans. Ahmad Misbach (Jakarta: Rabbani Press, 2001), vii.

[30] Hidayat Nurwahid and Untung Wahono, *Pengaruh Sekularisasi dan Globalisasi Barat Terhadap Harakah Islamiyah di Indonesia* (Jakarta: Pustaka Tarbiatuna, 2001), 21.

[31] Ahmad Firman Yusuf, foreword to *Pimikiran Politik Kontemporer Al-ikhwan Al-Muslimun: Studi Analitis, Observatif, Dokumentatif*, by Taufiq Yusuf al-Wa'iy, trans. Wahid Ahmadi and Arwni Amin (Solo: Era Intermedia, 2002), 6.

[32] In the Qur'an VI: 60 it states: "Have you not seen those who claim to have believed in what was revealed to you, [O Muhammad] and what was revealed before you? They wish to refer legislation to "*taghut*" (false objects of worship), while they were commanded to reject it, and Satan wishes to lead them far astray."

[33] Yusuf, foreword to *Pemikiran Politik Kontemporer*, 10.

[34] Michael Gilsenan, *Saint and Sufi in Modern Egypt: an Essay on the Sociology of Religion*, (Oxford: The Clarendon Press, 1973), 4.

[35] Ibid.

[36] John Obert Voll, *Islam Continuity and Change in the Modern World* (Essex: Westview Press, 1982), 175.

[37] Ishak Musa Husaini, *The Muslim Brethren* (Westport: Hyperion Press, 1986), 25.

[38] Rabi, *Intellectual Origins of Islamic Resurgence*, 67.

[39] Al-Banna, *Memoar Hasan al-Banna*, 199.

[40] Mitchell, *The Society of Muslim Brothers*, 6.

[41] Aminuddin, *Strategi Dakwah Gerakan Islam*, 143.

[42] Al-Banna, *Risalah Pergerakan 2*, 227-229.

43 Mitchell, *The Society of Muslim Brothers*, 6.

44 Rabi, *Intellectual Origins of Islamic Resurgence*, 67.

45 Al-Banna, *Memoar Hasan al-Banna*, 42-43.

46 Ibid., 132

47 The Sufi model of brotherhood or family is the best way of disseminating Islamic teachings. The organised Sufis, under their charismatic leader, easily expanded their influence beyond national borders. Some *tarekat* also served as clandestine organizations that aimed to challenge the authority of an unjust ruler of the day. See Abu Bakar Acheh, *Pengantar Sejarah Sufi dan Tasauf* (Kelantan: Pustaka Amar Press, 1977), 313.

48 A member of the *tarekat* may stay in the *zawiyah* (contemplation room) or the house of *al-ikhwan*. See Martin van Bruinessen, *Tarekat Naqsyabandiyah di Indonesia* (Bandung: Mizan, 1992), 15.

49 Al-Banna, *Memoar Hasan Al-Banna*, 43.

50 Ibid., 116.

51 Gilsenan, *Saint and Sufi in Modern Egypt*, 73.

52 Martin van Bruinessen, *Tarekat Naqsyabandiyah di Indonesia* (Bandung: Mizan, 1992), 83.

53 Al-Banna, *Memoar Hasan al-Banna*, 80.

54 Brynjar Lia, *The Society of the Muslim Brothers in Egypt: the Rise of an Islamic Mass Movement 1928-1942* (Readings: Ithaca Press, 1998), 115.

55 Al-Banna, *Risalah Pergerakan 2*, 163.

56 Harris, *Nationalism and Revolution in Egypt*, 143.

57 Ibid., 152.

58 See Zakariyya Sulayman Bayumi, *The Muslim Brothers and the Islamic Associations in the Egyptian Political Life, 1928-1948* (Cairo: Maktabah al-Wahda, 1978) as quoted by Lia, *The Society of the Muslim Brothers in Egypt*, 9.

59 He wrote a book entitled *Hasan al-Banna: Mata, Kaifa wa Li-mada?* (Cairo: Maktabah Madbuli, 1977).

60 See his book *al-Harakiyah al-Siyasiyah fi Misri 1945-1952* (Cairo: Dar al-Tawzi wa al-Nashr al-Islamiyah, 1972).

61 Lia, *The Society of the Muslim Brothers in Egypt*, 7. The stance of the Muslim Brothers vis-a-vis the palace indicates a certain Sufi tradition more accommodating to rulers, and the way in which they gave their support to combat secular and foreign forces in the country.

62 Interview, anonymous, Jakarta, 23 April 2003.

63 Bruinessen, *Tarekat Naqsyabandiyah di Indonesia*, 87.

64 Gilsenan, *Saint and Sufi in Modern Egypt*, 95.

65 Mitchell, *The Society of Moslem Brothers*, 8.

66 Al-Banna formulated ten prerequisites of the covenant. These include understanding (*al-fahm*), sincerity (*al-ikhlas*), action (*al-'amal*), honest striving (*al-jihad*), sacrifice (*al-tadhiyyah*), obedience (*al-ta'ah*), perseverance (*al-thabat*)), authenticity (*al-tajarrud*), brotherhood (*al-ukhuwwah*) and trust (*al-thiqah*).

67 In his memoir, al-Banna includes a story which describes his goals after graduating from the University of Darul Ulum. He dreamed he became a great teacher who took on a responsibility to educate people through academic training and a great supervisor to extend spiritual guidance to people through the Sufi tradition. See Al-Banna, *Memoar Hasan al-Banna*, 96-100.

68 Majelis Pertimbangan Partai PK, *Panduan Organisasi Partai Keadilan* (Jakarta: DPP PK, 2001), 19.

69 In the practice of the Naqsyabandiyah order, students are supposed to sense their teacher's presence as much as they can in order to strengthen their spiritual connection with him.

70 Hasan al-Banna, *Al-Ma'tsurat Sughra: Doa & Dzikir Rasulullah SAW Pagi dan Petang* (Jakarta: Sholahuddin Press, 1996). Jemaah Tarbiyah activists have used this formula of prayer as part of their daily practice. Thousands of books of collections of al-Banna's prayers are widely distributed by the Prosperous Justice Party.

71 *Keadilan Online*, 20 May 2003

72 Hidayat Nurwahid, *Mengelolah Masa Transisi Menuju Masyarakat Madani* (Jakarta: Fikri Publishing, 2004), 109.

[73] See Hasan al-Banna, *Konsep Pembaruan Masyarakat Islam* (Jakarta: Media Dakwah, 1983).

[74] See Cahyadi Takariawan, *Rekayasa Masa Depan Menuju Kemenangan Dakwah Islam* (Jakarta: Pustaka Tarbiatuna, 2003).

[75] Al-Banna, *Risalah Pergerakan 1*, 175.

[76] Interview with Mahfudz Sidiq, Jakarta, 8 October 2003

[77] Damanik, *Fenomena Partai Keadilan: Transformasi 20 Tahun Gerakan Tarbiyah di Indonesia* (Bandung, Mizan, 2002), 269.

[78] Nurmahmudi Ismail, Hidayat Nur Wahid and Mahfudz Sidiq, for instance, were among respondents who preferred the establishment of a mass organization. However, they have become leading figures in the Prosperous Justice Party.

[79] Interview with Sholeh Drehem, Surabaya, 13 March 2003.

[80] *Zakat* is one of the five pillars of Islam. Muslims with the financial means are obliged to a give certain percentage. For instance, from a monthly salary, one is obliged to deduct about 2.5%.

[81] *Infaq* means dispensing moneys or gifts and is more voluntary than obligatory.

[82] *Shadaqah* means charity. Both *infaq* and *shadaqah* carry similar meanings but the former is a gift that can be dedicated to any specific purpose, such as building a mosque or other public facility, while *shadaqah* is mainly dispensed to the needy.

[83] Interview with Aus Hidayat, Depok, 13 March 2003.

[84] See DPP PK, *Kebijakan Dasar Partai Keadilan 2000-2005* (Jakarta: Pustaka Tarbiatuna, 2000), 11.

[85] Damanik, *Fenomena Partai Keadilan*, 111.

[86] Takariawan, *Rekayasa Masa Depan*, 9.

[87] Interview with Mustafa Kamal, Jakarta, 13 December 2005.

[88] Damanik, *Fenomena Partai Keadilan*, 269.

[89] Interview with Mustafa Kamal, Depok, 11 June 2003

[90] The Indonesian Islamic Student Movement, *Pergerakan Mahasiswa Islam Indonesia* (PMII) was founded in 1960 and is affiliated with NU.

[91] Aminuddin, *Strategi Dakwah Gerakan Islam*, 48.

[92] Memet Sosiawan, member of the Central Board Committee of PKS in charge of organising *dakwah* activities in East Java said that this policy aims to prevent infiltration by terrorist groups (Mojokerto - East Java, 6 December 2005).

[93] Ibid.

[94] Interview with Mustafa Kamal, Jakarta, 13 December 2005.

[95] Damanik, *Fenomena Partai Keadilan*, 117.

[96] Ibid.

[97] *PKS Online*, 1 June 2005.

[98] Roy, *The Failure of Political Islam*, 53.

[99] See *Republika*, 19 August 2003

[100] Interview with Nurmahmudi Ismail, Depok, 8 May 2003.

[101] Damanik, *Fenomena Partai Keadilan*, 168

[102] Ibid., 161

[103] Ibid., 169

[104] Al-Banna, *Risalah Pergerakan 2*, 162.

[105] *Tempo*, 18 January 1999.

[106] Takariawan, *Rekayasa Masa Depan*, 92.

[107] Ibid.

[108] See Mahfudz Sidiq, "Peran Serta Da'wah dalam Politik" (Paper presented at the Square House Building, University of New South Wales, 9 August 2002), 7.

[109] The organization must be neither an ideological nor a political one. See Aminuddin, *Strategi Dakwah Gerakan Islam*, 151.

[110] Takariawan, *Rekayasa Masa Depan*, 117.

[111] Ibid.

[112] Ibid.
[113] Ridha, *Negara dan Cita-Cita Politik*, 132.
[114] Ibid., 111.
[115] See "Tifatul Sembiring: Paranoid Syariat Islam," *Gatra*, 6 May 2006.
[116] Interview with Ahmad Musyaffa, Jakarta, 19 April 2003.
[117] See Martin van Bruinessen, "Post-Soeharto Muslim Engagements with Civil Society and Democratization," in *Indonesia in Transition: Rethinking 'Civil Society', 'Region', and 'Crisis'* (Jakarta: Pustaka Pelajar, 2004), 58.
[118] Ibid.

Chapter 7: A Vision of *Shariah*-Led Prosperity: PKS Attitudes to the Implementation of Islamic Law

Political openings and opportunities, particularly after the end of Soeharto's New Order regime, have allowed activists of Jemaah Tarbiyah to promote their agenda of Islamisation with a broader target in view. Under the New Order they had remained outside the formal system and kept their distance from political activities, but after the resignation of Soeharto in 1998 they found a way to participate in the democratic system, transforming Jemaah Tarbiyah from an underground religious movement into a legal political party. The issue of the implementation of Islamic law in Indonesia has become an integral part of PKS's agenda to make Indonesia more religious in nature.

The question often arises about PKS's attitude towards *shariah*. What exactly is the party's stance towards its implementation in Indonesia? PKS has made no plain statement in its political platform but this does not mean that it has no desire to implement *shariah*. PKS has been ambivalent in responding to this sensitive issue. On the one hand PKS has tried to deny allegations that it has a hidden agenda to Islamise the state and on the other hand it also has insisted its commitment to the struggle of Islam, including to applying *shariah*.

This chapter analyses the broad question the formalisation of *shariah* in Indonesia. PKS's understanding of the issue has a significant place in this discourse; however, explaining it is not an easy task, since we must deal with political rhetoric and PKS's strategy for achieving broad support. What is the ultimate goal of PKS, and how will it bring about the "re-Islamising" of Indonesian society? Another important question that needs to be posed is "what makes PKS's idea of implementing *shariah* distinct from those of other Islamic parties in Indonesia?" In fact, the debate among Muslim scholars and leaders on the merits of *shariah* has made PKS avoid the issue. Its main concern is how to revise the image of *shariah* and to popularise it by stressing the goals of prosperity and justice for the Indonesian people.

A. The Pros and Cons of *Shariah* Implementation

Since Indonesian independence and during Soekarno's Old Order, the debate on *shariah* was carried out between secular and Islamic factions. The first group rejected the idea of the formulisation of *shariah* and the second group promoted it. With the New Order, the debate was pushed aside; any discussion about reviving *shariah* as a broader source of law was discouraged. However, after the collapse of the New Order *shariah* discourses have re-emerged and have inevitably sparked controversy. Disputes about the implementation of *shariah* no longer take place just between secular and Islamic factions but also among Muslims themselves. On an earlier political stage, for instance, M. Natsir (of *santri* background) would engage in confrontation with Soekarno (non-*santri* in orientation) in dealing with *shariah* issues. Nowadays the proponents of *shariah*, Hamzah Haz (PPP) and Yusril Ihza Mahendra (PBB) face challenges from their fellow devout Muslims, such as Abdurrahman Wahid, former leader of NU and Indonesian President from 1999-2000.[1] The *shariah* "pros" and "cons" debate is intensively discussed within the Muslim community itself.

1. Those Opposed to *Shariah*

Secular oriented Muslims argue that it is impossible to implement *shariah* comprehensively and successfully in Indonesia. Rather than a positive contribution to society, it is seen as a source of division. The secularists argue that the implementation of *shariah* would be counterproductive for society,[2] since Indonesian Muslims are not monolithic but embrace many orientations and interests. The diversity of religious practice and jurisprudential schools in Indonesian Islam is a significant factor to be considered.[3] There is a main obstacle in determining which school should be preferred.

Some areas of dispute in the *shariah* discourse, which often draw criticism from scholars, revolve around issues concerning gender, criminal law and attitudes to non-Muslims. Muslim scholars who oppose the implementation of *shariah* claim that it brings inequality in the status of women and imposes over-severe punishments for the violation of moral laws and to the conversion to other religions. Any effort to implement *shariah* creates discrimination for Indonesian citizens who do not embrace Islam. Embracing a religion and upholding its obligations are individual choices and cannot be enforced. When Islam is imposed on others, it will lose its fundamental character of giving mercy to all creatures (*rahmatan li al-'alamin*).[4] Finally, it is not feasible for a nation to have two different laws, one for Muslims and another for non-Muslims.

Ulil Abshar-Abdalla, a leading opponent of *shariah*-isation in Indonesia, argues that not all Islamic laws are created by God, so that when it comes to human matters, religion is to be understood and formulated by human nature. It follows that human perceptions open up debate and criticism. Ulil adds that many aspects of *shariah* must be questioned; for example, some do carry the potential for discrimination against women. In the case of witnesses in a trial, for example, two women are considered to be equal to one man. Furthermore, in Islam, if someone accuses another of committing adultery but is not able to show valid evidence of the charge, the accuser will be lashed 80 times for calumny. Four male witnesses must be provided in order to support the allegation. When a woman is raped and she is not able to bring the four witnesses, she will not get justice. These questions are hardly discussed in Indonesia because "if we want to criticize, it will be seen as insulting *shariah* and religion itself."[5]

According to the secular-minded group, in order to prevent the violation of individual human rights, *shariah* must not be implemented in Indonesia beyond family law. Any effort to bring religion into an organic relation with the state must be rejected. If Indonesian Muslims want to live in accordance with *shariah*, they may, as long as they do not use the state to back up their will. All religions are equal before the state and each religious adherence must respect all others equally, making no exceptions regarding Islam.[6]

The rejection of the implementation of *shariah* varies from the strictly secular groups who promote a total separation of state and religion to the moderate secularists who merely oppose the formalisation of *shariah* into the Indonesian legal system. The first believe that a secular system is the appropriate solution for Indonesia, which is of a diverse socio-cultural nature, whilst the latter does not fully support the idea of radical secularism, but attempts to promote universal human values derived from Islam. Both share common ideas in their rejection of any effort leading to the formalisation of *shariah* in Indonesia. For the opponents of formalisation, secularism is a blessing for all religions, since it prevents conflict among different religious adherences and any opposition between religion and state power.[7] Liberal Muslims contend that pluralism, understood as the acknowledgement of the truth in all religions, is most appropriate for Indonesian society. When Muslims are ready to accept and practice democracy, they also need to adhere to the principle of pluralism. The group led by Ulil Abshar-Abdalla has promoted its commitment to secularism and pluralism with this renowned slogan: "In the name of Allah, the entirely merciful, and especially merciful, the Lord of all religions."[8]

2. Those For *Shariah*

Islamist groups believe that *shariah* must be implemented in order to bring about justice and to end the Indonesian multi-dimensional crisis. Those who believe in the role of *shariah* in solving Indonesian problems are divided into two orientations. The first group contends that the Indonesian people not only need *shariah* but that it should also be implemented immediately. They see *shariah* as a kind of "generic medicine" to cure all social, economic and political ills in the country. Indeed, crisis has occurred because of the very absence of *shariah*. They also believe that the entire political system of Indonesia and its institutions must be Islamic.[9]

The "immediate" *shariah*-oriented group comprises hardliner Islamists who usually appeal to non-political organisations, such Hizbut Tahrir, Salafi Groups and MMI but draw benefit from the issue of the autonomy of the provinces and districts. They have also appealed to the central government to implement *shariah* at the national level. According to this group, the secular system is responsible for all crises in Indonesia. A partial solution will not bring any benefit to the country; rather it will produce other problems in the future. The radical and fundamental solution lies in the upholding of *shariah* so that the Indonesian people live according to Islamic laws.[10]

This group also views the present application of cultural aspects of *shariah* in family affairs and regulations of Islamic charity (*zakat*) as insufficient.[11] *Shariah* must be implemented comprehensively, *kaffah*, meaning that the Islamic criminal laws must also be applied, since for this group the fundamentals of *shariah* lie in the application of such laws. Proponents of this idea often criticise the role of the mainstream Islamic organization in Indonesia, such as NU and Muhammadiyah, which have no intention to observe a comprehensive practice of *shariah*, including its Islamic criminal laws.[12]

Salafi movements and Hizbut Tahrir have become well known for their demand to implement a total *shariah* but not through democratic means. They do not believe there are any benefits in following a democratic system since it is against Islam. Other groups associated with Darul Islam, such as Majelis Mujahidin Indonesia (MMI) and Komite Persiapan Penegakan Syariah Islam (KPPSI) in South Sulawesi have worked consistently to push the central government and provinces to implement Islamic law.

The second pro-*shariah* group are moderate Islamists arguing that *shariah* is an alternative for Indonesia but that its implementation must be through a long term democratic process, using constitutional means. The re-emergence of Islamic parties in Indonesia after Soeharto's resignation is a response to accommodate this demand. PPP, PKS, PBB and other smaller Islamic parties have worked to promote the implementation of *shariah*. Even though this group share the one ideal of the significance of *shariah*, it differs in terms of its views of the methods of implementation.

PPP and PBB, for instance, stress the significance of promoting *shariah* in Indonesia through the acknowledgment of special status for Muslims by reviving the idea of the Jakarta Charter (Piagam Jakarta) as it was initiated by their predecessors. A constitution that explicitly recognises the status of *shariah* is a crucial issue. In contrast, PKS has sought a different approach in promoting *shariah* and no longer regards the Jakarta Charter as important. For PKS, the implementation of *shariah* should not rely on the constitution but must begin with the individual, family, society and the state.[13] A Constitution specifying the status of *shariah* is not a priority in gaining formal recognition from the state. The state must not be designed in the way that privileges Islam, since the 1945 Indonesian Constitution and the state ideology of Pancasila ensure the rights of all religions.[14]

Whereas hardline Islamists see the absence of *shariah* as the main cause of the Indonesian crisis, moderate Islamists take a different approach. They assert that the non-implementation of *shariah* is mainly because the Indonesian people do not yet understand the concept in full. Furthermore, the absence of welfare and justice, including education, are the main reasons for this lack; first, the people need to be educated and have their living standards and their security improved. So at this stage, implementing *shariah* is not a priority; rather meeting the basic needs of the people is the first step, while continuously encouraging the people to practise *shariah* in their lives.[15]

Even though it has downplayed the issue of *shariah*, PKS still considers it important to promote it through to the state level. Rather than pushing its implementation through a "top down" or radical approach, PKS has worked to educate Muslims to understand the essence of *shariah* so that they willingly practise it in their daily lives and subsequently extend it into governmental activities. PKS believes that when people become familiar with the practice of *shariah* they will not oppose its implementation. The main effort for PKS activists is how to revive the image of *shariah* and to relate it to the basic needs of ordinary people.[16]

B. Revising the Image of *Shariah*

Even though the implementation of *shariah* law is not publicly discussed by the activists of PKS, as a political party arisen out of a religious movement, PKS will not stray from its commitment to Islamise society and the state. The struggle of how to implement *shariah* still preoccupies its activists. One member of a PKS committee in East Java said, "Partai Keadilan has never denied the implementation of *shariah* in Indonesia because it would be foolish for an Islamic party to reject *shariah*."[17] In political platform, however, PKS uses the term *dakwah* instead of *shariah*

> ...using *dakwah* as a means of the purification of human beings based on their natural tendencies (*fitrah*). Becoming God's servants who also serve as good exemples and enjoin the good in order to strengthen moral foundations of the nation. Promoting freedom to all citizens to embrace and practise their religion with mutual respect.[18]

PKS's position on the implementation of *shariah* can be found in a book written by a PKS activist, entitled *Yang Nyata dari PK Sejahtera*.[19] The book emphasises that "*shariah* is mercy for all creatures and the proper implementation of *shariah* will not bring discrimination. PKS believes that its implementation in Indonesia will provide the solution for the current multi dimensional-crisis. However, it must be done in a peaceful and constitutional way, not through violence or compulsion."[20] Furthermore, in a different expression, which carries the same meaning, the chairman of PK in East Java has said, "We don't want to use *shariah* as a merely political commodity because it saddens us that many activists of political parties strongly demand the implementation of *shariah* in Indonesia but they themselves do not practise it."[21]

Believing that the lack of a proper understanding of *shariah* is the chief obstacle in promoting its application, the Jemaah Tarbiyah activists who occupy the central leadership within PKS have begun to formulate their strategy for promoting its positive image. Implementing *shariah*, according to PKS, is not merely the need to impose a set of Islamic laws but rather it entails all positive aspects of human values and behaviour. For PKS, universal morality and values must take first priority in solving Indonesian political and economic crises.

In order to gain popular support, the party has worked to make *shariah* more applicable to day-to-day matters. The meaning of *shariah* has been widened in scope to include more substantive and practical issues. *Korupsi* (corruption), *Kolusi* (collusion) and *Nepotisme* (nepotism) known by the acronym "KKN" are new areas to combat, so that clean government, justice and welfare are considered to be the main ideals deriving from *shariah*.[22] The campaign for *shariah* should be directed towards achieving prosperity, security, justice and peace in the world.[23] In its simplest form, preserving public facilities, such transportation, parks, roads and toilets is obligatory for members of the party. In fact, PKS has tried to spiritualise all profane activities within realm of Islamic values and indeed all can be justified by religious doctrine.

In order to provide the religious grounds for these issues, the arguments are based on the Qur'an and Hadith and as well as on the public interest (*maslahah*). The manual and training materials of PKS state that preserving individual and public rights is important, since Allah in the Qur'an (XXVIII: 77) states:" …and desire not corruption in the land. Indeed, Allah does not like corruptors."[24]

According to the activists of PKS, most people still have insufficient information about *shariah* and tend to see it from a negative point of view.[25] They understand it merely as a legal system that prescribes the severe punishment of crimes under the *hudud* laws.[26] Hidayat Nurwahid, former president of PKS and currently chairperson speaker of the People's Consultative Assembly (MPR) in 2004-2009 stated:

> The problem is that too many people talk about *shariah* and they mean cutting off hands and wearing (head) scarves. Our main programme is how to make people better off, how to get justice.[27]

> In order to make Indonesians, both Muslims and non-Muslims, comprehend the concept and essence of *shariah*, Dr. Salim Segaf al-Jufri, chairman of the *Shariah* Council of the Central Board of PKS, suggests three steps in socialising *shariah*: educating Muslims, providing good examples and creating dialogue with non-Muslims.[28]

1. Educating Muslims

PKS believes that educating people to be well informed about the proper meaning of *shariah* is an important step. *Shariah* must be seen as a model that promises prosperity to all human beings. If *shariah* is described by such acts as stoning adulterers and cutting off the hands of thieves, which alarms both Muslims and non-Muslims, according to PKS, this is a wrong understanding.[29] *Shariah* contains aspects that apply not only to the legal system but also to economic progress and social solidarity. Rofi' Munawwar, a chairman of PKS in the province of East Java (1999-2004) explained

> It is true that *hudud* is part of *shariah* but a just economic distribution for all people is also Islamic. Unfortunately, the aspects of punishment within *shariah* are more dominant than efforts to encourage wealthy people to help and lift up the poor. If this other aspect of *shariah* is truly implemented and people gain prosperity, there will be no thieves and consequently the cutting off of hands will never be implemented.[30]

In this regard, PKS has succeeded in reformulating the meaning of *shariah* into more practical avenues suitable to Indonesian society. Suryadarma, a PKS member of the legislature in the province of South Sulawesi said:

> I think a Muslim who understands his or her religion well will practise *shariah*. *Shariah* is very wide and not only related to the legal dimensions often exposed by the mass media in a threatening way, such as the cutting off of hands. We focus on a *shariah* that is related to the achievement of prosperity and the basic needs of the people. In addition, we need to uphold the law in order to ensure the equality of all people before it. Without considering both dimensions, prosperity and law, we think it is difficult to implement *shariah*. How do we practise a *hudud* law if the thieves are poor people? How do we observe *qisas* when we tend to agree with the abuse of politics and power? In short, when we campaign for justice and prosperity, all these are part of implementing *shariah*.[31]

By educating people about the "essence" of *shariah*, it is hoped that they will not hesitate to put it into practice. And when Indonesian society supports the implementation of *shariah*, PKS is ready to bring the aspirations of its constituents into the legislature. PKS attitudes are always determined by the acceptance of the people.

So at this stage, making people familiar with the day-to-day aspects of *shariah* is more important than promoting its formalisation. PKS activists observe that the majority of people are ignorant of the practice of the true *shariah*. West Sumatra, for instance, is widely known as a stronghold of Muslim scholars and religious observance, but one activist from this area has acknowledged that the ordinary people are actually far from *shariah*. The campaign for formalisation in this region will not gain much popular support

> PKS raises the issue of *shariah* not as a political commodity or to win votes. Our mission is to uphold *shariah* itself. In West Sumatra, this is not an issue which will win us popular political support. The impact of secularism in West Sumatra is very strong. A campaign to bring the people to live in accordance with *shariah* will face difficulties, since people feel threatened by it. The decline of the Islamic institutions in West Sumatra has made *shariah* uninteresting. We do not need to campaign for *shariah* but it does need to be socialised.

He further stated

> The important issues for West Sumatra are the economy, education and public health. What makes West Sumatra's people proud of their region in terms of economy and education? Nothing! We were strong because we had Central Sumatra, including Riau, which is well known for its petroleum. PRRI (Pemerintahan Revolusioner Republik Indonesia) was ready to confront the central government because they knew about the resources. When Central Sumatra was made a new province, we became very weak and poor. What we need is kind of a reformist Islam. Why did Partai Amanat Nasional (PAN) win success in the general elections in 1999 - because they were not too fanatic or too secular! Those who want to practise Islam rigidly and too radically will not put down roots in this society. The typology of the people is moderate, as represented by Muhammadiyah.[32]

2. Being Exemplars

Besides educating Muslims about the "true meaning" of *shariah*, PKS activists try to offer themselves as living examples. Every cadre is expected to practise the teachings of *shariah* and to ensure that Indonesians, Muslims and non-Muslims, feel secure and comfortable with its concept. They firmly believe that *shariah* must avoid any possibility of causing discrimination against people, regardless of religion, gender or political aspirations and that *shariah* must be seen as an alternative solution for Indonesians.[33]

Since ideas of the implementation of *shariah* are still far from the popular mind in Indonesia, PKS activists have not voiced it during campaigns for the general elections. Even though some districts in Indonesia, such as in some areas of West Sumatra, have issued district policies (*peraturan daerah,* Perda) requiring female students and civil servants to wear head scarves, the most appropriate issue regarding *shariah* is the campaign to combat against corruption.[34] One of the PK legislators in the Province of West Sumatra (DPRD I) emphasised:

PK cadres are persons who are in the very beginning expected to practise *shariah* in their daily activities and to demonstrate it to others around them. They must feel happy and satisfied carrying out *shariah* so that other people will be interested and follow them. *Shariah* must lead to achieve welfare and prosperity for all. For that reason PK now adds the word "*Sejahtera*" (prosperous) into its new name, Partai Keadilan Sejahtera.[35]

PKS has also begun to promote the inclusive nature of *shariah*. As an example of its conviction of the all embracing nature of *shariah*, PKS elected a non-Muslim as branch chairman of PKS in one of the districts in Papua, while another elected Member of a regional parliament in Papua representing PKS, Natalis Kamo is a Christian.[36] This decision to include non-Muslims within PKS was not an easy choice since it drew criticism from some members. For instance, a mailing list of PKS sympathisers, partai-keadilan-sejahtera@yahoogroups.com, on March 2004 was filled with questions and criticism of the party's decision to appoint non-Muslims as members of PKS committees in the Province of Papua and for nomination as legislators as well. The main concern was that this policy did not follow the Traditions of the Prophet and the pious ancestors (*al-s}alaf al-s}alih*). One argumentation is that "appointing non-Muslims means requiring loyalty to an infidel and it is really against the teachings of the Prophet. The Qur'an states 'let not believers take disbelievers as allies (i.e., supporters or protectors) rather than believers. And whoever (of you) doest that has nothing (i.e. no association) with Allah, except when taking precaution against them in prudence. And Allah warns you of Himself, to Allah is the (final) destination.'"[37] However, these objections did not last long, since most members of the mailing list advised those who had criticised the policy of Central Board of PKS to trust their leaders.

In order to persuade its members about the validity of its decision in this regard, the Central Board of PKS issues *bayanat* (explanations) in which it is stated that the prohibition for a Muslim against voting and electing a non-Muslim as a member of parliament is clear. However, the party considers the rights of non-Muslims within the Muslim community the same to observe their religion and to manage their affairs. This is clearly worded in the Medina Charter. The inclusion of non-Muslims within PKS committees and in the parliament reflects the policy of recognising the existence of non-Muslim communities and their representatives in Indonesia.[38]

In the case of the amendment of the 1945 Constitution, particularly chapter 29 regarding religion, the PK, together with Partai Amanat National (PAN) did not support the Jakarta Charter. While other Islamic parties, such as PPP and PBB view the phrase of "with obligation for Muslims to carry out *shariah*" added in the 1945 Constitution to be critical for the legal acknowledgement of implementing *shariah*, for PK such recognition of the privileged status of Islam was not a priority. When the Islamic parties in the 2000 legislature raised the issue of returning to the Jakarta Charter, PK neither supported nor rejected the move. Instead, its representatives preferred to propose what they called Piagam Madinah (the Medina Charter), which gives the same freedom to all religions of Indonesia to carry out their teachings.[39] The reason is that the party did not support any effort to impose the implementation of *shariah* because it would be undemocratic.[40] PK preferred to see the government and the Muslim community strongly committed to the upholding of Islamic values first.[41]

The Medina Charter was the first "constitution" regulated by the Prophet Muhammad to knit all the inhabitants of his community into a single polity.[42] However, the proposal of PK is not a new issue since Piagam Madinah was widely discussed by Nurcholish Madjid in promoting pluralism within Islam.[43] Even earlier, during the debates in the 1959 constituent assembly on the ideological direction of the state, Islamic parties had pushed for the legalization of the Jakarta Carter and they met the objections of non-Muslims and Muslims who were not members of Islamic parties. Even though not referring to the Medina Charter as such, Djamaluddin Malik, the Third Chairman of NU's Executive Board, proposed a sentence in addition to the Jakarta Charter that "followers of other religions are under obligation to abide by the doctrines of their respective religions."[44] In fact, the idea of proposing a new sentence by Djamaluddin Malik is similar to the idea brought by members of PKS in order to guarantee the plural religious character of Indonesian state.

PKS has shown a reluctance to promote the position of women in politics but it has started to give recognition to their role. It allows the same opportunities for women to be involved in politics and in the broader arenas of life. PKS has begun the empowerment of women by proposing them as members of the legislature. The Election Law of the 2004 elections stated that parties were required to have at least 30 per cent female legislative candidates, and PKS met this quota in 65 of 69 electoral districts.[45] Even though only four women were actually elected as legislators because most had been put low in the candidate list, their presence is a symbol of the political will of the party in this direction. Compared to PPP, PKS is still higher in terms of female representation in the legislature. Women elected to the 2004 DPR from PKS are 4 of 45 members (8.89%) and from PPP, 3 of 58 members (5.17).[46]

Furthermore, it is interesting that in the district of Gayo Luwes in Aceh, a woman named Nurhayati is the head of the district committee of PKS. She is the only woman in the party to reach such a level of leadership.[47] In addition, female members of the party, Nursanita Nasution and Aan Rohanah have also been appointed members of the Consultative Council, which holds the highest authority in determining the direction of the party. However, the role of women in PKS is still far from satisfactory, since most women on committees of the

Central Board have been placed in a special department of women's affairs. They have not yet been accommodated in other departments on the basis of their true capacity and expertise.

Opportunities have always been open to women but they have not often been ready to take them up. For instance, the PKS Provincial Board of Central Java in 2006 is open for a woman to be elected as chairperson. Members of PKS in that area are free to choose woman as a chairperson. "There are many female cadres in PKS. So it is allowable for woman to run as a candidate for PKS chairperson."[48]

In responding to the issue of a female president, PKS has revised its objections. Yet however much PKS might prefer a man, the case of Megawati as President of Indonesia, replacing Abdurahman Wahid in 2000, was problematic. PK was actively involved in the campaign to oppose Megawati in 1999. There were two reasons to oppose Megawati's appointment. The first was ideological and political; Megawati's party and its members had an inharmonious relation with the Islamic parties. The second was a normative reason: most Islamic parties, including PK, opposed a woman president on religious grounds.[49]

A large demonstration was held in 2000, involving thousands of PK cadres, in front of the National Parliament in Jakarta to request members of DPR/MPR not to choose Megawati. However, during the presidency of Abdurahman Wahid, cadres of PK also held simultaneous demonstrations to call for the resignation of Wahid, which indirectly gave a constitutional opportunity for Megawati to replace him. Why did PK change its stance in favour of a woman as president? They followed political expediency in the legal clause "that men and women are treated equal under the constitution."[50] Whenever the constitution guaranteed a practice, PK preferred to follow the constitution.

By the good example of its cadres, PKS intends to lead Indonesian Muslims to willingly practise *shariah*. Even though some Islamic movements that campaign for the implementation of Islamic law argue that the Indonesian people already practise the non-legal aspects of *shariah*, PKS still considers that its introduction is urgent. It is true that some parts of *shariah* have been adopted by the state, such as the regulation of marriage and the laws of inheritance and endowment, however, for PKS, the essence of *shariah* is still wanting.

3. Dialogue with Non-Muslims

PKS activists believe that in order to explain the "true" meaning of *shariah*, a dialogue with non-Muslim organizations and communities needs to be established; as long as non-Muslims are honest about their religion and understand the issue of *shariah* properly they will not oppose its implementation.[51] Through dialogue, common values among the religions in Indonesia will emerge. Salim Segaf al-Jufri, chairman of *shariah* board of PKS said

> By dialogue a communication is established among different parties, including non-Muslims, if they are fair in dealing with this issue and are not overwhelmed by suspicions. I believe that even though it may raise some dispute and disagreement, we will find common agreement. For instance, whoever lives in this country must agree on the need to combat corruption and to practise justice for all, Muslims and non-Muslims alike. To protect people's rights, property and souls is the basic thing that all people must agree upon. Is not respect for others' rights in worship and the practice of their religions part of Islamic teaching (*shariah*)?[52]

Nonetheless, dialogue has not been an easy task because the elite of PKS have had little experience in initiating dialogue with non-Muslims. Their experiments within Jemaah Tarbiyah activities in the past were confined to their inner groups and rarely did they socialise beyond with the broader society. However, this last step program is still far from applicable for the rank and file of PKS. The PKS has not engaged in the interfaith dialogue that is promoted by the government and other leaders of religious organizations in Indonesia and many PKS activists still hesitate to cooperate with non-Muslims.[53]

According to al-Jufri, the socialisation of the concept of *shariah* still faces obstacles, since *shariah* itself is still seen by certain Muslims and non-Muslims as well as something that may threaten sections of society.[54] This is because *shariah* is promoted by certain Muslim groups such as NII, MMI, FPI and many radical groups in unwise ways, tending towards force and violence. It is a real challenge for PKS to reform this image. As many PKS activists have often said, "it is true that *hudud* is part of *shariah* but people often forget that the distribution of wealth is also a significant element of *shariah*."[55] The problem is how to find a balance between promoting welfare and proposing *shariah*, and not to fall into the trap of formalising the sacred whilst abandoning the profane.

PKS's commitment to Islamic teachings has resulted in actions to "Islamise" non-religious issues and to use them as vehicles to promote its ideals. Other Islamic parties often tend to promote Islam from a legal point of view and "top-down" approach, but PKS starts from practical issues to lead people into the essence of *shariah*. The issue of the formalisation of *shariah* guarantees their presence in the political field, among more powerful secular parties, even though they can claim only a small number of votes.[56]

The problem is whether or not the party will retain its commitment to gradual steps towards the formalisation of *shariah* if it should gain significantly greater support than before. This question will be analysed by focussing on the issue of the implementation of *shariah* and various opinions on it among PKS activists.

C. Implementing *Shariah*

As a religious movement influenced by the society of Muslim Brothers, PKS regards Islam to be the totality of rules and norms guiding the daily lives of Muslims — embracing religious, economic, social, cultural and political dimensions. Political institutions are necessary to maintain and promote the existence of the teachings of Islam. As a political party, PKS struggles for the interests of Muslims, or at least to prevent any political moves to obstruct Muslim interests. The state must be able to guarantee its people the performance of their faith. The issue as phrased by PKS is that "if it is not the Islamic parties which are dominant in the government, the Muslim community will have difficulties in observing its faith."[57] It seems that the possibility of "trust building" between Indonesian secular and Islamist elites is still low - most of the political elites still do not trust one another.[58]

For PKS, the place of Islamic parties within the democratic system is necessary and the only possible way to carry out the "Islamisation of the state." Only by the people's support through general elections can the agenda of the Islamisation of Indonesia be realised.[59] The implementation of *shariah* must be carried out in a constitutional way, avoiding the use of force or violence.[60] A jurisprudential view of the Egyptian scholar, Yusuf Qaradawi has strengthened PKS's belief in the benefits of democracy. It was quoted in a PKS organisational manual to support the principle of embracing democracy to further Islamic interests. Qaradawi said

> There is nothing wrong for a nation, intellectuals and leaders to use any concept from others, they may even find them more perfect and suitable. However, before we are able to provide an alternative concept, it is better for us to take lessons from various concepts and principles of democracy in order to ensure justice, consultation and human rights, as well as to challenge all tyrant regimes in the world.[61]

In this context, PKS believes that the practice of *shariah* within the community must be supported by political structures. Any efforts to influence the state must be carried out by an involvement in political activities. The cultural approach in promoting Islam is insufficient for PKS. Even though PKS seats in the National Parliament remain few in comparison to the more established parties, their presence in the Legislative Body (DPR) is still a prerogative.[62] One activist of PKS in East Java confirmed the strategic role of being involved in politics

> A good Muslim will not be confused with our approach in carrying out *dakwah*, including in politics. If people consider politics dirty and good men do not want to be involved in politics because they are afraid of being contaminated, what will happen? Does it mean that we must keep our distance while this condition will go on as it is? In fact, we know

that all policies are decided through political process, not through sermons! We cannot expect good policies if people who claim themselves clean just speak out in sermons or in raising criticism.[63]

So the attitude of PKS towards the formalisation of *shariah* in Indonesia is still ambivalent. This is because the party formally has no clear direction on *shariah* and its core members have varied in their responses to the issue. They are divided into two streams.

First, there is the moderate mainstream. Most PKS activists believe that the implementation of *shariah* should be initiated from the level of the individual, society and only then the state. The role of the government is to maintain and ensure that all rules and laws derived from Islamic values have been properly implemented. This moderate approach, which is supported by the majority of PKS activists, is more accommodative and suitable for the Indonesian community, yet it does not satisfy conservative groups who are impatient to see the introduction of *shariah* in Indonesia.

Following this direction, the implementation of *shariah* will be carried out in a careful way. The people's criticism and aspirations will be considered in order to continue on to the next step of Islamisation. Islamic aspirations do not need to be consistent in a formal way, but sometimes Islamic values may be adopted to give spirit to national laws. The planned strategy is that when the people show themselves to be receptive; more parts of *shariah* will be proposed. PKS's philosophy in implementing *shariah* is to give people a "taste" first and if they like it, more can be given. "It is like orange juice; if people like it but it only contains 30% pure fruit, for instance, give it to them. It is a matter of appetite."[64] This gradual approach of formalisation of *shariah* is mainly derived from the experience of Turkey.[65]

The pragmatic approach comes from this stream of opinion. Even so, some members of PKS in parliament have argued that empowering the little people and raising their standard of living is more important than keeping busy with the issue of *shariah*. "The important thing is to promote a good image of the party before the people; whether or not party will propose *shariah* is another issue that will be talked about later."[66]

Secondly, a conservative group comprises a small stream of PKS activists. They believe it is necessary to implement *shariah* immediately, once the opportunity arises, regardless of the response by most Muslims. They say that as long as *shariah* is an alternative and comprehensive system they must dare to apply it in Indonesia, regardless of the consequences. They maintain that since the application of secular laws introduced by the Dutch colonial regime in Indonesia did not consider broad social realities of the time, so the implementation of *shariah* should also not be dependent on the condition of the people. As long as the state is able and willing to implement it, the possibility will be there.[67] However, these radical views are not apparent within PKS, in particular within PKS representatives in the legislature. They are mostly heard from the section of Jemaah Tarbiyah not directly involved with current political issues.

In contrast to the supporters of partial Islamisation, this second group is more interested in bringing in Islamic laws first and other aspects later. They believe that the complete implementation of *shariah* will automatically bring the people into prosperity and justice - for religion itself promises such. Any partial application of *shariah*, however, will not give benefits but rather it will lead to further crisis. If ever the party should gain an electoral majority and is able to hold on to power, this faction will not hesitate to demand the complete implementation of *shariah*.

Yet the call for the immediate implementation of *shariah* has faced much resistance. Most PKS activists disagree with it because it is regarded as an obstacle for the party to survive in the future. To bring a change towards a more Islamic society and state, PKS prefers to rely on the gradual process that rests on a paradigm change within individuals.[68] Imposing *shariah* would be a counterproductive of cultural process and entail the risk of loosing political support from the grassroots whenever the party fails to comply with the people's interests. All the political investment of PKS will be devalued and the chance to implement *shariah* slip far away, perhaps even be impossible.[69]

Most PKS activists agree that the moderate stance is the only practicable way to introduce *shariah*. This is congruent with the fundamental *dakwah* principles of Jemaah Tarbiyah. *Dakwah* itself is understood as a slow process but with an ultimate goal, "*dakwah* is an estafet, not a sprint - it has steps."[70] Hilmi Aminuddin explains how PKS formulates its strategies in implementing *shariah* in Indonesia:[71]

First, practising *shariah* within the individual and the family. Before taking further steps towards having *shariah* observed by the government, this condition must really be met. The government will not have the power to regularise and ensure the practice of *shariah* unless the Muslim community voluntarily puts it into practice. The role of government is only to uphold practice and correct some deviations. Muslims' own readiness to accept *shariah* as part of their legal system will be the guarantee of its survival.

Second, drafting and legalising laws based on *shariah*. Legislators are responsible for introducing Islamic laws into the national legal system. By no means all laws are to be based on *shariah*, in some case it only requires the effort to make sure the laws are not in contradiction with *shariah*, or that they do not violate it. The law itself does not have to be obviously Islamic.

Third, formalising *shariah* as the fundamental source of law. At this stage, an institution responsible for the carrying out of all Islamic laws must be formed. It must be able to carry out the responsibilities associated with *shariah* guidance. The government is expected to perform this function after being Islamised.

The support of PKS in the case of the Proposal of Pornography Regulations, *Rancangan Undang-Undang Anti Pornografi dan Pornoaksi* (RUU APP) is evidence on how PKS sees this proposal as an effort to make the laws in accordance with the spirit of Islamic law. However, so far there is no precedent to suggest that PKS is willing to follow the three strategies above since it has attempted to downplay the demand for the implementation of *shariah* during the 1999 and 2004 general elections and it seems that it will maintain the same attitude in the next elections. For the next two general elections at least, we will not see any significant change in the terms of the formalisation of *shariah* at the national level. This is because activists of PKS believe that such an aspiration only can be achieved through the total support of people in Indonesia.[72] They believe that at present there is no guarantee that the people in general or the mainstream Islamic organisations support it.[73]

The most feasible way open to PKS is by encouraging the formalisation of *shariah* at the district level, relying on the political opportunities of autonomous districts whenever popular voices at the grassroots level sound in favour of *shariah*. Thus strategically, PKS has not pushed for formalisation at the national level, but it has consistently worked to support the implementation of *shariah* at the district level. For instance, most activists of KPPSI in South Sulawesi are also activists of PKS and in favour of *shariah*.[74] The logic behind this strategy is that once the district governments are islamised, the central government will simply have to adjust its policies to these realities.

Nonetheless, the problem is that not all districts in Indonesia have the same aspiration for *shariah*. A notable exception is the Province of Aceh and some districts, such as Cianjur (West Java), Pamekasan (East Java), Bulukumba and Maros (South Sulawesi), Padang (West Sumatra), Riau and East Lombok (NTB) have implemented some aspects of *shariah,* varying from the obligation to wear Muslim dress on Fridays, up to the regulation of *zakat* and other charitable activities.[75] However, in these regions the district regulations (Peraturan Daerah, Perda) consisting of some aspects of *shariah* were not initiated by PKS but by Golkar. In the province of West Sumatra, which has been known as the stronghold of modernists, the people are far from the ideal of implementing *shariah*. One PK representative at the provincial level suggested

> It is true that PK wants the practice of *shariah* to prevail in the West Sumatra but it is not an easy task to do it. The *dakwah* must be carried in gradual ways whilst we continue to struggle for the introduction of regulations that are closer to *shariah*, such as the head scarf for women

and prohibiting immoral activities (*perbuatan-perbuatan maksiat*). However, the application of *shariah* considers the reality of the people and the stages of *dakwah*.[76]

Even though PKS has started to introduce its "new perspective" on *shariah* by emphasising its universal values, such as advancing justice and prosperity and fighting against corruption and injustice, PKS still faces challenges in implementing its agenda. These come not only from outside but also from internal factors, in particular the hypothetical question of when it gains real political power.

D. Challenges

The important issue regarding the implementation of *shariah* is PKS' stance if the party gains majority support. Will it immediately impose *shariah* or remain committed to its gradualist approach? As long as there are no political obstructions, such as military or government intervention, to impede the achievements of PKS, most activists believe their ideal for promoting *shariah* will still be valid. PKS has felt compelled to be committed toward democracy since it believes that democracy guarantees its existence.[77]

Many Muslims and non-Muslims in Indonesia have not been able to obtain a clear picture of the PKS position on the application of *shariah*. Even though the issue has been discussed within PKS circles and in its publications, it has not been conveyed explicitly in its political platforms. Discourse on formalisation, including the idea of a "*shariah*-led prosperity" is conveyed in interviews or written about selectively in party training manuals. As a result, there is confusion among Muslims themselves towards PKS. For liberal Muslims, PKS is embedded in a fundamentalist image because of its links with the Muslim Brothers of Egypt, its source of inspiration and model of organization. PKS is accused of having a hidden agenda, pretending to be an open and pluralistic party while adhering to fundamentalist ideas, including the establishment of an "Islamic state."[78] In contrast, Muslim hard liners in Indonesia criticize PKS for not being serious in promoting the implementation of *shariah*, even accusing its activists of lacking the courage to uphold the struggle for *shariah*. According to this group, PKS plays no more than a pragmatic role at every political moment.

This ambivalent image of PKS indicates a lack of preparation by the party in responding to religious ideals and socio-political realities in Indonesia. The discourse has never been aired comprehensively or elaborated within the party. It is understandable that the question of *shariah* is not an attractive one in political campaigns, but the failure to take sides on this issue will have its impact in the loss of support in popular votes. Imposing *shariah* for the sake of religious commitment to the Indonesian people who are mostly far from a perceived proper understanding of *shariah* will result in tensions, even chaos in society, since the party has not properly informed the public on the issue.

The head of Politics and Defence Department of the Central Board of PKS, Untung Wahono, issued a clarification *(bayan)* regarding the ambiguity of the party towards *shariah*. However, this clarification was not in the official form issued by the party, it was instead "partly formal" for the purpose of guidance to the activists and not a political statement by the party itself.[79] Wahono stated that "it is strange for our party which, since the beginning, proclaimed its Islamic ideology, that it should be accused of rejecting the implementation of *shariah*. This allegation must be wrong, and if we take the issue seriously, it has been merely based on the Piagam Jakarta matter, which PKS did not support."[80]

As long as the more moderate elements of Jemaah Tarbiyah activists occupy the central leadership of PKS, the demand to implement *shariah* will be managed in such ways that enable them to consider the needs of Indonesian people. The people become the main factor in dealing with the formalisation of *shariah*. When the majority of people are willing to be ruled by *shariah*, the party will simply follow their demands. The presence of campus activists in great numbers in the party has been significant in directing it into more accommodative and realistic ways in negotiating their demands. As was suggested by Mahfudz Sidiq, who was in charge of PKS recruitments and caderisation from 1999 to 2004, "PKS wants to struggle for Islam through politics as a complement to the cultural approach in order to build a strong political basis in the grassroots level."[81]

The problem is that some activists of PKS assume that their achievement in politics is solely a reflection of their success in education at the grassroots level, mainly evident in an increase in membership. The education *(tarbiyah)* given by PKS activists that aims to enlighten Indonesian Muslims about the meaning of *shariah* will be important for the party to ensure its implementation. Nonetheless, the success of PKS in politics is not always accompanied by success in caderisation. Besides getting support from regions where numbers of Jemaah Tarbiyah's activists are dominant, PKS also has an impressive achievement in the areas where Islamic communities are not most numerous.[82] For instance, in the urban areas such as Jakarta, Tangerang, Bekasi, Depok and Cibinong PKS won the 2004 general elections. These are areas mostly inhabited by the lower middle class who are not necessarily religious in character – and yet these areas have become strongholds of PKS.

Even if PKS were involved in sharing power within an existing government and had the chance to formalise Islamic law, it is unlikely that it would immediately take the opportunity. PKS activists believe that the implementation of *shariah* is not only determined by legislative and popular support but must also involve the approval of other parties and executives, including the military.[83] The experience of an Islamic party in Algeria, the Islamic Salvation Front (FIS) that won the elections in 1990 but saw its triumph immediately aborted by the army has become a valuable lesson for PKS. PKS activists always try to ensure that their political moves will not tempt non-democratic powers to interrupt the political process.[84]

Despite the issue of ways to implement *shariah,* another important issue that will become a challenge for PKS is the sensitive aspects of the Islamic criminal laws, such as the punishments of the amputation of limbs, stoning and lashing. These are the areas which concern and worry many Indonesian Islamic scholars. PKS has shown a reluctance to deal with these particular issues. In fact, if we consider the doctrine of Jemaah Tarbiyah and its attempts to practise a total Islam, the signs are that the party will be willing to apply all of the laws prescribed in the Qur'an and Hadith, these two being the bases and sources of the Islamic legal system. But if we consider the composition of the elites currently holding high positions in PKS leadership, we will find another possibility.

In order to strike a compromise between the ideal of implementing *shariah* and responding to political and social realities in Indonesia, PKS has tried to keep a balance between its Islamism and flexibility. *Shariah* is to be the main inspiration for Indonesia national laws while local customs and Western laws are still accommodated.[85] To eliminate possible resistance from parts of Indonesian society, PKS has set aside its discussion on sensitive issues, such as the *hudud laws*. Neither Muhammadiyah nor NU supports the idea of formalising *shariah*.[86] Nonetheless, the problem is not merely caused by such resistance alone but it is also related to the party which is not fully prepared to discuss the issue at academic, theoretical or practical levels.[87]

At least in the short term, the implementation of the harsh punishments of *hudud* is not priority. Even if PKS institutes the Islamic criminal laws, they will try to avoid them in practice, in order to retain sympathy from the wider international community. Usually, these laws will be set up as "maximum" laws, while other alternatives that are not in conflict with them will be provided. For instance, instead of exacting the punishment of hand amputation, education and rehabilitation for the criminal will be preferred. Thieves will not be immediately charged, but rather they will be conditioned against their criminal activities. Only if they continue to re-offend will they face the maximum punishments of *hudud*. The precedent for this practice was applied by the great companion of the prophet, Umar ibn al-Khattab (634-644) when the criminal laws were not observed because of economic disasters during the term of his caliphate.[88]

So PKS has attempted to promote *shariah* from its own stand point. It will start by empowering people with prosperity and welfare and will subsequently introduce the Islamic laws. However, up to now some cadres of PKS who hold high governmental positions in certain districts have not demonstrated progress, although Nurmahmudi Ismail, a former President of PK who was elected mayor in the district of Depok, West Java has struggled to manage the district and to bring economic progress. It seems that PKS is not yet prepared to play the game at the expense of its success. It has been well aware that it cannot impose *shariah* when the people's interests are focused on the economy. The key issue is not simply that PKS needs the back-up of political power, but that there is an economic dimension as well. Any success in implementing *shariah* will be dependent on success in accelerating the economic growth of Indonesia and its people

> PKS sees that the implementation of *shariah* must be carried out step by step, not by force, unless for Muslims who really understand the concept of *shariah*. This country is not an Islamic state. We consider ourselves exemplars in terms of implementing *shariah* in our daily life, reflecting it in the practices of individual, family, society and state. *Shariah* is not a matter of implementing criminal laws, such as cutting off hands, stoning and the like. We eat using the right hand and maintain good character, for instance, these are other important aspects of shariah. We need to participate in order to establish justice for the people. If the people want *shariah* and it is a reflection of justice, it is OK. We want to see individuals, not merely as a political commodities and slogans, practising *shariah*. We are tired of promise and slogans, but in reality we are not the best examples in our community.[89]

Another crucial aspect in the implementation of *shariah* that needs to be addressed seriously is the party's position on the issue of pluralism. Pluralism is understood as an acceptance of the fact that Indonesian society contains a variety of religious affiliations. What will be the party's commitment towards the non-Muslim communities if they gain power?

Some observers worry about the possibility of PKS imposing their religious beliefs on others,[90] or if persuasion that claims Islam as the only true religion will prevent the party from accommodating non-Muslim groups in government. Furthermore, this attitude will lead to the inability of the party to share power with others in Indonesia, wherever power distribution is most likely to take place. Experience has shown that a lack of the preparation of political Islam in certain Islamic countries to respond to such issues has created great problems. Clashes occur not only between different religious professions, but also among Muslims who follow different schools and sects. How will PKS deal with this crucial question?

It seems that PKS has anticipated the issue by implementing the concept of *musharakah*. The term *musharakah* means "participation" and co-operation is a major concern among most of the activists of Jemaah Tarbiyah. The term indicates the need to make coalition in order to form government. However, not all members of Jemaah Tarbiyah are able to acknowledge the reality of diverse communities in Indonesia. PKS has attempted to steer its course carefully in order to satisfy the needs of Indonesian people on one hand and the religious demands of its cadres on the other.

PKS has been able to overcome theological issues regarding political participation within a non-Islamic system through the concept of *musharakah*, yet it needs to engage further with the political and social realities of Indonesia. The involvement of Islamic movements in an un-Islamic system is justified on grounds of the mission to reform the system from within, or at least in order to prevent further deterioration by the regime. The Qur'anic story of Joseph is well known among PKS activists as justification that political participation in a tyrant's regime is permitted if its aim is to bring a change for the better.[91] The story tells how Joseph nominated himself for appointment as treasurer in the infidel kingdom of Egypt. The Qur'an states

> [Joseph] said, "Appoint me over the storehouse of the land. Indeed, I will be a knowing guardian." And thus We established Joseph in the land to settle therein wherever he willed. We touch with Our mercy whom We will, and We do not allow loss of the reward of those who do good."[92]

Referring to this story, Abdi Sumaithi, a PKS representative in parliament (2004-2005) and a prominent leader of Jemaah Tarbiyah argues that the decision of a religious movement to take part in politics is essential in order to conceptualise and exercise the fundamental freedoms of people.[93] Basic freedoms that must be protected are religious, individual and organisational. Diversity and the plurality of the people are natural realities that must be kept in mind by all activists of religious movements. Each individual and group must be allowed to express its own character and to participate in the political process without restriction. Abdi Sumaith further elaborates upon the commitment to protect the freedom of religion

> It seems that it is crucial to stress that the commitment of Islamic movements towards the implementation of human rights is not simply a concept and slogan for political convenience. The guarantee for non-Muslims who live in an Islamic state to enjoy the same status as citizens is important. Non-Muslims (*ahl al-zimmi*) who acknowledge the Muslim ruling are considered as permanent citizens.[94]

In line with the concept of *musharakah,* the party also reserves the right to enter into coalition with other political parties, regardless of their religious background. However, similarity of ideology becomes a priority in forming such a coalition, above the question of making alliances based on strategic and tactical considerations. In practice, in coalition it is not always necessary to give priority to parties with Islamic platforms; sometimes PKS prefers to form coalition in local districts with secular parties.[95] In Boyolali, Central Java PKS made a coalition with a Christian party, The Prosperous Peace Party, Partai Damai Sejahtera (PDS).[96] Hilmi Aminuddin, the chairman of the consultative assembly (Majelis Syura) of PKS, says that the new paradigm of PKS enables its activists to form coalition with any broader elements of Indonesian society. He further stated

> It is not a hidden agenda and strategy but it is a matter of belief. *Shariah* can be applied in our daily life by promoting good deeds and caring for unfortunate people. I interact and work together with my Christian friends and they are not afraid of me.[97]

Acknowledging the reality of Indonesian pluralism is unquestionable. For PKS, whenever it enters democratic system, it automatically has to respect this pluralism.[98] Nonetheless, even though the issue has been solved at the structural level of the party, not all cadres of Jemaah Tarbiyah can easily follow this new paradigm. Some of them, even though a small portion, still envision the idea of an Islamic system and the immediate application of *shariah*. This is a real challenge for PKS and the notion of the implementation of *shariah* based on prosperity still needs to be negotiated among PKS members and with other parties in Indonesia. In fact, as was acknowledged by Tifatul Sembiring, the president of PKS (2005-2010) the implementation of *shariah* must be pursued through democratic means and needs to be negotiated with others.[99] In responding to the issue of the implementation of *shariah* in some regions he said: "*Kalau terlalu berat, tawarlah. Jangan anarkhis dan jangan terjadi penyesatan pemahaman*" ("If it is too difficult, strike a bargain. Do not be anarchic and let there be no misunderstandings").[100]

ENDNOTES

[1] Saiful Mujani, "Syariat Islam dalam Perdebatan," in *Syariat Islam Pandangan Muslim Liberal* (Jakarta: Sembrani Aksara Nusantara, 2003), 43.

[2] See "Azyumardi Azra: Penerapan Syariat Bisa Kontroprouduktif, " *Islamlib.com*, 5 August 2001.

[3] Ibid.

[4] Ibid. In the Qur'an there is a verse that states the freedom to embrace a religion, "there is no compulsion in [acceptance of] the religion." See the Qur'an II: 256.

[5] See Ulil Abshar Abdalla, "Syariat Islam," *Suara Karya*, 23 March 2004.

[6] Ibid.

[7] See Lutfi Assyaukanie, "Berkah Sekularisme," *Islamlib.com*, 11 April 2005.

[8] See opening statement at the website of a liberal Islam group, *Islamlib.com*.

[9] Jamhari, ed., *Gerakan Salafi Radikal di Indonesia* (Jakarta: Rajawali Press, 2004), 52.

[10] Ismail Yusanto, "Selamatkan Indonesia dengan Syariat Islam," in *Syariat Islam Pandangan Islam Liberal*, 147.

[11] Ibid.

[12] Ibid.

[13] Wawancara with Untung Wahono, Canberra, 12 July 2005.

[14] Ibid.

[15] Interview with Rofi' Munawar, Surabaya, 7 March 2003.

[16] Interview with Zulkieflymansyah, Canberra, 30 August 2004.

[17] Interview with Rofi' Munawar, Surabaya, 7 March 2003.

[18] Dewan Pimpinan Partai Keadilan Sejahtera, *Menyelamatkan Bangsa Platform Kebijakan Partai Keadilan Sejahtera* (Jakarta: Al'Iktishom Cahaya Umat, 2004), 126.

[19] Satria Hadi Lubis, *Yang Nyata dari PK Sejahtera* (Jakarta: Miskat Publication, 2003).

[20] Ibid., 20.

[21] Interview with Rofi' Munawar, Surabaya, 7 March 2003.

[22] Nandang Burhanuddin, *Penegakan Syariat Islam Menurut Partai Keadilan* (Jakarta: Al-Jannah Pustaka, 2004), 149.

[23] Ibid.

[24] Tim Departemen Kaderisasi DPP Partai Keadilan Sejahtera, *Manajemen Tarbiyah Anggota Pemula* (Jakarta: DPP PKS, 2003), 234.

[25] Interview with Rofi' Munawar, Surabaya, 7 March 2003.

[26] Islamic laws divides punishments into two categories: *hudud* laws, mandatory punishments imposed for crimes against God, and *ta'zir*, punishments under the judgment of a *qadi* (judge). *Hudud* punishments are clearly prescribed by the Qur'an and imposed to cases of morality (adultery, fornication, and false allegation of adultery), property (theft and robbery), and apostasy. For instance, the Qur'an says about the punishment for adultery and fornication: "The [unmarried] woman or [unmarried] man found guilty of sexual intercourse – lash each one of them with hundred lashes, and do not be taken by pity for them in the religion [i.e. law] of Allah, if you should believe in Allah and the Last Day. And let a group of the believers witness their punishment (Qur'an XXIV:2). See John L. Esposito, ed., *The Oxford Encyclopedia of the Modern Islamic World 2* (New York and Oxford: Oxford University, 1995), 137.

[27] *Reuters*, 7 April 2004.

[28] Burhanuddin, *Penegakan Syariat Islam*, 150-151.

[29] Interview with Rofi' Munawar, Surabaya, 7 March 2003.

[30] Ibid.

[31] Interview with Suryadarma, Makasar, 17 September 2003.

[32] Interview with Marfendi, Padang, 20 June 2003.

[33] Burhanuddin, *Penegakan Syariat Islam*, 159

[34] Interview with Rafqinal, Padang, 19 June 2003.

[35] Interview with Marfendi, Padang, 20 June 2003.

[36] *Jawa Pos*, 2 August 2005.

[37] Qur'an III:28.

[38] See "*Bayan* DPP PK Sejahtera" dated 27 March 2004.

[39] *Panjimas*, 20 Feb – 05 March 2003.

[40] Elizabeth Fuller Collins, "'Islam is Solution:' *Dakwah* and Democracy" (Paper presented at Ohio University, 20 June 2004).

[41] Mutammimul Ula, *Perpektif Syariat Islam di Indonesia* (Jakarta: Pustaka Tarbiatuna, 2001), 41.

[42] John L. Esposito, ed., *The Oxford Encyclopedia of the Modern Islamic World* (New York: Oxford University Press, 1995), 92.

[43] Nurcholish Madjid argued that the Madinah Charter is the first constitution that consisted of principles of ruling a state based on collective interests and humanity. See Nurcholish Madjid, "Agama dan Negara dalam Islam," in *Kontekstualisasi Doktrin Islam dalam Sejarah* (Jakarta: Paramadina, 1994), 590.

[44] See Allan S. Samson, "Islam and Indonesian Politics," *Asian Survey* 8 no. 12 (December 1968), 1011.

[45] See Greg Fealy and Virginia Hooker, ed., *Voices of Islam in Southeast Asia: a Contemporary Sourcebook* (Singapore: Institute of Southeast Asian Studies, 2006), 323.

[46] See Alan Wall, "The Indonesian Political Landscape Post General Election" (Report presented at ICWA meeting, 10 May 2004).

[47] See *Saksi*, 20 May 2003, 28.

[48] *Detikcom*, 11 January 2006.

[49] See Damanik, *Fenomena Partai Keadilan*, 301-302.

50 Ibid.

51 Burhanuddin, *Penegakan Syariat Islam*, 150-151.

52 Ibid.

53 The reason is that activists of PKS still focus their efforts to unite and cooperate with Muslim groups; when they succeed in bringing unity among Muslims they will begin to cooperate with non-Muslims. Interview, anonymous, Jakarta, 24 March 2003.

54 Burhanuddin, *Penegakan Syariat Islam*, 151.

55 Ibid.

56 Mujani, "Syariat Islam dalam Perdebatan," 41.

57 Lecture presented by Hidayat Nurwahid in Jakarta, 13 June 2003

58 Martin van Bruinessen, "Post-Suharto Muslim Engagements with Civil Society and Democracy," in Indonesia in Transition: Rethinking 'Civil Society', 'Religion', and 'Crisis' (Yogyakarta: Pustaka Pelajar, 2004), 37-66.

59 See Lubis, *Yang Nyata dari PK Sejahtera*, 4.

60 Ibid., 8.

61 See Anonym, "Panduan Pengambilan Kebijakan dalam Musyawarah Partai Keadilan," (Majelis Jakarta: Pertimbangan Partai Keadilan, December 2000), 48.

62 Interview with Irwan Prayitno, Jakarta, 14 June 2003.

63 Interview with Rofi' Munawar, Surabaya, 7 March 2003.

64 One member of PKS even stated that for the time being the issue is not necessary. It will become the responsibility of the party to Islamise when it has gained the people's attention. Interview, anonymous, Depok, 22 March 2003.

65 Interview with Mahfudz Sidiq, Jakarta, 8 October 2003.

66 Interview with Zulkieflimansyah, Canberra, 30 August 2004.

67 Daud Rasyid, *Indahnya Syari'at Islam* (Jakarta: Usamah Press, 2003), 55.

68 Interview with Mahfudz Sidiq, Jakarta, 8 October 2003.

69 Ibid.

70 Muhammad Sa'id, "Hatmiyah At Tarbiyah: Tarbiyah Suatu Kemestian", in *Tarbiyah Berkelanjutan* (Jakarta: Pustaka Tarbiatuna, 2003), 50.

71 *PK- Sejahtera.org*, 22 August 2002

72 Ula, *Perpektif Syariat Islam di Indonesia*, 43.

73 Ibid., 32-33.

74 Interview with Suryadarma, Makasar, 17 September 2003.

75 See "Syariat Islam yang Bagaimana," *Panjimas*, 27 November – 12 December 2002. For details see also *Gatra*, 6 May 2006.

76 Interview with Ahmad Shiddik, Padang, 19 June 2003

77 Interview with Mahfudz Sidiq, Jakarta, 8 October 2003.

78 See Ahmad Najib Burhani,"Piagam Jakarta dan Piagam Madinah", *Kompas*, 31 September 2004.

79 See *Saksi*, 31 December 2003.

80 Ibid.

81 Interview with Mahfudz Sidiq, Jakarta, 8 October 2003.

82 Interview with Razikun, 23 December 2005.

83 Interview with Budi Darmawan, Canberra, 12 December 2004.

84 Interview, anonymous, Jakarta, 25 June 2003.

85 Ula, *Perpektif Syariat Islam di Indonesia*, 21.

86 See "Perda Syariah Tidak Diperlukan," *Media Indonesia*, 16 June 2006.

87 Al Yasa Abu Bakar, "Hukum Pidana Islam dan Upaya Penerapannya di Indonesia," in *Penerapan Syariat Islam di Indonesia: Antara Peluang dan Tantangan* (Jakarta: Globalmedia, 2004), 118.

88 Surahman Hidayat, "Tahapan Pelaksanaan Syariat dalam Perspektif Dakwah," in *Penerapan Syariat Islam di Indonesia*, 199.

89 Interview with Aus Hidayat Nur, Depok, 13 May 2003.

90 Burhani,"Piagam Jakarta dan Piagam Madinah", *Kompas*, 31 September 2004.
91 Abu Ridha, *Saat Dakwah Memasuki Wilayah Politik* (Bandung: Syaamil, 2003), 97.
92 Qur'an XII: 55-56.
93 Ridha, *Saat Dakwah*, 70.
94 Ibid., 70-71.
95 See "PKS telah Praktikkan Pluralisme di Pilkada Termasuk Berkoalisi dengan PDS," *Kompas*, 1 August 2005.
96 See "PKS-PDS Tetapkan Pasangan," *Suara Merdeka*, 18 March 2005.
97 *Tempo*, 7 August 2005.
98 Ibid.
99 See "Tifatul Sembiring: Paranoid Syariat Islam," *Gatra*, 6 May 2006.
100 Ibid.

Conclusion

This study has shown the emergence of Jemaah Tarbiyah as a covert religious movement in the mid 1980s that was transformed in 1998 into a political party, the Justice Party (PK), further to evolve into the Prosperous Justice Party (PKS) in 2003. This study also shows how the influence of a trans-national Islamic movement, the Muslim Brothers of Egypt, has played a role in shaping the dynamics of Islam and politics in Indonesia. Jemaah Tarbiyah and PKS have entered an ideological experiment and have made a unique contribution to current Indonesian politics by testing the nature of the relationship between Islam-based politics and the secular state. In order to survive, the activists of Jemaah Tarbiyah have domesticated their ideals into the Indonesian context under the rubric of *maslahat dakwah* (Ar. *maslahah al-da'wah*, the benefit of *dakwah*).

The role of PKS as an Islam-based party in Indonesia has been determined by the need to balance Islamic aspirations with the socio-political realities of the times. The aims of PKS in politics are to achieve justice, social care and good governance for all Indonesians. Thus, Islamic symbols and slogans have been modified in order to meet the expectations of the masses. Religious and political accomodation has become a necessary choice for PKS. Its pragmatism is aimed at attracting popular support from the Indonesian people at large. PKS accommodation has been apparent in the following respects:

First, as an informal religious movement influenced by the Muslim Brothers of Egypt, Jemaah Tarbiyah has contributed to the process of Islamisation in Indonesia since the 1980s. Even though its followers have been distinguished from mainstream Islam and have displayed global inclinations (as global *santri*) they have sought to domesticate their appeal to Indonesian society. Their adoption and adaptation of the Muslim Brothers' ideas have not led them to totally distance themselves from the established traditionalist or modernist associations. They took the decision to form a political party in Indonesia when other Islamic movements, such as Hizbut Tahrir, Salafi and NII groups denounced politics. PKS has begun to develop relations with mainstream Islam in Indonesia, even though both NU and Muhammadiyah, to a certain extent, have indicated their resistance.

Second, the pattern of Islamisation carried out by members of Jemaah Tarbiyah has brought about a new phenomenon which combines two orientations: purification and accommodation. A commitment to the practice of orthodox Islam, firmly based on the teachings of the Prophet Muhammad, and the movement's hope to be accepted by broader Indonesian society have made possible the co-existence of various orientations within Jemaah Tarbiyah. Even though Jemaah Tarbiyah has been known for strongly promoting the spirit of return to the Qur'an and Hadith, most activists have proceeded in careful manner in order to maintain the unity of the Muslim community. They have also tried to value the traditionalist element of Indonesian Islam.

Third, in responding to the Soeharto regime's oppression in the 1980s, Jemaah Tarbiyah pursued non-violent avenues, avoiding open confrontation with the regime. This strategy enabled Jemaah Tarbiyah's rapid expansion on the university campuses. The movement was able to divert religious disillusionment among certain Muslim groups into *dakwah* activities. When the collapse of Soeharto's New Order finally came, political openness supplied the opportunity for Jemaah Tarbiyah to formally organise its activities into a political party.

Fourth, the transformation of an informal religious movement into a political party has made accommodation necessary for Jemaah Tarbiyah's activists to survive. Interestingly, this pragmatism has not only been determined by political realities but has also been guided by the writings of Hasan al-Banna, in which there is to be found a strong Sufi influence. These Sufi aspects are the most neglected areas in studies of the Muslim Brothers movement so far. Sufi practices, long familiar to traditionalist Islam in Indonesia, have meant that the movement has flexibility in responding to religious and political issues. Within PKS itself, in contrast to its "superficial modernist image", activists of Jemaah Tarbiyah in the past, and nowadays PKS, surpisingly show remarkable numbers of activists from a traditionalist background.

In addition, the presence of a great number of traditionalist *ikhwan* and former student activists has reinforced moderate attitudes in PKS. It is indisputable that the campuses of the secular universities of Indonesia have become strongholds of and the chief source of political caderasation for PKS. Experience gained in student politics has helped in directing PKS's political orientations and strategies.

Fifth, in responding to the issue of *shariah* in Indonesia, PKS has tried to position itself among moderate Islamic groups. The idea of the Medina Charter proposed by PKS representatives in the national parliament in 2000 is an example of how PKS sought to rein in its Islamic aspirations in order to gain wider sympathy from the public. Rather than aggressively campaigning for the application of *shariah*, PKS has preferred to reformulate the concept of *shariah* through a campaign for justice and public welfare. At the grassroots level, PKS activists, through *dakwah* activities, have started to educate Indonesian Muslims about the essence of *shariah*. By doing so, PKS hopes that the demand for the application of *shariah* will come of itself from the grassroots and not need to be imposed by the state. In fact, this strategy has resulted in a dual policy towards *shariah* in order to maintain relations with both secular factions and Islamist groups in Indonesia.

However, the ambiguity on the part of PKS in responding to the issue of the implementation of *shariah* in Indonesia is due to the following factors: first, the significant influence of mainstream Islam in Indonesia has made PKS calculate with care its impact on society in general. Since NU and Muhammadiyah do not support the implementation of *shariah* at the national level, PKS does not try to isolate itself from the mainstream. As a new party that has not yet put down strong roots in society, PKS has tried to build rapprochement with Muhammadiyah and NU. PKS will not sacrifice its popularity among a particular section of Indonesian Muslims by following radical approaches that will jeopardise its image. By following democratic means, PKS has focussed on attracting popular support. This is only to be achieved by offering programs that meet the interests of constituents. However, not all PKS's activists support this pragmatic approach; there is still a small stream among Jemaah Tarbiyah members that prefers the immediate application of *shariah*.

Second, the pragmatic-realist approach of PKS is also determined by jurisprudential precepts that stress the unity of the Muslim *ummah* and the benefit of *dakwah* (*maslahah al-da'wah*). Other the jurisprudential principles adopted by PKS in justifying its political decisions, such as *akhaffud durarain* (choosing the lesser of two evils), *ma la yudraku kulluh laa yutraku kulluh* (something that cannot be wholly attained does not mean it can be entirely left out) permit a spectrum of moderate approaches. Marginal influence and success is valued over nothing gained. These considerations have made PKS appear to blur its position on the pros and cons of introducing *shariah*.

Third, the dominant political role of secular groups Indonesia has narrowed the domain for the Islamic parties, including PKS, to win public sympathy. To rule Indonesia, a single majority power is unlikely. Coalition and co-operation must be developed, particularly with the nationalist parties. In order to be involved within the system PKS has entered coalitions with nationalists and Christian parties to form government. This coalition has required considerable political accommodation and negotiation by PKS and has forced PKS to compromise its Islamic aspirations, including not spelling out its demands for *shariah*.

The religious and political maneuvres by PKS mentioned above have posed more of a dilemma for members of Jemaah Tarbiyah who hold to the principle of *al-jama'ah hiya al-hizb wa al-hizb huwa al-jama'ah"*, "the movement is the party and the party is the movement." The unity of Jemaah Tarbiyah and PKS has become an obstacle for the party in expanding its influence and maintaining the solidity of the cadres at same time. In addition, their concept of "to interact but not to dilute" (*yakhtalituna walakinna yatamayyazun*) is too abstract to be consistent with political accommodation. The result is that the performance of PKS in politics has never satisfied all of its constituents.

This study of the development of PKS has also revealed the fact of the solidity of PKS cadres compared to those of other Islamic parties. So far, PKS has been known by its discipline in running organizational activities. Most cadres are highly committed to supporting the party during elections. They often have had to spend their own money to support the party in its campaigns. Tarbiyah training has been able to create solid cadres with a strong loyalty to the party and a high standard of personal morality to strengthen PKS.

Nonetheless, this condition changed when PKS grew into a party large enough to give political incentives to its cadres by awarding positions in parliament and the government bureaucracy. However, cadres from lower socio-economic levels with a lack of education and of a lower social status who have received no opportunities for political mobilisation have become critical of the party. For this reason, when PKS cadres in parliament or in government are not able to live up to their ideals and tend to be co-opted by power, cadre solidity faces a great challenge. The support given by PKS for the increase in oil prices in 2004 drew tremendous criticism from its constituents.

In addition, some cadres of Jemaah Tarbiyah, even though only small in number, who have been critical of the party and have disagreed with the concept of integration between the movement and the party (*al-hizb huwa and al-jama'ah hiya al-hizb*) have begun to consolidate.[1] They criticise the performance of PKS and any lack of commitment to the movement's ideals through a website called "PKS Watch." A loss of trust among cadres towards their representatives in the legislative and executive bodies will also influence the affectiveness of the party to direct its members to follow party decisions. If this happens, PKS will not only lose support from its own cadres but also on the popular front.

Since most Islamist groups in Indonesia have not been tested in holding power, the case of PKS has provided a good example of how a political party based upon an Islamic religious movement has faced the dilemma of keeping faith with its ideology after forming a coalition with nationalist and secular parties. PKS has placed its three cadres as ministers: Minister of Youth and Sport, Minister of People's Housing and Minister of Agriculture. Many Indonesians have been dissatisfied with the performance of the government. A current survey conducted by the Institute of Indonesian Survey, Lembaga Survei Indonesia (LSI) in December 2005, asking Indonesians which political party they would choose if a general election was held today, indicated the drastic decline of PKS from 10.1% in January 2005 to 2.7% in December 2005.[2] The decline of PKS in this survey was the result of the inability of the party to voice the people's interests and to bring about prosperity.[3]

Observing the performance of PKS in the 2004 general elections as a interesting phenomenon, it is also important to consider its success by analysing the ability of its activists in relating Islam to the basic and popular needs of the people. The party can come closer to the grassroots, especially those who live in marginalised urban areas, by promising a better life, prosperity and justice. PKS has consistently shown care for the less fortunate and for those who have suffered from natural disasters by providing free medications, shelter, food and social services. PKS has also campaigned for clean government and against corruption. PKS activists and particularly its reprensentatives in DPR RI and at the district level have the image of clean figures.

Thus the social, economic and political realities of Indonesia have influenced PKS's political orientation, keeping its ideology and promising betterment for the Indonesia people. The General Secretary of PKS (2004-2009) Anis Matta stated as much in order to win political legitimacy and to attract support for the party.[4] However, according to Matta, the ability to manage the state is also important and PKS must be able to develop the economy and manage resources, not merely to spend money for social care.[5] General elections are the only means to test the party's ability in power and gives the opportunity for people to vote it out of power.[6] The struggle for Islam through the democratic system has entailed the sacrifice of some Islamic aspirations because those aspirations need to be negotiated by the party in order to survive in the longer term. Within PKS itself, this strategy comes under jurisprudential precepts and the concept of *maslahah al-dakwah*.

ENDNOTES

[1] The more critical attitudes by anonymous cadres who have created *PKS Watch* to criticise the party (http://pkswatch.blogspot.com). See an interesting article regarding their disagreement with the concept of integration between the movement and the party entitled "Partai Jamaah, Jamaah Partai," http://pkswatch.blogspot.com/, 26 October 2005.

[2] See Andrew Steele, "The Decline of Political Islam in Indonesia," *Asia Times Online*, 28 March 2006.

[3] See Graham E. Fuller, "Islamism(s) in the Next Century," in *The Islamism Debate* (Tel Aviv: Moshe Dayan Center for Middle Eastern and African Studies, 1997), 143.

[4] See Anis Matta, *Menikmati Demokrasi: Strategi Dakwah dan Meraih Kemenangan* (Jakarta: Pustaka Saksi, 2002), 269-173.

[5] Ibid.

[6] Fuller, "Islamism(s) in the Next Century,"155.

Appendix 1: Piagam Deklarasi Partai Keadilan

Bahwa sesungguhnya Bangsa Indonesia telah melintasi gelombang pasang naik dan pasang surut, menghela beban berat penjajahan, penindasan dan pengkhianatan.

Tahap demi tahap perjuangan panjang mengantarkan bangsa ini ke gerbang kemerdekaan dan kedaulatan, yang pada mulanya dicitakan untuk mewujudkan Negara yang melindungi segenap bangsa Indonesia dan seluruh tumpah darah Indonesia untuk memajukan kesejahteraan umum, mencerdaskan kehidupan bangsa, dan ikut melaksanakan ketertiban dunia yang berdasarkan kemerdekaan, perdamaian abadi dan keadilan sosial, sesuai dengan semangat Proklamasi 1945. Namun selama lima dekade berikutnya, garis sejarah itu mengalami berbagai penyimpangan, sehingga cita-cita besar bangsa menjadi kabur.

Kejatuhan rejim Orde Lama, diikuti dengan keruntuhan rejim Orde Baru, merupakan tragedi yang seharusnya menyadarkan kembali bangsa ini akan cita-cita luhurnya semula. Seluruh kekuatan bangsa wajib bergandeng tangan dengan landasan persaudaraan, keadilan, dan berpacu dalam kebaikan, seraya meninggalkan permusuhan, kedhaliman, dan pertikaian antar kelompok.

Gerakan mahasiswa, yang disokong penuh rakyat Indonesia, telah mengobarkan "Reformasi Mei 1998" sebagai peretas jalan bagi terbentuknya "Orde Reformasi";orde yang diikat dengan nilai-nilai fitri kemanusiaan berupa keimanan, moralitas, kemerdekaan, persamaan, kedamaian, dan keadilan. Berkat rahmat Allah SWT, kemudian dipicu semangat reformasi, tercetuslah momentum untuk membangun kembali negeri yang besar ini, dengan cara pandang yang benar dan meninggalkan segala bentuk kesalahan generasi terdahulu. Mari bersatu dalam kebenaran untuk mengisi lembaran sejarah baru agar bangsa Indonesia senantiasa berdiri tegak dan berperan serta dalam mewujudkan masyarakat international yang berperadaban.

Kejayaan atau kehancuran suatu negeri merupakan buah dari kepatuhan atau keingkaran penduduknya terhadap nilai-nilai religius dan universal, terutama nilai keadilan. Pada titik ini fitrah insani bertemu dengan tuntutan reformasi dan peluang demokratisasi. Maka perjuangan menegakkan keadilan pun menjadi keharusan, sebagai manifestasi misi utama Islam untuk menjadi rahmat bagi seluruh alam.

Demi mewujudkan cita-cita sejati Proklamasi, mengisi kemerdekaan, mempertahankan kedaulatan dan pe rsatuan, serta berbekal semangat reformasi dan dukungan umat dari berbagai daerah, kami selaku anak bangsa dengan ini mendeklarasikan berdirinya PARTAI KEADIL AN.

Semoga Allah Yang Maha Kuasa membimbing dan memberi kekuatan untuk menegakkan keadilan, mewujudkan kesejahteraan dan kemakmuran bagi seluruh bangsa Indonesia.

"... Berbuat adillah, karena adil itu lebih dekat kepada taqwa ..." (Al-Qur-an, Surah Al-Maidah: 8)

Dinyatakan di Jakarta

Ahad, 15 Rabi'ul Tsani 1419 / 9 Agustus 1998

Dewan Pendiri

PARTAI KEADILAN

Dr. M. Hidayat Nurwahid, M.A.
Ketua

Luthfi Hasan Ishaaq, M.A.
Sekretaris

Anggota

Dr. Salim Segaf Aljufri, M.A.
Dr. Mulyanto, M.Eng.
Dr. Ir. H. Nur Mahmudi Isma'il, M.Sc.
Drs. Abu Ridho, A.S.
Mutammimul Ula, S.H.
K.H. Abdul Hasib, Lc.
Fahri Hamzah, S.E.
Dr. Daud Rasyid Sitorus, M.A.
Dr. Agus Nurhadi
Igo Ilham, Ak.
Chin Kun Min (al-Hafizh)
Drs. Arifinto
Nursanita Nasution, S.E., M.E.
H. Rahmat Abdullah
Dr. Ahmad Satori Ismail
Ir. Untung Wahono
Ir. Suswono
Mashadi
Dra. Sri Utami
Nurmansyah Lubis, S.E., Ak., M.M.
dr. Naharus Surur
Drs. Muhroni
Drs. H. Suharna S., M.S.
H.M. Ihsan Arlansyah Tanjung

H. Aus Hidayat
Ir. H. Tifatul Sembiring
Drs. Al Muzammil Yusuf
Drs. Mukhlis Abdi
Maddu Mallu, S.E., M.B.A.
H.M. Nasir Zein, M.A.
K.H. Acep Abdus Syakur
Dr. Ahzami Samiun Jazuli, M.A.
K.H. Yusuf Supendi, Lc.
Hj. Yoyoh Yusroh
M. Anis Matta, Lc.
Ahmad Zainuddin, Lc.
Dra. Zirlirosa Jamil
Syamsul Balda, S.E., M.M.
Habib Aboe Bakar Al-Habsyi
Sunmanjaya Rukmandis, S.H.
Ahmad Heriawan, Lc.
Drs. Erlangga Masdiana, M.Si.
Didik Akhmadi, Ak. Mcom.
K.H. Abdur Roqib, Lc.
H. Abdullah Said Baharmus, Lc.
Ahmad Hatta, M.A., Ph.D.
Makmur Hasanuddin, M.A.
Dra. Siti Zainab

Appendix 2: Deklarasi Partai Keadilan Sejahtera

Bismilllahirrahmaanirrahiim

Bangsa Indonesia telah menjalani sebuah sejarah panjang yang sangat menentukan dalam waktu lebih dari lima dekade ini dengan sebuah perjuangan yang berat dan kritis. Setelah lepas dari penjajahan Belanda dan Jepang selama tiga setengah abad, Indonesia memproklamirkan kemerdekaannya pada tanggal 17 Agustus 1945.

Kebangkitan ini berjalan hingga tahun 1959 ketika upaya untuk membangun bangsa yang demokratis dan sejahtera mengalami kebuntuan dengan dikeluarkannya Dekrit Presiden 5 Juli 1959 yang menandai awal diktaktorisme di Indonesia. Orde Baru muncul pada tahun 1966 tetapi ternyata hanya merupakan sebuah perpanjangan tangan kekuasaan militer yang benih-benihnya sudah mulai bersemi pada masa Orde Lama.

Pada tanggal 21 Mei 1998 bangsa Indonesia mengukir kembali harapannya untuk hidup dalam suasana yang mampu memberi harapan ke depan dengan digulirkannya Reformasi Nasional yang didorong oleh perjuangan mahasiswa dan rakyat. Reformasi Nasional pada hakekatnya adalah sebuah kelanjutan dari upaya mencapai kemerdekaan, keadilan dan kesejahteraan bagi bangsa Indonesia dari perjuangan panjang yang telah ditempuh selama berabad-abad.

Demokratisasi menjadi tulang punggung perjuangan tersebut yang mewadahi partisipasi masyarakat dalam keseluruhan aspeknya. Bertolak dari kesadaran tersebut, dibentuklah sebuah partai politik yang akan menjadi wahana dakwah untuk mewujudkan cita-cita universal dan menyalurkan aspirasi politik kaum muslimin khususnya beserta seluruh lapisan masyarakat Indonesia umumnya. Partai tersebut bernama Partai Keadilan Sejahtera.

Semoga Allah SWT memberikan hidayah dan inayah-Nya kepada kita, mengikatkan hati diantara para pengikut agama-Nya dan menolong perjuangan mereka dimana pun mereka berada. Amin.

Jakarta, 20 April 2002

Atas Nama Pendiri Partai Keadilan Sejahtera

(Drs. Almuzzammil Yusuf)

Ketua

(Drs. Haryo Setyoko)

Sekretaris Jenderal

DAFTAR NAMA PENDIRI PARTAI KEADILAN SEJAHTERA

Abdullah
Achyar Eldine, SE
Ahmad Yani, Drs.
Ahmadi Sukarno, Lc., MAg
Ahzami Samiun Jazuli, MA, DR
Ali Akhmadi, MA
Arlin Salim, Ir
Bali Pranowo, Drs
Budi Setiadi, SKH
Bukhori Yusuf, MA
Eddy Zanur, Ir, MSAE
Eman Sukirman, SE
Ferry Noor, SSi
H. Abdul Jabbar Madjid MA
H.M Ridwan
H.M. Nasir Zein, MA
Harjani Hefni, Lc
Haryo Setyoko, Drs
Herawati Noor, Dra
Herlini Amran, MA
Imron Zabidi, Mphil
Kaliman Iman Sasmitha
M. Iskan Qolba Lubis, MA
M. Martri Agoeng
Muttaqin
Mahfudz Abdurrahman
Martarizal, DR
Mohammad Idris Abdus Somad, MA, DR
Muhammad Aniq S, Lc.
Muhammad Budi Setiawan, Drs
Muslim Abdullah, MA
Musoli, MSc, Drs
Musyafa Ahmad Rahim, Lc
Nizamuddin Hasan, Lc
P. Edy Kuncoro, SE. Ak
Ruly Tisnayuliansyah, Ir
Rusdi Muchtar
Sarah Handayani, SKM
Susanti
Suswono, Ir

Syamsu Hilal, Ir
Umar Salim Basalamah, SIP
Usman Effendi, Drs
Wahidah R Bulan, Dra
Wirianingsih, Dra
Mahmudi, MA
Yusuf Dardiri, Ir
Zaenal Arifin
Zufar Bawazier, Lc
Zulkieflimansyah, DR.

Appendix 3: Anggaran Dasar Partai Keadilan Sejahtera

MUQADDIMAH

Bangsa Indonesia telah menjalani sebuah sejarah panjang yang sangat menentukan dalam waktu lebih lima decade ini dengan sebuah perjuangan yang berat dan kritis. Setelah lepas dari penjajahan Belanda dan Jepang selama tiga setengah abad, Indonesia memproklamirkan kemerdekaannya pada tanggal 17 Agustus 1945. Kebangkitan ini berjalan hingga tahun 1959 ketika upaya untuk membangun bangsa yang demokratis dan sejahtera mengalami kebuntuan dengan dikeluarkannya Dekrit Presiden 5 Juli 1959 yang menandai awal diktaktorisme di Indonesia. Orde Baru muncul pada tahun 1966 tetapi ternyata hanya merupakan sebuah perpanjangan tangan kekuasaan militer yang benih-benihnya sudah mulai bersemi pada masa Orde Lama. Pada tanggal 21 Mei 1998 bangsa Indonesia mengukir kembali harapannya untuk hidup dalam suasana yang mampu memberi harapan ke depan dengan digulirkannya Reformasi Nasional yang didorong oleh perjuangan mahasiswa dan rakyat.

Reformasi Nasional pada hakekatnya adalah sebuah kelanjutan dari upaya mencapai kemerdekaan, keadilan dan Sejahtera bagi bangsa Indonesia dari perjuangan panjang yang telah ditempuh selama berabad-abad. Demokratisasi menjadi tulang punggung perjuangan tersebut yang mewadahi partisipasi masyarakat dalam keseluruhan aspeknya. Bertolak dari kesadaran tersebut, dibentuk sebuah partai politik yang akan menjadi wahana dakwah untuk mewujudkan cita-cita universal dan menyalurkan aspirasi politik kaum muslimin beserta seluruh lapisan masyarakat Indonesia, dengan Anggaran Dasar sebagai berikut.

BAB 1
NAMA, PENDIRIAN, ASAS, KEDUDUKAN DAN LAMBANG PARTAI

Pasal 1

Nama dan Pendirian

Partai ini bernama Partai Keadilan Sejahtera. Didirikan di Jakarta pada hari Sabtu, tanggal 9 Jumadil Ula 1423 H bertepatan dengan tanggal 20 April 2002 M.

Pasal 2

Asas

Islam.

Pasal 3

Kedudukan

1. Pusat Partai berkedudukan di ibu kota negara Republik Indonesia.
2. Pusat partai dapat dipindahkan dalam kondisi tertentu atas keputusan Majelis Syuro.
3. Partai dapat membuka cabang-cabang di seluruh wilayah hukum negara Republik Indonesia dan perwakilan di luar negeri bagi Warga Negara Indonesia.

Pasal 4

Lambang

Gambar dua bulan sabit dengan untaian padi tegak lurus ditengah berwarna kuning emas dalam perisai segi empat persegi panjang berwarna hitam bergambar Ka'bah. Di bagian atas tertulis **PARTAI KEADILAN** dan bagian dalam kotak Ka'bah tertulis **SEJAHTERA** berwarna kuning emas.

Bab 2

TUJUAN DAN USAHA

Pasal 5

Tujuan

Partai Keadilan Sejahtera adalah Partai Da'wah yang bertujuan mewujudkan masyarakat yang adil dan sejahtera yang diridlai Allah Subhanahu Wata'ala, dalam negara kesatuan Republik Indonesia yang berdasarkan Pancasila.

Pasal 6

Usaha

Untuk mencapai tujuan tersebut diusahakanlah hal-hal sebagai berikut :

1. Membebaskan bangsa Indonesia dari segala bentuk kezaliman.
2. Membina masyarakat Indonesia menjadi masyarakat Islami.
3. Mempersiapkan bangsa Indonesia agar mampu menjawab berbagai problema dan tuntutan masa mendatang.
4. Membangun sistem kehidupan bermasyarakat dan bernegara yang sesuai dengan nilai-nilai Islam.
5. Membangun negara Indonesia baru yang adil, sejahtera dan berwibawa .

Bab 3

KEANGGOTAAN

Pasal 7

Keanggotaan

Setiap warga negara Indonesia dapat menjadi anggota partai.

Bab 4

STRUKTUR ORGANISASI

Pasal 8

Struktur Organisasi

Organisasi tingkat pusat Partai Keadilan Sejahtera adalah sebagai berikut

1. Majelis Syuro
2. Majelis Pertimbangan Partai.
3. Dewan Syari'ah Pusat
4. Dewan Pimpinan Pusat
5. Lembaga Kelengkapan Partai

Pasal 9

Masa Jabatan Pimpinan

Batas maksimal jabatan Ketua Majelis Syuro, Ketua Majelis Pertimbangan Partai, Ketua Dewan Syari'ah Pusat dan Ketua Umum Partai adalah 2 (dua) periode.

Pasal 10

Akhir Masa Jabatan Pimpinan

1. Telah selesai menjalani masa jabatannya sesuai dengan masa kerja yang telah ditetapkan.
2. Apabila tidak dapat lagi melaksanakan kewajiban-kewajibannya sebagai Pimpinan Partai , maka Majelis Syuro hendaknya mempelajari kondisi tersebut dan mengambil keputusan yang sesuai. Jika terlihat bahwa penghentian Pimpinan Partai tersebut akan membawa maslahat bagi Partai, maka hendaknya Majelis Syuro mengadakan pertemuan khusus untuk itu. Dan keputusan penghentian Pimpinan partai tersebut harus mendapatkan persetujuan lebih dari dua pertiga anggota Majelis Syuro.
3. Apabila ada Pimpinan Partai mengajukan pengunduran dirinya, maka Majelis Syuro hendaklah mengundang anggotanya untuk mempelajari latar belakang pengunduran diri tersebut dan mengambil keputusan yang sesuai. Dan apabila yang bersangkutan mendesak mengundurkan diri maka pengunduran diri itu dapat diterima berdasarkan keputusan suara terbanyak secara mutlak anggota Majelis Syuro.

4. Apabila terjadi kevakuman pada jabatan ketua dan wakil ketua Majelis Syuro dalam waktu yang sama, maka Majelis Syuro melakukan pemilihan penggantinya.
5. Apabila Ketua Umum Partai meninggal dunia atau berhalangan tetap, maka Majelis Pertimbangan Partai menunjuk salah seorang Ketua Dewan Pimpinan Pusat untuk mengambil alih seluruh tugas dan wewenang Ketua Umum hingga Majelis Syuro menetapkan Ketua Umum baru.
6. Apabila Ketua Dewan syari'ah Pusat meninggal dunia, maka wakilnya mengambil alih seluruh wewenangnya hingga habis masa jabatannya.
7. Ketentuan lain yang terkait dan atau sejalan dengan pasal ini akan ditetapkan oleh Majelis Syuro Partai

Bab 5
MAJELIS SYURO

Pasal 11
Fungsi Majelis Syuro

Majelis Syuro adalah lembaga tertinggi partai yang berfungsi sebagai Lembaga Ahlul Halli wal-Aqdi Partai Keadilan Sejahtera.

Pasal 12
Anggota Majelis Syuro

1. Anggota Majelis Syuro terdiri dari sekurang-kurangnya tiga puluh lima orang yang dipilih melalui pemilihan raya yang melibatkan seluruh anggota kader inti partai.
2. Pemilihan anggota Majelis Syuro dilakukan melalui pemilihaan raya yang penyelenggaraannya dengan membentuk kepanitiaan oleh Majelis Syuro yang sekurang-kurangnya terdiri dari: -Seorang ketua berasal dari anggota Majelis Syuro. -Seorang wakil ketua berasal dari anggota Dewan Syari'ah Pusat. -Seorang sekretaris berasal dari Dewan Pimpinan Pusat. -Dan beberapa orang anggota.
3. Pengesahan dan pelantikan anggota Majelis Syuro terpilih dilakukan oleh Musyawarah Nasional.

Pasal 13
Tugas Majelis Syuro

1. Majelis Syuro bertugas menyusun Visi dan Missi Partai, ketetapan-ketetapan dan rekomendasi Musyawarah Nasional, dan memilih Pimpinan Pusat Partai serta keputusan-keputusan strategis lainnya.

2. Membentuk Majelis Pertimbangan Partai sebagai Badan Pekerja Majelis Syuro dan Dewan Syari'ah Pusat.

Bab 6
MAJELIS PERTIMBANGAN PARTAI

Pasal 14
Tugas Majelis Pertimbangan Partai

Majelis Pertimbangan Partai adalah lembaga pelaksana harian tugas-tugas Majelis Syuro, dalam hal mengawasi jalannya partai agar sesuai dengan tujuan-tujuan Partai, Ketetapan-Ketetapan yang telah dikeluarkan oleh Majelis Syuro dan Musyawarah Nasional.

Bab 7
DEWAN SYARI'AH

Pasal 15
Struktur dan Anggota Dewan Syari'ah Pusat

1. Jumlah anggota Dewan Syari'ah Pusat sebanyak-banyaknya sepertiga anggota Majelis Syuro.
2. Ketua, Wakil Ketua dan beberapa orang anggota Dewan Syari'ah Pusat dipilih oleh Majelis Syuro dari anggotanya.
3. Dewan Syari'ah diberi wewenang membentuk struktur kepengurusan, mengangkat Mudir Idarah dan melengkapi keanggotaannya.

Pasal 16
Struktur dan Anggota Dewan Syari'ah Wilayah

1. Jumlah anggota Dewan Syari'ah Wilayah sekurang-kurangnya tiga orang.
2. Ketua, Wakil Ketua dan anggota Dewan Syari'ah Wilayah dipilih oleh Musyawarah Wilayah.
3. Struktur Dewan Syari'ah Wilayah sedapatnya mengikuti Dewan Syari'ah Pusat
4. Dewan Syari'ah Wilayah diberi wewenang melengkapi keanggotaannya dan mengangkat Mudir Idarah.

Pasal 17
Tugas Dewan Syari'ah

Dewan Syari'ah adalah lembaga fatwa dan qadha yang bertugas merumuskan landasan syar'i terhadap partai dalam melaksanakan aktifitasnya dan memberikan jawaban syar'i terhadap berbagai permasalahan yang dihadapi partai dan anggotanya serta masyarakat.

Bab 8

DEWAN PIMPINAN PUSAT

Pasal 18

Struktur Dewan Pimpinan Pusat

Struktur Dewan Pimpinan Pusat sekurang-kurangnya beranggotakan sebagai berikut

1. Ketua Umum
2. Sekretaris Jendral.
3. Bendahara Umum.
4. Departemen-departemen yang diperlukan.

Pasal 19

Tugas Dewan Pimpinan Pusat.

Dewan Pimpinan Pusat adalah lembaga tanfiziyah partai pada tingkat pusat yang bertugas melaksanakan kegiatan-kegiatan partai dengan masa kerja selama lima (5) tahun qomariyah.

Bab 9

STRUKTUR ORGANISASI WILAYAH, DAERAH,

CABANG DAN RANTING

Pasal 20

Organisasi Tingkat Wilayah

1. Organisasi Wilayah didirikan pada tingkat propinsi yang berkedudukan di ibukota propinsi.
2. Struktur Organisasi tingkat wilayah terdiri dari Dewan Syari'ah Wilayah - Dewan Pimpinan Wilayah.
3. Besarnya lembaga atau badan-badan tersebut disesuaikan dengan kebutuhan wilayah.

Pasal 21

Organisasi Tingkat Daerah, Cabang Dan Ranting

1. Dalam lingkup organisasi tingkat wilayah didirikan organisasi Daerah pada tingkat kabupaten / kotamadya yang berkedudukan di ibukota kabupaten / kotamadya.
2. Dalam lingkup organisasi tingkat Daerah didirikan organaisasi cabang dan dalam lingkup organisasi tingkat cabang pada tingkat kecamatan didirikan organisasi Ranting.
3. Struktur organisasi yang disebutkan ayat 1 dan 2 pasal ini disusun sesuai dengan Anggaran Rumah Tangga.

Bab 10
FORUM PENGAMBILAN KEBIJAKAN

Pasal 22

Musyawarah

1. Musyawarah adalah forum pengambilan kebijakan yang diselenggarakan oleh semua elemen struktural Partai Keadilan Sejahtera.
2. Jenis dan jenjang musyawarah diatur dengan ketentuan tersendiri yang ditetapkan oleh Majelis Syuro.

Pasal 23

Musyawarah Nasional

Musyawarah Nasional adalah pemegang kekuasaan tertinggi Partai Keadilan Sejahtera yang diselenggarakan oleh Majelis Syuro.

Bab 11
KEUANGAN

Pasal 24

Sumber Keuangan

Keuangan partai terdiri dari sumber-sumber berikut :

1. Iuran rutin anggota.
2. Sumbangan dan hibah dari para anggota dan simpatisan
3. Sumber-sumber lain yang halal dan tidak mengikat.

Bab 12
HUBUNGAN KEORGANISASIAN

Pasal 25

Hubungan dan Koalisi Partai

1. Ummat Islam Indonesia merupakan bagian dari ummat Islam sedunia. Partai Keadilan Sejahtera sebagai Partai Da'wah menyatakan dirinya merupakan bagian tak terpisahkan dari gerakan da'wah di berbagai kawasan dunia.
2. Untuk merealisasikan kemaslahatan ummat dan bangsa, Partai melakukan hubungan baik dan kerjasama dengan berbagai pihak di dalam maupun di luar negeri.
3. Majelis Syuro adalah lembaga yang berwenang memutuskan koalisi partai dengan partai atau organisasi lain.

Pasal 26

Hubungan Antar Struktur

Hubungan antar lembaga-lembaga partai tingkat pusat dan lembaga-lembaga partai tingkat pusat dengan lembaga-lembaga di bawahnya diatur dalam Anggaran Rumah Tangga.

Bab 13

KETENTUAN PENUTUP

Pasal 27

Perubahan Anggaran Dasar

Perubahan Anggaran Dasar dilakukan sebagai berikut:

1. Permintaan perubahan berikut alasan-alasannya diajukan melalui mekanisme struktural kepada Majelis Syuro untuk dinilai kelayakannya.
2. Pengubahan dianggap sah bila disetujui oleh dua pertiga anggota Majelis Syuro.

Pasal 28

Ketentuan Anggaran Rumah Tangga

1. Hal-hal yang belum ditetapkan dalam Anggaran Dasar ini diatur dalam Anggaran Rumah Tangga.
2. Anggaran Rumah Tangga adalah tafsir dan penjabaran Anggaran Dasar yang direkomendasikan oleh Majelis Syuro.

Pasal 29
Pengesahan Anggaran Dasar

1. Anggaran Dasar ini disahkan oleh Majelis Syuro Partai Keadilan Sejahtera berdasarkan Rapat Pendirian Partai tanggal 24 Maret 2002
2. Anggaran Dasar ini berlaku sementara sejak tanggal ditetapkan sampai diselenggarakannya Musyawarah Nasional Pertama.

Appendix 4: Anggaran Rumah Tangga Partai Keadilan Sejahtera

BAB 1

TAFSIR LAMBANG PARTAI

Pasal 1

Arti Lambang Partai

Bentuk lambang partai memiliki arti sebagai berikut :

1. Kotak persegi empat berarti kesetaraan, keteraturan dan keserasian.
2. Kotak hitam berarti pusat peradaban dunia Islam yakni Ka'bah
3. Bulan sabit berarti lambang kemenangan Islam, dimensi waktu, keindahan, kebahagiaan, pencerahan dan kesinambungan sejarah.
4. Untaian padi tegak lurus berarti keadilan, ukhuwah, istiqomah, berani dan ketegasan yang mewujudkan keejahteraan.

Warna lambang partai memiliki arti sebagai berikut :

1. Putih berarti bersih dan kesucian.
2. Hitam berarti aspiratif dan kepastian.
3. Kuning emas berarti kecermelangan, kegembiraan dan kejayaan.

Pasal 2

Makna Lambang Partai

Makna lambang partai secara keseluruhan adalah menegakkan nilai-nilai keadilan berlandaskan pada kebenaran, persaudaraan dan persatuan menuju kesejahteraan dan kejayaan ummat dan bangsa.

Bab 2

SASARAN DAN SARANA.

Pasal 3

Sasaran

Untuk mencapai tujuan partai dirumuskan sasaran berikut :

1. Terwujudnya pemerintahan yang jujur, bersih, berwibawa, dan bertanggung jawab berdasarkan nilai-nilai kebenaran dan keadilan.
2. Tegaknya 'Masyarakat Islami' yang memiliki kemandirian berdasarkan sebuah konstitusi yang menjamin hak-hak rakyat dan bangsa Indonesia.

Sasaran partai yang dimaksud ayat (1) pasal ini diupayakan dalam bingkai Kebijakan Dasar Periodik dan Agenda Nasional Partai Keadilan Sejahtera, yang merupakan bagian tak terpisahkan dari Anggaran Dasar dan Anggaran Rumah Tangga Ini.

Pasal 4
Sarana dan Prasarana

Dalam mewujudkan tujuan dan sasarannya partai menggunakan cara, sarana dan prasarana yang tidak bertentangan dengan norma-norma hukum dan kemaslahatan umum, antara lain:

1. Seluruh sarana dan manajemen politik, ekonomi, sosial, budaya dan IPTEK yang dapat mengarahkan dan mengatur kehidupan masyarakat serta dapat menyelesaikan permasalahan-pernasalahannya.
2. Ikut serta dalam lembaga-lembaga pemerintahan, badan-badan penentu kebijakan, hukum dan perundang-undangan, lembaga swadaya masyarakat, dan lain sebagainya.
3. Menggalakkan dialog konstruktif disertai argumentasi yang kuat dengan semua kekuatan politik dan sosial.
4. Aktif berpartisipasi dalam berbagai lembaga dan organisasi serta yayasan yang sesuai dengan tujuan partai.

Bab 3
KEANGGOTAAN

Pasal 5
Sistem dan Prosedur Keanggotaan

Anggota Partai Keadilan Sejahtera terdiri dari :

1. Anggota Kader Pendukung, yaitu mereka yang terlibat aktif mendukung setiap kegiatan kepartaian.
2. Anggota Kader Inti, yaitu anggota yang telah mengikuti berbagai kegiatan pelatihan kepartaian dan dinyatakan lulus oleh panitia penseleksian.
3. Anggota Kehormatan yaitu mereka yang berjasa dalam perjuangan partai dan dikukuhkan oleh Dewan Pimpinan Pusat.

Sistem dan prosedur keanggotaan serta hal-hal yang terkait dengan keanggotaan partai diatur dalam ketentuan tersendiri yang ditetapkan oleh Majelis Syuro.

Bab 4
MAJELIS SYURO

Pasal 6

Anggota Majelis Syuro

1. Syarat keanggotaan Majelis Syuro sebagai berikut:
   a. Umur tidak kurang dari 30 tahun qomariyah
   b. Telah menjadi anggota kader inti dengan status anggota ahli Partai
   c. Melaksanakan asas dan tujuan partai
   d. Komitmen dengan kewajiban-kewajiban anggota
   e. Berkelakuan baik dan tidak mendapatkan sangsi dalam 3 tahun terakhir.
   f. Berwawasan syar'i.
   g. Bersifat amanah dan berwibawa
2. Jika ada anggota Majelis Syuro berhalangan tetap maka majelis berhak mengangkat dan mensahkan pengantinya.
3. Majelis Syuro berhak menambah keanggotaannya dengan orang-orang yang dibutuhkan oleh Partai, terdiri dari para pakar dan tokoh dengan catatan tambahan itu tidak lebih dari 15 % anggotanya.
4. Jika anggota Majelis Syuro telah dipilih, maka masing-masing mengucapkan janji setianya di hadapan Musyawarah Nasional, dengan bunyi sebagai berikut:

'Saya berjanji kepada Allah yang Maha Agung untuk berpegang teguh pada syari'at Islam dan untuk berjihad di jalan-Nya, menunaikan syarat-syarat keanggotaan Majelis Syuro Partai Keadilan Sejahtera, melak sanakan tugas-tugas darinya dan untuk mendengar serta taat kepada pemimpinnya dalam keadaan lapang maupun sempit -selain untuk maksiat-, sekuat tenaga melaksanakannya. Dan saya bersumpah kepada Pengurus Majelis Syura untuk itu, dan Allah menjadi saksi atas apa yang saya ucapkan.

Pasal 7

Tugas Majelis Syuro

1. Memilih dan menetapkan Ketua majelis, Wakilnya dan SekretarisMajelis dan menetapkannya sebangai ketua, wakil dan sekretaris Majelis Pertimbangan Partai.
2. Memilih dan menetapkan anggota Majelis Pertimbangan Partai.
3. Memilih, dan menetapkan Ketua, Wakil dan Anggota Dewan Syari'ah Pusat
4. Memilih, dan menetapkan Ketua Umum, para Ketua, Sekretaris Jendral dan Bendahara Umum serta beberapa orang Anggota Dewan Pimpinan Pusat.
5. Menyusun tujuan-tujuan Partai, keputusan-keputusan dan rekomendasi Musyawarah Nasional.
6. Menetapkan klausul-klausul perubahan Anggaran Dasar/Anggaran Rumah Tangga (AD/ ART) dan kebijakan politik.

7. Menetapkan anggaran tahunan dan evaluasi akhir dari laporan keuangan.
8. Menetapkan rencana kerja periodik partai, dan mengawasi serta mengevaluasi pelaksanaannya.
9. Mengambil sikap tegas dan bijak dalam hal pencemaran nama baik, kritik, pengaduan, dan tuduhan-tuduhan yang berkaitan dengan partai.

Bab 5
MAJELIS PERTIMBANGAN PARTAI

Pasal 8

Anggota Majelis Pertimbangan Partai

Majelis Pertimbangan Partai terdiri dari sebanyak-banyaknya sepertiga anggota Majelis Syuro yang dipilih oleh Majelis Syuro dari anggotanya.

Pasal 9

Majelis Pertimbangan Partai

1. Menjabarkan ketetapan-ketetapan Musyawarah Nasional dan Majelis Syuro
2. Mengarahkan dan mengawasi pelaksanaan ketetapan-ketetapan Musyawarah Nasional dan Majelis Syuro
3. Menentukan sikap Partai terhadap permasalahan-permasalahan umum dan perubahan-perubahan politik secara regional, dunia Islam atau internasional bersama Dewan Pimpinan Pusat.
4. Mempersiapkan penyelenggaraan Musyawarah Nasional dan Sidang-sidang Majelis Syuro.
5. Merekomendasikan kebijakan program pemilihan umum dan melegalisir calon-calon partai untuk Dewan Perwakilan Rakyat/ Majelis Permusyawaratan Rakyat.
6. Menunjuk perwakilan (wakil) Partai pada lembaga-lembaga, organisasi dan kongres-kongres di dalam dan luar negeri bersama Dewan Pimpinan Pusat.
7. Meratifikasi langkah-langkah yang terarah untuk melaksanakan program kerja politik (strategis).
8. Meratifikasi anggaran proyek yang diajukan Dewan Pimpinan Pusat sebelum diajukan ke Majelis Syuro.
9. Meratifikasi pengajuan struktur dan personil Bidang Dewan Pimpinan Pusat.
10. Mengambil tindakan tegas dalam hal fitnah, kritik, aduan, dan tuduhan yang berkaitan dengan partai dan anggotanya.
11. Mejelis berhak membentuk komisi ad-hoc yang terdiri dari unsur anggota Majelis Syuro dan pakar-pakar sesuai dengan bidangnya.

Bab 6

DEWAN SYARI'AH

Pasal 10

Syarat Anggota Dewan Syari'ah

1. Umur Ketua dan wakil ketua Dewan Syari'ah Pusat tidak kurang dari 35 tahun qomariyah.
2. Umur Ketua dan Wakil ketua Dewan Syari'ah Wilayah tidak kurang dari 30 tahun qomariyah.
3. Telah menjadi kader inti partai dengan status anggota ahli Partai.
4. Berpegang dan komitmen kepada nilai-nilai moral dan kebenaran universal, adil, bertaqwa, sabar, jujur dan bijaksana.
5. Memiliki pengetahuan hukum-hukum syariat yang memadai, bersifat amanah dan berwibawa.
6. Memiliki pengetahuan di Bidang peradilan dan menguasai mekanisme pengambilan keputusan.

Pasal 11

Fungsi Dewan Syari'ah

1. Sebagai Lembaga Fatwa.
2. Sebagai Lembaga Qadha yang keputusan-keputusannya mengikat.
3. Pelaksana tugas-tugas khusus yang ditetapkan oleh Majelis Syuro.
4. Lembaga Peradilan Banding.

Pasal 12

Tugas dan Wewenang Dewan Syari'ah

1. Memberikan landasan syar'i terhadap kebijakan-kebijakan dan persoalan-persoalan yang dihadapi partai.
2. Melakukan pembinaan terhadap Dewan Syari'ah Wilayah.
3. Melakukan kajian terhadap perkara-perkara yang tidak terselesaikan di Dewan Syari'ah Wilayah.
4. Melakukan investigasi terhadap isu, pengaduan, tuduhan, evaluasi dan kesewenangan yang berkaitan dengan Pimpinan Partai dan mengungkapkan hasilnya kepada Majelis Syuro. Khusus yang berkenaan dengan Ketua Umum Partai atau Ketua Majelis Syuro atau Ketua Majelis Pertimbangan Partai atau Ketua Dewan Syari'ah Pusat untuk kasus yang menyangkut dirinya dilakukan oleh komisi khusus yang dibentuk oleh Majelis Syuro.
5. Dewan Pimpinan Pusat, atau Dewan Syari'ah Wilayah kepadanya.

6. Menyusun program dan anggaran tahunan untuk Dewan Syari'ah Pusat kemudian mengajukannya kepada Majelis Syuro.
7. Mengajukan laporan kerja setiap dua bulan kepada Majelis Syuro.

Pasal 13

Klasifikasi Pelanggaran dan Hukuman

1. Setiap perbuatan anggota yang menodai citra partai atau bertentangan dengan prinsip-prinsip kebenaran dan Anggaran Dasar atau Anggaran Rumah Tangga partai adalah pelanggaran yang harus dikenakan sangsi hukum.
2. Klasifikasi pelanggaran berikut hukuman dan cara pelaksanaannya, di atur oleh ketentuan Dewan Syari'ah yang ditetapkan oleh Majelis Syuro.

Bab 7

TUGAS DEWAN PIMPINAN PUSAT

Pasal 14 :

Tugas Konsepsional

1. Menyusun program dan anggaran tahunan untuk Dewan Pimpinan Pusat dan lembaga-lembaga struktural di bawahnya kemudian mengajukannya kepada Majelis Pertimbangan Partai.
2. Mengajukan rancangan perubahan Anggaran Dasar/Anggaran Rumah Tangga kepada Majelis Pertimbangan Partai.
3. Menetapkan Produk-produk konsepsional untuk Bidang-bidang tugas dan lembaga-lembaga struktural di bawahnya.

Pasal 15

Tugas Stuktural

1. Menerima waqaf, hibah dan dana sukarela yang legal.
2. Menyerahkan laporan keuangan dan evaluasi akhir kepada Majelis Pertimbangan Partai.
3. Mengusulkan daftar nama calon sementara anggota legislatif kepada Majelis Pertimbangan Partai.
4. Mengajukan laporan kerja setiap dua bulan kepada Majelis Syuro.

Pasal 16

Tugas Manajerial

1. Menunjuk ketua-ketua Bidang dengan persetujuan Majelis Pertimbangan Partai.

2. Memimpin, mengesahkan dan mengawasi lembaga-lembaga struktural di bawahnya.
3. Membentuk dan mengkoordinasikan lembaga-lembaga pendukung partai.
4. Mensahkan struktur kepengurusan Dewan Pimpinan Wilayah
5. Mengawasi dan mengevaluasi pelaksanaan program kerja tahunan
6. Dewan Pimpinan Wilayah dan lembaga terkait lainnya.

Pasal 17
Tugas Operasional

1. Melaksanakan kebijakan-kebijakan yang ditetapkan oleh Musyawarah Nasional dan Majelis Syuro.
2. Menerbitkan pernyataan-pernyatan resmi.
3. Mempersiapkan kader partai dalam berbagai Bidang.
4. Melaksanakan koordinasi anggota legislatif, eksekutif dan yudikatif yang berasal dari anggota kader partai.

Bab 8
DEWAN PIMPINAN WILAYAH

Pasal 18
Struktur Dewan Pimpinan Wilayah

Dewan Pimpinan Wilayah adalah lembaga eksekutif tingkat propinsi yang berkedudukan di ibukota propinsi dengan struktur sebagai berikut :

1. Ketua Umum dan beberapa ketua.
2. Sekretaris dan wakil sekretaris
3. Bendahara dan wakil bendahara
4. Deputi-deputi.

Pasal 19
Tugas Dewan Pimpinan Wilayah

1. Melaksanakan kebijakan-kebijakan yang ditetapkan oleh Musyawarah Wilayah dan Dewan Pimpinan Pusat.
2. Menyusun program dan anggaran tahunan untuk Dewan Pimpinan Wilayah dan lembaga-lembaga strutural di bawahnya kemudian mengajukan kepada Dewan Pimpinan Pusat.
3. Memimpin, mengesahkan dan mengawasi lembaga-lembaga struktural di bawahnya.
4. Menyiapkan laporan keuangan dan evaluasi akhir dan mengajukannya kepada Musyawarah Wilayah dan Dewan Pimpinan Pusat.

5. Menyusun sidang-sidang Musyawarah Wilayah sesuai dengan ketentuan yang terkait dengan hal tersebut.
6. Mengajukan laporan kerja secara terperinci setiap tiga bulan kepada Dewan Pimpinan Pusat.

Pasal 20
Syarat-syarat Ketua Umum dan Ketua Dewan Pimpinan Wilayah

1. Telah menjadi kader inti partai dengan status anggota ahli.
2. Berpegang teguh kepada nilai-nilai moral dan kebenaran, adil, bertaqwa dan kuat dalam (membela) kebenaran, serius dalam kemaslahatan dan persatuan bangsa, jauh dari fanatisme kepentingan pribadi dan golongan.
3. Memiliki wawasan politik, hukum dan syari'at yang memungkinkannya melaksanakan tugas.
4. Umur tidak kurang dari 25 tahun qomariyah.

Bab 9
DEWAN PIMPINAN DAERAH

Pasal 21
Struktur Dewan Pimpinan Daerah

Dewan Pimpinan Daerah didirikan pada tingkat kabupaten/kotamadya yang berkedudukan di ibukota kabupaten/kotamadya dengan struktur sebagai berikut

1. Ketua Umum dan beberapa ketua.
2. Sekretaris dan wakil sekretaris
3. Bendahara dan wakil bendahara
4. Bagian-Bagian.

Pasal 22
Tugas Dewan Pimpinan Daerah

1. Melaksanakan kebijakan-kebijakan yang ditetapkan oleh Musyawarah Daerah dan Dewan Pimpinan Wilayah.
2. Menyusun program dan anggaran tahunan untuk Dewan Pimpinan Daerah dan lembaga-lembaga struktural di bawahnya kemudian mengajukan kepada Dewan Pimpinan Wilayah.
3. Memimpin, mengesahkan dan mengawasi lembaga-lembaga struktural di bawahnya.
4. Menyusun laporan keuangan dan evaluasi akhir dan mengajukannya kepada Musyawarah Daerah.

5. Menyusun sidang-sidang Musyawarah Daerah sesuai dengan ketentuan yang terkait dengan hal tersebut.
6. Mengajukan laporan kerja secara terperinci setiap tiga bulan kepada Dewan Pimpinan Wilayah.

Pasal 23
Syarat-syarat Ketua Umum dan Ketua Dewan Pimpinan Daerah

1. Telah menjadi kader inti partai yang sekurang-kurangnya dengan status anggota dewasa.
2. Berpegang teguh kepada nilai-nilai moral dan kebenaran, adil, bertaqwa dan kuat dalam (membela) kebenaran, serius dalam kemaslahatan dan persatuan bangsa, jauh dari fanatisme kepentingan pribadi dan golongan.
3. Memiliki wawasan politik, hukum dan syari'at yang memungkinkannya melaksanakan tugas.
4. Umur tidak kurang dari 25 tahun qomariyah.

Bab 10
DEWAN PIMPINAN CABANG

Pasal 24
Struktur Dewan Pimpinan Cabang

Dewan Pimpinan Cabang didirikan pada tingkat kecamatan yang berkedudukan di ibukota kecamatan dengan struktur sebagai berikut

1. Ketua dan Wakil ketua.
2. Sekretaris dan wakil sekretaris
3. Bendahara dan wakil bendahara
4. Seksi-Seksi.

Pasal 25
Tugas Dewan Pimpinan Cabang

1. Melaksanakan kebijakan-kebijakan yang ditetapkan oleh Musyawarah Cabang dan Dewan Pimpinan Daerah.
2. Menyusun program dan anggaran tahunan untuk Dewan Pimpinan Cabang dan lembaga-lembaga struktural di bawahnya kemudian mengajukan kepada Dewan Pimpinan Daerah.
3. Memimpin, mengesahkan dan mengawasi lembaga-lembaga struktural di bawahnya.

4. Menyusun laporan keuangan dan evaluasi akhir dan mengajukannya kepada Musyawarah Cabang.
5. Menyusun sidang-sidang Musyawarah Cabang sesuai dengan ketentuan yang terkait dengan hal tersebut.
6. Mengajukan laporan kerja secara terperinci setiap tiga bulan kepada Dewan Pimpinan Daerah.

Pasal 26

Syarat Ketua dan Wakil Ketua Dewan Pimpinan Cabang

1. Telah menjadi kader inti partai yang sekurang-kurangnya dengan status anggota madya.
2. Berpegang teguh kepada nilai-nilai moral dan kebenaran, adil, bertaqwa dan kuat dalam (membela) kebenaran, serius dalam kemaslahatan dan persatuan bangsa, jauh dari fanatisme kepentingan pribadi dan golongan.
3. Memiliki wawasan politik, hukum dan syariat yang memungkinkannya melaksanakan tugas.
4. Umur tidak kurang dari 20 tahun qomariyah.

Bab 11

DEWAN PIMPINAN RANTING

Pasal 27

Struktur Dewan Pimpinan Ranting

Dewan Pimpinan Ranting didirikan pada tingkat kelurahan/desa dengan struktur kepengurusan sebagai berikut :

1. Ketua dan Wakil ketua.
2. Sekretaris dana wakil sekretaris
3. Bendahara dan wakil bendahara
4. Unit-Unit.

Pasal 28

Tugas Dewan Pimpinan Ranting

1. Melaksanakan kebijakan-kebijakan yang ditetapkan oleh Musyawarah Ranting dan Dewan Pimpinan Cabang.
2. Menyusun program dan anggaran tahunan untuk Dewan Pimpinan Ranting kemudian mengajukan kepada Dewan Pimpinan Cabang.
3. Menyiapkan laporan keuangan dan evaluasi akhir dan mengajukannya kepada Musyawarah Ranting.

4. Menyusun sidang-sidang Musyawarah Ranting sesuai dengan ketentuan yang terkait dengan hal tersebut.
5. Mengajukan laporan kerja secara terperinci setiap tiga bulan kepada Dewan Pimpinan Cabang.

Pasal 29

Syarat-syarat Ketua dan Wakil Ketua Dewan Pimpinan Ranting

1. Telah menjadi kader pendukung partai dengan status anggota muda.
2. Berpegang teguh kepada nilai-nilai moral dan kebenaran, adil, bertaqwa dan kuat dalam (membela) kebenaran, serius dalam kemaslahatan dan persatuan bangsa, jauh dari anatisme kepentingan pribadi dan golongan.
3. Memiliki wawasan politik, hukum dan syariat yang memungkinkannya melaksanakan tugas.
4. Umur tidak kurang dari 18 tahun qomariyah.

Bab 12

KEUANGAN

Pasal 30

Sumber Keuangan

Kekayaan Partai diperoleh dari:

1. Iuran, infaq wajib, dan shadaqah yang berasal dari anggota.
2. Infaq dan shadaqah dari luar anggota.
3. Sumbangan dan bantuan tetap atau tidak tetap dari masyarakat atau orang-orang atau badan-badan yang menaruh minat pada aktifitas Partai yang bersifat sukarela dan tidak mengikat.
4. Waqaf, wasiat dan hibah-hibah lainnya.

Pasal 31

Pemungutan Iuran dan Infaq Anggota

Partai mempunyai hak untuk mengambil iuran, infaq dan shadaqah dari anggotanya.

Pasal 32

Penyaluran/Pengalokasian Dana

1. Partai mempunyai hak untuk menentukan penyaluran dan atau pengalokasian dana Partai.

2. Dana Partai yang tidak segera digunakan untuk kepentingan aktifitas Partai, pengaturannya ditentukan oleh Majelis Syuro.

Pasal 33
Tugas Bendahara Partai

1. Mengatur kekayaan Partai.
2. Mencatat semua harta Partai dan membukukan pengeluaran dan pemasukannya.
3. Mengawasi semua jenis kegiatan keuangan dan akuntansinya serta melaporkannya kepada Dewan Pimpinan Pusat secara periodik.
4. Menyusun anggaran dan penyiapan evaluasi akhir.

Bab 13
HUBUNGAN KEORGANISASIAN

Pasal 34
Asas Hubungan Keorganisasian

1. Hubungan dengan oragisasi yang sejenis baik vertikal maupun horizontal atas asas wala' dan ta'awun.
2. Hubungan dengan organisasi Islam atas asas ukhuwah dan ta'awun.
3. Hubungan dengan organisasi umum atas asas kemanusiaan dan kemaslahatan umum yang dibenarkan Islam.

Pasal 35
Hubungan Antar Struktur

1. Hubungan lembaga tertinggi partai dengan lembaga-lembaga di bawahnya bersifat langsung.
2. Hubungan antar lembaga tinggi partai tingkat pusat bersifat langsung, melalui Pimpinan masing-masing.
3. Hubungan lembaga tinggi partai dengan lembaga organisasi partai tingkat wilayah bersifat langsung sesuai tingkat wewenangnya.
4. Hubungan departemen di Dewan Pimpinan Pusat dengan deputi terkait di Dewan Pimpinan Wilayah bersifat langsung sesuai tingkat wewenang dan kebutuhan, dengan sepengetahuan Dewan Pimpinan Wilayah.
5. Apabila departemen di Dewan Pimpinan Pusat tidak mempunyai turunannya di Dewan Pimpinan Wilayah maka departemen tersebut dapat berkoordinasi dengan Dewan Pimpinan Wilayah.
6. Hubungan antar pimpinan partai tingkat wilayah dengan struktur di bawahnya, mengikuti pola hubungan antar level kepemimpinan partai seperti tersebut dalam ayat 2 sampai dengan 5 pasal ini.

7. Hubungan lembaga-lembaga struktural di tingkat bawah dengan lembaga-lembaga di atasnya mengikuti mekanisme struktural yang telah ditetapkan.

Bab 14
KETENTUAN TAMBAHAN

Pasal 36

Ketentuan Tambahan

1. Untuk memperluas jaringan kerja dan menampung aspirasi pendukung partai, maka:
   - - Dewan Pimpinan Pusat dapat membentuk kepengurusan Majelis Kehormatandan Dewan Pakar,
   - - Dewan Pimpinan Wilayah dapat membentuk kepengurusan Dewan Pakar, - Dewan Pimpinan Daerah dapat membentuk kepengurusan Dewan Penasehat, dan - Dewan Pimpinan Cabang dapat membentuk kepengurusan Dewan Pembina, yang diatur oleh peraturan khusus yang ditetapkan Majelis Syuro.
2. Apabila persyaratan kepengurusan tingkat Dewan Pimpinan Wilayah, Dewan Pimpinan Daerah serta kelengkapan strukturnya tidak terpenuhi, maka dimungkinkan pembentukan struktur dan pengangkatan kader dari jenjang keanggotaan di bawahnya, dengan sepengetahuan Dewan Pimpinan Pusat dan Majelis Pertimbangan Partai.
3. Apabila persyaratan kepengurusan tingkat Dewan Pimpinan Cabang, Dewan Pimpinan Ranting serta kelengkapan strukturnya tidak terpenuhi, maka dimungkinkan pembentukan struktur dan pengangkatan kader dari jenjang keanggotaan di bawahnya, dengan sepengetahuan Dewan Pimpinan Wilayah dan Dewan Pimpinan Pusat.
4. Didirikan perwakilan Partai di kalangan warga negara Indonesia di luar negeri sesuai dengan peraturan khusus yang diterbitkan Dewan Pimpinan Pusat dengan memperhatikan peraturan perundang-undangan yang berlaku di negara bersangkutan.

Bab 15
KETENTUAN PENUTUP

Pasal 37

Penutup

Dalam hal belum dilaksanakannya Musyawarah Nasional I, maka para pendiri partai bertindak dan melaksanakan tugas selaku Majelis Syuro.

Appendix 5: Susunan Pengurus Pusat PKS 205-2010

Ketua Majelis Syuro / Ketua Lembaga Tinggi Partai : K.H. Hilmi Aminuddin. Presiden Partai : Ir. H. Tifatul Sembiring. Sekretaris Jenderal : H.M. Anis Matta Lc. Bendahara Umum : H. Mahfud Abdurrahman. Badan Pemenangan Pemilu : H.M. Razikun, Ak, MS. Ketua : DR. H. Surahman Hidayat.

Lembaga Tinggi Partai

Ketua Majelis Syuro / Ketua Lembaga Tinggi Partai : K.H. Hilmi Aminuddin

Mas'ul Maktab Hay-ah Syar'iyyah/Ketua Dewan Syariah Pusta : Drs. H. Suharna Surapranata, MT.

Mas'ul Maktab Tanfidzi/Ketua Dewan Pimpinan Pusat/Presiden Partai : Ir. H. Tifatul Sembiring

Aminul 'Aam/Sekretariat Jenderal : H.M. Anis Matta

Amin Maali / Bendahara Umum : H. Mahfudz Abdurrahman

Badan-Badan di Lembaga Tinggi Partai :

Badan Pertimbangan Tugas dan Jabatan : ex officio
Ketua : Drs. H. Suharna Supranata, MT.
Anggota : Ketua Bidang Pembinaan Kader, Ketua Bidang Pembinaan Wilayah, Wilda terkait, Ketua Departemen Kaderisasi, Sekjen, Wasekjen Bidang Organisasi.

Badan Penegak Disiplin Organisasi :

Ketua : H. Luthfi Hasan Ishaq, MA

Anggota : Ketua Wilayah Dakwah terkait, Ketua Bidang Pembinaan Wilayah, Ketua Bidang Pembinaan Kader, Ket.Dept. Kaderisasi, Sekjen, MPP.

Dewan Pimpinan Pusat

Presiden Partai : Ir. H. Tifatul Sembiring

Sekretaris Jenderal : H.M. Anis Matta Lc.
Wakil Sekjen I : Ir. H. Suswono, MMA.
Wakil Sekjen II : Ir. Ade Barkah
Wakil Sekjen III : Ir. Aboe Bakar Alhabsy
Wakil Sekjen IV : Dr. Mardani
Wakil Sekjen V : H. Fahri Hamzah, SE.
Wakil Sekjen VI : Nurhasan Zaidi, S.Sos.I
Sekjen VII : Riko Desendra : SSI.

Bendahara Umum : H. Mahfud Abdurrahman

Bendahara I : P. Edy Kuncoro
Bendahara II : Masfuri, Ak.
Bendahara III : Taruna Wiyasa
Bendahara IV : H. Kiemas Taufik
Bendahara V : H. Didin Amaruddin, Ak.

Bidang Pembinaan Kader : Ahmad Zainuddin, Lc
Departemen Kaderisasi : Abdul Muiz, MA
Departemen Dakwah : Thahhah Nuhin, Lc.
Departemen MDI (Ma'hid dan Dirosah Islamiyyah) Samin Barkah, Lc

Bidang Pembinaan Wilayah : H. Aus Hidayat Nur
Departemen Wilayah Dakwah Sumbagut : Drs. Chairul Anwar, Apt.
Departemen Wilayah Dakwah Sumbagsel : Drs. M. Syahfan Badri
Departemen Wilayah DakwahBanten, DKI Jakarta, Jawa Barat : Ir. Syamsu Hilal
Departemen Wilayah Dakwah Jawa Tengah dan Jogjakarta : Zubeir Syafawi, SH.I
Departemen Wilayah Dakwah Jawa Timur dan Bali : Ir. Sigit Sosiantomo
Departemen Wilayah Dakwah Kalimantan : Abdurrohman Amin
Departemen Wilayah Dakwah Maluku, Maluku Utara, Irian : Ahmad Zaki, Ak.
Departemen Wilayah Dakwah Sulawesi : drs. Cahyadi Takariawan, Apt.
Departemen Wilayah Dakwah NTB, NTT : Triono, SH.

Bidang Kewanitaan : Ledia Hanifa, MS
Departemen Kajian Wanita : dra. Sri Utami, MM
Departemen Jaringan Lembaga Wanita : Netti Prasetyani
Departemen Pemberdayaan Wanita : Dwi Septiawati

Bidang Kesejahteraan Rakyat : drs. H. Musholi
Departemen Pendidikan dan SDM : drs. Fahmi Alaydroes, Psi, MM, Med.
Departemen Kesehatan dan Sosial : dr. H. Agoes Koos Hartoro
Departemen Kemahasiswaan : Ahmad Ariyandra, Ak.
Departemen Seni dan Budaya : H. M. Ridwan

Bidang Politik, Hukum dan Keamanan (POLHUKAM) : Ir. H. Untung Wahono, Msi.
Departemen Politik dan Hankam : drs. H. Almuzammil Yusuf
Departemen Hukum dan HAM : Fitra Arsil, SH, MH.
Departemen Pemerintahan dan Otonomi Daerah : Achyar Eldine, SE,MM

Bidang Ekonomi, Keuangan, Industri dan Teknologi (EKUINTEK): DR. Mohammad Sohibul Iman
Departemen Ekonomi, Keuangan, Perbankan : Sigit Pramono, SE,MSE.
Departemen Pembinaan UKM : Ir. H. Ruly Tisna Yuliansyah
Departemen Teknologi, Industri, LH : DR. Edi Syukur
Departemen Buruh Tani, Nelayan : Edy Zannur, MSAE.

Bidang Pembinaan Pemuda : Ir. Ahmad Faradis
Departemen Kepeloporan Pemuda: Slamet Nurdin
Departemen Kepanduan : Cahya Zailani
Departemen Olahraga : Unggul Wibawa

Badan-Badan di Bawah DPP

Badan Pemenangan Pemilu : H.M. Razikun, Ak, MS.
Badan Legislatif : Hermanto, SE, MM.
Badan Penelitian dan Pengembangan, drs. H. Mahfudz Siddiq, MSE.
Badan Hubungan Luar Negeri : H. Lutfi Hasan Ishaq, MA

Dewan Syariah Pusat

Ketua : DR. H. Surahman Hidayat
Amin Maktab (Mudir Idarah) : H. Bukhari Yusuf, MA.
Amin Mali : H. Kastiri

Laznah Qadha :
Amin Lajnah (Panitera) : drs. Muhroni
Anggota : DR.H. Muslih A. Karim, Dr. H. Mu'inuddin, H. Abdul Hasyib Hasan, Lc, H. Amang Syarifuddin, Lc, Msi.

Lajnah Tahqiq :
Koordinator : H. Iskan Qolban Lubis, MA.
Anggota : DR. H. Idris Abdu Shamad , H. Aunurafiq Saleh Tamhid, Lc, Hj. Herlini Amran, MA, Dra. Suzy Mardiani

Lajnah Ifta
Amin Lajnah : Harjani Hefni, MA
Anggota : DR. H. Muslih Abdul Karim, DR. H. Muiduddin, H. Abdul Hasib Hasan, Lc, H. Abdul Aziz Arbi, MA, H. Abdul Ghani Kasuba, Lc

Lajnah Tabrib
Amin Lajnah : H. Abdul Raqib, Lc
Anggota : A. Zairofi, Lc, drs. H. Amad Yani

Staf Sekretariat/Teknologi Informasi : Ridho Kurniawan

Majlis Pertimbangan Pusat

Ketua : Drs. H. Suharna Surya Pranata, MT.
Sekretaris : Drs H. Arifinto

Komisi Organisasi dan Kewilayahan
Ketua : Ir. Memed Sosiawan
Anggota : Najib Subroto, SE, H. Refrizal

Komisi Pembinaan Kader dan Kewanitaan
Ketua : Drs. H. Abdi Sumaithi

Anggota : Mustafa kamal, Hj. Aan Rohana, Mag., H. Yoyoh Yusroh, Sag.

Komisi Kebijakan Publik
Ketua : H. TB. Sunmandjaja
Anggota : Hj.Nursanita Nasution, SE, ME., Didik Akhmadi, Ak.,M.Com, Mutammimul Ula, SH.

Komisi Kajian Strategis
Ketua : H. Ahmad Firman Yusuf
Ketua : H. Suripto, SH, H. Ahmad Relyadi.

Dewan Pakar
Ketua : H. Suripto, SH.

Appendix 6: Susunan Penempatan Anggota F-Pks Di Alat-Alat Kelengkapan Dpr/Mpr Ri Dan Kabinet Periode Tahun 2004/2005

Hidayat Nurwahid : Ketua MPR 2004-2009

Komisi I: Pertahanan, Luar Negeri dan Informasi

- Hilman Rasyad Syihab
- Suripto
- Muhammad Anis Matta
- Untung Wahono

Komisi II: Pemerintahan Dalam Negeri, Otonomi Daerah, Aparatur Negara dan Agraria

- Jazuli Juwaini
- Muhammad Nasir Jamil
- Mahfudz Sidik
- RB Suryama MS

Komisi III: Hukum dan Perundang-undangan, HAM dan Keamanan

- Agus Purnomo
- Almuzammil Yusuf
- Mutamimul Ula
- Abdul Aziz Arbi

Komisi IV: Pertanian, Perkebunan, Kehutanan, Kelautan, Perikanan dan Pangan

- Syamsu Hilal
- Suswono
- Umung Anwar Sanusi
- Tamsil Linrung

Komisi V: Perhubungan, Telekomunikasi, Pekerjaan Umum, Perumahan Rakyat, Pembangunan Pedesaan dan Kawasan Tengah

- Abdul Ghani Kasuba
- Habib Aboe Bakar Al-Habsyi
- Ahmad Chudori
- Abdul Hakim

Komisi VI: Perdagangan, Perindustrian, Investasi, Koperasi UKM dan BUMN

- Refrizal
- Ahmad Najiyulloh
- Zulkieflimansyah
- Fahri Hamzah

Komisi VII: Energi, Sumberdaya Mineral, Riset dan Teknologi, dan Lingkungan Hidup

- Wahyudin Munawir
- Muhammad Idris Luthfi
- Irwan Prayitno
- Ami Taher

Komisi VIII: Agama, Sosial dan Pemberdayaan Perempuan

- DH Al-Yusni
- Djalaluddin Asy-Syatibi
- Ma'mur Hasanuddin
- Yoyoh Yusroh

Komisi IX: Kependudukan, Kesehatan, Tenaga Kerja dan Transmigrasi

- Chairul Anwar
- Mustafa Kamal
- Anshori Siregar
- Andi Salahuddin

Komisi X: Pendidikan, Pemuda, Olahraga, Pariwisata, Kesenian dan Kebudayaan

- Aan Rohanah
- Abdi Sumaithi
- Yusuf Supendi
- Zubeir Syafawi

Komisi XI: Keuangan, Perencanaan Pembangunan Nasional, Perbankan dan Lembaga Keuangan Bukan Bank

- Nursanita Nasution
- Luthfi Hasan Ishaq
- Andi Rahmat
- Rama Pratama

Menteri-Menteri Kabinet

- Anton Apriyantono : Menteri Pertanian

- Adhyaksa Dault : Menteri Negara Pemuda dan Olahraga
- Muhammad Yusuf Ashari : Menteri Negara Perumahan Rakyat

Duta Besar

- Salim Segaf Al-Jufri : Duta Besar RI untuk Kerajaan Saudi Arabia dan Kesultanan Oman

Bibliography

A. Primary Sources

1. Interview with Prosperous Justice Party Leaders.

Abu Ridha, member of DRR RI, Jakarta, 11 October 2003.

Ahmad Mudzafar Jufri, Chairman of Consultative Body in East Java, Surabaya, 17 March 2003.

Ahmad Shidik, chairman of PKS in West Sumatra, Padang, 19 Juni 2003.

Akswendi, chairman of PKS in South Sumatra, Surabaya, 13 March 2003.

Aus Hidayat Nur, head of Wilda PKS, Depok, 13 May 2003

Budi Darmawan, member of the Expert Council of PKS, Canberra, 24 May 2004.

Fahri Hamzah, member DRR RI, Jakarta, 23 December 2005

Hilmi Aminuddin, head of Consultative Body, Jakarta, 23 December 2003.

Irwan Prayitno, member of DRR RI, Jakarta, 14 June 2003.

Ismail Yusanto, Hizbut Tahrir Spokesperson, Canberra, 1 August 2004.

Mahfudz Sidiq, member of DPR RI, Jakarta, 13 August 2003 and 8 October 2003.

Marfendi, member of DRR I West Sumatra, Padang, 23 June 2003.

Muhammad Arif, head of caderarisation section in West Sumatra, Padang, 19 June 2003.

Muslikh Abdul Karim, member of Shariah Council, Depok, 9 September 2003.

Mustafa Kamal, member of DRR RI, Jakarta, 11 June 2003.

Mutammimul Ula, member of DPR RI, Jakarta, 16 June 2003.

Nurmahmudi Ismail, former president of PK, Jakarta, 8 May 2003.

Nursanita Nasution, member of DPR RI, Canberra, 25 October 2005.

Rofi' Munawar, member of DPR I East Java, Surabaya, 7 March 2003.

Rafqinal, head of Wilda I West Sumatra, Padang, 19 June 2003.

Rahmat Abdullah, member of DPR RI, Jakarta, 11 May 2003.

Razikun, head of general election section of PKS, Jakarta, 23 December 2005.

R.B. Suryama, member of DPR RI, 11 June 2003.

Sholeh Drehem, member of Shariah Council in East Java, Surabaya, 13 March 2003.

Sigit Susiantomo, vice chairman of PKS in East Java, Surabaya, 17 March 2003.

Suryadarma, member of DPR I South Sulewesi, Makasar, 17 September 2003.

Untung Wahono, member of DPR RI, Canberra, 12 July 2005.

Zulkieflymansyah, member of DPR RI, Canberra, 30 August 2004.

I also conducted some interviews with members of Jemaah Tarbiyah and Prosperous Justice in DKI Jakarta, East Java, West Java, West Sumatra, and South Sulawesi but for some reason they did not want their name to be cited in this thesis.

2. Books written by Jemaah Tarbiyah and PKS activists

Al-Jufri, Salim Segaf forward to *Politik Da'wah Partai Keadilan*, by Syamsul Balda, Abu Ridha, and Untung Wahono. Jakarta:DPP Partai Keadilan, 2000.

Alynudin, Suhud, et.al. *Partai Keadilan Sejahtera Menjawab Tudingan dan Fitnah*. Jakarta: Pustaka Saksi, 2004.

Akbar, Subhan, et.al. *Mereka Melawan Korupsi: Jihad Wakil Rakyat PK Sejahtera*. Jakarta: Pustaka Saksi, 2003.

Aminuddin, Hilmi. *Strategi Dakwah Gerakan Islam*. Jakarta: Pustaka Tarbiatuna, 2003.

Balda, Syamsul, Abu Ridha and Untung Wahono. *Politik Da'wah Partai Keadilan*. Jakarta: DPP Partai Keadilan, 2000.

Ismail, Ahmad Satori. *Tarbiyah dan Perubahan Sosial*. Jakarta: Pustaka Tarbiatuna, 2003.

Kurmarwanti and Nugroho Widiyantoro. *Dakwah Sekolah di Era Baru*. Solo: Era Intermedi a, 2002.

Lubis, Satria Hadi. *Yang Nyata dari PK Sejahtera*. Jakarta: Miskat Publication, 2003.

Matta, Anis. *Menikmati Demokrasi: Strategi Dakwah dan Meraih Kemenangan*. Jakarta: Pustaka Saksi, 2002.

Nasrullah, et.al (ed). *Geliat Dakwah di Era Baru: Kumpulan Wawancara Da'wah*. Jakarta: Izzah Press, 2001.

Nurwahid, Hidayat and Untung Wahono. *Pengaruh Sekularisasi dan Globalisasi Barat Terhadap Harakah Islamiyah di Indonesia*. Jakarta: Pustaka Tarbiatuna, 2001.

_____. *Mengelolah Masa Transisi Menuju Masyarakat Madani*. Jakarta: Fikri Publishing, 2004.

Pusat Konsultasi Syariah. *Penerapan Syariat Islam di Indonesia: Antara Peluang dan Tantangan*. Jakarta: Globalmedia, 2004.

Prayitno, Irwan. *Tarbiyah Islamiyah Harakiyah*. Jakarta: Pustaka Tarbiatuna, 2001.

Rasyid, Daud. *Indahnya Syari'at Islam*. Jakarta: Usamah Press, 2003.

_____. *Pembaruan Islam dan Orientalisme*. Jakarta: Usamah Press, 2003.

Rahmat, Andi and Mukhammad Najib. *Gerakan Perlawanan dari Masjid Kampus*. Surakarta: Purimedia, 2001.

Ridha, Abu. *Negara & Cita-Cita Politik*. Bandung: Syaamil, 2004.

_____. *Saat Dakwah Memasuki Wilayah Politik*. Bandung: Syaamil, 2003.

_____. *Amal Siyasi Gerakan Politik Dalam Dakwah*. Bandung: Syaamil, 2004.

_____. *Islam dan Politik: Mungkinkah Bersatu?* Bandung: Syaamil, 2004.

Sa'id, Muhammad. "Hatmiyah At Tarbiyah: Tarbiyah Suatu Kemestian," in *Tarbiyah Berkelanjutan*. Jakarta: Pustaka Tarbiatuna, 2003. 45-54.

Sidiq, Mahfudz. "Peran Serta Da'wah dalam Politik," Paper presented at the Square House Building, University of New South Wales, 9 August 2002.

_____. *Dakwah & Tarbiyah di Era Jahriyah Jamahiriyah*. Jakarta: Pustaka Tarbiatuna, 2002.

_____. *KAMMI dan Pergulatan Reformasi: Kiprah Politik Aktivis Dakwah Kampus dalam Perjuangan Demokratisasi di tengah Krisis Nasional Multidimensi*. Solo: Era Intermedia, 2003.

_____. *Pemikiran dan Manhaj Politik Ikhwanul Muslimin*. Jakarta: Pustaka Tarbiatuna, 2003.

Takariawan, Cahyadi. *Rekayasa Masa Depan Menuju Kemenangan Dakwah Islam*. Jakarta: Pustaka Tarbiatuna, 2003.

Tamhid, Ainur Rofiq Foreword to Syekh Abdur Rahman Abdul Khaliq, *Penyimpangan-Penyimpangan Tasawuf*, trans. Ahmad Misbach. Jakarta: Rabbani Press, 2001.

Tandjung, M. Arlansyah "Tarbiyah, Perjalanan dan Harapan," in *Tarbiyah Berkelanjutan*. Jakarta: Pustaka Tarbiatuna, 2003. 12-19.

Ula, Mutammimul. *Perpektif Syariat Islam di Indonesia*. Jakarta: Pustaka Tarbiatuna, 2001.

Waluyo, Sapto. *Kebangkitan Politik Dakwah: Konsep dan Praktik Politik Partai Keadilan Sejahtera di Masa Transisi*. Bandung: Harakatuna Publishing, 2005.

Wahono, Untung. "Piagam Jakarta, PKS, dan Demokratisasi Referensi." Kompas, 14 December 2004.

Yasmin, Ummu. *Materi Tarbiyah: Panduan Kurikulum bagi Da'i dan Murabbi.* Solo: Media Insani, 2002.

Yusuf, Ahmad Firman foreword to *Pimikiran Politik Kontemporer Al-Ikhwan Al-Muslimun: Studi Analitis, Observatif, Dokumentatif*, trans. Wahid Ahmadi and Arwani Amin. Solo: Era Intermedia, 2002.

Zulkieflimansyah. "Overcoming the Fear: PKS and the Democratization," *Jakarta Post*, 12 December 2005.

3. Official Documentations

Bayan DPP PK Sejahtera, 27 March 2004.

Bayan DPP PK Sejahtera, 1 June 2004.

DPP Partai Keadilan. *Kebijakan Dasar Partai Keadilan 2000-2005*. Jakarta: Pustaka Tarbiatuna, 2000.

_____. *Manajemen Tarbiyah Anggota Pemula*. Jakarta: DPP Partai Keadilan, 2003.

_____. *Menyelamatkan Bangsa Platform Kebijakan Partai Keadilan Sejahtera*. Jakarta: Al'Iktishom Cahaya Umat, 2004.

_____. *Panduan Organisasi Partai Keadilan*. Jakarta: DPP PK, 2001.

Press release DPP PKS, 21 Maret 2005

Press release issued by FPKS, 15 Maret 2004.

Press release issued by FPKS, 4 Maret 2004

B. Secondary Sources

1. Books and Journals

Abaza, Mona. Islamic Education: Perception and Exchanges Indonesian Students in Cairo. Paris: Cahier Archipel, 1994.

Abduh, Umar. *Al-Zaitun Gate: Investigasi Mengungkap Misteri Dajjal Indonesia Membangun Negara Impian Iblis*. Jakarta: LPDI, 2002.

_____. *Pesantren AL-Zaitun Sesat? Investigasi Mega Proyek dalam Gerakan NII*. Jakarta: Darul Falah, 2001.

Abdullah, Taufiq. "The Formation of a New Paradigm: A Sketch on Contemporary Islamic Discourse" in Toward New Paradigm: Recent Developments in Indonesia Islamic Thought. Tempe: Arizona State University, 1996. 47-88.

Abuza, Zachary. "Politics and Violence in Indonesia: an Emerging Jihadist-Islamist Nexus?" NBR Analysis 15 no. 3 (September 2004): 1-54.

Acheh, Abu Bakar. *Pengantar Sejarah Sufi dan Tasauf*. Kelantan: Pustaka Amar Press, 1977.

Ahmadsumadi, Sugiat. "HMI, LMD, AMT, ICMI, DI dan Akhirnya Sufi," in Bang 'Imad Pemikiran dan Gerakan Dakwahnya. Jakarta: Gema Insani Press, 2002. 247-251.

Al-Banna, Hasan. Al-Ma'tsurat Sughra: Doa &Dzikir Rasulullah SAW Pagi dan Petang. Jakarta: Sholahuddin Press, 1996.

_____. Usrah dan Da'wah. Kuala Lumpur: Ikhwan Agency, 1979.

_____. Risalah Pergerakan Ikhwanul Muslimin 1, tran. Anis Matta et.al. Solo:Era Intermedia, 2001.

_____. Risalah Pergerakan Ikhwanul Muslimin 2, tran. Anis Matta et.al. Solo: Era Intermedia, 2001.

_____. Memoar Hasan Al-Banna Untuk Dakwah dan Para Dainya, trans. Salafuddin Abu Sayyid and Hawin Murtadho. Solo: Era Intermedia, 2004.

Ali, Daud. "Fenomena Sempalan Keagamaan di PTU: Sebuah Tantangan Bagi Pendidikan Agama Islam," in Dinamika Pemikiran Islam di Perguruan Tinggi. Jakarta: Logos, 1999. 249-257.

Anon. Buku Islam Sejak 1945. Jakarta: Yayasan Masagung, 1988.

_____. Diskusi Buku Agama. Jakarta: Tempo, 1987.

Anwar, Syafi'i. Pemikiran dan Aksi Islam Indonesia: Sebuah Kajian Politik Tentang Cendekiawan Muslim Order Baru. Jakarta: Paramadina, 1995.

Aspinall, Edward. "Students and the Military: Regime Friction and Civilian Dissent in the Late Suharto Period," Indonesia 59 (April 1995): 21-44.

Assidiqie, Jimly eds. Bang 'Imad Pemikiran dan Gerakan Dakwahnya. Jakarta: Gema Insani Press, 2002.

Awwas, Irfan. S. (ed). Dialog Internet: Aksi Sejuta Ummat dan Issu Negara Islam. Yogyakarta:Wihda Press, 2000.

Aziz, Abdul. "Meraih Kesempatan dalam Situasi Mengambang: Studi Kasus Kelompok Keagamaan Mahasiswa Univesitas Indonesia," Penamas No. 20 (1995): 3-20.

Azra, Azyumardi. Jaringan Global dan Lokal Islam Nusantara. Bandung: Mizan, 2002.

_____."Kelompok Sempalan di Kalangan Mahasiswa PTU: Anatomi Sosio Historis" in Dinamika Islam di Perguruan Tinggi Wacana Tentang Pendidikan Agama Islam. Jakarta: Logos, 1999. 233-246.

_____."Melacak Pengaruh dan Pergeseran Orientasi Tamatan Cairo," Studia Islamika 2 no. 3, (1995): 141-177.

Barton, Greg. "Islam and Politics in the New Indonesia," in Islam in Asia Changing Political Realities. New Brunswick and London: Transaction Publishers, 2002. 1-89.

Bayumi, Zakariyya Sulayman. The Muslim Brothers and the Islamic Associations in the Egyptian Political Life, 1928-1948. Cairo: Maktabah al-Wahda, 1978.

Benda, Harry J. "Christian Snouck Hurgronje and the Foundations of Dutch Islamic Policy in Indonesia," The Journal of Modern History 30 no. 4 (December 1958): 338-347.

Bertrand, Jacques. "False Starts Succession Crises, and Regime Transition: Flirting with Openness in Indonesia," Pacific Affairs 69 no. 3 (Autumn, 1996): 319-340.

Boland, B.J. The Struggle of Islam in Modern Indonesia. Leiden: KITLV, 1982.

Bruinessen, Martin van. "Genealogies of Islamic Radicalism in Post-Suharto Indonesia," South East Asia Research 10 no. 2 (2002): 117-154.

_____. "Post-Suharto Muslim Engagements with Civil Society and Democratisation," in Indonesia in Transition: Rethinking 'Civil Society', 'Religion', and 'Crisis.' Yogyakarta: Pustaka Pelajar, 2004. 37-66.

_____. Tarekat Naqsyabandiyah di Indonesia. Bandung: Mizan, 1992.

_____. "Global and Local in Indonesian Islam", Southeast Asian Studies 37, no.2 (1999): 158-175.

_____. "Gerakan Sempalan di Kalangan Umat Islam Indonesia: Latar Belakang Gerakan Sosial Budaya," in Artikulasi Islam Kultural: dari Tahapan Moral ke Periode Sejarah. Jakarta: RajaGrafindo Persada: 2004. 206-261.

Burhanuddin, Nandang. Penegakan Syariat Islam Menurut Partai Keadilan. Jakarta: Al-Jannah Pustaka, 2004.

Castori, James P. ed. Introduction to Islam in the Political Process. London: Cambridge University Press, 1983.

Crouch, Harold. "Islam and Politics in Indonesia" in Politics, Diplomacy and Islam: Four Case Studies. Canberra: Department of International Relations the Australian National University, 1986. 15-30

Damanik, Ali Said. Fenomena Partai Keadilan:Transformasi 20 Tahun Gerakan Tarbiyah di Indonesia. Bandung, Mizan, 2002.

Dhume, Sadanand "Radical March on Indonesia's Future," Far Eastern Economic Review 168 No. 5 (May 2005): 11-19.

Dobbin, Christine. "Islamic Revivalism in Minangkabau at the Turn of the Nineteenth Century," Modern Asian Studies 8 no. 3 (1974): 319-345.

Dodge, Bayard. Al-Azhar: A Millenium of Muslim Learning. Washington DC: The Middle East Institute, 1961.

Douglas, Ramage. Politics in Indonesia: Democracy, Islam and the Ideology of Tolerance. New York: Routledge, 1995.

Douglas, Stephen A. Political Socialization and Student Activism in Indonesia. Urbana: University of Illinois Press, 1970.

Effendy, Bahtiar. Islam dan Negara: Transformasi Pemikiran dan Praktik Politik Islam di Indonesia. Jakarta: Paramadina, 1998.

_____. Teologi Baru Politik Islam Pertautan Agama, Negara dan Demokrasi. Jakarta: Galang Press, 2001.

Esposito, John L. and John O Voll. Islam and Democracy. New York: Oxford University Press, 1996.

Esposito, John L. ed. The Oxford Encyclopaedia of the Modern Islamic World. New York: Oxford University Press, 1995.

Fealy, Greg and Greg Barton, ed. Nahdlatul Ulama, Traditional Islam and Modernity in Indonesia. Clayton: Monash Asia Institute, 1996.

Fealy, Greg and Virginia Hooker, ed. Voices of Islam in Southeast Asia: a Contemporary Sourcebook. Singapore: Institute of Southeast Asian Studies, 2006.

Feillard, Andree. "Traditionalist Islam and the State in Indonesia" in Islam in an Era of Nation States: Politics and Religious Renewal in Muslim Southeast Asia. Honolulu: University of Hawaii Press, 1997. 129 – 156.

Fischer, Joseph and Sudarsono, Juwono. "Indonesian Student Activism," Pacific Affairs 44 no. 1 (Spring, 1971): 92-96.

Fuller, Graham E. "Islamism(s) in the Next Century," in The Islamism Debate. Tel Aviv: Moshe Dayan Center for Middle Eastern and African Studies, 1997. 140-173.

Furkon, Aay Muhammad. Partai Keadilan Sejahtera Ideologi dan Praksis Politik Kaum Muda Muslim Indonesia Kontemporer. Bandung: Teraju, 2004.

Gayatri, Irene H. "Arah Baru Perlawanan Gerakan Mahasiswa 1989-1993," in Penakluk Rezim Orde Baru. Jakarta: Pustaka Sinar Harapan, 1999. 64-125.

Geertz, Clifford. Islam Observed Religious Development in Morocco and Indonesia. Chicago and London: University of Chicago Press, 1968.

_____. The Religion of Java. New York: The Free Press, 1960.

Gilsenan, Michael. Saint and Sufi in Modern Egypt: an Essay on the Sociology of Religion. Oxford: The Clarendon Press, 1973.

Hadi, Setyo (ed). Masjid Kampus Untuk Umat & Bangsa. Jakarta: Masjid ARH UI and LKB – Nusantara, 2000.

Hafez, Mohammed M. and Quintan Wiktorowicz. "Violence as Contention in the Egyptian Islamic Movement," in Islamic Activity: a Social Movement Theory Approach. Bloomington and Indianapolis: Indiana University Press, 2004. 61-88.

Harris, Christina Phelps. *Nationalism and Revolution in Egypt: the Role of the Muslim Brotherhood*. The Hague: Hoover Institution Publication, 1964.

Hasan, Muhammad Kamal. Muslim Intellectual Responses to New Order Modernisation in Indonesia. Kuala Lumpur: Dewan Bahasa and Pustaka, 1980.

Hassan, M. Zein. *Diplomasi Revolusi Indonesia di luar Negeri: Perjuangan Pemuda/Mahasiswa Indonesia di Timur Tengah*. Jakarta: Bulan Bintang, 1980.

Hefner, Robert W. "Islamising Java? Religion and Politics in Rural East Java," Journal of Asian Studies 46 no. 3 (Augustus, 1987), 533-554.

_____. "Islam, State, and Civil Society: ICMI and the Struggle for the Indonesian Middle Class," Indonesia 56 (October 1993): 1-35.

_____. Civil Islam: Muslim and Democratisation in Indonesia. Princeton and Oxford: Princeton University Press, 2000.

Howell, Julia Day. "Sufism and the Indonesian Islamic Revivalism" The Journal of Asian Studies 60 no. 3 (Augustus 2001): 701-729.

Husaini, Ishak Musa. The Moslem Brethren: The Greatest of Modern Islamic Movements. Westport: Hyperion Press, 1956.

Ismail, Faishal. "Pancasila as the Sole Basis for all Political Parties and for all Mass Organizations; an Account of Muslim's Responses, Studia Islamika 3 no. 4 (1996): 1-87.

Jamhari ed. Gerakan Salafi Radikal di Indonesia. Jakarta: Rajawali Press, 2004.

Jenkins, David. Suharto and His General: Indonesian Military Politics 1975-1983. Ithaca: Cornel Modern Indonesian Project, 1984.

Johns, A.H. "Islam in Southeast Asia: Problems of Perspective," in Readings on Islam in Southeast Asia. Singapore: Institute of Southeast Asian Studies, 1985. 304-320.

Jones, R. "Ten Conversion Myths from Indonesia," in Conversion to Islam. New York: Holmes and Meier, 1979. 129-158.

Jones, Sidney "Indonesia Backgrounder: Why Salafism and Terrorism Mostly Don't Mix," ICG Asia Report no. 83 (13 September 2004).

_____. "Radical Islam in Central Asia: Responding to Hizb Ut-Tahrir" ICG Asia Report, no. 58 (30 June 2003).

_____. "The Recycling Militants in Indonesia: Darul Islam and the Australian Embassy Bombing" ICG Asia Report no. 92 (22 February 2005).

_____. "It Can't Happen Here: A Post-Khomeini Look at Indonesian Islam," Asian Survey 20 no. 3 (March 1980): 311-323.

_____. "Al-Qaedah in Southeast Asia: the Case of the Ngruki Networks in Indonesia," Indonesia Briefing (8 August 2002).

_____. "Indonesia: Violence and Radical Muslims" ICG Indonesia Briefing (10 October 2001).

Karim, M. Rusli. HMI MPO dalam Kemelut Modernisasi Politik di Indonesia. Bandung: Mizan, 1997.

Koentjaraningrat, Javanese Culture. Singapore: Oxford University, 1985.

Kramer, Martin, ed. The Islamism Debate. Ramat Aviv: Tel Aviv University, 1997.

Kuntowijoyo, Muslim Tanpa Masjid. Bandung: Mizan, 2001.

Lapalombara, Joseph and Jeffrey Anderson, "Political Parties," in Encyclopedia of Government and Politics Vol. 1. London and New York: Roudledge, 1992. 393-412.

Levtzion, Nehemia. "Towards a Comparative Study of Islamisation," in Conversion to Islam. New York: Holmes and Meier, 1979. 1-23.

Lia, Bryanjar. The Society of Muslim Brothers in Egypt: The Rise of Islamic Mass Movement 1928-1942. Reading: Ithaca Press, 2002.

Liddle, R. William. "Soeharto's Indonesia: Personal Rule and Political Institutions," Pacific Affairs 58 no. 1 (Spring, 1985): 68-90.

_____. "Media Dakwah Scriptualism: One Form Islamic of Political Thought and Action in New Order Indonesia" in Toward a New Paradigm: Recent Developments in Indonesian Islamic Thought. Tempe: Arizona State University, 1996. 323-356.

_____. "The Islamic Turn in Indonesia: A Political Explanation," The Journal of Asian Studies 55 no. 3 (August, 1996): 613-634.

Lim, Merlyna. "Cyber-Civic Space in Indonesia: From Panopticon to Pandemonium?" IDPR 24 no. 4 (2002): 383-400.

Lufhfi, AM. "Gerakan Dakwah di Indonesia," in Bang Imad Pemikiran dan Gerakan Dakwah. Jakarta: Gema Insani Press, 2002. 158-163.

McAdam, Doug, et.al., ed., Comparative Perspectives on Social Movements: Political Opportunities, Mobilizing Structures, and Cultural Framings. Cambridge: Cambridge University Press, 1996.

Machmudi, Yon. Partai Keadilan Sejahtera: Wajah Baru Islam Politik Indonesia. Bandung: Harakatuna Publishing, 2005.

Madjid, Nurcholish. "Agama dan Negara dalam Islam," in Kontekstualisasi Doktrin Islam dalam Sejarah. Jakarta: Paramadina, 1994. 588-594.

Madjid, Nurcholish. "Cita-Cita Politik Kita" in Aspirasi Umat Islam di Indonesia. Jakarta: Leppenas, 1983. 7-36.

Mahmud, Ali Abdul Halim. Perangkat-Perangkat Tarbiyah Ikhwanul Muslimin, trans. Wahid Ahmadi, et.al. Solo: Era Intermedia, 1999.

Mandaville, Peter. Transnational Muslim Politics: Reimagining the Umma. London and New York: Routledge, 2001.

Means, Paul B. "The Religion Background of Indonesian Nationalism," Church History 16 no. 4 (December 1947). 234-247.

Mehden, Fred R. von der Two Worlds of Islam: Interaction between Southeast Asia and the Middle East. Gainesville: the University Press of Florida, 1993.

Mitchell, Richard. The Society of the Muslim Brothers. New York and Oxford: Oxford University Press, 1993.

Mujani, Saiful. "Syariat Islam dalam Perdebatan," in Syariat Islam Pandangan Muslim Liberal. Jakarta: Sembrani Aksara Nusantara, 2003. 19-51.

Mun'im, Abdul DZ, "Gerakan Mahasiswa 1966 di Tengah Pertarungan Politik Elit," in Penakluk Rezim Orde Baru. Jakarta: Pustaka Sinar Harapan, 1999. 17-44.

Naipaul, V.S. Among the Believers: an Islamic Journey. New York: Vintage Books, 1982.

_____. Beyond Belief: Islamic Excursions among the Converted Peoples. London: Little, Brown and Company, 1998.

Nieuwenhuijze, C.A.O. Van. Aspects of Islam in Post-Colonial Indonesia. Bandung: Van Hoeve Ltd, 1958.

Nock, A.D. Conversion: The Old and the New in Religion from Alexander the Great to Augustine of Hippo. New York: The Oxford University Press, 1961.

Pauker, Guy J. "Indonesia in 1980: Regime Fatigue?" Asian Survey 21 no. 2 (Feb, 1981), 232-244.

Peacock, James L. Muslim Puritans: Reformist Psychology in Southeast Asian Islam. University of Berkeley: California Press, 1978.

Pranowo, Bambang. "Islam and Party Politics in Rural Java," Studia Islamika I no. 2 (1994): 1-19.

Putra, Heddy Shri Ahimsa. "Ramadhan di Kampus, PNDI, dan Safari Ramadhan: Beberapa Pola Islamasasi di Masa Order Baru" in Agama Spiritualisme dalam Dinamika Ekonomi Politik. Surakarta: Universitas Muhammadiyah Surakarta, 2001. 11-22.

Qardhawi, Yusuf. Umat Islam Menyongsong Abad 21, trans. Yogi Prana Izza and Ahsan Takwim. Solo: Era Intermedia, 2001.

Rabi, Ibrahim M. Abu Intellectual Origins of Islamic Resurgence in the Modern Arab World. Albany: State of New York Press, 1996.

Rahardjo, M. Dawam foreword to Islam Garda Depan: Mosaik Pemikiran Islam Timur Tengah by M. Aunul Abied Shah, ed. Bandung: Mizan, 2001.

_____. Islam dan Transformasi Budaya. Yogyakarta: PT Dana Bhakti Prima Yasa, 2002.

Reid, Anthony. "Nineteenth Century Pan-Islam in Indonesia and Malaysia," The Journal of Asian Studies 26 no. 2 (February 1967): 267-283.

Ricklefs, M.C. "Islamization in Java" in Islam in Asia II. Boulder: Westview Press, 1984. 36-43.

_____. A History of Modern Indonesia since C. 1200. Hampshire: Palgrave, 2001.

Roff, William R. The Origins of Malay Nationalism. Kuala Lumpur: Universiti Malaya, 1980.

Roy, Olivier. The Failure of Political Islam, trans. Carol Volk. Massachusetts: Harvard University Press, 1994.

_____. The Globalised Islam: the Search for a Global Ummah. London: C. Hurst, 2002.

Saidi, Ridwan. "Dinamika Kepemimpinan Islam," in Islam in Indonesia: Suatu Ikhtiar Mengaca Diri. Jakarta: CV Rajawali, 1986. 81-96.

Samson, Allan A. "Army and Islam in Indonesia," Pacific Affairs 44 no. 4 (Winter, 1971-1972): 545-565.

_____. "Islam and Indonesian Politics," Asian Survey 8 no. 12 (December 1968): 1001-1017.

Sanit, Arbi. "Gerakan Mahasiswa 1970-1973: Pecahnya Bulan Madu Politik," in Penakluk Rezim Orde Baru Gerakan Mahasiswa '98. Jakarta: Pustaka Sinar Harapan, 1999.

Schrieke, B.J.O Indonesian Sociological Studies I. Den Hag and Bandung: Van Hoeve, 1995.

Schwarz, Adam. A Nation in Waiting: Indonesia's Search for Stability. St. Leonards: Allen and Unwind, 1999.

Syam, Firdaus. Ahmad Sumargono:Dai dan Aktifis Pergerakan Islam Yang Mengakar di Hati Umat. Jakarta: Millenium Publiser, 2004.

Tamara, Nasir. Indonesia in the Wake of Islam: 1965-1985. Kuala Lumpur: Institute of Strategic and International Studies, 1986.

Tanter, Richard. "The Totalitarian Ambition: Intelligence and Security Agencies in Indonesia" in State and Civil Society in Indonesia. Clayton: Monas University, 1990.

The American Heritage® Dictionary of the English Language, 4 rd ed. Boston: Houghton Mifflin, 2000.

Tholkhah, Imam and Abdul Aziz. "Gerakan Islam Kontemporer di Indonesia: Sebuah Kajian Awal," in Gerakan Islam Kontemporer di Indonesia. Jakarta: Pustaka Firdaus, 1996. 1-20.

Tibbi, Bassam. Islam and the Cultural Accommodation of Social Change. San Francisco: Westview Press, 1991.

Tim Amnesti Internasional. Fakta Diskriminasi Rezim Soeharto Terhadap Umat Islam, trans. Mohammad Thalib. Yogyakarta: Wihda Press, 1988.

Tim Litbang Kompas. Wajah DPR dan DPD 2004-2009. Jakarta: Kompas, 2005.

Voll, John Obert. Islam Continuity and Change in the Modern World. Essex: Westview Press, 1982.

Waardenburg, Jacques. "Muslim and Other Believers: The Indonesian Case Towards a Theoretical Research Framework," in Islam in Asia II. Boulder: Westview Press, 1984. 24-66.

Wahid, Abdurahman. "Pribumisasi Islam," in Islam Indonesia Menatap Masa Depan. Jakarta: P3EM, 1989. 81-96.

_____. "Islam, the State, and Development in Indonesia," in Islam in South and South- East Asia. New Delhi: Ajanta Publications, 1985. 75-125.

Ward, Ken. The 1971 Election in Indonesia: An East Java Case Study. Clayton: Centre of Southeast Asian Studies Monash University, 1974.

Wasis, Widjiono. Geger Talangsari: Serpihan Gerakan Darul Islam. Jakarta: Balai Pustaka, 2001.

Yusanto, Ismail. "Selamatkan Indonesia dengan Syariat Islam," in Syariat Islam Pandangan Islam Liberal. Jakarta: Sembrani Aksara Nusantara, 2003. 139-171.

2. Articles in Newspaper or Magazines

Abdalla, Ulil Abshar. "Syariat Islam," Suara Karya, 23 March 2004.

____. "Muhammad Nabi dan Politikus", Media Indonesia, 04 May 2004.

Anon. "Anggota DPRD Depok dari PKS Dipecat," Kompas, 6 June 2006.

____."Banyak Jalan Menuju Kehidupan Islami," Suara Hidayatullah, August 2000.

____. "Barat atau Timur; Tetap Islam," Tempo, 3 April 1993.

____. "Belasan PSK Hadiri Kampanye PKS," Jawa Pos, 18 March 2004.

____. "Beragam Jalan Menempuh Dunia," Tempo, 3 April 1993.

____. "Cikal Bakal PKS," Dewan Rakyat, 3 October 2003

____. "Comparing Islamic Leftist and Rightist," The Jakarta Post, 21 September 2002.

____. "Demonstrasi itu Tertib dan Damai," Media Indonesia, 15 September 2003.

____. "Dinas Rahasia Susupi PKS," Dewan Rakyat, 3 October 2003.

____. "Gerakan Islam Kontemporer: Sebuah Sketsa tentang Gerakan Salafi dan Laskar Jihad di Jogyakarta," www.lkis.org/islam_kontemporer.php.

____. "Historical Development of Methodologies al-Ikhwan al-Muslimeen and Their Effect and Influence upon Contemporary Salafee Dawah," Salafi Publication, March 2003.

____. "Jalan Pintas ke Surga, Katanya," Tempo, 14 July 2002.

____. "Jamaah Partai, Partai Jamaah," pkswatch.blogspot.com, 26 October 2005.

____."Kader Muhammadiyah Tergiur 'Rumah Yang Lain'" Suara-Muhammadiyah.or.id, 5 October 2005.

____. "Klaim di Luar Survei LSI," Jawa Pos, 26 March 2006.

____. "Mahasiswa RI di Mesir Mencapai Rekor Terbanyak," Gatra, 5 November 2005.

____. "PCNU Depok Deklarasikan Dukung Nurmahmudi," PKS Online, 10 June 2005.

____. "Perda Syariah Tidak Diperlukan," Media Indonesia, 16 June 2006.

____. "PKS-PDS Tetapkan Pasangan," Suara Merdeka, 18 March 2005.

____. "PKS Perkirakan Raih 48 Kursi DPR," Gatra, 21 April 2004.

____. "PKS Ancam Recall Anggotanya," Jawa Pos, 17 April 2005.

____. "PKS telah Praktikkan Pluralisme di Pilkada Termasuk Berkoalisi dengan PDS," Kompas, 1 August 2005.

_____. "Profesional dari Mujahid Kampus" Hidayatullah, April 2000.

_____. "Sejarah Kebangkitan dan Perkembangan PII," PelajarIslam.or.id.

_____."Survey PKS Yogya: Citra PKS Turun Gara-Gara Dukung SBY," Tempointeraktif.com, 24 November 2005.

_____. "Syaikhut Tarbiyah, KH Rahmat Abdullah: Ikhwanul Muslimin Inspirasi Gerakan Tarbiyah," Hidayatullah, August 2001.

_____. "Syariat Islam yang Bagaimana," Panjimas, 27 November – 12 December 2002.

_____. "Tegar Juga Ayah yang Sabar," *WWW. PK-Sejahtera.org*, 01 Oktober 2001.

_____. "Tertunda, Pencarian Dana Kompensasi BBM," Kompas, 8 March 2005.

_____. "Tidak Mudah Bagi Pemerintah Penuhi Amanat UU Sisdiknas," Kompas, 17 June 2003.

_____."Transkrip Pidato Dr. Amien Rais di FSLDK Nasional XI di Universitas Indonesia," Ukhuwa.or.id, 2000.

_____."Ulil Abshar: NU akan Mengalami Penggundulan Generasi," Media Indonesia Online, 30 April 2005.

_____."61 dari 112 Pilkada telah Direbut PKS," Gatra, 10 June 2006.

Assyaukanie, Lutfi. "Berkah Sekularisme," Islamlib.com, 11 April 2005.

Azra, Azyumardi. "Fenomena Hidayat Nurwahid dan Politik Islam," Media Indonesia, 11 October 2004.

Basyaib, Hamid. "Dilemma Partai Agama," Islamlib.com, 19 April 2004.

Burhani, Ahmad Najib. "Piagam Jakarta dan Piagam Madinah," Kompas, 31 September 2004

Dhume, Sadanand. "PKS and the Future of RI's Democracy," Jakarta Post, 5 December 2005.

Khamami, Rizqon "Kebangkitan Neo-Wahabisme," Duta Masyarakat, 16 August 2005.

Mulkhan, Abdul Munir. "Sendang Ayu: Pergulatan Muhammadiyah di Kaki Bukit Barisan," Suara-Muhammadiyah.or.id, 2 January 2006.

Salahuddin. "Menelusuri Kelompok Sempalan, Detik.com, 10 January 2001.

Steele, Andrew. "The Decline of Political Islam in Indonesia," *Asia Times Online*, 28 March 2006.

Yusanto, Ismail. "LDK: Antara Visi, Misi dan Realitas Sejarah Perkembangannya," www.fsldk.20m.com.

3. Newspapers, Magazines and other Publications

Berita Keadilan, Bulletin of the Prosperous Justice Party District Jombang, 2003.

Bulletin Al-Islam no. 45, 2000.

Detik.com, 10 January 2001.

Eramuslim.com, 14 November 2002.

Gatra, 7 October 1995.

http://www.metareligion.com/Extremism/Islamic_extremism/muslim_brotherhood.htm.

Jawa Pos, 2 August 2005.

Jawapos, 27 December 2004.

Keadilan Online, 18 Maret 2005.

Keadilan Online, 20 Mei 2003.

Kompas, 21 April 1981.

Kontan Online, 16 November 1998.

Mertju Suar, 4 April 1968

Muslim Executive and Expatriate Newsletter, volume 1 Issue 3.

www.islamic-path.org.

Panjimas, 20 Feb – 05 March 2003.

PKS Online, 1 June 2005.

PKS Online, 1 Juni 2005.

PKS Online, 22 August 2002

Republika, 19 August 2003

Reuters, 7 April 2004.

Saksi, 20 May 2003, 28.

Saksi, 31 December 2003.

Salafy, no. 30 (1999).

Suara Karya, 21 April 1981

Sriwijaya Post, 21 January 2002.

Syariahonline.com, 01 January 2003.

Tempo 30 September 1978.

Tempo, 11 April 1981.

Tempo, 14 July 2002.

Tempo, 18 January 1999

Tempo, 3 April 1993.

Tempo, 7 August 2005.

Tempo, May 30, 1987.

Tempo, 19-25 June 2006.

Ulumul Qur'an 2 no. V (1994).

www.salafy.or.id

Christian Science Monitor, 2 Jan 1986.

4. Unpublished Materials

Anon. "Pemilih Islam dan Partai Keadilan Sejahtera (PKS): Hasil Survey LSI tentang Partai Politik dan Calon Presiden 2004," LSI, September 2004.

_____."Tanya Jawab Estapeta Pemimpin NII dalam Darurat Perang," 14 September 2002.

Abduh, Umar. "Konspirasi Gerakan Islam & Militer di Indonesia." Jakarta: Cedsos, 2003.

Azra, Azyumardi. "Islam in Southeast Asia: Tolerance and Radicalism," Paper presented at The University of Melbourne, 6 April 2005.

Bamualim, Chaidar S. "Radikalisme Agama dan Perubahan Sosial di DKI Jakarta." Jakarta: Tim Peneliti Pusat Bahasa dan Budaya, 2000.

Imdadun, Muhammad. "Tansmisi Gerakan Revivalisme Islam Timur Tengah ke Indonesia 1980-2002: Studi Atas Gerakan Tarbiyah dan Hizbut Tahrir Indonesia," Master's thesis, University of Indonesia, 2003.

Collins, Elizabeth Fuller. "'Islam is Solution:' *Dakwah* and Democracy." Paper presented at Ohio University, 20 June 2004.

Kraince, Richard Gordon "The Role of Islamic Student Activists in Divergent Movements for Reform during Indonesia's Transition from Authoritarian Rule, 1998-2001," Ph.D. diss., Ohio University, 2003.

Kurniawan, Hendra "Realitas Gerakan Hizbut Tahrir di Indonesia: Wacana Hegemonik dan Praksis Ideologi." Master thesis, University of Indonesia, 2003.

Kurtogle, Gul M. "Toleration of the Intolerant? Accommodation of Political Islam in the Muslim World." Ph.D. diss., University of Chicago, 2003.

Rosyad, Rifki. "A Quest for True Islam: A Study of the Islamic Resurgence Movements among the Youth in Bandung, Indonesia." Master thesis, the Australian National University, 1995.

Samson, Allan A. "Islam and Politics in Indonesia." Ph.D. diss, University of California, 1972.

Santosa, Candra June. "Modernization, Utopia and the Rise of Islamic Radicalism in Indonesia." Ph.D diss, Boston University, 1996.

Uhlin, Anders. "Indonesian Democracy Discourses in a Global Context. The Transnational Diffusion of Democratic Ideas," Working Paper 83, the Centre of Southeast Asian Studies Monash University, 1993.

Wall, Alan. "The Indonesian Political Landscape Post General Election." A report presented at ICWA meeting, 10 May 2004.

www.ingramcontent.com/pod-product-compliance
Lightning Source LLC
Chambersburg PA
CBHW060928170426
43192CB00031B/2863